CREATIVITY, COGNITION, AND KNOWLEDGE

**Recent Titles in
Perspectives on Cognitive Science**

CREATIVITY, COGNITION, AND KNOWLEDGE

AN INTERACTION

EDITED BY
TERRY DARTNALL

Perspectives on Cognitive Science
Peter Slezak, Series Editor

Westport, Connecticut
London

British Library Cataloguing in Publication Data is available.

Copyright © 2002 by Terry Dartnall

ISBN: 0–275–97680–7
       0–275–97681–5 (pbk.)

First published in 2002

Praeger Publishers, 88 Post Road West, Westport, CT 06881
An imprint of Greenwood Publishing Group, Inc.
www.praeger.com

Printed in the United States of America

The paper used in this book complies with the
Permanent Paper Standard issued by the National
Information Standards Organization (Z39.48–1984).

10 9 8 7 6 5 4 3 2 1

Copyright Acknowledgment

The editor and publisher gratefully acknowledge permission for the use of the following material:

A version of "Staring Emmy Right in the Eye—and Doing My Best Not to Flinch"
first appeared in VIRTUAL MUSIC: COMPUTER SYNTHESIS OF MUSICAL
STYLE, edited by David Cope, published by The MIT Press, 2000.

To Wendy

Contents

Foreword

The broad interdisciplinary field of cognitive science encompasses research in psychology, linguistics, neuroscience, artificial intelligence, and philosophy. The existence and content of this series reflect the exciting growth and scientific importance of this eclectic field, even if it cannot claim to be a single, unified domain of inquiry. Indeed, the very diversity and intense controversies are evidence of the intellectual vitality of a flourishing enterprise. The volumes in this series reflect the ferment of ideas, the range and depth of explanatory theories, and the methods and approaches that are the exciting fruits of the "cognitive revolution."

This volume typifies the ferment in the field. Terry Dartnall argues that cognitive science needs a new epistemology that re-evaluates the role of representations in cognition and that accounts for the flexibility and fluidity of creative thought. Such an epistemology, he proposes, is implicit in some leading edge models of human creativity. One of his main aims in this volume is to bring this epistemology into the light of day. He argues for his position in a long, meticulous Introduction and engages in lively debate with the contributors in a discussion section at the end of each chapter. This is an unusual and original volume that is a significant contribution to cognitive science.

Peter Slezak

Preface

I considered calling this volume *Creativity, Cognition, and Knowledge: An Exploitation.* A quick flip through the pages will show that it is not an ordinary collection. I outline my position in the Introduction and argue with the contributors in a discussion section at the end of each chapter. Sometimes I use a chapter to illustrate what I think is wrong with some aspect of cognitive science, and sometimes I use a chapter to illustrate the direction in which I think cognitive science should be going. When I was putting the collection together, I kept asking myself how I would feel if the tables were turned. How would I feel if someone included my chapter in a collection and said, "This beautifully illustrates what is wrong with the field"? I decided that I would be flattered, so I continued. (The nicest thing a reviewer has ever said to me is, "This is analytic philosophy, but it's as good as it gets.")

The dialectical, discuss-it-with-the-contributors style of the book began with Doug Hofstadter (as many things do). I asked him and his co-author, Gary McGraw, if they would clarify something in their chapter. "Why don't we write a discussion about it?" Doug said. "It'll be more interesting that way." We wrote a discussion, and he was right, of course—it was more interesting that way. If they had just expanded their chapter to cover my comments, our exchange of ideas would never have happened.

So I decided to have a discussion at the end of each chapter. At one time I wanted all the contributors to chip in whenever they thought it was appropriate, and I wanted a final chapter in which we looked back and discussed

what we had learned. I gave up on these ideas because they were too difficult, but I am sure that somebody with more energy and determination
could have pulled it off.

Nevertheless, there is an argument that runs throughout this book. I
argue that cognitive science needs a new epistemology that re-evaluates the
role of representations in cognition, one that accounts for the flexibility and
fluidity of creative thought. My optimistic message is that such an epistemology is already with us in some leading edge models of human creativity.
One of my main aims in this volume is to focus on this epistemology and
bring it into the light of day.

ACKNOWLEDGMENTS

At this point it is customary to thank people for their contributions and
help. This is an easy job for me because this book literally wouldn't exist
without the contributions and the discussions at the end of them. A thousand tiny dancing thank-yous to the contributors, for your contributions
and patience.

There are many others I would like to thank, but the list would be too
long. I will limit myself to my wife Wendy and son Adam, who put up with
me while I was compiling the volume, and to the staff at Greenwood and
at Shepherd, who have specially adapted rods and cones for spotting typos
and bad grammar. You are unsung heroes.

Introduction

Terry Dartnall

Consider some fairly common creative acts. Suppose that we are watching an artist or sculptor or potter at work. The artist applies paint to the canvas. The sculptor chisels a form out of a block of marble or granite. The potter shapes a pot or vase out of a lump of clay. In each case we see a created product emerging, not out of a combination of basic elements, as we might build a house or put a Lego kit together, but out of the artist's knowledge of his subject and his ability to manipulate his medium. Similarly, when we perform the simplest feats of imagination, such as imagining funny faces, we do not assemble a set of basic elements or features, as we put together a face out of an identikit. We can imagine faces of any size, shape and color, with the most peculiar features, by virtue of our knowledge and imaginative abilities. What we can imagine is not limited (or so I shall argue) by the size and combinatorial capabilities of a set of atomic ingredients (an "identikit" of eyes, ears, noses, etc.), but by what we know about the properties of faces, and our ability to vary these properties in our minds.

I think that these simple scenarios give us insights into human cognition. They show us that at least some cognition is not atomistic or combinatorial: it is not limited to a combination or recombination of atomic elements. Consequently, atomistic, combinatorial accounts of creativity and cognition that characterize these things as the rule-governed manipulation of inner elements completely miss the mark. And yet the main models and explanatory stories put forward by cognitive science and people trying to explain creativity are atomistic, combinatorial ones.

Our imagined scenarios suggest that we need a non-atomistic, non-combinatorial theory of knowledge that can account for the fluidity and flexibility of human thought. Such an epistemology must be able to account for the way in which we can understand the properties of objects and vary them in the imagination. I call this epistemology "knowledge-about," or "property epistemology," because to know about something is to know its properties and to be able to vary them in the imagination.

This volume is an edited collection of papers that addresses central issues in creativity and cognitive science: mundane creativity, representational redescription, analogical thinking, fluidity and dynamic binding, input versus output creativity, recursion and feedback loops, relational learning, runaway learning, emergent memory and emergence broadly construed—to name only some of them. But it is held together by the theme I have outlined above—that cognitive science needs a new epistemology to account for the fluidity and flexibility of creative thought. In the next section I argue that there are strong independent reasons for adopting such an epistemology, and I argue that these reasons go to the heart of the Cartesian Paradigm that underlies and drives much of cognitive science. Such an epistemology is not only non-atomistic and non-combinatorial, but broadly non-representational as well. It is non-representational in the sense that it downplays the importance of representations, while at the same time recognizing that they play a role in cognition. I argue that, to the extent that we have representations at all, they are *constructed* in our minds by the knowledge and conceptual capabilities that we acquire in making sense of the world. They are not copies of experience, however attenuated or transduced, which is the story that cognitive science has inherited from Classical Empiricism.

Such a constructive epistemology avoids the traditional problem of the representational veil or "the veil of perception." This problem, which has played a major role in epistemology since Descartes and Locke, arises when we say that representations are the direct and immediate objects of experience, from which we problematically infer the existence and properties of the external world. If this was true, we would be cut off from reality by the impenetrable curtain of our own ideas. The alternative story is that we first learn to make judgments about the world and then deploy this ability off-line to construct representations in our minds: we acquire our cognitive abilities in problem solving and making sense of the world, in what Partridge and Rowe in their chapter call "input creativity," and we deploy these abilities off-line to generate and manipulate representations in the imagination. This can be a recursive process, in which the output of one constructive cycle is the input to the next. McGraw and Hofstadter, and then John Rehling, call it the "Central Feedback Loop of Creativity."

Such an epistemology captures the active, constructive spirit of Classical Rationalism, without inheriting any of its metaphysical baggage, and it stands in contrast to the passive, copy-and-combine epistemology of Classical

Empiricism. It is influenced by the work of the later Wittgenstein, but it is more optimistic about cognitive science than he would have been—or than his followers are. (In a recent issue on Wittgenstein and cognitive science, I waved the cognitive science flag in splendid isolation [Dartnall, 1999a].)

These are the broad theoretical brushstrokes of the epistemology I shall propose. But what does such an epistemology look like in practice, when we get down to the serious stuff of modeling and implementation? My optimistic message is that this epistemology is already with us in some of the leading-edge models of human creativity, and one of my main aims in this volume is to use the chapters as triangulation points to get a fix on it and bring it into the light of day.

There is a more general message in the volume, which is that studying creativity gives us insights into cognition, representation and knowledge broadly construed, and that these insights have implications for cognitive science. The principal paradigms of cognitive science and what we might call "creativity theory" are really very similar. The "computational metaphor," "rules and representations" approach that underlies and drives classical cognitive science says that cognition is the rule-governed, syntactic manipulation of formally specified inner entities, which (nevertheless) are interpreted and represent things in the world. The fact that they are interpreted guarantees the good semantic behavior of the system (even though the manipulation that is driving it is syntactic). A pocket calculator gives us a simple example of syntactic manipulation producing good semantic behavior: the operations performed inside the system are formal and syntactic, but the tokens are interpreted and the calculator exhibits semantic good behavior: it does sums for us. Classical cognitive science says that we are like calculators: cognition is the syntactic manipulation of formally specified, but interpreted, inner elements called "representations." I shall call this "representationism."

The main model that we find in creativity theory is very similar: creativity is the combination or recombination of what we already have, and "what we already have" is usually seen as a set of atomic elements. I shall call this "combinationism."

There are obvious differences between the two positions. Combinationism is not necessarily computational, although it lends itself to computational interpretation (see, for example, Boden, 1990). For this reason it is uncluttered by the baggage of the computational metaphor, so that it is easier to see. Also, its elements or building blocks do not have to be interpreted. A combinationist will say that good music is a creative combination of notes, and that the Taj Mahal is a creative combination of bricks and stones, where neither the notes nor the building materials are "interpreted." We will see in section three that this is significant, because representationism says that representations carry the cognitive load precisely because they are interpreted—because they carry or contain the relevant information.

Combinationism shows us that this is not always the case. It is what the musician *knows about* the notes in a musical score that matters: the notes do not represent anything in themselves.

Despite these differences, representationism and combinationism are very similar. We can bring this out by comparing them with what I think is a more realistic account. Let us go back to the case of the potter. The pot does not come about through a combination or recombination of elements. It emerges out of the potter's skill, knowledge, inspiration, insight, and other difficult notions such as these. This case is relatively straightforward, because pots and vases do not have components. But the same thing applies in the case of music or poetry, where we do have elements: it is trivially true (and completely uninformative) to say that a mazurka is a combination of notes, or that a poem is a combination of words. We want to know how these things emerge out of the musician's and poet's skill, knowledge, inspiration, and so on. The same thing applies to cognition in general: we want to know how cognition emerges out of our knowledge about a domain and our ability to express this knowledge as explicit, accessible thoughts.

My more general message, then, is that studying creativity gives us insights into cognition, representation and knowledge generally conceived, and that these insights have major implications for cognitive science. Some of these may already be apparent. Representationism has nothing interesting to say about pottery or poetry, and this, I shall argue, is the thin end of the wedge.

It would be possible to treat either the epistemological or the more general issue next. I shall look at the epistemological issue, because the history of cognitive science is to a large extent the history of an epistemology. I shall provide independent reasons (independent of the issues outlined above) for abandoning the representational story and for adopting a "knowledge-about" approach. Because the issues are interwoven I could equally have looked in more detail at the commonalities between creativity studies and cognitive science, and this, in turn, would have forced us to focus on epistemology.

So in the next section I shall look at epistemology. Then I shall return to the relationship between creativity theory and cognitive science. Subsequent sections will outline the plot as it is played out in the chapters. In the last two sections we will look back and see what we have learned and then take a look at creativity and emergence.

KNOWLEDGE AND REPRESENTATION

The Origins of an Epistemology

Let us begin at the beginning. It is early in the seventeenth century, and the old worldview is being questioned. Montaigne has published his *Essays* and his *Apology for Raimond Sebond* has reintroduced Pyrrhonian skepticism to the West. To find certainty in troubled times, Pierre Charron advocates faith,

Francis Bacon advocates observation and experience, so that the new "experimental philosophy" is struggling to its feet, and René Descartes (1596–1650) advocates reason.

It is Descartes who interests us here. To establish "certain and indubitable" foundations for knowledge, he uses his Method of Doubt. He says that he can consistently doubt everything, except the fact that he is doubting. From this he believes that he can establish three things: (a) that he exists, (b) that he exists as a thinking thing (a consciousness or mind), and (c) that he is imperfect, since he is capable of doubt. He says that these are the only things he can be certain of, and he will use them as the foundations of his epistemology. But now he has a problem. Having established that he is a consciousness, or a mind, he has to say which contents of consciousness he can trust and which he cannot. Can he, for instance, trust any of the ideas that seem to tell him about the existence and properties of the external world?

How Descartes tried to extricate himself from this tarpit need not concern us here. What matters is that he set Western epistemology on a course from which it has never fully recovered. Descartes' disservice to epistemology was to give us the Cartesian Paradigm, or the Way of Ideas, according to which the royal road to knowledge starts with the contents of consciousness, and works outwards from there. The immediate and direct objects of experience are ideas, or representations, in the mind.

The Cartesian Paradigm emerges in various forms from the seventeenth century to the present day. In the Classical Empiricism of John Locke (1632–1704) it is wedded to an atomism that Locke gets from "the incomparable Mr. Newton." Locke says that experience, or sensory impressions, gives rise to simple, atomic ideas, that combine together in the mind to form complex, molecular ones. In a typically homely metaphor, Sir Karl Popper calls this the "bucket theory of the mind" (Popper, 1972, esp. p. 61). The mind is like a bucket with holes in it. At birth it is empty. Sensory impressions, or experiences, give rise to simple ideas. These enter the bucket through the holes, which correspond to the senses, and combine together inside the bucket to form complex ideas. This, according to Locke, is the way that our minds fill up with knowledge.

Locke's problem is now the same as Descartes': from the point of view of the experiencing subject, how do we know which ideas correspond to reality and which do not? Locke argues that some of our ideas (the ideas of primary qualities such as number, velocity, mass and shape) correspond to properties of things in the world, whereas the ideas of secondary qualities, such as color, taste and smell, do not. These ideas are brought about in us by objects in the external world affecting our senses. According to such a picture, external objects have properties such as number, shape and mass, but they are not red, sweet or aromatic—these are ideas that are generated in us by objects in the external world affecting our senses. (An alternative reading is that objects in the external world *do* have secondary qualities, inasmuch as they can bring about ideas of secondary qualities in us. On this reading, secondary qualities are causal capabilities of objects, that they have by virtue of their primary qualities. The broad picture remains the same.)

Locke's idea of an idea is extremely vague. He defines it as "whatsoever is the object of the understanding when a man thinks" and "whatever it is which the mind can be employed about in thinking" (Locke, 1690, I.i.8). An idea is any object of consciousness or awareness—literally, anything that we care to think about.

It is interesting to compare this with the contemporary notion of a representation in cognitive science, which is no less vague. Locke's ideas at least have to be conscious, and they are intermediary objects between us and the external world. These are not very good constraints, but at least they are constraints. Representations in cognitive science, on the other hand, can be conscious or unconscious, symbolic or nonsymbolic, mental or physical. Aaron Sloman (1996) says:

We need a label to cover all the various kinds of information stores, irrespective of what their structures are, or how they are created, or whether we are aware of using them or not. The word 'representation' seems to me to come closest to meeting this requirement, even if some people normally use it in more restricted ways. (p. 119)

Locke's theory is called Representational Realism, because it says that some of our ideas represent properties of objects in the world (whereas others, of course, do not). The notorious problem for this theory is that it cuts us off from reality. According to the theory we have no independent access to the external world, and so cannot know whether our ideas correspond to it or not. Strictly speaking we have no grounds for believing that there is an external world at all, for all that we are acquainted with our ideas in our minds. It is not surprising that Locke's "Idea-ism" became Berkeley's "Idealism," according to which objects simply *are* clusters of ideas in minds, so that what exists are ideas and the minds that have them.

The Standard Account of Cognition in Cognitive Science

Now let us wind the tape forward to the present day. The standard account of cognition in cognitive science is that cognition begins with sensory experiences, or sensory impressions, which are transduced (that is, transformed) into inner symbols or representations. These are then combined and manipulated by inner rules in the symbol-handling part of the system. In such a way, cognition begins with sensory experiences, which are converted, stored and manipulated in increasingly complex ways. We become adept at manipulating inner representations that originated as copies, or close cousins, of sensory experience.

This standard story is a marriage of the Cartesian Paradigm, as it appears in Classical Empiricism, with the computational model of the mind. Classical Empiricism says that sensory impressions give rise to simple ideas, which can combine to form complex ones. The computational model of the mind replaces ideas with representations and characterizes cognition as the rule-governed manipulation of these inner entities. This gives us the "rules and representations" approach, according to which cognition is computation over a fixed set of inner, formally specified elements. It is also known as the "computational theory of the mind" (Fodor, 1980), the "representational-computational view of the mind" (Shanon, 1993), the "computational-representational understanding of the mind" (Thagard, 1996), and the "computer between the ears" approach (Torrance, 1997). Even connectionism succumbs to a version of this story, since it replaces symbols with subsymbolic states, which it typically sees as representational, whether local or distributed (e.g., Smolensky, 1988).

This story can be made to seem not only plausible, but almost inevitable. The sales pitch goes like this:

We begin with thoughts and experiences about objects and events that are spatiotemporally present. I am able to think about my dog in her presence because I can see her there in front of me. But how am I able to think about her in her absence? Obviously I must have made an inner copy of her that stands in for her as a surrogate. And this must be the case with cognition in general. Representations become increasingly important as cognition becomes more abstract, complex and uncoupled from the context. As cognition becomes more sophisticated we become increasingly adept at manipulating and combining inner representations that stand in for their referents.

According to this story, representations become increasingly important as cognition uncouples from the context. Focusing on these inner entities encourages a computational account of cognition, according to which rules iterate over inner representations. The problem of the representational veil conveniently recedes into the background, because the computations are performed on formally specified elements, and their interpretation or meaning (in terms of the outside world or anything else) is irrelevant to the execution of the program.

Retelling the Standard Story

This standard story is defended by Clark and Toribio (1994), who argue that what they call "representation-hungry problem domains" demonstrate the need for inner representations. These domains involve reasoning about absent, nonexistent or counterfactual states of affairs, and states of affairs that are highly relational or abstract. Representations, they say, play an increasingly important role in cognition as it becomes more flexible and uncoupled from the context. This argument is the centerpiece of their criticism of the anti-representationism found in Rodney Brooks' work on mobile robots (Brooks, 1991) and Randall Beer's work on leg controllers for robot insects (Beer, 1990, 1995; Beer & Gallagher, 1992). They also discuss Robert Port and Tim van Gelder's work on dynamical systems (van Gelder, 1995; Port & van Gelder, 1995). Clark and Toribio argue that the problem domains addressed by these projects are not sufficiently "representation-hungry." Representationism, they say, might succumb to a concerted attack on the Cartesian Paradigm that underlies Classical Empiricism, but it will not fall to robots, insects and their ilk.

I agree that robots, insects and Watt governors do not put pressure on representationism, but I also believe that a concerted attack on the Cartesian Paradigm can begin with a reevaluation of just those "representation-hungry problem domains" that Clark and Toribio think vindicate representationism. And ironically, it is Descartes who gives us the key.

In the Sixth Meditation, Descartes says that we cannot have a representation of a chiliagon (a plane figure with a thousand angles), because it is too detailed and complex for the mind's eye to focus on. We can *understand* such a notion, but we cannot have an image or representation of it. Or at least, we cannot have one that will be of any use to us. Descartes says that we are accustomed to having some sort of a representation when we think, so that we may use an arbitrary one, but it cannot carry the cognitive load.

So what does carry the cognitive load? I think that we find the answer in Norman Malcolm's distinction between factual and pictorial memory (Malcolm, 1963). Factual memory is remembering *that* such and such: that Bill has a spotty face and red hair, for instance. No images or pictures are needed here. Pictorial memory, on the other hand, is remembering Bill's face: it is having an inner image or picture of it. Malcolm points out that we can have factual memory without pictorial memory, but that we cannot have pictorial memory without factual memory. If I have an image of Bill's face I do not know that it is a *memory* of Bill's face unless it is accompanied by factual knowledge to this effect. In this sense, factual memory is more basic than pictorial memory. In the same way, unless an image is accompanied by the factual knowledge that it is an image of Bill's face, I cannot know that it is an image of Bill's face. (Bear with me while I talk about images and pictures. I am *not* equating representations with images.)

What carries the cognitive load in the case of the chiliagon, then, is our factual knowledge *about* chiliagons: we know *that* a chiliagon is a plane figure with a thousand angles. We cannot have images of complex objects like chiliagons, and we do not *need* them because our factual cognition supplies us with the information and carries the cognitive load.

The same analysis carries over to the highly relational and the abstract. Whereas we cannot *practically* have images of complex objects, we cannot *even in principal* have images of abstract ones, such as truth, beauty, and electricity. Of course, we can have arbitrary representations of them (such as a lightning bolt for electricity), accompanied by factual knowledge ("this stands for electricity"), but such representations are not images. Again, it is the factual knowledge that does the work here, and not the representations.

Finally, factual knowledge does most of the work in the cases of the absent, the nonexistent and the counterfactual. We might have images of these things, but we do not need them. After all, if we can think about the complex and the abstract without having images, why should less complicated cases require such things? And they would still need to be accompanied by factual knowledge ("this is Bill's face," "this is Pegasus, the winged horse that sprang from Medusa's blood," "this is Hitler invading London").

So far I have talked about pictures or images, but implicit in the distinction between factual and pictorial knowledge is a more general distinction between what we might call "factual" and "representational" cognition. Images and pictures resemble their objects, but, following Haugeland (1991) and, in fact, Clark and Toribio (1994), I take a *representation* to be any item that stands in for something else, whether it resembles it or not. Representations are always accompanied by factual knowledge, and we typically say things like, "let this salt cellar represent Napoleon and this pepper pot represent Wellington."

Representational and factual knowledge range along a continuum. If we have an image of Bill's face it is the image (the representation) that does most of the work, although I shall argue later that images are constructed in the imagination by our factual knowledge. They are not copied from experience. At the other end of the continuum we have, for want of a better word, "abstract" cognition, where representations play no significant role at all—as when we think about truth, beauty or electricity, or when we say that if Attila the Hun was alive today he would not approve of the welfare state.

We can now see that, in contrast to Clark and Toribio's claim, cognition becomes *less* representational as it becomes more abstract and flexible. As representations are increasingly removed from the context, they contain *less* information in themselves, and the cognitive load is transferred to our knowledge *about* them, *about* what they represent, and *about* the mapping relationship between these two. So the standard story has it exactly backwards: the road to representations and the road to abstraction and flexibility run in opposite directions.

Moreover, this *has* to be the case. Our earliest ancestors *must* have been able to make judgments about the immediate context in order to survive. They had to know that this food is good and that that stuff is poisonous, that this route is safe and that that one leads to danger. They must have been able to make judgments about the immediate context before they ostensibly acquired the ability to store pale copies of it—and these copies, anyway, would have been useless unless they were accompanied by judgments that made them relevant to survival.

Constructing Representations in the Imagination

So far I have argued that inner items cannot function as representations unless they are accompanied by non-representational judgments, and that it is these judgments that do the hard cognitive work. As cognition becomes increasingly complex, these judgments take over and representations wither away.

I shall now argue for a stronger case—that representationism has it backwards even for relatively simple cognition, such as remembering or imagining sights and sounds. I shall argue that such relatively uncomplicated cognition is only possible because our non-representational capabilities enable us to *generate* images and memories. To the extent that we have representations at all, they are constructed by our knowledge-about, and we will see later that it is this constructive ability that gives us the flexibility and fluidity that we need for creative cognition. We can imagine anything that we want to, and we are limited only by the limitations of our knowledge and imaginative abilities—not by the combinatorial properties of a set of inner elements.

I shall focus on imagination and fantasy rather than memory. An example used in neuropsychology is to imagine your favorite politician riding a donkey, and to see if she can see over the donkey's head (Behrmann et al., 1995, reviewed in Dartnall, 1997). This requires us to know *about* politicians and donkeys: we need to know that politicians can sit on donkeys, and that donkeys do not combust or decrepitate when sat upon. Here our imaginative, representational abilities depend on our judgmental, nonrepresentational ones.

Now imagine your favorite politician with red hair and an evil grin. How did you do that? Did you first access a stored image of his face and then change it (this is the story that classical cognitive science is committed to), or did you directly construct a representation out of what you know about him? When I conduct this thought experiment, I am not aware of first remembering the face and then altering it. It seems to me that I perform the imaginative process in a single step, but my introspection might be playing me false.

Here the neuropsychological literature comes to our aid. Kosslyn, Maljkovic et al. (1995) refer to earlier research which demonstrates that "images are *constructed* [my emphasis] a portion at a time, with portions corresponding to individual perceptual units" (p. 151). (An example of a perceptual unit is a segment of a block letter, the strokes and curves that we put together to form a capital. We shall return to this later in the chapter.) They argue that information about perceptual units and information about the spatial relationships holding between them are stored in different parts of the brain. Kosslyn, Holtzman et al. (1985) assume that spatial relations between microfeatures are stored using language-like, symbolic representations in the left hemisphere, but Kosslyn, Maljkovic et al. (1995) cite evidence against the left hemisphere hypothesis and argue that both hemispheres can generate images, but that they do so in different ways.

It now begins to look as if we *construct* representations out of stored atomic features or microfeatures, using our non-representational abilities. This is a far cry from the standard story in cognitive science, which says that we make copies of experiences, store them in memory, retrieve them, and modify them in the imagination.

But even this account cannot be correct. What are these stored, atomic microfeatures meant to be? Here we need to distinguish between microfeatures and *micropictures*. Identikits work because they use micropictures— pictures of eyes, ears, noses, and so on. These succumb to exactly the same analysis as representations of whole faces. In the same way that we can imagine any kind of face, by virtue of our knowledge about faces, we can imagine any kind of eyes, ears and noses: we are not limited to a fixed inner repertoire. Here are some brown eyes. Imagine that they are green. Now how did you do that? Not by looking in an inner box marked "types of eyes" and accessing a representation of green ones! It is unfathomably unlikely that you have stored representations that perfectly match the eyes you are looking at, except for their color. No, you drew on your non-representational knowledge *about* eyes and how they can vary. Denis et al. (1995) say:

A recent extension of imagery research has been the investigation of images which are not constructed from a perceptual experience of specific objects, but from a text or a verbal description of these objects. Several experiments have shown that individuals are not only able to construct mental images from verbal descriptions, but that these images have properties which are similar to those of images derived from perception. (p. 178)

(They go on to say, "Little information is available on the brain structures that are involved in imagery based on verbal inputs." They also say that, having used verbal descriptions to construct images, we can then scan them. We shall return to this later on.)

There are other ways of coming to this conclusion. An ancient and obvious one, that goes back to Plato, is to try to explain how we are able to recognize things. Plato said that we are able to recognize things because we were acquainted with their archetypes or forms before birth, and we are now able to recognize them because they partake in these archetypes. Thus, for instance, we are able to recognize an animal as a dog because it partakes in the Idea or Archetype "Dog." Representationism is not greatly different. It says that we have stored inner representations that enable us to recognize things in the world. How do we recognize faces? We do so by comparing them with inner representations!

First, this leads to problems of storage. Every time that we see a face it looks different to us, so we would need to store a representation of every face from every possible angle and with every type of nuance—and we would run out of storage. Second, if we cannot recognize a face, how can we recognize a *representation* of that face? It is difficult to see how we can avoid a regress here. How am I able to recognize Bill? The standard story is that I summon up a representation of him. But if I cannot recognize Bill, how can I recognize a representation of him? How can I know that it is a representation of Bill? It might be replied that I know *about* the representation that it is a representation of Bill. But in that case I could have applied this knowledge directly to Bill, so that the representation is redundant. This is stronger than the first argument. The first argument shows that there are practical limits to how many representations we can store. The present argument shows that *any* representation is redundant in explaining how recognition is possible.

My claim is that the freedom and flexibility that enables us to recognize things, in all their varieties, and in all the variable conditions of experience, also enables us to generate representations of them in the imagination. I am not saying, of course, that we can imagine sounds, sights and colors without first having had sensory experience of these things. I do not believe that a congenitally blind person can have visual fantasies. I am saying that sensory experience must be accompanied by judgmental, non-representational knowledge, or just plain *judgment,* and that we can subsequently deploy this knowledge off-line to generate representations in the imagination.

It is a curious historical irony that someone who recognized that we have this ability was Hume, the last of the Classical Empiricists. At the beginning of *A Treatise of Human Nature* (first published in 1739), he says, following Locke, that all simple ideas are derived from simple impressions. He then asks whether it is possible for someone to imagine a shade of blue that he has not seen before:

Now I ask, whether it is possible for him, from his own imagination, to supply this deficiency, and raise up to himself the idea of that particular shade, though it had never been conveyed to him by his senses? I believe there are few but will be of opinion that he can; and this may serve as a proof, that the simple ideas are not always derived from the correspondent impressions. (*A Treatise of Human Nature,* Vol. I, Book I, Part I)

He goes on to say that "the instance is so particular and singular, that it is scarce worth our observing, and does not merit that, for it alone, we should alter our general maxim." But this single instance, this blue torpedo, sinks the ship! Here is a counterexample to the claim that all simple ideas are derived from impressions, and a clue to much else besides. The point, of course, is that we know that shades of color can vary, and this knowledge enables us to imagine the missing, intermediate shade of blue. Hume failed to appreciate the importance of this fact.

Now let us return to microfeatures and micropictures. I said that there is a confusion between microfeatures and micropictures. Identikits use micropictures, and these succumb to the same analysis as whole faces. So do micropictures consist of microfeatures, such as lines, shapes and colors?

Here we come to the end of the line. Such features are *properties,* not components or entities. They do not exist independently of what they belong to. This is the point of Lewis Carroll's famous joke about the grin of the Cheshire Cat, which remains when everything else has faded away. The grin is a property, or feature, of the cat. It does not exist independently of the cat. That is the point of the joke! In just the same way, the cat's face has a shape, but the shape does not exist independently of the face. The shape could not remain while the face faded away. We can *know about* the shape of the face, but we cannot store it as an inner entity. I will return to this later on.

Wittgenstein

At the beginning of the Introduction, I said that in some ways this knowledge-about epistemology draws on the work of the later Wittgenstein. Wittgenstein's influence may now be apparent. Malcolm got his pictorial/factual distinction from Wittgenstein. In Wittgenstein's early work, the *Tractatus Logico-Philosophicus,* picturing is the prototypical way in which cognition hooks onto the world. Propositions picture the logical structure of reality. The logical structure of a proposition is isomorphic with the facts that it represents. Wittgenstein says: "*That* is how a picture is attached to reality: it reaches right out to it" (Wittgenstein, 1961, 2.1511).[1]

By the time of the *Philosophical Investigations,* the best known work of his later period, all of this has gone. Any connection that exists between a representation and an object is now a cultural convention. Any sign can be variously interpreted—even pictures. Consequently, for something to function as a representation it must be accompanied by *knowledge about it* and about what it represents (although Wittgenstein himself does not explicitly talk about knowledge-about). The lines of projection that project a representation onto the world only function in the context of a method or convention of projection, and once we understand this, Wittgenstein says, "the [inner] object drops out of consideration as irrelevant" (Wittgenstein, 1963, § 293).[2] As I have put it, *representations wither away.* It is our knowledge *about* them and about the world that matters, knowledge that we can run off-line in the absence of its referents, and that enables us to construct representations in the imagination, *as created entities.* This ability has been consistently misinterpreted, from Classical Empiricism to the present day, as evidence that we store pale copies of experience and manipulate them in the imagination, and that this is somehow the essence of cognition.

In this section I have outlined independent reasons for abandoning a passive, atomic, copy-and-combine epistemology in favor of an active, constructive epistemology that emphasizes the importance of the knowledge we bring to experience: we know *about* the domain, and we deploy this knowledge off-line to construct representations in the imagination and created products in the external world. Why did we take such an elaborate detour?

When we look at creativity we see how manifestly inadequate representationism really is. We saw the tip of the iceberg in the first paragraph of the Introduction. In the case of pottery and sculpture there are simply no components or elements to combine, let alone interpreted, meaningful elements that can be computationally manipulated through their syntax or morphology. (Where, after all, are such elements in a lump of clay?) In music, architecture, and elsewhere, there are components, but they are not interpreted. If we build a house or compose a piece of music, we do not think that the bricks and the notes are *interpreted*. We do not say that this brick or this particular note has a *meaning*.

In the next section I shall suggest that there are three distinct types of productive, or output, creativity (as opposed to input, or problem-solving, creativity),[3] and I shall show that representationism can at best play a role in only one of them. Knowledge-about, on the other hand, is indispensable for all three. A separate but related point is that knowledge-about gives us the fluidity and flexibility that we need for creative cognition. Under these circumstances I thought it best to provide an account of knowledge-about before moving on to the broader canvas.

CREATIVITY AND COGNITIVE SCIENCE

We now turn to the broader canvas of creativity and cognitive science. I shall first show that creativity provides an acid test for cognitive science: cognitive science cannot succeed if it cannot model creativity, and it is here that it is most likely to fail. Later in the section we will see that creativity paints on a broader canvas, for it covers cases where there are not only no interpreted elements (as in the case of music), but where there are no elements at all (as in the case of the potter and the lump of clay).

I will then argue that not only creativity, but standard attempts to explain creativity, cast light on cognition and cognitive science. This is because these attempts typically subscribe to *combinationism,* which is the belief that creativity is the creative combination or recombination of previously existing elements.

Combinationism and representationism clearly have much in common. From a logical point of view, representationism is a special case of combinationism, in which the elements are interpreted. Both positions subscribe to atomism, so that reading Poincaré, writing about creativity in the twentieth century, is very much like reading Locke, writing about human knowledge in the seventeenth. Both ultimately derive from the same intuition, that *nothing can come of nothing,* so that what we have must be a *combination or recombination of what we already had.* I will examine this notion, which is absolutely crucial, and I will look very briefly at the historical origins of atomism and contrast its appropriateness in the context of explaining change in the physical world with its inappropriateness for explaining creativity.

The Acid Test for Cognitive Science

A major issue in cognitive science is the viability of the computational metaphor. This is the notion, as Thagard puts it, that "thinking can best be understood in terms of representational structures in the mind and computational procedures that operate on these structures" (Thagard, 1996). With the re-emergence of connectionism in the mid-1980s, and the more recent emergence of artificial life and genetic algorithms, cognitive science has to reassess its assumption that cognition is computation over text-like inner entities in the mind.

Cognitive science is also under attack for its belief that thinking is a computational process that occurs in the mind, since (it is claimed) this ignores the fact that our intellectual capabilities are grounded in our interaction with the world (Clancey, 1997). Finally, a rival to computationalism has emerged in the shape of dynamic systems theory (Port & van Gelder, 1995).

Let us stand back from this picture. The computational metaphor captures a sentiment that has been increasingly with us since La Mettrie's *L'Homme Machine* (Man A Machine) in the French Enlightenment. This is the intuition that people are machines, and that cognition is computation. But we have an equally strong intuition that machines cannot be creative (or, equivalently, that computation cannot be creative). Lady Lovelace, the friend and colleague of Charles Babbage, voiced this sentiment when she said that computers cannot be creative because they "have no pretensions whatever to *originate* anything." Consequently we have the conflicting intuitions that people are machines, and yet that they can do things that machines cannot do (they can be creative). This gives us an inconsistent triad:

1. People are creative.
2. People are machines.
3. Machines cannot be creative.

These cannot be true together. If two of them are true, the third one is false. Number 1 seems to be true, so either numbers 2, 3, or both, must be false. If number 3 is true it would be a fatal blow to the computational metaphor, for then number 2 would be false, and we would have to accept that people are not machines. In other words, we would have to accept that cognition is not computation. It could still be argued that *some* cognition is computation whereas some is not (so that we are part mechanism and part something else). I think that this would be a difficult position to defend. And the interesting question would then be, "what is the nature of our *non-computational* cognition?"

It is difficult to say what the consequences would be for cognitive science (as opposed to the computational metaphor) if number 3 was true. It might be argued that there is a difference between *modeling* creativity and *being* creative. Searle (1980, 1990), for instance, points out that there is a difference between simulation and duplication. Models of the digestive system do not digest pizzas, and models of hurricanes are not themselves wet and windy. So it might be argued that computers can model creativity, even though they cannot be creative themselves. I am not as clear as I would like to be about this distinction. I am not aware of any models of human creativity that are not also claimed to be creative in themselves, and I am not sure what it means to say that something is a model of a human creative process but is not creative in itself. I am simply not sure what such a model would look like.

Cognitive science is heavily influenced by the functionalist belief that it is cognitive *processes* that matter. If computers cannot be creative, then either (a) it is not cognitive processes that matter (so that functionalism is false), or (b) it *is* cognitive processes that matter, but these cannot be performed by computers. If (a) is true, then Searle's claim might be correct, that silicon is not the "right stuff" and lacks the causal powers to generate cognition and consciousness. It is not at all clear to me what would happen to cognitive science if this turned out to be the case. If (b) is true, then dynamic systems theory might give us the right framework for studying cognition. Either way, the result would be of enormous significance for cognitive science, and we would have got the result by asking questions about creativity and computation.

The point here (to labor the obvious) is that we can restore a focus to cognitive science by looking at what we are told *computers cannot do*—and yet which they must be able to do if they are to be intelligent. Good science does not test theories by looking at easy cases, since it is always possible to find data that will fit. A crucial part of the methodology of science is to test theories by exposing them to maximum risk—a point that has been made famous by Popper. We know some of the things that computers are good at. They can perform rapid search, and can do so far more efficiently than people. Consequently they can do things such as play chess and backgammon. They are adept at formulating and deploying complex bodies of rules, so that they can diagnose diseases of the blood and configure computer systems. Now the time has come to test them against the things that it is claimed they cannot do, and it is here that creativity provides us with the acid test.

I shall return to this issue in my discussion of the first chapter, in which Douglas Hofstadter looks at David Cope's program Emmy. Emmy produces music that is hard to distinguish from that of the great masters. Hofstadter is deeply disturbed by this because he believes that music comes from the depths of the human soul.

Creativity and Combinationism

We can gain insights into cognition and cognitive science by looking, not only at creativity, but at attempts to explain it. These attempts are typically combinatorial. The driving intuition is that we cannot get something out of nothing, so that creativity must be the combination of elements or matrices that we already had. Poincaré says, "the future elements of our combinations" are "something like the hooked atoms of Epicurus." Ideas have hooks on them, and "flash about in every direction . . . [like] a swarm of gnats, or, if you prefer a more learned comparison, like the molecules of gas in the kinematic theory of gases. Then their mutual impacts may produce new combinations" (Poincaré, 1982, p. 393).

A more recent account of creativity is provided by Margaret Boden (1990, 1993, 1994a, 1994b). Boden argues that creativity involves the mapping, exploration and transformation of what she calls "conceptual spaces." A conceptual space is a space of structures defined by the rules of a generative system. We explore it and map it by combining the elements according to the rules, and we transform it by exploring and mapping it, and then modifying the rules to generate different types of structures. She calls the first kind of creativity "improbabilist" and the second kind "impossibilist."

Boden argues for her thesis by examining the notion that creativity involves the novel combinations of old ideas—in other words, combinationism. Combinationist accounts, she says, do not tell us *which* combinations are novel, nor how novel combinations can come about.

Right. Combination theories only give us well-formedness criteria for structures. They define a space of structures, such as a space of sentences or sonnets, or pieces of music. They do not tell us which of these structures are novel or valuable, nor how to navigate the space to find novel or valuable structures. We can put this differently by saying that combination theorists need to say either that creativity involves the *creative* search of a combination space, or that it involves the search of a limited, "creative" combination space. Mozart was consistently more successful than Salieri in searching the musical space of his day, so a combinationist would have to say that he either searched the space more creatively, or that his space was limited to a subset of creative cases. Either way, creativity pops up on the wrong side of the equation and remains to be analyzed.

I think that Boden's criticism of combinationism is correct. It is ironical, therefore, that her own account is really a combinationist one, and falls to her own criticism. Consider the two types of creativity that she proposes. Improbabilist creativity maps and explores the space of structures defined by a generative system. This is just standard combinationism. All the structures in the space will be well-formed, by definition, but the vast majority will be dull and humdrum. We can use heuristics to prune the space, but the question will recur: how do we find *creatively interesting structures* in the pruned space?

It is not only a combinationist position. It is an atomistic one as well. The space of structures is defined by a generative system. A simple example of a generative system is a phrase structure grammar. A phrase structure grammar generates a set of sentences out of a finite set of atomic elements, using a finite number of rules. If the rules allow for recursion, the set of sentences will be non-finite, otherwise it will be finite. The rules iterate over a set of *atomic elements,* which are combined into structures of varying degrees of complexity.

Now look at her second type of creativity, impossibilist creativity. She says that impossibilist creativity employs heuristics to modify the original rule-set. This will give the rule-set a different generative ability, which will enable it to "break out" of the confines of the conceptual space. Euclidean geometry was transformed by abandoning the assumption that the angles of a triangle add up to 180 degrees, and Newtonian physics was transformed by abandoning the assumption that light travels in straight lines.

But so what? All that we have done here is to introduce new rules, or heuristics, at a higher level. We are still combining elements to get new structures. It is just that we have changed the rules that generate the structures.

Boden's own criticism of combinationism now recurs at a higher level. Modifying a rule-set will give us a new conceptual space, but it will not necessarily give us a more creatively interesting one. We need to know which modifications to a rule-set, and hence which new spaces, are creatively interesting and which are not. "Creative" pops up again on the wrong side of the equation.

Combinationism and Representationism

Combinationism and representationism are clearly very similar. Representationism has its origins in Descartes and Locke, as we saw previously. Locke tried to apply Newton's atomism to epistemology and cognition, and claimed that simple, atomic ideas combine together to give us complex molecular ones. Poincaré's combinationism says that ideas are like Epicurus' hooked atoms, and that "their mutual impacts may produce new combinations."

The only real difference between combinationism and representationism is that representationism is committed to the manipulation of *interpreted* elements, whereas combinationism is not. Representationism, in fact, is a special case of combinationism—that case where manipulated inner entities *represent,* where they have a semantics. In both cases the manipulation is syntactic. In both cases the theories try to account for the generated product in terms of the combination of simple elements into more complex wholes.

We can now see that there are three distinct types of creativity. The first trades in interpreted components. Such creativity ranges along a continuum from components that represent in themselves to representations that represent largely as a matter of convention, as when we say, "let this pepper pot represent Napoleon." In these cases, it is our knowledge-about that carries the cognitive load. The second type of creativity has components, but they are uninterpreted. Examples are music and architecture. The third type does not have components at all. Examples are pottery and sculpture.

The best-case scenario for representationism is that it can account for the first type of creativity, which has interpreted components. It cannot account for the other types of creativity, because the second type of creativity does not have interpreted components, and the third type does not have components at all. The best-case for combinationism is that it can account for the first two types of creativity, both of which have components. It cannot account for the third type of creativity, which does not have components.

Getting Something Out of Nothing

The driving intuition behind combinationism is that we cannot get something out of nothing, so creativity must be a combination or recombination of what we already had. Johnson-Laird says, "First, like all mental processes, [creativity] starts from some given building blocks. One cannot create out of nothing" (Johnson-Laird, 1988). Thornton says:

The starting point for any study of creativity is generally the observation that creativity involves the creation of something new. This observation is qualified with the observation that creation *ex nihilo* is a logical impossibility. (You can't create something out of nothing.) Therefore creativity must be the creation of something new out of things that already exist. But if this fact is logically necessary then it seems to imply that combination theories of creativity (i.e., theories which propose that creativity involves combining old stuff to make new stuff) must be essentially correct. (Thornton, 1994, p. 211)

Johnson-Laird talks about building blocks. Thornton says that creativity is the creation of something new out of things that already exist. But the pot was not made out of building blocks, or things that already existed, and neither was Michaelangelo's David. On the other hand, it is trivially true that Hamlet consists of words and that Verdi's Requiem consists of musical notes. These statements are not only uninformative and inane. They misdirect our attention away from the knowledge, experience and skill that really gave rise to these things. It is a tautology to say that nothing can come of nothing. But creativity does not begin with nothing. It begins with knowledge, skills and abilities—the full panoply of human cognition. The challenge is to explain how we can get one type of thing out of another type of thing, for it is a commonplace that we get explicit artifacts, created products, out of implicit knowledge and skill: the painting emerges from the painter's brush, the pot emerges in the hands of the potter, poems and stories emerge from the writer's mind. These are the palpable products of our knowledge and ability, so that there really is something there when there was *nothing of the kind* there before, but not when there was *nothing at all* there before!

The kind of explanation provided by combinationism might be appropriate for the physical world, but it is inappropriate for the world of human invention. It is so inappropriate that I will look, very briefly, at the historical origins of atomism, so that we can contrast its original relevance with its current misuse.

Atomism

Atomism was introduced by the Greeks to solve the Problem of Change. Parmenides and the Eleatics believed (and it was entirely appropriate in this context!) that "nothing can come of nothing," and concluded that everything that exists has always existed. They also believed that nothing that exists can become nothing, so that everything is eternal. Democritus and the other Greek atomists took this further and argued that if nothing can come out of nothing, and if nothing is ever lost, then change must consist of the *combination and recombination* of tiny, indivisible, eternal, immutable elements, which they called *a-toms* (meaning "un-cuttables").

These people were materialists, inasmuch as they believed that all that exists is atoms and the void. They did not believe in an intelligence guiding the natural course of events.

Now wind the clock forward to the seventeenth century. Locke is taken with the new experimental method, and especially with "corpuscular philosophy." He tries to provide an atomistic account of the acquisition of knowledge. At birth, he says, the mind is a *tabula rasa,* an empty slate, but is written on by the hand of experience. Sensory impressions give rise to simple, atomic ideas, which form together in the mind to give us complex, molecular ones.

The Greeks introduced atomism to account for the changes that we see going on in the world around us, on the assumption that the world consists of some basic, underlying stuff that has always been there, and on the assumption that there is no intelligence guiding the natural course of events.

Under these circumstances, change and innovation can *only* consist of combinations and recombinations of what we already have. But human cognition is totally different to this, for here we have active, constructive intelligence and we are not limited to the combination and recombination of what we already have (that is, to a fixed set of passive elements). On the one hand we have the material world, with no guiding intelligence behind it, and in this context it is entirely appropriate to say that nothing can come of nothing. On the other, we have active, constructive intelligence generating new creative output. Atomism is appropriate for explaining the material world, where all that we have is the material world, but it is inappropriate for explaining creativity, which is driven by intelligence and mind.

The challenge is to show how creative products can emerge, not out of a combination of basic elements, but out of our knowledge and skill—out of what we know about them and their domains. How this is possible will unfold as we work our way through the chapters, to which we now turn.

EMMY—COMBINATIONISM AT WORK?

In Chapter 1, Douglas Hofstadter talks about David Cope's program, Emmy, which produces music that is hard to distinguish from that of the great masters. Hofstadter says that, as a rule, about two-thirds of the audience can distinguish between Emmy and Johann Sebastian Bach, while the other third gets it wrong. He adds, "it is by no means always the sophisticated audience members who make the wrong classification." Moreover, Emmy is evolving all the time.

Emmy poignantly illustrates our conflicting intuitions that we are machines, and that machines cannot be creative. Hofstadter is deeply disturbed by her. This is not because Emmy is a machine. He says that he has long been convinced that we are machines. What worries him is that she is such a simple machine. He believes that music comes from the depths of the human soul, and he believes that a human soul depends on "intricate biological machinery."

Emmy is a challenge to me as well, because she seems to present an excellent case for combinationism, and Cope himself says that she produces what he calls "recombinant music." I shall argue that the emotions of the input pieces retain their power and integrity because of the subtle, systematic labeling that is assigned to their components. This labeling provides *knowledge about* the components, that determines their location in the local and global contexts. Emmy effectively reverse engineers the pieces she is given as input. I will return to this.

Hofstadter says that Emmy's "central *modus operandi*" is *chop up and reassemble*. In the local context, pieces must hook onto one another and snuggle up against each other in the way that they do in the input music.

Hofstadter calls this *syntactic meshing,* and he likens it to the way in which the pieces of a jigsaw puzzle fit snugly together. What he calls *semantic meshing* concerns the *content* of the pieces, and is similar to the way in which we put jigsaw pieces together by looking at the picture we are building up. Pieces have labels attached to them that locate them in the local and global contexts. A local fragment of an input piece has its own label, plus that of the fragment of which it is a part, plus that of the fragment of which *that* is a part, and so on up. These tell us "where we are" inside a piece, and enable us to locate the fragment "in the same place" in the piece that is being composed. Hofstadter suggests that this may "constitute a significant new contribution to music theory." Emmy uses other mechanisms, but these are her main ones.

In our discussion at the end of the chapter (after Doug's question and answer session), I suggest that it is Emmy and David Cope, together, who produce the music, so that the question is: who contributes the most? Doug's reply is that Cope has "striven mightily to diminish his own role in her composition," and that his participation in Emmy's compositional process is becoming less and less.

So let us imagine that Cope gets to the point where Emmy is completely autonomous, inasmuch as he doesn't twiddle her dials as she is composing. He gives her some Bach or Chopin, and she produces pieces that are equally as good, at least pretty often, in the same way as a human composer. What would we say under these circumstances?

We might say that Emmy is autonomous, but that she is autonomous only because she has been taught and trained by a human being. And for this reason (we might say) she is a mimic and a parasite. She is a mimic because she can only copy musical styles, rather than having a style of her own, and she is a parasite because she mimics and has been *trained* to mimic by a human being.

In Emmy's defense, creativity in music, or in any of the other arts, often begins with copying and imitation. This is simply how we learn the trade: we copy and create in the style of others who have excelled in the past, and only later do we acquire a voice of our own. Emmy doesn't have a voice of her own yet, but we would be impressed by a *person* who could imitate as well as she does. The same thing applies to her being trained by a human being. We might train a person to compose like Bach or Chopin, and we would be delighted if they were as successful as Emmy.

That is one thing we might say. But the Devil is in the detail. We train people and programs in very different ways. In fact, strictly speaking, Emmy isn't trained at all (not even in the way that a neural network is trained). Emmy is *programmed.* I think that it comes down to what kind of a system Emmy is, compared to what kind of systems people are. In my discussion with Doug I point out that in Hofstadter and FARG, 1995, he says that if a computer generated a deeply moving new piece of music he would not know how to assign credit unless he knew about its innards. What is now worrying him is that Emmy's innards are so simple. So on the one hand he says that the innards tell us how to assign credit, and on the other he is surprised that relatively simple innards can produce music that seems to come from a soul. He can avoid this inconsistency by sticking to his original intuition and saying that Emmy's innards are so simple that the music does not come from a soul—that the credit does not lie with her.

Etiology (the question of causal origins) is vitally important in judging creativity. A monkey on a typewriter might just turn out a good poem, which might move us and show us something about the human condition. But it would not be *creative,* any more than it would be creative if the words had just tumbled together. This shows that we judge creativity at least partly in terms of causal origins. For this reason it seems to me that Emmy might be the *final failure* of combinationism (and, for that matter, of the Turing Test). Rather than agonizing about the fact that she produces beautiful music, we might say, "This shows that *even a relatively simple machine* can be a successful combinationist. Although the elements have been successfully combined, *there is no creativity here.*" So either we can say that Emmy is creative, on the basis of her output—and then we have to ask how a relatively simple machine can be creative—or we can say that she is not creative, because she is a relatively simple machine. In this case, recombinant music is not creative: it is merely syntactic manipulation. And in this case, music can come from the human soul, but it can *also* be produced by a relatively simple machine (but then it is not creative).

Where does this leave Doug's fear that Chopin or Bach might have been consummate craftsmen, who didn't really *feel* what they were composing— that in some sense they might have been operating at a shallow, syntactic, combinatorial level? I think the answer is that this is possible, but that we have no reason to believe that it is true. It is actually a modal fallacy to say that we do not know something because it is possible that it is false (in this case, that we do not know that Bach and Chopin composed from their souls, because it is *possible* that they didn't). It is consistent to say, "I know that Bach's music came from his soul, but it is possible that it didn't." If this wasn't a fallacy we would only be able to know things that are necessarily true. We would not be able to know things that are only contingently true.

But the question remains: How does Emmy produce deep and moving music? Even if she is not creative, we still need to know how she can compose such wonderful stuff. How can she compose 'music that would come from the soul if it was created by a human'? What is the magic in her innards that enables her to retain the soulfulness of her input, down to a fine level of granularity, and then to recombine these "music molecules," as Doug calls them, in such an effective way? How can combinationism do this?

I think that the answer lies in the labels. When Emmy is given an input piece, she systematically labels its components, on a hierarchy of levels from local to global, so that every piece is highly conceptualized. Every piece is labeled with information about its immediate, local context, and it inherits the labels attached to the higher-level fragments of which it is a part. This is exactly what a knowledge-about theory would expect to find: labeling, or knowledge-about, that enables Emmy to *reconstitute* new musical pieces. I am not well-acquainted with Emmy's innards, but it seems to me that input pieces could be decomposed into very small fragments, and new pieces constructed out of them, just so long as the fragments were adequately labeled.

How far can this process go? Why shouldn't pieces be analyzed down to fragments that have no structure at all, where all of the information is carried in the labels, where the structure is reduced to pure content and idea? This would give us plans, or genotypes, from which new phenotypes (new musical pieces) could be built.

This is reverse engineering, from product to pattern to plan. Input pieces are reverse engineered down to a set of plans or instructions. In the old black-and-white movie, *The Ghost Goes West*, a Scottish castle is dismantled, labeled block-by-block, and taken to America. (The castle contains the ghosts of a father and son, and the son says, "Father, I don't want to go to America."). The information to rebuild the castle is in the labels that are attached to the building blocks, and in other, more general knowledge about the structure of the castle.

Notice that the more knowledge-about we have, the smaller the pieces can be, and the more flexible we become. This is not the vacuous flexibility of having no constraints at all. We would have that kind of flexibility if we had a pile of blocks without any information about how to assemble them! Positive flexibility comes with plenty of knowledge-about, that tells us how to put Humpty together again, and how to create lots of other Humpties as well. This underscores the vital relationship between knowledge-about and flexibility: the greater the knowledge-about, the greater the flexibility. The limiting case, where we have the most flexibility, is where we have no building blocks to begin with, but where we know how to construct them, in any shape or size. Now our ability is not constrained by the combinatorial capabilities of a fixed set of elements, for we can change the set of elements. Or we might know how to avoid building blocks altogether by carving a castle out of the rock, or sculpting a glass castle out of the sand—think up your own science fiction scenario! After all, the more we know, the more we are able to do. As we saw earlier, the building blocks "wither away" as our conceptual knowledge becomes more sophisticated. As Wittgenstein says, "the object drops out of consideration as irrelevant."[4]

RETELLING THE EMPIRICIST STORY

In Chapter 2, Jesse Prinz and Larry Barsalou set out to revitalize the empiricist tradition of perceptual symbol systems. This is a tradition that originates with Aristotle, but which is most commonly associated with Classical Empiricism. The Classical Empiricists (Locke, Berkeley, and Hume) stressed the importance of experience and perception in the acquisition of concepts and knowledge, and said that we derive our concepts, or "ideas," from corresponding percepts, or "impressions" (roughly, experiences). Percepts give rise to simple ideas, which are combined to form complex ones. This account is commonly believed to have failed, and one of its many problems is that it does not adequately distinguish between ideas and impressions: ideas are seen as pale copies of impressions, differing from them only in terms of what Hume called "force and liveliness."

Prinz and Barsalou believe that this traditional account has failed because it embodies a naive belief about the nature of perception. It sees ideas as relatively unstructured, conscious images that are close copies of the experiences from which they have been derived. In contrast, Prinz and Barsalou believe that what they call "perceptual symbols" are structured, or schematized, and are inaccessible to consciousness. Such symbols, they say, *must* be schematized to account for our ability to recognize commonality across very different inputs—for instance, to recognize Great Danes and Chihuahuas as dogs, while excluding rats, cats and possums. Equipped with this account of perceptual symbols, they set out to rehabilitate the traditional account, *and* to formulate a symbolic theory of cognition that is quite different to the standard symbol-handling account that we find in cognitive science. That account treats symbols as arbitrary: the word "cow" refers to a large, milk-producing bovine, but in principle it could refer to anything. In contrast, what Prinz and Barsalou call the *perceptual* symbol of a cow is extracted from perceptual representations of cows: it *looks* like a cow, and for this reason is non-arbitrary. Prinz and Barsalou provide an account of perceptual symbols and how they can be combined in a perceptual symbol system to give us concepts and cognition.

What has this got to do with creativity? First, Prinz and Barsalou argue that creativity is a litmus for the viability of a cognitive theory: a cognitive theory has to be able to account for our ability to be creative. Second, they set out to "domesticate" creativity by distinguishing between what they call "mundane" and "exceptional" creativity. Exceptional creativity is what we normally mean by "creativity." Mundane creativity is our ability to acquire concepts and combine them into new and original thoughts. They provide an account of how we can do this, in terms of their theory of perceptual symbol systems.

I begin our discussion by asking Prinz and Barsalou how idealization, or schematization, can possibly turn the trick. They say that perceptual systems are schematized inasmuch as they "abstract away the irrelevant details of incoming signals, separate aspects of a signal that are independent, and introduce a significant amount of structure." This schematization is demanded by "behavioral evidence that we can recognize commonality across very different inputs." They say that we can recognize this commonality because we have highly structured, schematized inner symbols. But (I ask) how can *any* symbols be flexible enough to pick out the relevant commonalities? How can we have a "general idea" of a dog (in the sense of some kind of inner copy of a percept, whether schematized or not), which picks out Great Danes and Chihuahuas, but doesn't pick out rats, cats, and possums?

Their reply to this question comes in three parts. First, they say that categories have multiple representations. Then they say that each representation can be modified to achieve a high degree of flexibility. Finally they say that representations of dogs refer to dogs not only because they resemble dogs, but because they are causally related to dogs.

Let us take these in turn. First, they say that they do not want to give the impression that all categories can be represented by a single perceptual symbol. A category may have multiple representations. We may, for instance, have a family of different dog representations stored in memory corresponding to dogs we have experienced (one for Cujo, another for Benji, etc.). These "exemplars," as they call them, may be similar enough to co-classify in memory, but distinct enough to warrant storage of separate symbols.

It seems to me that this is the beginning of a regress. Dogs come in so many different shapes and sizes that it is difficult to see how a single schematized representation can cover all of them. Consequently (they say) we need a family of different representations to cover all the dogs we have experienced. Now either we will have a very large number of representations, say, one for each dog, in which case we will need to be able to recognize that they are all representations of dogs. In that case the problem recurs, and we have a regress. Or we will have a small number of representations, say, one for small dogs, one for large dogs, and so on. But then the schematization problem recurs: how can a single representation cover all small dogs, or all large ones? Prinz and Barsalou seem to prefer the first option. It seems to me that the only way to stop the regress is to say that we *know about* the representations (that is, we know about them that they are all representations of dogs). But in that case we know about dogs already and do not need internalized copies, and in that case the regress does not have to begin in the first place.

This brings us to the second part of their reply, which is that representations can be modified to achieve a high degree of flexibility. Their example is that schematization might give us a decomposable representation of a normal, four-legged dog, which can be used to identify or simulate a three-legged dog, by simply removing a part. This same basic mechanism enables us to "spontaneously create new category representations during online processing" by "mixing and combining parts of existing perceptual symbols."

This suggests that we have a great deal of dexterity at manipulating our representations, and this in turn suggests that we know a great deal about them. I will return to this later.

Finally, Prinz and Barsalou say that representations refer not only by virtue of resemblance, but by virtue of causal connection: dog representations refer to dogs by virtue of the fact that they were initially created as a result of encounters with dogs, or by virtue of their ability to reliably detect dogs when they are present.

What is the evidence for this? Of course there is a causal story. Our representations of dogs are causally related to our experiences and interactions with dogs. But *how* are they causally related? Why does causality favor one story over another? The story that I am arguing for is that we learn about the world, and run this knowledge off-line to construct representations in the imagination, so that representations are constructions rather than copies. There is a causal story here as well. Why does causality favor Prinz and Barsalou's theory?

Next, consider this scenario. You have had causal encounters with dogs, as a result of which you have a rich repertoire of doggy representations. Now you get amnesia and forget all that you ever learned about dogs. You have a rich internal repertoire, which you acquired through a causal process, but the representations mean nothing to you, because you have forgotten about dogs. This would be like having a collection of family photographs but being too old and doddery to know who they are photographs of. Being causally connected to canines doesn't help you to understand representations of canines, any more than being causally connected to the people in the photograph helps you to understand the photograph and to know about your family. Without the relevant knowledge-about, representations are of no use to us, whatever their causal origins. (On the other hand, we can know about aardvarks or dodos, or old John Brown of Osawatomie, without having any causal connections with them at all.)

Another issue that we talk about is *cognitive flexibility,* which brings us back to our ability to manipulate representations. It is a crucial aspect of creativity that we can imagine pretty much anything. We can imagine our favorite politician riding a donkey, we can imagine him with a green face, we can imagine him with red hair and horns, etc. I claim that an active, constructive, knowledge-about account of cognition can account for this ability. It can say that we construct representations in the imagination, deploying our knowledge about things in the world, and that we modify them by using our general knowledge of the properties of things in the world (for instance, that shapes and colors can vary). Prinz and Barsalou, on the other hand, say that we make copies of experience—schematized copies, but copies nonetheless. Now they can either stick with this copy-and-schematize account or they can amplify it by introducing knowledge-about, as generalized, nonperceptual knowledge. If they stick with it, they will be stuck with a fixed representational repertoire that will give them very little cognitive flexibility.

In fact they do not stick with it. They amplify it with knowledge-about. They say that, for instance, the differences between the representation of a lion running and an armadillo running can be extrapolated from our *knowledge about* the differences between the anatomies of the two animals (e.g., our knowledge about the length of their legs).

Now I think that they have two problems. They have the problem about general symbols and they have to provide an account of what it is to know about something (in this case, the anatomy of the two animals). Since they have to provide an account of knowledge-about *anyway,* why not let it do *all* the work? Since we know about the anatomy of the animals, why can't we know about running? In fact we *do* know about running: we know about bodies and legs, and how we move them to get from one place to another. Since we have this knowledge, why do we need general perceptual symbols at all? They are problematic anyway.

In their reply, Prinz and Barsalou first outline the cognitive mechanisms that enable us to "freely recombine perceptual symbols to form representations of novel objects and events." Perceptual symbols, they say, are "neural states in our input systems." These states have complex parts. The visual system, for example, processes color, motion, and form separately. The brain, they say, can generate combinations of perceptual features not found together in experience, which it typically does by taking features that are found in experience (say, the color red and a person's face) and putting them together. When we imagine a red face we call up a face shape from memory by reactivating a pattern in the face-shape center in our visual system. Then we reactivate the neural pattern for red in our color system, and finally we bind them together. Accumulating perceptual symbols can be a passive process in the first instance, but once acquired the symbols can be creatively and constructively recombined.

I find some of this surprising. Prinz and Barsalou say that perceptual symbols are neural states. I thought that perceptual symbols were, well, perceptual symbols, as illustrated in Figure 2.2. But our positions do seem to be converging. Prinz and Barsalou say that we can "generate combinations of perceptual features not found together in experience." I agree that we can do this. I think that what drives this ability is our knowledge about perceptual features: we can imagine a red face or a green face because we know about faces and colors. But, I maintain, we can do more than merely combine (back to the identikit again!). We can *genuinely* imagine. We can imagine shades and hues and subtleties, and all sorts of nuances, that we have never encountered in experience and never thought of before. We have already seen the implications of Hume's missing shade of blue. Also, I agree that the learning process can be passive, whereas the knowledge, once acquired, can be dynamically deployed. This is a theme we shall return to in later chapters. But we disagree about the details—and about other things. I am deeply skeptical about face shapes being stored in separate parts of the brain. Face shapes are *properties,* not *parts* or *components,* and do not exist independently of faces, any more than the smile of the Cheshire Cat exists independently of its face.

Finally, Prinz and Barsalou address what I see as the redundancy of perceptual symbols. Since they have to provide an account of knowledge-about *anyway,* why not let it do *all* the work? Well, they say, suppose that you have never seen an armadillo run. You do, however, know about running, because you have seen what other creatures look like when they run. And you know what armadillos look like. You can now combine the two, to predict what a running armadillo will look like. You have a general knowledge of what running looks like, and what armadillos look like, and you creatively combine the two.

It seems to me that in this case you do not have a general knowledge of running at all: all that you have are more perceptual symbols of animals running. A general knowledge of running, I take it, would be a knowledge of what these symbols have in common by virtue of which they symbolize or depict running (for instance, they depict the way that animals rapidly move their legs in contact with a surface to propel themselves along). An alien who knew nothing about running might not be able to make sense of them, even if they were moving pictures. Compare this with the way in which we might not be able to understand any complex process, even though it is going on before our eyes. We might need to have it explained to us, to be talked through it, so that it makes sense to us. But once we understand it, we no longer need to see it in action, although our knowledge enables us to imagine it. Napoleon said that a picture is worth a thousand words—yes, but only if we understand the picture.

REPRESENTATIONAL REDESCRIPTION AND ACCESS

In Chapter 3, Donald Peterson talks about what he calls "explicitation." Explicitation is the process of acquiring new knowledge by explicitating (making explicit) knowledge that was already available to the system in principle, but which it could not access in practice. He identifies two broad types of explicitation: *representational redescription,* which is the explicitation of knowledge that is implicit in inner cognitive structures, and *notational explicitation,* which is the explicitation of knowledge that is implicit in external notations. An example of the first kind of explicitation is the way that a young child acquires thousands of water-pouring skills, which eventually blossom forth as an explicit theory about the behavior of fluids. The knowledge that is implicit in the child's behavioral capabilities is explicitated as an accessible theory that she can reflect upon and change. An example of the second form of explicitation is re-representing a list structure as a tree, or going from Roman to Arabic notation in order to facilitate the multiplication of numbers. Peterson identifies subspecies within these genera and analyzes their structure and complexity.

In this section I focus on the first kind of explicitation: representational redescription. The Representational Redescription Hypothesis (RRH) says that the mind is endogenously driven to go beyond what Annette Karmiloff-Smith calls "behavioral mastery" and to redescribe, or re-represent, its knowledge to itself in increasingly abstract forms (Karmiloff-Smith, 1992, 1993, 1994). It does this "under its own steam," without need of exogenous pressure. Initially the knowledge is implicit in the system's procedures and abilities. It is not available to other procedures, nor to the system as a whole: Karmiloff-Smith says that it is *in* the system but is not available *to* the system. In the course of development it is redescribed as explicit, declarative knowledge that becomes available to other procedures and to the system as a whole. We continue to redescribe it on increasingly abstract levels, all of which are retained and may be accessed when necessary. Peterson explains the levels of representation and outlines some of the experimental evidence.

The RRH gives us a rich picture of knowledge, native endowment, creativity, and mental life. Here are some of its implications:

1. At the individual level it claims that we go from skills to structured thoughts (from *knowing how* to *knowing that*). Philosophers have known about this distinction for a long time, but here it is being claimed that knowing how can *become* knowing that.

   This has implications for Artificial Intelligence (AI). AI has been held up for the last 15 to 20 years by the problem of commonsense knowledge. How do we get a system to understand that water flows out of a container when we tilt it, or that things fall when we let go of them? Classical, symbol-handling AI tries to give knowledge and belief to AI systems by putting knowledge structures and belief structures into knowledge bins and belief bins, possibly endowing the structures with causal efficacy, so that the system behaves in the right kind of way. Children, on the other hand, acquire commonsense knowledge by interacting with the world. Their knowledge and symbolisms are grounded in skills and abilities that apparently *become* declarative structures. Can we implement this process?

2. Representational redescription seems to give us an epistemological third route: knowledge can be innate or learned *or* it can be a re-representation of what we already knew. This revives the rationalist claim that knowledge can develop from within. It counters, in a way reminiscent of both Kant and Popper, the dreary empiricism that says that science and experience start with observation and slowly and cautiously proceed towards theory. But the Kantian story is subtly

retold. Out goes innate content. In comes an innate propensity to construct theories and to re-represent to ourselves what we already knew.

3. At the species level, the RRH points to a joint in the natural order between creatures that have thoughts and a mental life and creatures that do not: something has a mental life if it can present its knowledge to itself as explicit structures (that is, as *thoughts*).

4. Most importantly for our purposes, the RRH provides an account of creativity: a system is creative if it can articulate its domain-specific skills as accessible structures that it can reflect upon and change, and map onto structures in other domains.

   This is precisely what we need for an account of creativity, for it says that our creative products emerge, not out of a combination of elements, but out of our knowledge and skill—just as we believed that they did before we began doing cognitive science.

Consequently, the RRH solves problems, generates solutions, and leaps mighty buildings at a single bound. The problem is that we do not know how to implement it (Clark and Karmiloff-Smith, 1993). We do not know what an implementation would even look like. We do not know what kinds of neural processes support it and make it possible. Nor do we know how it could have evolved. In fact, as the problem is stated, it looks like magic. We spontaneously go from one representational format to another, without exogenous pressure. Arguably it is even worse than this. We go from skills and abilities, where it is not clear to me that we have underlying representations *at all*, to declarative, text-like inner items. On the one hand we have skills and abilities, on the other we have structured thoughts and theories, and in between is what we might call "the Great Epistemological Divide." It is not entirely unfair to say that the RRH only restates the problem. We want to know how we can get palpable products (thoughts, theories, pots, paintings, poems) out of our knowledge and skill. The RRH says that we get them by going from implicit, procedural representations to explicit declarative ones. But how do we do so?

I think that we have arrived at this impasse because we have the wrong epistemology. In its present formulation, representational redescription requires a mysterious emergence of new, inner formats. We go from the representations that allegedly underlie our implicit procedural capabilities to the explicit, declarative representations that constitute thoughts and theories. Following Dartnall (1996), Peterson suggests a different way of explaining the data: rather than generating new forms of representation, we get increasingly better access to one and the same internal structure. The argument goes like this. To explain our increasing cognitive flexibility, Karmiloff-Smith says that we introduce new representational structures. An analogy is that we begin with something like a stack or a queue, which is only accessible sequentially, one item at a time, starting at one end. As a result we are constrained, for instance, to drawing stick figures by drawing the head, drawing the body, drawing the arms, and so on—always in the same sequence, and we subsequently find it easier to access and modify sub-skills at the beginning and end of the sequence. We then (to continue with our analogy) redescribe the data as a list, where it can be accessed orthogonally, in any sequence at all. This enables us to put feet on the end of arms, hands on the end of legs, and so on. That is, Karmiloff-Smith proposes a change in inner representational format in order to explain our ability to access information and abilities that we could not have accessed before. But in that case, why not say that it is *just* a question of access? We get better at accessing the information and abilities—and that's it. There is no need to talk about representational change.

The details of this alternative epistemology will emerge as we work through the chapters, but a first approximation is that three phases of learning give rise to three types of creativity:

1. The first phase is the *input-creative*, problem-solving phase, during which we learn about the domain. We solve problems, learn to understand music and poetry, and generally learn about the world.

2. In the second phase we use the knowledge-about acquired during the first phase to generate representations of what we know about the domain. The child draws a stick figure of a person. We write a word on a piece of paper to see how it is spelled. The child already knows about people, and we already know how to spell the word. We explicitate our knowledge in order to freely access it and to familiarize ourselves with what we already know by running it before the mind's eye. I call this *Type 1 output creativity*.

3. We become proficient at accessing and modifying our representations and at creating new and original ones: we draw funny men, produce music and poetry, and come up with thoughts and theories of our own. I call this *Type 2 output creativity*.

This is a first approximation, painted in broad brushstrokes. It will presumably be punctuated by periods during which performance deteriorates before it improves, as we attend to inner processing and pay relatively little attention to external input. Karmiloff-Smith distinguishes between *representational change* and *behavioral change*. Representational change is a story of ongoing success: the learning graph goes steadily up (Karmiloff-Smith, 1992, p. 16). Behavior, or performance, on the other hand, goes through three phases and deteriorates before it improves, giving us a U-shaped curve. Karmiloff-Smith says that this deterioration is because the system is focusing on the process of inner representational change, to the detriment of external input.

There are two crucial differences between Karmiloff-Smith's theory and my own. First, she begins her investigations where other developmental psychologists stop, with behavioral mastery, at which point the child has acquired its basic skills. I think that if we are to explain what happens after behavioral mastery we need to look at what preceded it—to see how the knowledge acquired during the input phase generates representations that are Type 1 output creative.

The second crucial difference is that I maintain that a representation is not a hidden, inner structure. Rather, it is the output itself, the created product that is generated by our knowledge about the domain. The child knows about people and articulates this knowledge to itself by creating a representation in its imagination or on paper. This process of articulating our knowledge to ourselves is creative in itself, because it generates a structure out of our knowledge and skill.

In my discussion with Peterson I suggest that representational redescription and notational explicitation are so different that it is hard to see how they can belong to the same family. Representational redescription is driven from within. Notational change is conscious and willing and deliberate. Notational change requires a change in representational format, whereas (or so we both believe) representational redescription does not. What seems to follow is that representational redescription and notational change are very different, and that it is some sort of category mistake to try to explain one in terms of the other. By articulating the two types of explicitation, Peterson enables us to see the differences between them, and, I believe, to see that so-called "representational redescription" does not involve representational change at all.

REPRESENTATIONAL RANKS

In the previous section, we saw that representational redescription gives us a rich picture of knowledge, native endowment, creativity and mental life. A system is creative if it can articulate its domain-specific skills to itself as structures that it can reflect upon and change. This is precisely what we need to account for creativity, because it provides an in-theory explanation of how our creative products emerge, not out of a combination of elements, but out of our knowledge and ability. It provides an in-theory explanation of how we can come up with thoughts and theories, pots and paintings, almost, but not entirely, *ex nihilo*. It also begins to explain how we can access and update our knowledge, and to cross-pollinate it across domains. The problem, as we saw, is that we do not know how to implement this process.

To some extent Graeme Halford and William Wilson take up the challenge in Chapter 4. They begin by discussing representational redescription, and agree that creativity requires explicit representations that are accessible to, and modifiable by, other cognitive processes without need of external input. More specifically, they say that creativity requires the ability to represent and recursively modify explicit, complex relations in parallel.

In order to define this ability at a more theoretical level, they outline a hierarchy of six levels, or ranks, of representation, show how they relate to performance at different cognitive levels, and assess their effectiveness at mediating creativity.

The first two levels, Ranks 0 and 1, employ mechanisms that are traditionally identified with associationist psychology, and that only process associations, whereas Ranks 2–6 can process relations. There are no representations at all at Rank 0, which is concerned with reflexes, stimulus-response associations, and perceptuo-motor skills. There are no representations of *relations* at Rank 1. Infants apparently represent features of objects, such as height, and their distance from other objects, but there is no evidence that they can relate such representations to other representations, so presumably they have no explicit representations of relations.

Ranks 2–6, in contrast, embody the relational knowledge that Halford and Wilson believe underlies higher thought. At Rank 2, simple propositions can be expressed: a predicate can be represented with one argument, for example HAPPY(John). At Rank 3, the predicate can have two arguments, for example LOVES(Mary,John). And so on, with increasingly sophisticated cognition emerging at each new level. The ability to represent propositions, relations and variables emerges at Rank 3, and the ability to represent x as varying as a function of y, as in $R(x,y)$, emerges at Rank 4.

Evidence from the literature suggests that these ranks are associated with phylogenetic and ontogenetic development. The ability to represent relations and to change representations dynamically seems to be a factor that differentiates species at different points in the phylogenetic scale. Similarly, the ability to represent relational concepts increases with the age of the individual.

Halford and Wilson now unpack their claim that creativity depends partly on the ability to represent the relational structure of a task. Relational representations, they say, have properties such as explicitness and accessibility to other cognitive processes, which enable them to be processed recursively. For this reason, Halford and Wilson suggest that representational redescription can be explained at least in part by the transition from associative to relational representations. Explicit, high-level representation gives us dynamic binding, higher-order relations, and the ability to change strategies. An argument is dynamically bound to a predicate if the binding can change in the course of reasoning, so that, for example, LIKES(John,Tom) can change to HATES(John,Tom). An example of a higher-order relation is "It's good that Peter returned," which can be expressed as GOOD(RETURNED[Peter]), where GOOD is a higher-order predicate that has RETURNED(Peter) as its argument. Higher-order relations allow us to express structure at a high level of abstraction, and so enable analogies to be formed between situations that are similar in structure but different in content. Finally, high-level representations enable us to represent the structure of a task, which guides the development of efficient skills, strategies and procedures.

Halford and Wilson explore these aspects of creativity in the Transitive Inference Mapping (TRIM) and the Structured Tensor Analogical Reasoning (STAR) computational models.

I said at the beginning of this section that Halford and Wilson to *some* extent take up the challenge of modeling representational redescription. This is because they limit themselves to what they see as the preliminary process of modeling representational ranks, before trying to model the process of ascending from one rank to another. They say that research has been more concerned with modeling phenomena that belong to particular levels, rather than making the transition between levels, so they have limited themselves to defining the levels with more precision.

What would an explanation of representational redescription look like in terms of relational complexity and rank theory? Following Phillips et al. (1995) and Halford et al. (2001), Halford and Wilson suggest that it can be explained at least in part by the transition from associative to relational representations (from Rank 1 to at least Rank 2). One way of formulating the question is to consider the transition from Rank 1 to Rank 2 neural networks. This is basically to change from a three-layered net to a tensor net, and Halford and Wilson say that they know of no published algorithm that can do this. Another way is to consider the transition as it occurs in nature. This is so-called "learning-set" acquisition, in which the structure underlying a set of isomorphic discrimination tasks is acquired. Learning becomes progressively faster as more problems are experienced. Participants learn something more general, more "abstract," than the properties of the individual stimuli. Halford and Wilson say that there is almost no understanding of how this improvement occurs.

Halford and Wilson have to say that the child who can draw a stick figure, but who cannot redescribe its representation, is at Rank 1. Here is what they say about Rank 1: "At this level there is internal representation, but it is undifferentiated, and is unrelated to other representations. Many features, and quite a large amount of information, can be represented, but no relations with semantic interpretations are defined between components of the representation."

Surely this is not true of the child who can draw stick figures. This child knows about people, knows about their parts and properties, knows that they have arms and legs, etc. Moreover, she knows about the relationship between these things. If we asked her about arms and legs and the relationship between them, she would be able to tell us.

I think that one of the problems here is that we have a monolithic concept of a skill. Hoverflies have skills. They can meet and mate in mid-air. These are hard-wired skills and the behavior is principally driven by information that is in the environment, rather than in the hoverfly (Dreyfus, 1979). The beaver has skills, and knows how to build a dam. But it has no access to the knowledge that drives this ability. It is trapped in a procedure, doing what its rules tell it to do: first you put in stones, then you put in big logs, then you put in small ones. Halford and Wilson, following Dartnall (1994), agree with this. They say that humans can articulate rules at the explicit level and modify them, whereas animals that are phylogenetically more primitive lack this ability. The beaver can build a dam, but has no explicit knowledge of dam building, so that it is not an engineer. Even if a beaver and an engineer were to build precisely the same dam, they say, their mental processes would be very different. The differences would become apparent if modifications had to be made to the dam-building procedure, and the more fundamental the modifications, the more the differences would become apparent.

I think that there is something wrong here. I agree with Halford and Wilson that there is a phylogenetic difference between beavers and people, especially engineers (engineers will be gratified by this piece of information). This is for the reasons that Halford and Wilson provide: the engineer knows what she knows, and can change it, whereas the beaver is trapped in a procedural rut. But according to Karmiloff-Smith the redescription takes place after the child has achieved behavioral mastery. The child learns to draw stick figures and *then* redescribes its knowledge by changing its representational format. I suggest that the child's ability at the level of behavioral mastery is *already* different to that of the beaver. If we quizzed her about stick figures, she would be able to answer our questions. She would be able to tell us about their parts and properties, and about the relationships holding between them. We could not have such an exchange with the beaver. So the child already knows about stick figures, in a way that the beaver does not know about dams. The difference is already in place at the level of behavioral mastery, although it may not be apparent in overt behavior. The seeds of creativity are planted in the learning phase and have already born their first fruits by the output creativity-1 phase (the level of behavioral mastery). The child can draw stick figures because she already knows about their parts and properties: she can draw them because she knows about them. Consequently it is crucial to understand how this knowledge-about is acquired in the first place, and what happens to it after that.

What does happen after the child has drawn her stick figure representation of a man? Such a drawing gives her immediate, orthogonal access to what she knows about people. She is no longer stuck in a procedural rut in which she has to construct one component at a time, in a fixed sequence. She can see the whole person, all of its components, and all of the relationships between them, at a glance. (Previously we saw Denis et al., 1995, say that we can use verbal descriptions to construct images, and that we can then scan them.) At the same time, she can see what she is capable of drawing, so that she has articulated her skills to herself.

She can now, iteratively, modify the representation. How is she able to do this? Well, she now knows about the representation. This is the same knowledge that enabled her to draw the representation in the first place: it is her knowledge about people. She knows about the figure that it represents a person, so that figure means something to her. She can now modify it. Without this knowledge the figure would be a meaningless cipher, an incoherent combination of lines. This is archetypal knowledge-about, where a representation means something to us by virtue of the knowledge that we bring to it.

In the same way we are able to write a word because we know how to spell it. The word means something to us because we can spell it, and we can then meaningfully modify it in various ways. If we did not know how to spell it—or if we did not know about writing—we would know nothing about the word. We would bring no knowledge to it, and it would be a series of meaningless squiggles to us.

So how do we manipulate and modify our representations, when we have them? And (the big, hard questions) what is knowledge-about, and how do we acquire it? One way in which we can meaningfully manipulate and modify our representations is through analogical thinking. This takes us on to the next section.

ANALOGY, STORAGE AND ACCESS

One way to be creative is to map a problematic situation onto a structurally similar situation that we are more familiar with. A common example of this kind of analogical thinking is when we compare the behavior of electricity with the flow of water (Gentner & Gentner, 1983). We map the flow of the current onto the flow of the water, the conductor onto the water pipe, the voltage onto the pressure pushing the water through the pipe, and so on. In his famous analogy between the atom and the solar system, Rutherford mapped the nucleus of the atom onto the sun, and the electrons onto the planets. In both cases (electricity and water, and atoms and solar system) we map a target situation that we do not properly understand onto a structurally similar source or base that we are more familiar with. Typically, we map relationships but not attributes (Gentner, 1983). We do not, for instance, map the fact that water is wet onto any of the properties of electricity.

The most obvious point about analogies is that they enable us to draw inferences, in the sense of generating hypotheses. Having mapped the structure of the atom onto the structure of the solar system, Rutherford argued that, because the sun's attraction of the planets causes them to revolve around the sun, then, similarly, the nucleus' attraction of the electrons causes them to revolve around the nucleus.

In Chapter 5, John Hummel and Keith Holyoak outline what they see as the four major components of analogical thinking: (a) access a potentially useful source analog (water flow, or the solar system), (b) map this onto the target, (c) use the mapping to draw inferences about the target, (d) induce a generalized schema that captures the commonalities between the target and the source, as an abstraction that can be stored in long term memory for future use. For instance, "Mary owns the book" maps onto "Bill has an apple." Here the people and the objects differ, but in both cases a person possesses an object, so that the schema might be "Someone possesses an object." The induction of schemata is important for our understanding of creativity because, among other things, it creates new structures and abstractions that can be stored and used in subsequent reasoning. Hummel and Holyoak say, however, that although many computational models of analogy have been developed in recent years, schema induction has largely been left as a promissory note. Their own model, LISA, aims at providing an integrated account of all four components of the analogical process, including schema induction. LISA is a symbolic-connectionist model that combines the generalizing capabilities of neural networks with some of the symbol-handling capabilities of classical architectures. On the one hand it represents predicates and their objects as patterns of activation distributed over units in a neural network. On the other, it actively binds these units into propositional or sentential structures, so that it has the systematicity (the ability to handle explicit structure) of traditional systems.

Figure 5.3 shows how the target analog "Mary owns a book" retrieves the source analog "Bill has an apple" from long term memory. "Mary owns the book" is represented in working memory by two "sub-proposition" units, *Mary-as-owner* and *book-as-owned*, that are bound together by synchronous firing. *Mary-as-owner* and *book-as-owned* are in turn represented by synchronously firing predicate and object units: *Mary* and *own1* for *Mary-as-owner*, and *book* and *own2* for *book-as-owned*. Working memory communicates with long term memory through a layer of semantic units, or semantic primitives. When the sub-proposition unit *Mary-as-owner* fires in working memory, it activates *Mary* and *own1*, which in turn activate their semantic units, such as *human, female, adult* and *state1, possess1,* and *legal1*. These now activate predicate and object units in the long-term memory network, and after a complex process of activation and inhibition, "Bill has an apple" is retrieved as an analog for "Mary owns a book."

The scene is now set for inducing schema that capture the commonalities between the analogs. What the analogs have in common, of course, are their shared semantic primitives (see Figure 5.4). In the "Mary owns a book"/"Bill has an apple" example, the shared primitives are *human* and *possess1*, so that the schema is "possess(person,object)," or simply "Somebody possesses an object." LISA can combine primitives to form new, novel predicates, and she can make inferences about the target analog based on its analogical mapping with the source.

Hummel and Holyoak's Chapter 5 is a natural sequel to Halford and Wilson's, Chapter 4, because they claim that Halford and Wilson's model is limited in the following way. It seems reasonable to say that we can map the transitive inference "Abe is taller than Bill, and Bill is taller than Charles" onto the sequence "top, middle, bottom," where we think of Abe being at the top, Bill in the middle, and Charles at the bottom. This is mapping binary ordered pairs from a set of three objects onto a three-place array. Hummel and Holyoak argue that Halford and Wilson's model, and, indeed, "all computational models of mapping prior to LISA," cannot account for this ability because they are limited by "an inviolable 'n-ary restriction': a predicate with n arguments can only map to another predicate with n arguments." They say that this restriction is sensible to a first approximation, but that it makes the above kind of mapping problem unsolvable. LISA avoids this problem, principally by virtue of her distributed representations of meaning.

LISA provides us with an enticing model of at least one kind of knowledge-about. As Hummel and Holyoak say, analogical reasoning is a prominent example of how we "access and use relevant prior knowledge from outside the immediate domain of the problem at hand." This is a kind of knowledge-about. As a model of analogical reasoning, LISA shows how we can modify existing representations, and consequently provides us with an account of Type 2 output creativity. She also appears to provide us with an account of the more basic, and in some ways more elusive, Type 1 output creativity that gives rise to explicit representations in the first place. This is because propositional content is not stored as explicit data in long term memory (LTM). It is encoded in LTM by a hierarchy of structure units (proposition units, sub-proposition units, object and predicate units), and only becomes explicit at the level of working memory, in the synchronized distributed patterns of activation over semantic units that represent an active proposition. As Hummel and Holyoak say in the discussion, "these patterns make both the semantic content and the structure (i.e., role bindings) of a proposition explicit." This appears to be an account of explicitation, where content is not explicitly stored in LTM, but where it is explicitated in working memory. In our discussion I say that LISA certainly seems to be able to explicitate her implicit knowledge as accessible symbol structures. But I ask how implicit her "implicit" knowledge really is. Is it really just stored propositional knowledge, in which synchronous firing stands in for syntactic structure? Can she give us anything like representational redescription? Hummel and Holyoak say that they do not know whether the particular symbolic connectionist architecture embodied in LISA can give rise to representational redescription. In her current state they say that she cannot do this, but "the problem seems well within the domain of the approach."

LISA's architecture also begins to account for the relationship between Type 1 and Type 2 output creativity. In the previous section I suggested that the knowledge-about that generates the representation of a stick figure is iteratively applied to that representation, so that we know about the representation. This, in turn, enables us to modify it. If I understand LISA's architecture correctly, we can make a case for saying that the knowledge in the system that enables a proposition to be explicitated in working memory, also assigns a structure to the proposition. This structure then plays a role in accessing a source analog, on the basis of which the present proposition can be modified. I am not as clear about this as I would like to be, but I think there is a sense in which the knowledge that generates the target analog assigns a structure to it that, in turn, plays a role in modifying it.

The problem that I have with LISA is that she does not really know about her domain. In my discussion with Hummel and Holyoak we talk about the following two scenarios. In the first, a child is shown a picture of hay and horses and a picture of some seeds. She has to work out the relationship between hay and horses ("eats"), and find an analog for seeds. In the second, she has to work out the analogy: hot is to cold as heavy is to [what?]. I suggest that there is no relevant structural information available in either of these scenarios. There is nothing, for instance, in the picture of hay and horses, or seeds and birds, that enables the child to find an isomorphism between them.

Hummel and Holyoak agree. They say that the relevant structure is found, not in the pictures (i.e., in the representations), but in the child's knowledge about the domains. The child knows about hay and horses, and seeds and birds (she knows that horses eat hay and that birds eat seeds), and she knows about heat, cold, heaviness, and so on. They say "LISA would need to embed 'hot,' 'cold,' and 'heavy' in a richer *external* structure." In the same way, "the "eats' relation is in an important sense *external* to hay and horses (it links the two, rather than being an internal *feature* of either)."

We agree, then, that the relevant structure is found, not in the representations, but in the child's knowledge about the domains. But LISA does not have any knowledge about her domains and so cannot model the child's ability. Presumably Hummel and Holyoak will say that she can *explicitly represent* this knowledge (she can explicitly embed it "in a richer external structure"). I have no doubt that she can have such explicit representations. But the key to the child's knowledge is found, not in her representations, but in her *knowledge about* the representations and the domains. Whatever representations LISA has, they will not be accompanied by this essential knowledge-about. Any attempts to give her such knowledge will simply give her more representations.

The situation might be different if LISA operated in a microworld in which she had criteria for applying concepts to objects, so that she could be said to know about the objects in some sense. These concepts could be activated by the contents of her microworld and dynamically bound by hierarchical synchronous firing into propositions, that could be stored in long term memory. These could subsequently be explicitated in working memory, in a process that would look very much like representational redescription. I think that we could make a case for such knowledge, in both its implicit and explicit forms, being knowledge about the domain, since it would be grounded in the domain and would have a semantics. We will return to this issue later.

INPUT AND OUTPUT CREATIVITY

In Chapter 6, Derek Partridge and Jon Rowe identify two competing psychological theories of human creativity and implement them as minor variations of the same computational framework, based on Minsky's "Society of Mind" model of agents, or "k-lines" (Minsky, 1985). In this paradigm, low-level, self-contained pieces of code called "agents" cooperate to construct representations. Partridge and Rowe's specific implementation, GENESIS, also features what they call "a 'representationally fluid' emergent memory mechanism." When GENESIS solves a problem it stores the syntax, or structure, of the representation in memory. When it comes across a similar problem later on—specifically, when half of the structure's components are activated by the input data—it activates the other components in the structure. Partridge and Rowe say that this is a form of memory that enables a society of agents to dynamically interact and cooperate in problem-solving situations. They say that the system has analogical capability, because the syntax, or structure, of a representation is activated when only some of its components are relevant to the current context. Analogies *emerge* under these circumstances.

Partridge and Rowe importantly distinguish between input and output creativity. They say that we are input creative when we solve problems and make sense of the world—during perception, or when we listen to music or poetry, for instance—and that we are output creative when we deploy this mechanism off-line, free from external constraints, to *produce* music or poetry. They say that GENESIS is creative in both senses, and we shall return to this. Their aim, however, is not only to provide a system that is creative in itself. They also wish to provide a platform for evaluating two rival theories of human creativity: the Cortical Arousal Theory and the No Special Mechanism Theory.

The Cortical Arousal Theory says that there is a special mechanism for the creative process. When we cannot solve a problem we sometimes unfocus, or dilate, our attention and access a wider range of ideas. If we find relevant ideas, we form connections with them and import their schemata into the present problem-solving context. We dilate our attention, make new associations, import them, and refocus on the task. The No Special Mechanism Theory, on the other hand, says that there is no special mechanism involved in creativity. Creativity is normal problem solving, plus a great deal of knowledge.

Partridge and Rowe model these theories with two versions of GENESIS. GENESIS-TS models the Cortical Arousal Theory, using a search method based on what Hofstadter calls a "terraced scan" (see his explanation in the discussion at the end of Chapter 8). GENESIS-BF models the No Special Mechanism theory, using best-first search. Partridge and Rowe empirically tested these versions of GENESIS in the domain of Eleusis, a card game that models some aspects of theory-discovery in science. The programs had to discover the rule underlying a sequence (this required input creativity), and invent rules for sequences of cards (this required output creativity). They say that the programs exhibited "significant creativity" at both of these tasks.

One of the reasons for proposing the Cortical Arousal Theory is to account for the "aha!" phenomenon often associated with creative behavior and flashes of insight. Measurable cortical arousal occurs on these occasions, and the Cortical Arousal Theory says that this is the creative mechanism kicking in. In the simulation, GENESIS-BF (which simulates the No Special Mechanism Theory) exhibited the "aha!" phenomenon, whereas, perhaps surprisingly, GENESIS-TS did not. This happened when GENESIS-BF abandoned an unfruitful pathway and suddenly replaced it by a more profitable one, sometimes of a quite different sort. Consequently, Partridge and Rowe suggest that the "aha!" phenomenon is *caused* by the registration of creative breakthrough, rather than by a special mechanism that causes the breakthrough. This rules in favor of the No Special Mechanism Theory.

Two of the main motifs in Chapter 6 are (a) that we generate representations, rather than copy them or transduce them from experience, and (b) that we need to distinguish between input and output creativity. Both of these claims chime with my own position, so I shall consider them in turn.

In the input-creative process, GENESIS has to determine the rule underlying and generating a sequence of cards. It has a sample sequence to guide it, and it can experiment by playing a card. The solution will be a finite state automaton (FSA) that correctly encodes the rule. An FSA consists of a set of states, including a starting state and one or more final or "accept" states. Given an input sequence, an FSA processes one element at a time, which might cause it to transition from one state to another. If the final element leaves it in an accept state, it has successfully recognized the input sequence. (As I understand it, GENESIS deviates from this definition by having no final state: the rule specifies an indefinitely long and repeatable sequence of cards.)

GENESIS represents an FSA as a list of labeled arcs. Partridge's example in the discussion is:

[[1 2 [red even]] [2 1 [red odd]]]

The labeled arc [1 2 [red even]] says "playing red-even transitions from state 1 to state 2," and the labeled arc [2 1 [red odd]] says "playing red-odd transitions from state 2 to state 1." Consequently the FSA says, "alternate red-even, red-odd as many times as you like."

Partridge and Rowe say that there are two kinds of agents: builders and k-lines. Builders are labeled arcs, such as [1 2 [red even]], and k-lines are sequences of builders from which the transitions on the arcs (such as "red even") have been removed. A sequence is stored in memory and is activated in its entirety when half of its components are activated by the incoming data. The idea, of course, is that it will be activated in the presence of a structurally similar problem—structurally similar because the specific transitions on the arcs have been removed. The above FSA would be stored as:

[[template 1 2] [template 2 1]]

The crucial factor here is that GENESIS *generates* representations. It actively constructs them, rather than copies or transduces them from the data in the fashion of Classical Empiricism. Here, of course, I entirely agree. Nevertheless, Partridge and Rowe are not as clear as they might be about the nature of agents (ironically, they say that although Minsky "proposes the idea of agents that form links between other agents, to create memories," he "gives no details as to how such agents might operate"). Sometimes they say that builders "construct representations" and that k-lines group successful agents together. In Partridge and Rowe (1994) they say, "A builder is a procedure" (p. 60). This is certainly what we would expect. We would expect builders to be micro-procedures that parse the input and use the gathered information to construct a representation. I would have thought that this is obviously true in our experience of the external world: in perceiving an object, such as a person or a house, we "parse" it (determine and label its structure). We can then use this information to create a copy, or some other form of representation, in the imagination or the external world.

Sometimes, however, Partridge and Rowe say that builders are the representations themselves, so that k-lines are sequences of builders stripped of their content. Partridge's example of a k-line in the discussion is simply:

[[template 1 2][template 1 2][template 2 1][template 2 1]]

which is the stored, stripped version of the FSA:

[[1 2[red even]] [1 2[red odd]] [2 1[black even]] [2 1[black odd]]]

This lack of clarity about the nature of agents seems particularly unfortunate to me, for it seems that we are close to seeing how representations are constructed. What *are* the procedures, the small pieces of code, the microskills, that generate representations? As usual, representations steal the show and make it difficult for us to get *behind* them to the knowledge that generates them. Nevertheless, the main point remains: Partridge and Rowe say that representations are generated rather than copied from experience.

Previously, I said that we generate representations as a way of presenting to ourselves what we already know. It is not that this knowledge is stored or contained in representations, so that we have to *retrieve* the representations in order to discover what we know. Rather, our knowledge drives and *generates* the representations, so that they are creative products that show us what we know.

My broad-brushstroke claim was that we first present our knowledge to ourselves in the Type 1 output phase. This is what behavioral mastery consists of: it is the ability to generate representations of a domain, that (as a matter of fact) enable us to inspect (and in a sense, to discover) what we already know. At this stage we are not sufficiently familiar with this knowledge to be fluently creative. That greater flexibility comes with time and attention paid to inner processing, in which we become adept at deploying our knowledge to generate creative output. At that later stage, of course, we achieve Type 2 output creativity.

I also said that in order to understand output-1 creativity we need to understand input creativity. In the light of Partridge and Rowe's chapter we can now see things more clearly. The first thing is this. Input creativity already requires an iterative process of generating a representation and testing it against the data. This representation is a creative product of what we know or have conjectured thus far, that we can inspect and test against the data. If it passes the test we can test it against new data, or generate more representations and test them in turn. If it fails, we can modify it, or generate a new representation.

Second, and just as important, we can now see that output creativity is a natural consequence of this generate-and-test process that is already in place. Partridge and Rowe are surprisingly circumspect about this claim, which I think is a key insight into creativity. They say that input and output creativity are related, and they "suggest" that this relationship resolves a paradox: "If a result has been derived from previous experience, then it is hard to see how it can be novel. If on the other hand a creative act contains something new, that is not derived from experience, then it is difficult to see where it could have come from." Their solution is that we store structures during the input creative phase, which we retrieve in the output creative phase. These are only structures. They have been stripped of their labels. They are not complete solutions (that is, complete FSAs). And they are activated when only half of their components apply to the current context. Partridge and Rowe say, "a representation [could] be built which contained elements of two previous experiences and would be in some ways analogous to each. But the representation itself would be new and could be used, by motor agents, to construct a novel external object. This is output creativity." It is not clear to me how this would work in the case of GENESIS, since all that is stored in memory are structures. No labels are stored, and I do not see how stored structures can cross-pollinate one another and be melded together.

Nevertheless, the idea is clear enough: mechanisms and inner capabilities that were put into place during the input creativity phase are redeployed in the output creativity phase. Partridge and Rowe say that the constraints are reduced in the case of output creativity. In input creativity, "the constraints on problem solving are external: they are inherent in the structure of the problem." The constraints on output creativity "are much less rigid." (I think that this is questionable. In understanding a sonnet we become aware of the constraints, but in composing a sonnet we are *subject* to them: they force themselves upon us.)

This transition from input to output creativity seems inevitable to me. Given that we *are* output creative, where could this ability have come from other than from a redeployment of our input-creative abilities to solve problems in the world? In the next section we will look at some results from machine learning and see that this transition from input to output creativity is in fact surprisingly easy: output creativity can be seen as a natural consequence of the learning process.

CREATIVITY AND RUNAWAY LEARNING

In Chris Thornton's Chapter 7, he argues that creativity can be seen as a natural consequence of the learning process. Learning and generative creativity, he says, lie at opposite ends of the same dimension, and this type of creativity may be the result of learning processes "running away" beyond the normal point of termination.

Thornton begins by saying that all learning is either relational or non-relational. Non-relational learning is learning about objects as they are in themselves. Relational learning is learning about relationships between objects. If, for instance, we are learning non-relationally about numbers, we might learn about integer values, but if we are engaged in *relational* learning we will learn about relationships between numbers—for instance, that some numbers are bigger than others.

Relational learning can be recursive: the output of one iteration of the learning process can be the input data for the next iteration of the same process. In fact, Thornton argues that relational learning must be recursive if the output data is at a level of description above the level of the original input data. In order to learn about boxes, for instance, we first need to learn about surfaces. Then we can learn that a box is made up of surfaces arranged in certain relationships.

Thornton invites us to imagine what will happen if this recursive learning process continues unchecked—if it becomes what he calls a "runaway process." He provides a detailed example of a system that is given the task of learning poker hands. The system is programed to look for certain relationships between cards, such as sameness-of-suit and integer-sequence. First it discovers straights and flushes (a straight is a sequence of cards, such as 3, 4, 5, 6, 7; a flush is a hand in which all cards belong to the same suit). It then recurses and looks for relationships between straights and flushes, and discovers straight flushes (straights in which all the cards belong to the same suit).

Now suppose that it "runs away" and is not terminated at this point. It would then look for relationships between the patterns generated in previous learning cycles and come up with imaginary hands, such as a "full house" consisting of a three-card and a two-card run (we might call this a "strange full house," or a "straight house"). At this stage it has gone beyond its original learning task, and has begun to explore the space of "poker-like" hands.

Thornton stresses that this analysis is a priori. The notion of there being a connection between learning and creativity is not a new one, he says, and here he cites Hummel and Holyoak's Chapter 5. Previous studies, however, have been empirical, whereas his is a logical analysis that applies to *any* learning situation. The upshot is that at least one type of creativity can be a natural consequence of learning, so that people who wish to devise artificial, creative agents should pay close attention to work currently going on in the learning sciences.

Thornton's analysis is closely related to a number of themes we have already touched on. For instance, it is related to Halford and Wilson's claim that creativity requires the ability to represent and recursively modify explicit, complex relations in parallel. Thornton says that if recursive, relational learning (that is "modification") continues unchecked it can become a creative process. (See Halford 1997 for an exchange with Clark and Thornton on the relevance of recoding to learning.)

Here I shall focus on the themes (a) that representations are generated in the imagination rather than copied from experience, and (b) that this productive capability derives from our input-creative ability to make sense of the world. In our discussion, Thornton agrees that we construct representations, and that in doing so we are redeploying capabilities that we originally used in the context of immediate experience. On the other hand, he rejects the more coarse-grained claim that we can distinguish between input and output creativity. We cannot do this, he says, because "Input creativity is going to produce new concepts that will feed directly into your creative output (look at the way that the concept of a requiem feeds straight into the production of a requiem)." It is not clear to me why we cannot acquire new concepts and simply leave it at that. I acquired the concept of a requiem some time ago, but I have not yet written one. If I did write one, of course, I would lean heavily on my acquired concept of a requiem, but I do not see what follows from this.

Perhaps Thornton's point is that the broad-brushstrokes distinction between input and output creativity (say, between understanding poetry and writing it) disguises a more fine-grained, on-going interaction between input and output creativity. We saw in the last section that a generate-and-test process is already in place during input creativity, in which we produce output as part of the learning process. Thornton similarly says that the output of the learning process can be the input data (so to speak, "creatively recoded") for the next iteration of the same process. In fact he says that the learning process *has* to be recursive under some circumstances, as we have seen. This iterative process, broadly construed as learning but in fact consisting of multiple input-output sequences, can subsequently become the operational core of output creativity. Such a story sees the transition from learning to behavioral mastery to fluid and flexible output creativity as an ongoing, continual process (punctuated, presumably, by periods of introspection during which we familiarize ourselves with what we already know). In the poker example, the system begins by discovering pairs. It then iteratively discovers pairs of pairs. So far it has discovered what we might call "standard combinations" in what, broadly construed, is a learning process. But if the input-output microdynamics continues unchecked it will begin to produce creative products that are not standard combinations at all: it will become output creative broadly construed. According to this story, learning flows naturally into creativity. Type 1 creativity, the initial output that characterizes behavioral mastery, now looks like a falsely frozen moment in what is really a fluid and ongoing process from learning to behavioral mastery to fluent and flexible creativity. The apparently unbridgeable divide between implicit, procedural knowledge and explicit, declarative knowledge has disappeared, and left us with a more or less smooth, continuous process.

But we still have the distinction between input and output creativity, on both the microdynamic and broad-brushstroke levels. On the microdynamic level this is the distinction between being able to parse (assign a labeled structure to) an input and use this knowledge to generate an output. On the broad-brushstroke level it is the distinction between learning and creating, where we are unaware of, or not concerned about, the underlying, ongoing microdynamics.

We will look at both processes in more detail in the next section.

OF LOOPS AND LOOPINESS

In Chapter 8, Gary McGraw and Douglas Hofstadter discuss the Letter Spirit project; in Chapter 9, John Rehling discusses its first full implementation. Letter Spirit is the most ambitious project in a long line of research by Hofstadter and the Indiana University Fluid Analogies Research Group (FARG) into what we might call "agent-based analogy engines." The central theme of this research is the idea of nondeterministic, stochastic processing distributed over a large number of small computational agents, which work on different aspects of an analogy problem simultaneously, thereby achieving a kind of differential parallelism. Processing occurs through the collective actions of the agents working together, without any higher-level, executive process directing the overall course of events. Letter Spirit's two main predecessors were Copycat (Mitchell, 1993) and Tabletop (French, 1995), although Letter Spirit pays more attention to the internal structure of concepts and focuses on a much larger-scale creative process that unfolds over an extended period of time. Hofstadter and FARG (1995, p. 8) say that Letter Spirit is "almost certainly FARG's most ambitious computer model, . . . which attempts to model creativity on a far larger scale than our previous projects have."[5] There are some similarities between Letter Spirit and Partridge and Rowe's GENESIS (McGraw, 1995, pp. 106–107).

The Letter Spirit Chapters 8 and 9 show how the project has unfolded over time. The project was conceived some years ago, but around 1990 Gary McGraw "started agitating for a project to get his teeth stuck into" (Hofstadter & FARG, 1995, p. 405). Hofstadter felt that this was premature, but he relented and the project began. In 1995 they said, "We shall see, over the next few years, how it goes" (p. 406).

We are now in a position to see how it has gone, at least so far. McGraw and Hofstadter's Chapter 8 was written in 1995, when McGraw had completed the first part of the project, the Examiner. Rehling's Chapter 9 was written in late 1999, when Letter Spirit was implemented and up-and-running for the first time (although not as originally envisaged, as we shall see).

Letter Spirit is a system that aims to model the way in which the lowercase letters of the Roman alphabet can be rendered in different but internally coherent styles. Starting with one or more seed letters representing the beginnings of a style, it attempts to create the rest of the alphabet in such a way that all 26 letters share the same style, or *spirit*. Consequently, it "tries to do in one framework something that has already been done in a significantly different framework."

As originally envisaged, Letter Spirit has four global memory structures. The *Conceptual Memory* includes Letter Spirit's knowledge about letters. This consists of "core knowledge" about "what the letter consists of" and an *associative halo* that specifies its relationships to other concepts. The core knowledge specifies the building blocks, or *roles*, out of which a letter is built. Roles are things such as posts, bowls, loops, cross bars, slashes, angle brackets, and so on, so that the letter *b* might be thought of as consisting of a post on the left side attached in two places to an open bowl on the right. Roles, in turn, consist of smaller components called "parts." The associative halo consists of links of varying lengths connecting the letter to related concepts. These links provide relational information, such as resemblances between letters and analogical relationships between roles.

The *Visual Focus* is where the recognition of letterforms takes place. Letters consist of short line segments called "quanta," drawn on a fixed grid of points arranged in an array. Letters are recognized in the Visual Focus by quanta being chunked together, bottom-up, into parts. To begin with this process is purely syntactic, but as structures are built up, top-down influences appear and guide the docking of syntactic parts into semantic slots (into the roles that, when put together, constitute letters). The *Thematic Focus* is where stylistic attributes are stored and scored. The more that an attribute is found as letters are examined, the greater is its chance of being elevated to the status of a guiding principle, or a *theme*. The *Scratchpad* is where letters are created and stored during a run.

The 1995 architecture envisaged four interacting emergent agents. The *Imaginer* would play with the concepts behind letterforms. The *Drafter* would convert ideas for letterforms into graphical realizations. The *Examiner* would combine bottom-up and top-down processing to perceive and categorize letterforms, and the *Adjudicator* would perceive and dynamically build a representation of the evolving style. These agents would engage in an iterative process of guesswork and evaluation that for a long time Hofstadter has called the "central feedback loop of creativity."

McGraw and Hofstadter provide us with an example of how these agents might work together. We begin by giving Letter Spirit a highly stylized seed letter, such as an *f* without its crossbar, and ask it to construct other letters in the same style.

Letter Spirit first has to identify the category of the letter. The Examiner chunks components together by focussing on part of the letter. The discovered structures are labeled and wake up the semantic roles *post* and *hook*, which in turn activate the letter categories *f* and *l*. The letter *f* wins, with the attached stylistic note "crossbar suppressed."

Letter Spirit now moves from its perceptual to its generative phase. The letters *f* and *t* are linked as similar letters in the Conceptual Memory, so it will probably tackle *t* next. The Drafter draws a crossbar-less *t* on the Scratchpad. The Examiner examines it, but, knowing that a *t* was attempted, rejects the attempt as a failure. This information, together with "crossbar suppressed" is now sent back to the Imaginer. The Imaginer is now between a rock and a hard place, torn between Spirit pressure ("suppress the crossbar, to make the *t* more like the *f*") and Letter pressure ("if you do that, it won't be a *t* any more"). To resolve this conflict, it looks at the conceptual halo of related concepts around "suppress" and finds the concept "underdo." It slips from "suppress" to "underdo," and makes a short crossbar on the left side of the stem (with nothing on the right side). McGraw and Hofstadter say that this slippage from "suppress" to "underdo" is "the key creative breakthrough," since it resolves the conflict between letter and spirit, and allows a new structure to emerge. Creativity, they say, is an automatic outcome of the existence of sufficiently flexible, context-sensitive concepts, that allow new creative forms to emerge from the resolution of conflict between inner forces. Here, of course, this is the conflict between Spirit pressure and Letter pressure.

McGraw and Hofstadter's original proposal was that the Imaginer would create an abstract plan for each gridletter, that would not be concerned with the actual grid. The Drafter would then render a grid-based version of the plan. In Rehling's full implementation there is only one module, called the Drafter, which carries out its work directly on the grid. Letter Spirit is given some seed letters. The Examiner identifies them and the Adjudicator assesses their style. This information is passed to the Drafter, which generates different letters of the same, or similar, style. In fact there is a loop here: the Drafter generates many versions of the same letter, each of which is judged by the Examiner and Adjudicator, and the best one is retained.

It is probably significant that McGraw and Hofstadter initially envisaged Letter Spirit's knowledge as abstract and that Letter Spirit would plan first and execute later—and that this idea was later abandoned in favor of the Drafter carrying out its work directly on the grid. Of course, it might just be that it was easier to implement this way. But the fact is that the current architecture presents us with a picture of knowledge that is integrated with skill, in which we don't plan everything first and execute it later, but constantly evaluate our creative products. Hofstadter and Rehling say that we might need to have the Examiner permanently peering over the Drafter's shoulder, so that knowledge and skill of execution are tightly integrated. I shall return to this.

I now want to stand back and look at the big picture.

At the beginning of Chapter 8, McGraw and Hofstadter say that many AI programs that purport to model creativity, "*don't know anything about what they're doing*" (their emphasis). They have no knowledge about the domains in which they are working, and they have "no internal representations of the actions [they are] taking, and no awareness of the *products* [they are] creating." McGraw and Hofstadter say that for a program to be creative:

- Its knowledge must be rich, in the sense that its concepts must be nontrivial and explicitly connected.
- Concepts and their interrelationships must be flexible and context-dependent.
- It must be able to judge and modify its own output.
- It must be able to converge on a solution through a continual process of suggestion and evaluation.

If a program can do these things then it will "know what it is doing."

I think that this is both too bold and too modest. It is too bold because it is implicitly talking about Type 2 output creativity, for which, yes, a repertoire of richly interconnected concepts that enable conceptual slippage may well be necessary. But we do not need conceptual slippage for Type 1 output creativity, the initial, basic, articulation of form or structure, in which we generate a representation as a created product. For this we need a mechanism that shows how explicitation is a natural consequence of the learning, or recognition, process. It seems to me that Letter Spirit gives us precisely this, and this is why I think that the claim is too modest. Letter Spirit, as well as some of the other FARG programs and some of the programs we have considered in this volume, pioneers a new epistemology in which representations, rather than being copied or transduced from experience, are generated "in the imagination" by our knowledge about a domain. They are the created products of such knowledge, rather than stored repositories or representations of what we know. Now, at last, we can see how they are constructed.

Here it is again. Letter Spirit first determines the structure of a letter by chunking some of its quanta into parts and labeling the products. Another way of saying this is to say that it focuses on the parts and labels them. This bottom-up, syntactic process generates simple, labeled structures that activate semantic roles such as "bowl," "post," and so on. These letter components are chunked together and labeled in turn, and activate the appropriate letter concept. The letter has now been recognized (along with its stylistic attributes). Control is handed over to the Drafter, which tries to draft an analogous letter in the same style. This involves fluid representations and the subtleties of conceptual slippage, and (if it is successful) will give us Type 2 output creativity, the output of a new created form. But, trivially, once control has been handed over to the Drafter, it can draft another identical letter in the Visual Focus. It knows how to do this because it knows about the letter and its stylistic properties: it knows about the roles that constitute the letter, and the parts that constitute the roles (it also knows about its stylistic properties, such as "crossbar suppressed"). The Drafter, so to speak, only has to peel the labels off the letter (the labels assigned to it by the Examiner), and it has the wherewithall to generate another copy of the letter in the Visual Focus. In doing so it generates a representation of the letter out of its knowledge about it—knowledge that the Examiner acquired in the recognition phase. This gives us Type 1 output creativity.

The relationship between input and output creativity, between recognition and reproduction, is almost endlessly subtle. In personal correspondence, Hofstadter and Rehling have suggested that we need a "loop within a loop": ideally, the Examiner should peer over the Drafter's shoulder as the Drafter draws on the grid, and say "fine, keep going, I recognize that," or "no, that's wrong." This is the loop-within-a-loop that I suggested in the last section: there is trial-and-error generation and evaluation going on *during the recognition phase,* on a microdynamic scale. I have suggested that this accounts for the origins of human creativity, because it gives us an ongoing, iterative process of guesswork and evaluation that does not have to terminate in recognition, but which can carry on into the output creativity phase. As Thornton says, generative productivity can be seen as a natural consequence of the learning process. It is now beginning to look as if the high-level process of guesswork and evaluation emerges out of the ongoing microdynamic guess-and-evaluate cycle that so naturally takes us from learning and recognition, on the one hand, to broad-brushstroke productive creativity, on the other—the big loop emerges out of the small one. Perhaps this is what McGraw and Hofstadter mean when they say that Letter Spirit's agents are emergent: "it must be borne in mind that these modules are in some sense convenient descriptive fictions, in that each is simply an emergent by-product of the actions of many codelets, and their activities are so intertwined that they cannot be disentangled in a clean way." My impression, however, is that they are rather more than descriptive fictions in Letter Spirit's present incarnation.

I want to stress that representations are generated rather than copied or transduced. The Examiner parses a letter by labeling it. When we parse a sentence we assign a labeled bracketing to it. When we recognize an object in the world we presumably do something very similar. We recognize tables and chairs by "parsing" them into configurations of legs and horizontal surfaces. If we merely copied the objects of perception we would be stuck with a regress, for how would we know what the copies were about?

Our knowledge about the sentence, or the object, now enables us to generate a representation of it in the imagination. This is what Letter Spirit does. It recognizes letters by assigning a labeled bracketing to them ("this letter consists of a bowl and a post, which in turn . . . ," etc.). This knowledge enables the Drafter to generate a representation, or an analogue, of the letter in the Visual Focus.

As I understand it, information about letters is not stored as representations—as surrogates of the letters. It is stored as knowledge *about* the letters—for instance, that a *b* consists of a bowl and a post, etc. In turn, knowledge about these roles is not stored as representations, but as knowledge about the roles—that a bowl consists of such-and-such parts, and so on. Parts are not stored, and neither are quanta.[6] Quanta are constructed by joining points together on the grid. As Rehling says in describing the work of the Drafter, "Then quanta are drawn, one by one, as though a pen were drawing the role filler on the grid." This gives us a non-representational knowledge about letters, that enables Letter Spirit to generate them out of its knowledge about them. And this is creativity!

SO WHAT HAVE WE LEARNED?

I began by saying that when we look at some fairly common creative acts, such as a sculptor chiseling a form out of a block of marble or granite, or a potter shaping a pot out of a lump of clay, we see a created product emerging, not out of a combination of components or elements, but out of the artist's knowledge about his subject and his ability to manipulate his medium. Similarly, when we perform the simplest feats of imagination, such as imagining funny men, what we can imagine is not limited by the size and combinatorial abilities of a set of elements or components, but by what we know about the properties of faces and our ability to vary them in our minds. These simple scenarios suggest that there is something seriously wrong with the combinatorial accounts of creativity and cognition endorsed by cognitive science and researchers into human creativity, and they strongly suggest that we need a new epistemology to account for the fluidity and flexibility of creative thought. I have called this epistemology "knowledge-about," and I said in the opening section that such an epistemology is already with us in some leading-edge models of human creativity: my main aim in the volume is to bring it into the light of day.

We then looked at the standard, representational, copy-and-combine account of knowledge and cognition in classical cognitive science, and I laid the foundations for an alternative story: it is our knowledge about a domain that does the hard cognitive work, and representations, to the extent that we have them at all, are constructed out of this knowledge. They wither away as cognition becomes more sophisticated, and finally they play no role in cognition at all.

A similar combinationist story is commonly told by researchers into human creativity. Because we cannot get something out of nothing, it is assumed that creative products must be combinations of elements or components that already existed. From the tautology that we cannot get something out of nothing, it is concluded that creative products are just combinations of components or elements—even when we had knowledge, experience and skill to begin with. Again, we need an account of how creative products can emerge, not out of a combination of elements or components, but out of our knowledge, experience and skill.

Representational redescription promises to provide us with such an account because it says that palpable products emerge out of our implicit, procedural knowledge. We begin with implicit, procedural knowledge and redescribe it into explicit, declarative structures that we can access, reflect upon and change. The problem is that we do not know how to implement this process, we do not know what kinds of neural processes support it, and we do not know how it could have evolved. Representational redescription really only restates the problem. It tells us that we can get palpable products out of our knowledge and skill (which we already knew), but it does not tell us how we do so.

I believe that the problem lies in the implicit representational epistemology. Annette Karmiloff-Smith says that a change in inner representational format ("representational redescription") enables us to access information and abilities that we could not have accessed before. I suggest that we simply get better at accessing information and abilities that we already had. To sustain this story I suggest that we have to look at what happens before behavioral mastery in order to explain what happens after it, because the knowledge that is acquired during the learning phase can be deployed to generate representations about what has been learned. I also exorcise representations as inner entities that encapsulate our knowledge. Rather than underlying and driving our knowledge, representations are the creative products of our knowledge.

This enables us to distinguish between two types of output creativity. Type 1 output creativity is the generation of a representation out of our implicit knowledge: it is the emergence of a created product out of our implicit knowledge and skill. Type 2 output creativity is what we normally think of as creativity: it is the generation of imaginative products that are more than mere representations of what we already know.

The story, however, is more complex than this. The input-creative, learning phase already requires an iterative process of generating a representation and testing it against the data. This representation is a creative product of what we know or have conjectured thus far. Output creativity is a natural consequence of this generate-and-test cycle. Indeed, the transition has an air of inevitability about it. Given that we *are* output creative, this ability could only have come from a redeployment of input-creative abilities acquired in learning about the world. This conjecture is supported by a priori results from machine learning, which show that at least some creativity can be seen as a consequence of the learning process "running away" beyond its normal point of termination.

In the case of human cognition we sometimes talk about "compiled knowledge." We are often taught a skill by being given complex instructions—when we are taught a tennis serve, or how to hit a golf ball, or how to drive a car. To begin with we are often bewildered by this information, but after a while we "compile it down" to an automatic ability. Here representational redescription runs in the opposite direction. We begin with explicit, declarative knowledge and "redescribe" it (in reverse) into a compiled skill, so that we can get on with the job without having to think about how we do it. (A. N. Whitehead said that we can measure intelligence in terms of how much we can do without having to think about it, and we all know the joke about the centipede who was asked how he was able to walk, and then couldn't lift a single leg.) But although our declarative, conceptual, knowledge is compiled, it is still there, and we can access it when necessary. We do so when we need to examine or correct our ability, or when we have to pass it on to somebody else. Karmiloff-Smith tells the story of how she learned to do a Rubik's Cube as a compiled skill, and subsequently had to explicitate this knowledge in order to explain it to her daughter (Karmiloff-Smith, 1992, pp. 16–17).

Similarly, drawing and recognizing letters is a compiled skill. We might need to have the internal structure of letters explained to us when we first learn the alphabet ("a *b* has a bowl and a post, like this . . ."), but we soon compile this knowledge into automatic ability. The conceptual knowledge-about is still there, however, and we can explicitate it whenever we want to—when we want to tell somebody how to write the letter, or when we want to create a new form of the letter. Our implicit, compiled, conceptual knowledge drives our skill, and we typically access this knowledge by examining the created product ("now . . . what does a *q* consist of?").

The point here, of course, is that the road to representational redescription runs in both directions, so that, in redescribing or explicitating a skill, we are often revisiting and unwinding knowledge that we acquired in the learning phase. We compile our knowledge-about into a skill, so that we do not need to think about it and can just get on with the job, and we can uncompile, unpack, explicitate, and redescribe the skill back into an explicit structure. We *reverse engineer* our knowledge, as Emmy does when she accesses the labels she has assigned to a musical structure and uses them to generate new musical forms.

Of course, it remains to be seen whether an implementation of this story will give us the key characteristics of representational redescription, such as the U-shaped learning curve and the initial difficulty with modifying "inner" subprocedures. But accessing labels and structures assigned during the learning phase will take up processing time, during which it is likely that input data will be ignored, and it is plausible that "inner" labels, embedded in inner subprocedures, will be more difficult to retrieve than labels assigned at the beginning and end of a series of subskills.

Here are some brief notes about flexibility and fluidity, and about complex cognition.

Flexibility, fluidity, components, and properties.   When we know about something we know about its components, as we saw in the case of Letter Spirit. But components ultimately break down into sets of *properties*. Letter Spirit's components, such as "bowl" and "stem," break down into properties such as "straight" and "curved." Properties do not exist independently of what they are properties of, so that representations of them cannot be stored as separate entities (or, for that matter, as entities at all). This is the point about the smile of the Cheshire Cat. The smile does not exist independently of the cat (more specifically, it does not exist independently of certain components of the cat, such as its mouth and teeth), any more than the curve of a cheekbone exists independently of the cheekbone. Nevertheless we can know *about* properties and vary them continuously in the imagination. This gives us a fluid imaginative capability that stands in stark contrast to combinatorial accounts. *Any* combinatorial account must be granular at some level, depending on the granularity of the components. A combinationist might say that her model can capture the ability to vary properties, but, of course, it will only be able to do so to the extent that it *knows about* its representations. It seems to me that once you admit this kind of knowledge you should let it do all of the work.

I think that we are inclined to say that a factor in continuous, *temporal* fluidity is that we need to have the "examiner," the critical-feedback component, continuously peering over the "drafter's" shoulder. The feedback loop has to be as tight as possible—preferably instantaneous. We are inclined to say that this is what happens in real life: the pot or vase emerges fluidly in the hands of the potter because of continual critical feedback (if the internal critic fired spasmodically we would have a jerky generative-evaluative cycle). But the situation might be more interesting than this. John Rehling has suggested in personal correspondence that we need a loop in order to plan and anticipate the near future: "When I try to leap a stream about nine feet wide, I find myself somehow visualizing an attempted jump to see if it will work." Letter Spirit, he says, "needs to visualize a quantum and then how things might go from there, and see if it likes the result of the quantum." If this is the case, the potter imagines what will happen if he does such-and-such, before actually doing it.

This might seem to put representations back on center stage, because it now seems that we need them for planning and anticipating the future and, consequently, for any actions that we perform. But assuming that we have such representations, where do they come from? One thing is clear enough: they cannot have been copied from future experiences that we have not had! Instead, they must have been generated from what we know and conjecture about the future. They enable us to present to ourselves in a compact, inspectable format what we already know and conjecture.

Complex cognition. One of the main theoretical reasons for adopting a knowledge-about epistemology is to account for complex, sophisticated cognition where representations are not practically possible. Complex objects such as chiliagons (thousand-sided plane figures) provide a simple example. We cannot practically have representations of chiliagons. We can have dummy representations of them, but the real knowledge is carried in our knowledge about them—that they are thousand-sided plane figures. How we acquire this knowledge is a complex story, of course. We do not acquire it by looking at chiliagons and counting their sides! They are just too complex for that. Nevertheless, our knowledge as a whole must originate in parsing objects in the world. This requires us to assign labels. These labels subsequently take on lives of their own and can be used in their own right, neither in the presence of the original objects, nor to create representations of them. We often think about things that are not spatio-temporally present, and that we do not have representations of. In the terminology of traditional empiricism, we begin with experience, which requires concepts and percepts. We then run these concepts off-line and supply something like inner perceptual content that enables us to generate representations in the imagination. We do this in the case of the missing shade of blue that we talked about in the second section. Here we cannot have stored a copy of the color, because, *ex hypothesi*, we have never experienced such a color. We generate it in the imagination, and we can only do this by supplying some sort of quasi-perceptual content. Finally, we deploy the concepts without any perceptual content at all. We *have* to do this in the case of complex cognition, where perceptual content is just not practical: we cannot have representations of chiliagons. We lever labels off the world and deploy them as tokens in their own right. (Dare I suggest that this is the origin of language?)

That is the basic outline. It is little more than a sketch, and I have not even touched on major issues such as intentionality (which an account of knowledge-about obviously needs), the relationship between concepts and skills, and the deep difference between representations and labels. I have glossed over intentionality by talking rather loosely about semantics and concepts having criteria of application. The story also needs to distinguish between knowledge as content and knowledge as cognitive state. When we say that someone's belief is contradictory and four years old, we mean that the *content* of the belief is contradictory, and that the *state* of the belief is four years old. The same distinction applies to knowledge, where, however, it is less intuitively clear. See Dartnall (1999b, 2000) for an analysis.

Nevertheless, I think that the outline gets the big picture right. It avoids the problem of the veil of perception, because it says that representations are generated in our minds rather than being direct objects of experience that come between us and reality. Crucially, it recognizes that generating representations and other cognitive content is a creative act in itself: creativity inheres, not only in big ticket items like plays, poems and sonatas, but in the ability to produce cognitive content at all. It shows how these abilities are intimately related, and how there can be a smooth transition from learning to implicit knowledge to explicit knowledge that might provide us with the key to representational redescription. It accounts for the fluidity and flexibility of creative thought, and provides us with an in-principle explanation of the transition from cognition that is tied to the context, to representational cognition, to complex cognition where we do not use representations at all. This gives us the big picture, in which some of the mountains are just about visible above the mist. The details remain obscure. All of the hard work lies ahead.

EMERGENCE

In final Chapter 10, Richard McDonough takes up the issue of creativity and emergence. Emergence is an ongoing theme in the volume. McGraw and Hofstadter say that top-level behavior emerges from many low-level stochastic computational actions occurring in parallel: Letter Spirit's parallel stochastic processing constitutes *emergent computation* (Forrest, 1991), in which complex high-level behavior emerges as a statistical consequence of many small computational actions. Stylistic attributes are unpredictable emergent by-products of the creation of new letters. Conceptually separable types of large-scale activities emerge from the many small actions of low-level codelets. Partridge and Rowe say that GENESIS is an emergent memory model that reconstructs representations rather than storing them in toto ("GENESIS" stands for "Generation and Exploration of Novel Emergent Structures in Sequences"). Peterson says that the created product is emergent because, although it has a cause, this is not of its own type (it does not itself constitute an item of system output). Halford and Wilson say that representational ranks correspond to levels of conceptual complexity, and that new psychological processes emerge at each level. In talking about Emmy, Hofstadter says that he does not expect full human intelligence to emerge from something far simpler, architecturally speaking, than the human brain. I have said that the created product emerges out of our knowledge and ability. A palpable product emerges, and this is a different kind of thing to knowledge and ability. I have contrasted this with combinationism, where the created product is constructed out of components that were already there.

I have left this chapter until last because it paints on a broad canvas, in which the details of the smaller picture that I have outlined might have been lost.

McDonough begins by considering Lady Lovelace's intuition that machines cannot be genuinely creative because "they cannot originate anything." "Emergentism," he says, "offers the possibility of a kind of creativity that involves the birth of something genuinely new, and, therefore, would seem to provide a robust metaphysical answer which supports Lady Lovelace's intuition that organisms are creative in a sense in which mere machines cannot be." He sets out to define a sense in which the behavior of the organism is genuinely creative, in which more comes out of it than can be accounted for by what is mechanically internal to it. He limits himself to *emergent materialism,* which is the view that life and mind are emergent characteristics of matter. He says that a material system has a material base, and that it has emergent characteristics if these characteristics are more than the sum of the characteristics of the parts of the base. He also says that a characteristic is emergent if there is an explanatory gap between the properties of the base and the characteristic. He then outlines five types of emergence: (a) the emergence of epiphenomenal properties, (b) emergence based on indeterminism, (c) the emergence of configurational forces, (d) the emergence of new material substances, and (e) the emergence of persons. He uses this taxonomy to define "an ascending series of five 'degrees' of emergence-based freedom and creativity."

In our discussion at the end of Chapter 10, I ask him to clarify his position on whether people can be creative in a way that machines cannot be. He says in the chapter that the characteristics of a machine are just the sum of the characteristics of its parts. I ask him whether this isn't just a verbal account, that rules out machine intelligence and creativity by definition. If a material base can give rise to emergent properties, and if emergence gives rise to creativity, why can't we have creative machines? Saying that they are now no longer machines by definition doesn't seem helpful to me.

His reply is that he does not rule out creative machines by definition, because he has not provided a general definition of creativity in the chapter. Instead, he says, he has defined emergence, and defined kinds of creativity with reference to it. So, he says, the real question is, "Could we have emergence-machines (machines, perhaps the brain, on which meaning or intelligence emerge)?" His answer is that we probably could, but he stresses that because of the explanatory gap we would not be able to explain this meaning or intelligence in terms of the underlying mechanism. Moreover, he says, if meaning or intelligence emerged from brain mechanisms, the functioning of the mechanisms would be "downright mysterious," for meaning depends on cultural context. I assume that his point has to do with what philosophers call "broad" and "narrow" descriptions. When the hands of a clock show that it is two o'clock, there is nothing in the clock (in its innards, in the mechanism) that means that the hands are pointing to two o' clock. Reference to the innards will explain why the hands are here, why they are positioned thus and so, but that this means that it is two o'clock is a matter of cultural convention: the meaning "it is two o'clock" has not emerged from the machine. In the same way he would say that culturally sensitive things such as signing a check cannot be explained in terms of brain mechanism. Reference to such a mechanism might explain why my hands move the way they do when I am signing a check, but they will not explain how this constitutes signing a check. To understand this we have to understand the social context in which it takes place. Consequently, an explanation of mechanism cannot give us an explanation of meaning.

I find this issue extremely difficult. I shall make two points. First, if emergence involves an explanatory gap—especially an explanatory gap by definition—then we are stuck with this gap, and no amount of reference to the cultural context is going to make it go away. If there is such a gap, then

McDonough may well be right in saying that reference to the mechanism will not fully explain (emergent) meaning and intelligence. But the same thing applies to organisms. Suppose that a person is operating in a cultural context. Then there will an explanatory gap between their properties as gross, physical things and their emergent meaning and intelligence. So either there is an explanatory gap, in which case I do not understand the difference between an organism and a mechanism, and do not see what is gained by appealing to the cultural context. Or there is no explanatory gap, in which case, according to McDonough, there is no emergence. As I say, I find this very difficult, and I may well have missed the mark.

My second point is this. Some of the implementations outlined in this volume operate in microworlds which might be seen as very miniature, proto-, cultural contexts. I assume that "being culturally sensitive" means "being sensitive to cultural norms," and I assume that we need to distinguish between "being subject to a rule (or a norm)" and "being sensitive to one." Computers and most computer programs are subject to rules: the rules underlie and drive them, and there is no room for choice or cultural sensitivity. But programs such as Letter Spirit are becoming aware of their rules and what they know. That, anyway, is the intention. As we have seen, McGraw and Hofstadter say that many AI programs that purport to model creativity *"don't know anything about what they're doing"* (their emphasis), whereas they claim that Letter Spirit does. And I have said that explicitation enables us to know what we know, to present our knowledge to ourselves in a compact, accessible form. It is presumably through this kind of explicitation that we graduate from being subject to rules to being sensitive to them—whether they are part of our make up or part of the cultural context. In Letter Spirit we have a program that responds to an input, focuses on parts of it, tries to apply concepts, focuses harder if it succeeds, applies semantic concepts such as "bowl" and "stem," and finally applies concepts such as "b" or "d." These concepts have vertical criteria of application and horizontal links to one another in an interconnected framework of concepts, so it seems to me that they have a genuine semantics. There is a sense in which part of the system is receptive to something "outside itself," "in its world," as well as having an internally coherent network of concepts. And by inspecting what it has constructed in the Visual Focus it can become aware of what it knows. This is my gloss on the situation, not McGraw, Hofstadter, and Rehling's.

It may well be that we are orders of magnitude more sensitive to our cultural surroundings than machines will ever be (though living in Queensland I do wonder), but this is not an in-principle, and therefore not a philosophically interesting, objection to what "dry mechanisms" might be able to achieve, nor does it show that we are not machines.

Two points of clarification. In the discussion I say that we want an emergence that gives us not only something that is greater than the sum of its parts, but richness and complexity without any parts. McDonough says that this is a contradiction in terms, because saying that we want something that is greater than the sum of its parts implies that there are parts, which is inconsistent with saying that we want richness and complexity without any parts. What I meant, of course, was that we want to explain *both* those cases where something is greater than the sum of its parts *and* those cases where there are no parts.

Secondly, in talking about the relationship between creativity and emergence, I say that creativity *exploits* emergence. Emergence throws things up, and we evaluate them in terms of our knowledge-about. We then readjust our goals and repeat the process. This is essentially McGraw, Hofstadter, and Rehling's central feedback loop of creativity.

McDonough says that this combines the worst features of mechanism and emergentism. Most obviously, the notion of a "central feedback system" places a mechanism at the higher level, of judgment and knowledge-about, where it is hardest to justify. Rather than judgment and knowledge-about being embodied in mechanisms that exploit lower level emergence they are themselves candidates for characteristics that emerge, rather in the way that persons emerge. Surely, he says, these emergent characteristics exploit lower level "mechanisms," "much as I, the person, use my knowledge about the mechanical world to exploit the mechanical calculator in my pocket."

Well, I plead guilty. I have tried to outline a framework of explanation that shows how our creative products emerge out of our knowledge and skill, and this is the main kind of emergence I have focussed on. There are other kinds, and the emergence of macroscopic structures out of microscopic actions is, of course, only one of them.

Finally, a question. Does emergence always involve an explanatory gap? McDonough quotes Hempel as saying that the job of science is to "eliminate the appearance of emergence." Perhaps, rather than eliminating its appearance, we can actually explain it. But we will only be able to do so if there is no explanatory gap. An explanatory gap is something of a loose cannon, after all. Does McDonough really want to have explanatory gaps in all those places where we have emergence? Does he want to say that we cannot explain the emergence of knowledge, and that we cannot explain how knowledge and skill give rise to creative output? What I mean by "emergence" in this introduction is that one kind of thing, a created product, a representation, a poem, or a play, can emerge out of another kind of thing (our knowledge and ability), rather than out of a combination of components. But I am not opposed to explaining emergence. Rehling says that we can see Letter Spirit as a black box, out of which things mysteriously emerge. But when we look inside it we see how things are modularized, and how the final output is produced. When we don't look at the slow accrual of output during the loops, the final output surprises us, but when we look at each gradual increment we are not surprised at all. McDonough says, "the very notion of emergence involves an explanatory gap with respect to any underlying mechanism." But is this true? When the unit of heredity was explained in terms of DNA it opened up a world of wonders for us, by *explaining the emergence* of acquired characteristics in the individual. It was as if we had come up out of the dusty cellars of our ignorance into a room filled with sunlight. This was explaining the emergence of acquired characteristics, not eliminating emergence or explaining it away.

NOTES

1. The *Tractatus* was first published in 1921. The first English translation appeared in 1922.

2. *Philosophical Investigations* was first published in 1953.

3. These three types of output creativity are not to be confused with Type 1 and Type 2 output creativity, which I discuss in later sections.

4. An issue I have not had time to address is the crucial one of psychological reality: how psychologically real are the results of the reverse engineering? Emmy is given musical pieces that have been composed by humans. She decomposes them into labeled fragments, and reassembles them into new wholes. Do these fragments and rules of combination correspond to anything psychologically real in the minds of the original composers? One thing seems clear. Composers have to understand and analyze before they can compose and create. As Partridge and Rowe say in their chapter, we are *input* creative when we solve problems and make sense of the world—during perception, or when we listen to music or poetry—and we are *output* creative when we deploy this capability off-line, to produce music or poetry.

5. Hofstadter and FARG (1995) provide a detailed account of these projects. McGraw (1995) provides a detailed account of the implementation of Letter Spirit's Examiner. A more recent horse out of the FARG stable is James Marshall's Metacat (Marshall, 1999), which involves the idea of "self-watching"—the ability to perceive and remember patterns that occur in its processing as it solves analogy problems.

6. Some of the neuropsychological literature seems to suggest that the equivalent of quanta *are* stored when we recognize letters and form images of them. As we saw early in this Introduction, Kosslyn et al. (1995) agree that "images are *constructed* [my emphasis] a portion at a time, with portions corresponding to individual perceptual units, . . ." (p. 151). But they go on to say, "This finding is consistent with the claim that one encodes not only the overall shape of complex objects, but also high-resolution representations of at least some component parts. . . . If a high-resolution image is required to perform a task, stored representations of an object's parts are activated . . . when the image is formed. . . . There is evidence that the spatial relations among parts of a scene are stored separately from the parts themselves." "For present purposes," they say, "parts correspond *to segments of block letters* [my emphasis]." I am puzzled by the notion that segments of block letters are stored, especially in the context of the claim that images are constructed (a portion at a time). An uncharitable explanation is that this is atomism again—the notion that images and representations must be built out of basic elements, in the way that houses are built out of bricks. A more likely explanation is that I have misunderstood their meaning.

REFERENCES

Beer, R. (1990). *Intelligence and adaptive behavior.* San Diego, CA: Academic Press.

Beer, R. (1995). A dynamical system perspective on environmental agent interactions. *Artificial Intelligence, 72,* 173–215.

Beer, R. & Gallagher, J. C. (1992). Evolving dynamical neural networks for adaptive behavior. *Adaptive Behaviour, 1,* 91–122.

Behrmann, M., Kosslyn, S. M., & Jeannerod, M. (Eds.). (1995). *The neuropsychology of mental imagery.* Oxford: Pergamon. Special issue of *Neuropsychologia, 33* (11), 1335–1582.

Boden, M. A. (1990). *The creative mind: Myths and mechanisms.* London: Weidenfeld and Nicolson. (1991: Expanded edition, Abacus; American edition, Basic Books.)

Boden, M. A. (1993). Mapping, exploring, transforming. *Artificial Intelligence and Simulation of Behaviour Quarterly, 85.* Special edition on Artificial Intelligence and creativity, T. H. Dartnall (Ed.).

Boden, M. A. (1994a). What is creativity? In M. A. Boden (Ed.), *Dimensions of creativity.* Cambridge, MA: MIT Press.

Boden, M. A. (1994b). Creativity and computers. In T. H. Dartnall (Ed.), *Artificial Intelligence and creativity: An interdisciplinary approach.* Dordrecht: Kluwer.

Brooks, R. (1991). Intelligence without representation. *Artificial Intelligence, 47,* 139–159.

Clancey, W. J. (1997). *Situated cognition: On human knowledge and computer representations.* Cambridge: Cambridge University Press.

Clark, A., & Karmiloff-Smith, A. (1993). The cognizer's innards. *Mind and Language, 8,* 3.

Clark, A. & Toribio, J. (1994). Doing without representing. *Synthese, 101,* 401–431.

Dartnall, T. H. (Ed.). (1994). *Artificial Intelligence and creativity: An interdisciplinary approach.* Dordrecht: Kluwer.

Dartnall, T. H. (1996). Redescription, information and access. In D. Peterson (Ed.), *Forms of representation: An interdisciplinary theme for cognitive science.* Exeter: Intellect Books.

Dartnall, T. H. (1997). Imagine that! Or: How many images did you have before breakfast? *Metascience, 11,* 151–154.

Dartnall, T. H. (1999a). Normative engines: Stalking the wild Wittgensteinian machine. *Idealistic Studies: An Interdisciplinary Journal of Philosophy, 29,* 215–229. Special Issue: Wittgenstein and Cognitive Science, R. McDonough (Ed.).

Dartnall, T. H. (1999b). Content, cognition and the inner code, in J. Wiles & T. Dartnall (Eds.), *Perspectives on cognitive science.* Stamford: Ablex.

Dartnall, T. H. (2000). Reverse psychologism, cognition and content. *Minds and Machines, 10,* 1, 31–52.

Denis, M., Gonçalves, M.-R. & Memmi, D. (1995). Mental scanning of visual images generated from verbal descriptions: Towards a model of image accuracy. In M. Behrmann, S. M. Kosslyn & M. Jeannerod (Eds.), *The neuropsychology of mental imagery* (pp. 177–196). Oxford: Pergamon.

Descartes, R. (1970). Meditations on first philosophy, In E. Anscombe & P. T. Geach (Eds.), *Descartes, philosophical writings* (pp. 59–124). London: Nelson.

Dreyfus, H. (1979). *What computers can't do: The limits of artificial intelligence.* (2nd ed.) New York: Harper and Row.

Fodor, J. (1980). Methodological solipsism considered as a research strategy in cognitive psychology. *Behavioral and Brain Sciences, 3,* 63–110.

Forrest, S. (Ed.). (1991). *Emergent computation.* Cambridge, MA: MIT Press.

French, R. M. (1995). *Tabletop: An emergent, stochastic computer model of analogy-making.* Cambridge, MA: Bradford/MIT Press.

Gentner, D. (1983). Structure-mapping: A theoretical framework for analogy. *Cognitive Science, 7,* 155–170.

Gentner, D., & Gentner, D. R. (1983). Flowing waters or teeming crowds: Mental models of electricity. In D. Gentner & A. L. Stevens (Eds.), *Mental models.* Mahwah, NJ: Erlbaum.

Halford, G. S. (1997). Recoding can lead to inaccessible structures, but avoids capacity limitations. *Behavioral and Brain Sciences, 20* (1), 75. Peer Commentary on A. Clark and C. Thornton, Trading spaces: Computation, representation, and the limits of uniformed learning.

Halford, G. S., Phillips, S., & Wilson, W. H. (2001). *Structural complexity in cognitive processes: The concept of representational rank.* Manuscript in preparation.

Haugeland, J. (1991). Representational genera. In W. Ramsey, S. Stich, & D. Rummelhart (Eds.), *Philosophy and connectionist theory* (pp. 61–90). Mahwah, NJ: Erlbaum.

Hofstadter, D. and Fluid Analogies Research Group (FARG). (1995). *Fluid concepts and creative analogies: Computer models of the fundamental mechanisms of thought.* New York: Basic Books.

Hume, D. (1911). *A treatise of human nature.* London: Everyman, J. M. Dent & Sons.

Johnson-Laird, P. (1988). *The computer and the mind.* London: Collins/Fontana.

Karmiloff-Smith, A. (1992). *Beyond modularity: a developmental perspective on cognitive science.* Cambridge, MA: MIT/Bradford.

Karmiloff-Smith, A. (1993). Is creativity domain-specific or domain general? Clues from normal and abnormal phenotypes. *Artificial Intelligence and Simulation of Behaviour Quarterly, 85.* Special edition on Artificial Intelligence and creativity, T. H. Dartnall (Ed.).

Karmiloff-Smith, A. (1994). Digest of *Beyond modularity,* with Peer Reviews, *Behavioral and Brain Sciences, 17,* 4.

Kosslyn, S. M., Holtzman, J. D., Farah M. J., & Gazzaniga, M. S. (1985). A computational analysis of mental image generation: Evidence from functional dissociations in split-brain patients. *Journal of Experimental Psychology, 114,* 311–341.

Kosslyn, S. M., Maljkovic, V., Hamilton, S. E., Horwitz, G., & Thompson, W. L. (1995). Two types of image generation: Evidence from left and right hemisphere processes. In M. Behrmann, S. M. Kosslyn & M. Jeannerod (Eds.), *The neuropsychology of mental imagery* (pp. 151–176). Oxford: Pergamon.

Locke J. (1690). *Essay concerning human understanding.* London. There are many modern editions.

Malcolm, N. (1963). Three forms of memory. In N. Malcolm, *Knowledge and certainty.* Englewood Cliffs, NJ: Prentice Hall.

Marshall, J. (1999). *Metacat: A self-watching cognitive architecture for analogy-making and high-level perception*. Doctoral dissertation. Dept. of Computer Science and the Cognitive Science Program, Indiana University, Bloomington.

McGraw, G. (1995). *Letter Spirit (Part One): Emergent high-level perception of letters using fluid concepts*. Doctoral dissertation. Dept. of Computer Science and the Cognitive Science Program, Indiana University, Bloomington.

Minsky, M. (1985). *The society of mind*. New York: Simon & Schuster.

Mitchell, M. (1993). *Analogy-making as perception*. Cambridge, MA: Bradford/MIT Press.

Partridge and Rowe. (1994). *Computers and creativity*. Oxford: Intellect Books.

Phillips, S., Halford, G. S., & Wilson, W. H. (1995). *The processing of associations versus the processing of relations and symbols: A systematic comparison*. Seventeenth Annual Conference of the Cognitive Science Society, Pittsburgh, PA.

Poincaré, H. (1982). *The foundations of science: Science and hypothesis, the value of science, science and method*. Washington, DC: University Press of America.

Popper, Sir K. R. (1972). *Objective knowledge: An evolutionary approach*. Oxford: Clarendon Press.

Port, F. P. and van Gelder, T. (1995). *Mind as motion: Explorations in the dynamics of cognition*. Cambridge, MA: MIT/Bradford.

Searle, J. (1980). Minds, brains and programs. *Behavioral and Brain Sciences, 3*, 417–427.

Searle, J. (1990). Is the brain's mind a computer program? *Scientific American, 262* (1), 20–31.

Shanon, B. (1993). *The representational and the presentational: An essay in cognition and the study of mind*. London: Harvester.

Sloman, A. (1996). Towards a general theory of representations. In D. Peterson, (Ed.), *Forms of representation: An interdisciplinary theme for cognitive science*. Exeter: Intellect Books.

Smolensky, P. (1988). On the proper treatment of connectionism. *Behavioral and Brain Sciences, 11*, 1–74.

Thagard, P. (1996). *Mind: Introduction to cognitive science*. Cambridge, MA: MIT/Bradford.

Thornton, C. (1994). Creativity, connectionism and guided walks. In T. H. Dartnall (Ed.), *Artificial Intelligence and creativity: An interdisciplinary approach*. Dordrecht: Kluwer.

Torrance, S. (1997). A change of mind in cognitive science. *Metascience, 11*, 106–114.

van Gelder, T. (1995). What might cognition be, if not computation? *The Journal of Philosophy, XCI* (6), July, 345–381.

Wittgenstein, L. (1961). *Tractatus logico-philosophicus*. London: Routledge and Kegan Paul.

Wittgenstein, L. (1963). *Philosophical investigations*. Oxford: Basil Blackwell.

1

Staring Emmy Straight in the Eye—and Doing My Best Not to Flinch

Douglas Hofstadter

> Good artists borrow; great artists steal.
> —Douglas Hofstadter[1]

HOW YOUNG I WAS, AND HOW NAÏVE

I am not now, nor have I ever been, a card-carrying futurologist. I make no claims to be able to peer into the murky crystal ball and make out what lies far ahead. But one time, back in 1977, I did go a little bit out on a futurologist's limb. At the end of Chapter 19 ("Artificial Intelligence: Prospects") of my book *Gödel, Escher, Bach,* I had a section called "Ten Questions and Speculations," and in it I stuck my neck out, venturing a few predictions about how things would go in the development of Artificial Intelligence (AI). Though it is a little embarrassing to me now, let me nonetheless quote a few lines from that section here:

Question: Will there be chess programs that can beat anyone?

Speculation: No. There may be programs which can beat anyone at chess, but they will not be exclusively chess players. They will be programs of *general* intelligence, and they will be just as temperamental as people. "Do you want to play chess?" "No, I'm bored with chess. Let's talk about poetry." That may be the kind of dialogue you could have with a program that could beat everyone.

We all know today how very wrong that speculation was. What was it that so misled the author of *Gödel, Escher, Bach* back then?

Well, when I wrote those words, I was drawing some of my ideas from a fascinating article that I had read by my soon-to-be colleague at Indiana University, the psychologist and chess master Eliot Hearst (formerly Vice President of the United States Chess Federation [USCF], member of the U.S. Chess Olympics team, and once a frequent playing partner of Bobby Fischer). In his article, Hearst (who clearly knew infinitely more about chess than I ever could hope to) eloquently expressed the conviction that deep chess-playing ability depends in an intimate manner on such cognitive skills as the ability to sort the wheat from the chaff in an intuitive flash, the ability to make subtle analogies, and the ability to recall memories associatively. All of these elusive abilities seemed to lie so close to the core of human nature itself that I jumped to the conclusion that profoundly insightful chess-playing draws intrinsically on central facets of the human condition, and that mere brute-force searching of the rapidly branching lookahead tree, no matter how fast, broad, or deep, would not be able to circumvent or shortcut that fact.

I didn't realize—and perhaps no one did, at the time—that the USCF rankings of the best computer chess programs (all of which used brute-force search algorithms) were pretty much creeping up linearly with time, so that a simple-minded linear extrapolation on a plot of chess prowess versus time would, even back then, have suggested that computers would take over from humans somewhere around the year 2000. The first time I actually saw such a graph was in an article in *Scientific American* in the mid-1990s (written by the creators of Deep Blue, by the way), and I vividly remember thinking to myself, when I looked at it, "Uh-oh! The handwriting is on the wall!" And so it was.

CHESS TUMBLES TO COMPUTATIONAL POWER . . .

We now know that world-class chess-playing ability can indeed be achieved by brute-force techniques—techniques that in no way attempt to replicate or emulate what goes on in the head of a chess grandmaster. Analogy-making is not needed, nor is associative memory, nor are intuitive flashes that sort wheat from chaff—just a tremendously wide and deep search, carried out by superfast, chess-specialized hardware using ungodly amounts of stored knowledge. And thus, thanks to the remarkable achievements of the past decade, one can no longer look at a subtle, elegant, and stunning midgame chess move and say with confidence, "Only a genius could have spotted that move!" because the move could just as well have emanated from a mindless, lightning-fast full-width search as from the silent machinations of an insightful human mind.

I cannot say what goes on in the brain of a Bobby Fischer or a Garry Kasparov when they play championship-level chess. I have no idea whether their phenomenal chess-playing ability draws in some subtle way on their entire human existence, on their prior struggles with life and death, on their striving for personal identity, on their coping with dashed romances, on their hopes and fears in domains apparently remote from chess—or whether their chess-playing skill is in some sense totally isolated from the rest of their minds, fully contained in some little localized region of their brains that, at least in principle, could be neatly excised by a neurosurgeon, leaving the rest of their brains fully intact so that they could go on living normal lives while the little module, safely preserved and nourished in a vat, happily kept on playing world-level chess.

Eliot Hearst's article had led me to believe that the image of an isolated chess-playing module is wrong, and that, to the contrary, great chess-playing skill is of necessity deeply intertwined with all that being human is about. But as Deep Blue has taught us, that certainly need not be the case. Top-notch chess-playing does not necessarily depend on the full mental complexities that come from living life, facing death, and all those messy things that we experience. Top-notch chess playing *can* come from a pure chess engine, full stop. As for top-notch *human* chess-playing ability, one might still plausibly believe that it is necessarily tightly integrated with the rest of the brain and with the whole kit and caboodle of being human—but ever since Deep Blue's appearance on the scene, there is reason to doubt that romantic vision. Perhaps it is the case, but perhaps not.

I, in any case, have had to eat humble pie with respect to my 1977 speculation. But, I must say, having to swallow my words about chess doesn't upset me all that much, since, aside from writing that one speculation, I personally have never had any emotional stake in the notion that chess skill lies very near the pinnacle of that which is most truly human, and so I'm not crushed that my speculation was refuted. And even though people say that the game of Go is far less computer-tractable than chess is, I don't think I'd care to rewrite my speculation substituting Go for chess. I'll just admit my mistake.

So . . . chess-playing fell to computers? I don't feel particularly threatened or upset; after all, sheer computation had decades earlier fallen to computers as well. So a computer had outdone Daniel Shanks in the calculation of digits of pi—did it matter? Did that achievement in any way lower human dignity? Of course not! It simply taught us that calculation is more mechanical than we had realized. Likewise, Deep Blue taught us that chess is more mechanical than we had realized. These lessons serve as interesting pieces of information about various domains of expertise, but to my mind, they hardly seem to threaten the notion, which I then cherished and which I still cherish, that human intelligence is extraordinarily profound and mysterious.

It is not, I hasten to add, that I am a mystic who thinks that intelligence intrinsically resists implantation in physical entities—to the contrary, I look upon brains themselves as very complex machines, and, unlike John Searle and Roger Penrose, I have always maintained that the precise nature of the physico-chemical substrate of thinking and consciousness is irrelevant. I can imagine silicon-based thought as easily as I can imagine carbon-based thought; I can imagine ideas and meanings and emotions and a first-person awareness of the world (an "inner light," a "ghost in the machine") emerging from electronic circuitry as easily as from proteins and nucleic acids. I simply have always run on faith that when "genuine artificial intelligence" (sorry for the oxymoron) finally arises, it will do so precisely because the same degree of complexity and the same overall kind of abstract mental architecture will have come to exist in a new kind of hardware. What I do not expect, however, is that full human intelligence will emerge from something far simpler, architecturally speaking, than a human brain.

. . . AND SO, IS MUSICAL BEAUTY NEXT IN LINE?

My "Ten Questions and Speculations" section in *Gödel, Escher, Bach* (*GEB*) was an attempt to articulate just these kinds of pieces of faith, and at the time I wrote it, I was particularly proud of another one of them, which I now reproduce here in full:

Question: Will a computer program ever write beautiful music?

Speculation: Yes, but not soon. Music is a language of emotions, and until programs have emotions as complex as ours, there is no way a program will write anything beautiful. There can be "forgeries"—shallow imitations of the syntax of earlier music—but despite what one might think at first, there is much more to musical expression than can be captured in syntactical rules. There will be no new kinds of beauty turned up for a long time by computer music-composing programs. Let me carry this thought a little further. To think—and I have heard this suggested—that we might soon be able to command a preprogrammed mass-produced mail-order twenty-dollar desk-model "music box" to bring forth from its sterile [*sic!*] circuitry pieces which Chopin or Bach might have written had they lived longer is a grotesque and shameful misestimation of the depth of the human spirit. A "program" which could produce music as they did would have to wander around the world on its own, fighting its way through the maze of life and feeling every moment of it. It would have to understand the joy and loneliness of a chilly night wind, the longing for a cherished hand, the inaccessibility of a distant town, the heartbreak and regeneration after a human death. It would have to have known resignation and world-weariness, grief and despair, determination and victory, piety and awe. In it would have had to commingle such opposites as hope and fear, anguish and jubilation, serenity and suspense. Part and parcel of it would have to be a sense of grace, humor, rhythm, a sense of the unexpected—and of course an exquisite awareness of the magic of fresh creation. Therein, and therein only, lie the sources of meaning in music.

In recent years, when lecturing about Dave Cope's work, I have read this paragraph aloud so many times that I practically know it by heart. And what do I make of it now? Well, I am not quite sure. I have been grappling for several years now with these issues, and still there is no clear resolution. That, perhaps, is why I have been so fascinated by Cope's Emmy and the issues raised thereby. Let me explain.

In the spring of 1995, I was conducting a cognitive-science seminar at Indiana University called "AI: Hype versus Hope," whose purpose was for me and my students, working together, to try to sort the wheat from the chaff in this field so rife with brazen claims of human-level performance in one domain or another, most of which I knew were groundless, or nearly so. I was willing to concede, however, that even in a hopelessly hyped project, there might somewhere reside a nugget of value, and it was my idea that we would uncover those nuggets while at the same time chucking out the overblown claims. We discussed computer driving of cars, speech recognition, story understanding, machine translation, face recognition, and many other topics. One topic that particularly interested me was music, because I was convinced, a priori, that claims I'd heard here and there about high-quality music emanating from computers were hugely exaggerated, and I wanted to confirm this hunch. And so when a student in the seminar told me she had run across a book called *Computers and Musical Style* in the music library and wondered if she could present it to the seminar, I enthusiastically encouraged her to do so.

A couple of days later in class, this student described to us the ideas behind the program—Emmy, to be specific—but I found myself not terribly interested. It sounded like Emmy was dealing only with the surface level of music—with patterns, not with the deep emotional substrate—and I was pretty sure that little of interest could come of such an architecture. Then she said she could play for us some of Emmy's compositions on the piano in my research center, so I said "Fine!" We went in and listened as she played, and my skeptical ears were somewhat jolted. Although the two pieces she played—very short Mozart-aping and Brahms-aping pieces—sounded amateurish and flawed, they were by no means totally incoherent or absurd. I wondered how in the world they could have come out of this architecture, and so I asked if I could borrow the book for a day or two. She said yes, and I took it home and plunged into it with great interest.

I noticed in its pages an Emmy mazurka supposedly in the Chopin style, and this really drew my attention because, having revered Chopin my whole life long, I felt certain that no one could pull the wool over my eyes in this department. Moreover, I knew all 50 or 60 of the Chopin mazurkas very well, having played them dozens of times on the piano and heard them even more often on recordings. So I went straight to my own piano and sight-read through the Emmy mazurka—once, twice, three times, and more—each time with mounting confusion and surprise. Though I felt there were a few little glitches here and there, I was impressed, for the piece seemed to *express* something. If I had been told it had been written by a human, I would have had no doubts about its expressiveness. I don't know that I would have accepted the claim that it was a newly-uncovered mazurka by Chopin himself, but I would easily have believed it was by a graduate student in music who loved Chopin. It was slightly nostalgic, had a bit of Polish feeling in it, and it did not seem in any way plagiarized. It was *new,* it was unmistakably *Chopin-like* in spirit, and it was *not emotionally empty.* I was truly shaken. How could emotional music be coming out of a program that had never heard a note, never lived a moment of life, never had any emotions whatsoever?

The more I grappled with this, the more disturbed I became—but also fascinated. There was a highly counterintuitive paradox here, something that obviously had caught me enormously off guard, and it was not my style to merely deny it and denounce Emmy as "trivial" or "nonmusical." To do so would have been cowardly and dishonest. I was going to face this paradox straight on, and it seemed to me that the best thing to do was to look the monster right in the face. And thus I picked up my telephone and phoned the program's inventor, David Cope, in Santa Cruz. I reached him with ease, and as he was very friendly and open, I asked him about aspects of Emmy's architecture that I had not been able to glean from his book. After a lengthy and very informative conversation, we made a point of agreeing to get together next time I was in California. In the meantime, I continued to grapple with this strange program that was threatening to upset the apple cart that held many of my oldest and most deeply cherished beliefs about the sacredness of music, about music being the ultimate inner sanctum of the human spirit, the last thing that would tumble in AI's headlong rush towards thought, insight, and creativity.

THE PROOF OF THE PUDDING IS IN THE EATING

Of all the projects examined in my "Hype versus Hope" seminar, Emmy was the only one that made me reconsider deeply held beliefs. I have to confess, though, that had I only read about its architecture and not heard any of its output, I would have paid little or no attention to it. Although Cope has put in far more work on Emmy than most AI researchers ever do on any one project (he has worked on it for nearly 20 years now, and the program consists of some 20,000 lines of Lisp code that runs on his trusty Macintosh), the basic ideas in the design of Emmy simply did not sound radically new to me, or even all that promising. What made all the difference in the world for me was *carefully listening to Emmy's compositions.*

I don't think one can possibly judge Emmy without hearing some of "her" pieces. (Dave usually says "her," and, for fun, I sometimes go along with the anthropomorphism.) Some people will approach them open-mindedly, while others—often musicians—will come to Emmy's pieces with a strong pre-conceived idea that they will be weak or blatantly derivative, and so, however the pieces actually sound, such people will wind up putting them down, even pooh-poohing them, safe in their knowledge that they were done by a computer. For that reason, I think it best that one first hear a few of Emmy's pieces without knowing their provenance—perhaps without even having ever heard of Emmy. I don't like dishonesty, but perhaps it is best to misinform people about what they are about to hear, in order that they not listen with a pre-closed mind.

LECTURING ON EMMY IN MANY DIFFERENT VENUES

It was not too long after my first exposure to Emmy that I decided that I had to organize my many complex reactions to this strange project in a coherent fashion, and that meant preparing a well-rounded lecture on it all. I pulled together a set of thoughts, made a bunch of transparencies, and was lucky enough to find several venues where I could give this lecture. My set of transparencies evolved in many ways as these lectures took place, which was good, but one strange thing I soon discovered was that almost no one in my various audiences shared my profound sense of bewilderment or alarm. Hardly anyone seemed upset at Cope's coup in the modeling of artistic creativity; hardly anyone seemed threatened or worried at all. I felt kinship with but a few souls in the world who also were bewildered by similar triumphs. One of them was none other than Garry Kasparov, who had said, a year before being trounced by Deep Blue:

To some extent, this match is a defense of the whole human race. Computers play such a huge role in society. They are everywhere. But there is a frontier that they must not cross. They must not cross into the area of human creativity. It would threaten the existence of human control in such areas as art, literature, and music.

On one level, Kasparov's words sounded ridiculous to me. Saying "Computers *must not* cross into human creativity" seemed hopelessly naïve, almost like saying, "We must not let them do certain things, because they'll beat our pants off if we do, and that would be dreadful!" And Kasparov's last sentence, even sillier, raises the specter of computers trying to wrest control away from human beings, as if on the surface of our planet there were already raging some terrible battle between alien species for control of culture. Such a weird scenario may possibly come to be in the next few decades or next few centuries—who can say for sure?—but certainly it is not happening already. Today we control computers, and that is beyond doubt or dispute.

And yet . . . something of Kasparov's worried tone resonated with me. It was as if he had felt, and I now felt, something about the profundity of the human mind's sublimity being taken away, being robbed, by the facile victories of programs that seemed totally out of touch with the essence of the domains in which they were operating so well. It seemed somehow humiliating, even nightmarish, to me.

But no matter how I tried, I could not get my own sense of confusion and worry across to my audience. One thing I learned fairly soon was that few people have a visceral feeling about the centrality and depth of music. Indeed, I discovered that there is a rough trichotomy of people. There are some who, like me, feel that music is the most powerful drug in the world, and that it reaches in and touches one's innermost core like almost nothing else—more powerfully than art, than literature, than cinema, and so on. But such people are few and far between. A much more common attitude is, "Sure I like music, but it doesn't touch me at my very core. It's just fun to listen to, to dance to, and so forth." And then another attitude that came up surprisingly often in question-and-answer sessions after my lectures was this: "I'm kind of tone-deaf, and music's okay but I can take it or leave it, so I don't really relate to your deep love of music, but. . . ."

I soon realized that I was probably not going to reach the third group no matter what I said, and wondered if the "music enthusiasts" of the middle group were also beyond reach. But to my greater chagrin, even most people in the *first* group often couldn't relate to my worry! This I found utterly baffling.

A PERSONAL VIEW OF HOW EMMY WORKS

The basic idea behind Emmy is what Dave Cope terms "recombinant music"—the identification of recurrent structures of various sorts in a composer's output, and the reusing of those structures in new arrangements, so as to construct a new piece "in the same style." One can thus imagine feeding in Beethoven's nine symphonies, and Emmy coming out with Beethoven's Tenth (or Brahms' First, if you subscribe to the claims of some musicologists that in his First Symphony, Brahms carried on the Beethoven spirit beyond the grave).

Toward the beginning of *Computers and Musical Style,* his first book about Emmy, Cope says this about his personal pathway of exploration:

In 1981, during a moment of recklessness, I wrote the following in a daily journal:

> I envision a time in which new works will be convincingly composed in the styles of composers long dead. These will be commonplace and, while never as good as the originals, they will be exciting, entertaining, and interesting. Musicians and non-musicians alike will interact with programs that allow them to endlessly tinker with the styles of the composing programs . . . I see none of this as problematic. Machines, after all, only add and subtract. Programs that benefit from those operations are only as good as their creators.

This book describes many aspects of a program I have since devised for the replication of musical styles. . . . If there is a discovery here, it is that one way of defining style is through pattern recognition and that musical style can be imitated if one can find what constitutes musical patterns. (pp. xiii–xiv)

If one is to form an educated opinion of Emmy, one's first duty is obviously to familiarize oneself with how the program works. Cope, naturally, has his own ways of explaining Emmy, but I have found it useful to rephrase what I have learned over these past few years, and I think that hearing it from an outsider's viewpoint may help to clarify certain difficult points. Moreover, I found more than once, in talking with Dave, that he would provide highly revelatory answers to key questions—questions that were not answered anywhere in his writings, and in fact in most cases were not even posed in his books. Such interchanges gave me a kind of personal insight into some aspects of Emmy that I believe may be useful to share, and so, with that as my excuse, I now present my amateur's capsule portrait of Emmy's innards.

Emmy's central *modus operandi,* given a set of input pieces (usually all by a single composer and belonging to the same general form, such as *mazurka*) is:

1. Chop up
2. Reassemble

This, in three words, is what Cope means by the phrase "recombinant music." Caveat: The assembly phase, in contrast to Mozart's famous *Musikalisches Würfelspiel,* which produced waltzes by random shuffling of 3/4 measures, is anything but haphazard or willy-nilly (as if by throwing dice). There are significant principles constraining what can be tacked onto what, and these principles are formulated so as to guarantee coherence (at least to the extent that the input pieces themselves are coherent!). I summarize these two principles as follows:

1. Make the *local flow-pattern* of each voice similar to that in source pieces
2. Make the *global positioning* of fragments similar to that in source pieces

These could be likened to two types of constraints that a jigsaw-puzzle solver naturally exploits when putting together a jigsaw puzzle:

1. The *shape* of each piece meshes tightly with those of neighboring pieces
2. The *stuff* shown on each piece makes sense in the context of the picture

The former of these constraints might be characterized as *syntactic meshing,* or meshing based solely on form, while the latter could be characterized

as *semantic meshing,* or meshing based solely on content. In isolation, perhaps neither of them would be too impressive, but when used together, they
form a powerful pair of constraints. But how does my jigsaw-puzzle
metaphor translate into specific musical terms?

Syntactic Meshing in Emmy: Voice-Hooking and Texture-Matching

Let me first consider the first of these constraints—that involving form,
or what one might call "coherence of flow." This constraint in fact breaks
down into two facets:

1. Voice-hooking
2. Texture-matching

To understand these two distinct facets of syntactic meshing, one has to
imagine that a new piece is being put together note by note, in sequence,
and that to this end, short fragments of input pieces are being selected so as
to mesh with the current context. Imagine that we have just inserted a fragment f_1, and are considering whether to insert fragment f_2 right after it,
drawn from somewhere in the input. *Voice-hooking* would be the requirement that the initial note of the melodic line of fragment f_2 should coincide
with the next melodic note to which fragment f_1 led in its original context.
In other words, a given fragment's melodic line should link up smoothly
with the melodic line of its successor fragment. This is very much like saying that two puzzle pieces should fit together physically.

Of course, here I referred only to the melodic, or soprano, line of a piece.
One can also insist on voice-hooking of the bass line, and of intermediate
lines as well (tenor, alto, etc.). Ideally, voice-hooking can be carried out successfully on all voices at once, but if not, then the most logical voices to sacrifice are the inner ones, then the bass line, and last of all, the melodic line.
Usually, provided there is a sufficient quantity of input pieces, it will be possible to achieve a good deal of satisfaction in voice-hooking.

In addition, there is *texture-matching,* which is basically the idea that the
notes in a chord can be moved up or down pitchwise by full octaves and can
be spread out timewise so as to match some preexistent local pattern in the
piece being composed. Most typically, these two operations result in the
"spinning-out" of a simple chord into an arpeggio that matches some
preestablished arpeggiation pattern. Thus, a purely vertical C-E-G triad could
be spun out, for instance, into a C-G-E-G figure to be incorporated into an
Alberti-type bass line, or into a very wide E-C-G arpeggio to match the
widely arpeggiated pattern of the bass line of a Chopin-like nocturne. It could
even be turned into the very long sequence of notes "C-E-G-C-E-G-C-E;
C-E-G-C-E-G-C-E," which you may recognize as the melody in the first
measure of the C major prelude of Book I of Bach's *Well-Tempered Clavier.*

Basically, the pattern of that piece is so regular that it is a mechanical act to spin out a triad into a whole sixteen-note sequence.

Semantic Meshing in Emmy: Tension-Resolution Logic and *SPEAC* Labels

We now turn to the second constraint—that involving content, or what one might call "tension-resolution logic." This is where ideas devised by Cope as part of Emmy may in fact constitute a significant new contribution to music theory. The basic idea is that one wishes to insert a fragment into a new piece only if *the "location" of the insertion is similar to the "location" of the fragment where it occurred in some input piece.* The word "location" is put in quotes here because it is not clear what it means. Indeed, the italicized phrase forces one to ask the puzzling question, "How can a given fragment be 'in the same location' with respect to two different pieces? How can one compare 'locations' inside totally different pieces? What, indeed, might 'location' inside a piece be taken to mean (since, self-evidently, using measure number would be a pathetic travesty of an answer)?"

Cope decided that "location" must be defined in a way that involves both global and local contexts—in fact, a series of nested contexts, ranging from very local (notes, measures) to medium-range (phrases) to large-scale (periods) to global (sections). To a fragment on any of these distinct hierarchical levels (and there can be any number of such structural levels), Cope attaches a label—one of the five letters *S, P, E, A, C*—which attempts to capture what I have chosen to call the *tension-resolution status* of that fragment. These letters stand for the following words: *statement, preparation, extension, antecedent, consequent.* The label-assignment process proceeds from most local to most global, with the labels of larger sections dependent upon the labels already assigned to their component pieces.

Unfortunately, the details of the label-assignment process are unclear to me, but in essence it starts at the most local level, where the presence of specific scale degrees in the various voices is used as the main diagnostic for the labeling of a chord (co-presence of tonic and dominant, for instance, or tonic and mediant, suggests an "S" label at that level). From there on out, certain characteristic sequences of local labels are telltale cues that suggest specific higher-level labels, and so on, always moving upwards hierarchically. In the end one winds up with *SPEAC* labels attached to sections of many different sizes and, perforce, at many different structural levels.

The upshot of this many-leveled labeling process carried out by Emmy is that any local fragment of an input piece winds up with a set of labels—its own label, that of the larger fragment inside which it sits, then that of the next-larger fragment in which that one sits, and so on, and so on. Thus hypothetically, a given chord in an input piece could have the following set of labels (proceeding from most local to most global): A-C-C-E-P-A-S, and another chord might have the hierarchical series of labels E-S-C-S, and so on. In either case, such a series of letters basically tells you, on several different hierarchical levels, just what the tension-resolution status of the piece is at the chord concerned. And that—provided it really works well—would seem about as good a way of saying "where you are" in a piece as any I could imagine, since tension and resolution on many levels really do constitute the crux of musical meaning.

Now the trick is to use these labels to guide composition, and the basic idea is fairly straightforward. Suppose that in our piece-under-construction we find ourselves in a location whose tension-resolution status is PACSCS (moving from most local to most global). The letters "PACSCS" tell us "where we are," so to speak, inside our new piece. And so, in choosing a fragment to borrow from an input piece and to insert right here, our main criterion will naturally be that the chosen fragment's tension-resolution status inside its original piece was exactly PACSCS—in other words, that the fragment we are going to quote lies in "the same place" inside its original piece as in the new piece.

If in the input corpus we find several such "same-location" fragments, that is good, since it gives us a choice of how to continue, but we of course also want to satisfy the syntactic voice-hooking constraint. We thus throw away any fragments that don't match in this manner. If after this paring-down, there are still several potential fragments surviving and vying with each other for insertion, then we can choose one at random.

Suppose, on the other hand, that there is no input fragment that has exactly the desired multi-level tension-resolution status—how then to proceed? The only solution is to sacrifice something—but what? Cope decided that in such circumstances, global status is more sacrificeable than local, and so we lop off the final letter, leaving us with "PACSC," and now we try again to find an appropriate fragment in the input corpus. If this fails, we lop off one more letter (thus giving "PACS"), and we search again in the input corpus. Since through such lopping-off we are loosening ever further the constraint of matching tension-resolution status, we will eventually find one or more input fragments that match the labels that we seek, and then we can choose randomly among those fragments, provided that voice-hooking also works. And thus the piece gets extended a little bit. At this point, we restart the constrained search process and extend the growing composition a little bit more—and so forth and so on. Thus, like a crystal growing outwards, is built up a piece of music by Emmy.

In summary, here, in my own words, is the core of Emmy's composition process:

1. Sequential assembly of fragments that have the highest possible degree of agreement of *SPEAC* labels on all hierarchical levels

2. Stitching-together of fragments so as to respect voice-hooking constraints and so as to match local textures

Signatures

The preceding is the true core of Emmy, but in addition there are two other important mechanisms that should be described here as well. The first is what Cope calls *signatures*. A signature is a characteristic intervallic pattern that recurs throughout a composer's *œuvre*, the use of which lends a high degree of seeming authenticity to a freshly composed piece. To find signatures, Cope has Emmy scour all input pieces for pairs of short note-sequences (say, between four and twelve notes, although there is no strict cutoff) whose intervallic patterns match either exactly or approximately. Thus, for instance, C-B-C-G would *exactly* match F-E-F-C, and would be a *near* match for D-C-D-A (the difference being that the first and second intervals are semitones in C-B-C-G, and whole tones in D-C-D-A). Emmy scours the input for exact matches, and then gradually loosens up the search (relaxing the criteria governing interval-matching), until a satisfactory number of recurrent patterns have been found.

The parameters that determine whether a potential match is judged satisfactory or not are called "controllers," and during a search for signatures, one must adjust the controllers until just the right number of signatures is found—not too few but not too many either. I know that in the past, Cope tended to do this adjustment of controllers himself in order to increase the effectiveness of Emmy's search for signatures, but perhaps by now he has managed to automate that aspect of the process. In any case, among the subtlest of controllers are those that winnow "insignificant" notes out of a given passage, leaving just "significant" ones; thanks to such controllers, Emmy can then match a highly embellished melodic fragment that contains, say, 20 very rapid notes with another melodic fragment that contains only four slow notes, and can discover the core signature that they share. Thus signatures found by Emmy can be very subtle indeed.

An important point is that such matching of intervallic patterns must take place *across* pieces, rather than *within* a given piece—for the obvious reason that any given piece will reuse its own motifs many times, and Cope is not trying—indeed, he does not wish—to get Emmy to reproduce the melodic lines of a given piece, but rather he wishes Emmy to pick up on and to exploit the recurrent (but less obvious) melodic patterns that a composer tends to reuse from piece to piece, probably without even being aware of doing so.

It may not seem evident, needless to say, that all composers do have signature motifs, but this has turned out to be the case. One might tend to think that the existence of many signatures would show that a composer is rut-bound, and perhaps it does, but in any case, it is a universal fact,

revealed in undeniable fashion by Cope's work on Emmy, that each composer does employ interval-pattern motifs that recur in piece after piece.

Once such signatures have been identified in the input, they are stored in
a database, with each diverse instance of a given signature being stored
together with its underlying harmonies, thus all ready for insertion *as a
whole* inside a new piece. You might suppose that the insertion of prepackaged, precisely quoted chunks would risk producing passages that sound
like pure plagiarism, but surprisingly, these prepackaged chunks are usually
so generic-seeming and so small that, even to a highly astute listener, they
don't shout from the rooftops which precise piece they came from; they
merely sound like the given composer in a nonspecific, non-pinpointable
manner.

Templagiarism

The second mechanism that I wish to describe here is what I dub "templagiarism," short for "template plagiarism"—a fascinating, more abstract
version of the signature concept. If, in scanning a given input piece, Emmy
notes that a motif appears in quick succession two or more times (again with
some liberty taken in the matching, thus allowing variants of a given motif,
such as tonal entries of a fugue theme, to be counted as "equal" to each
other), it records the following data for these entries: (1) the *pitch displacement* of the new occurrence relative to the previous occurrence, and (2) the
temporal displacement of the new occurrence relative to the previous occurrence. In short, Emmy records, for any repeated motif, the "where and
when" pattern that characterizes the motif's repetitions. Emmy then
detaches this abstract pattern from the specific motif in question, and takes
it to be characteristic of the composer's style. Note that this is a higher-order
architectural stylistic feature than a mere signature, because it is concerned
not with any motif itself, but with how that motif recurs within a piece.

Templagiarism can be an astonishingly effective style-evoking device, as I
found out one day when listening, in Cope's living room, to "Prokofiev's
tenth sonata for piano" (as Dave humorously, or perhaps hubristically,
dubs one of Emmy's pieces, which I will talk more about later). As the second movement started, I heard a very striking chromatically descending
eight-note motif in midrange, then moments later heard the same motif way
up high on the keyboard, then once again a few notes lower, and then one
last time very deep down in the bass line. These widely spread entries gave
an amazing feeling of coherence to the music. Indeed, for me the passage
reeked of Prokofievian impishness, and I thought, "Good God, how in the
world did Emmy do *that?*" It sounded so well calculated (not in the computer sense of the term!), so inventive, so full of musical intelligence.

Astonished, I asked Dave what was going on, and he replied, "Well,
somewhere in one of the input movements on which this movement is

drawing, there must be some motif—totally different from *this* motif, of course—that occurs four times in rapid succession with exactly these same timing displacements and pitch displacements." Then he spelled out more explicitly the concept of templagiarism to me. It would have been pleasing if at that point we had scoured Prokofiev's scores until we found exactly such an episode, but we didn't take the trouble to do so. I'll take Dave's word for it that we would find it somewhere or other.

Cope's idea of templagiarism is itself brilliant and devilishly impish: it borrows a touch of genius from the composer at such a high level of abstraction that when the pattern is simply quoted lock, stock and barrel—plagiarized, no more, no less—it once again sounds like a touch of genius, but an utterly fresh and new one. The reason it sounds fresh and new is, of course, that in order to quote the template, you need to supplement it with a new "low-level" ingredient—a new motif—and so the quotation, though exact on the *template* level, sounds truly novel on the *note* level, even if one is intimately familiar with the input piece from which the template was drawn. New filler material has been spliced into an old template that bears the unmistakable stamp of a specific genius, and so the whole passage has a powerfully compelling feel to it—a deep musical mind seems to lie behind it.

It's a bit as if one were to use fancy speech-synthesis technology to make the very familiar voice and accent of, say, John Kennedy come out with utterances that Kennedy himself never made—perhaps nonsense statements, perhaps cheap rabble-rousing inanities that he would have despised, whatever. Despite their falsified content, they would still sound for all the world like Kennedy (at the voice level, at least), and such statements probably would seem genuine to most people.

I must admit that I don't have a clear understanding of how the very complex operation of templagiarism (or, for that matter, the somewhat simpler operation of insertion of signatures) is made to coexist harmoniously with the previously described syntactic and semantic meshing-operations, because I can easily imagine them conflicting with each other. Nor do I understand how Emmy composes a "motif" and deems it worthy of use as such in an extended movement. But of course, how could I? It would probably take many months of intense study of Emmy in order to understand such matters. I remain an intrigued outsider, and hope and expect that over time, Dave will explain Emmy's principles ever more lucidly.

The Acid Test: Hearing and Voting

The foregoing provides a summary of what I myself have absorbed about the workings of Emmy, both from reading Cope's books and from a good number of one-on-one conversations with him.

In my lecture, I have almost always had a live pianist—sometimes Dave's wife Mary Jane Cope, who is on the music faculty at UC Santa Cruz—perform a handful of small two-voice pieces for the audience. The listeners are fore-warned that there is at least one piece by Johann Sebastian Bach in the group, and at least one by Emmy in the style of Johann Sebastian Bach, and they should try to figure out which ones are by whom (or by what).

As a prelude and to set the proper tone, I first read aloud the following two short excerpts from Cope's *Computers and Music Style,* the first one describing a very simplified version of Emmy which Cope devised solely for pedagogical purposes, and the second one ushering in the chapter in which the full-strength Emmy—at least the Emmy of that vintage—is carefully discussed (though it is certainly not described in full detail):

It will create small two-part inventions similar in nature (not in quality) to those created by Bach. (p. 98)

For the true inheritance of Bach's style to take place, a much more elaborate program would be necessary. This more elaborate program is presented in the description of Emmy in the next chapter. (p. 136)

Make of that telling little phrase "the true inheritance" what you will. . . .

After the pieces have been performed, I tell the audience that they are now going to vote (with the proviso that anyone who has recognized a piece from their knowledge of the classical repertoire is disenfranchised). The result has usually been that most of the audience picks the genuine Bach as genuine, but usually it is only about a two-thirds majority, with roughly one-third getting it wrong. And it is not by any means always the less sophisticated audience members who make the wrong classification.

To *Sound* Like Bach and to *Speak* Like Bach

Emmy is evolving—it is a moving target. Cope began work on his program in 1981, and in all these years he has not let up on it. Emmy's early pieces are, like any fledgling composer's, pretty amateurish affairs, but her later output sounds increasingly impressive, and Cope has grown more and more ambitious over time. Whereas initially he was proud of Emmy's production of short two-part inventions and short mazurkas, he now has Emmy producing entire sonatas, concertos, and symphonies. There is even a "Mahler opera" under way or in the works—something that would certainly be a challenge for any human composer to carry off.

What exactly is the difference between stylistic imitation as carried out by a human being and stylistic imitation carried out by a computer program? My friend Bernard Greenberg has been writing music in the style of J. S. Bach (and other composers, but Bach most of all) for decades. Indeed, among my life's most amazing memories are visits to Bernie's apartment, where, as I listened to him play his own soulful pieces on the organ, filled with complex dissonances and marvelously unexpected turns of phrase, I felt as if I were in the presence of Old Bach himself. One time I brought along a mutual friend to listen, and he—also a gifted musician—made the following unforgettable remark to Bernie: "Gee, not only is your music in the Bach style but it *sounds* good, too!" I always found this remark extremely puzzling, since to me the very *essence* of Bach style is that it "sounds good." How could something possibly sound deeply *Bach-like* and yet also sound *bad*? The tone of the remark made no sense to me—and yet I must admit that Bernie himself once made a related remark about the secrets of capturing Bach's style:

The trick is to make music not that *sounds* like him, but that also *speaks* like him.

The Nested Circles of Style

Well, of course, what is being hinted at here, though in a blurry way, is that style is a multi-layered phenomenon. There are shallow aspects to style (how a piece "sounds," in Bernie's terms), and then there are deep aspects (how it "speaks"). It is quite possible that someone could be capable of capturing many of the shallower trademarks of a composer and yet miss the bull's-eye as far as essence is concerned. I always think of Schumann's short piano piece called "Chopin," which occurs in his *Carnaval*, which on one level "sounds like" a Chopin nocturne—it has the characteristic wide left-hand arpeggios and a lot of melodic embellishment—and yet on a deeper level, it quite misses the mark in terms of Chopin soul (at least to my ear).

This talk of different levels of style and of targets and bull's-eyes suggests the extremely simple yet seemingly inevitable diagram pertaining to stylistic imitation shown in Figure 1.1. Someone who glibly captures only the most obvious features of a composer's style—an Alberti bass, say, for Mozart—would fall in the outer ring but leave all inner rings untouched. A deeper imitator would add other outer layers of style but fail to penetrate all the way to the core, or stylistic bull's-eye. But only someone who had dedicated years to the art, and whose emotional makeup, moreover, bore a deep affinity to that of the composer in question (and this is how I see Bernie vis-à-vis Bach), could hope to come close to that elusive central core that constitutes true "Chopinity" or "Bachitude."

And yet . . . there is something most troubling to me about this diagram, as I have drawn it—namely, the fact that the ring with the greatest area is the outermost one, not the innermost one. This disturbs me because it suggests that you will get the most effect from the simplest and shallowest tricks. The diagram suggests that as you proceed further and further in—as your mastery of the art ever deepens—the area you are adding

FIGURE 1.1
Nested circles of style.

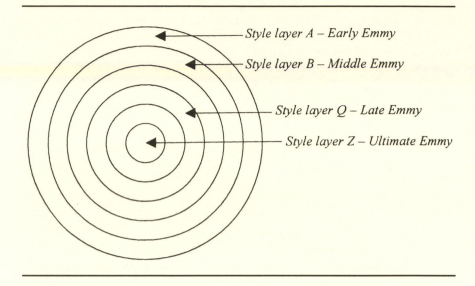

Style layer A – Early Emmy

Style layer B – Middle Emmy

Style layer Q – Late Emmy

Style layer Z – Ultimate Emmy

becomes smaller and smaller. When you have acquired but one layer of style mastery, your music will surely not fool experts, but it might fool 80 percent of the general populace. Work harder, add the second ring of mastery, and now you fool 90 percent. Add the third ring, and your fooling-rate goes up to, say, 95 percent, and the fourth ring gets you to 98 percent. There's still something missing, but sadly, the missing ingredient is getting subtler and subtler, tinier and tinier. . . . In the end, then, with all but the innermost circle, you may wind up reliably fooling all of the world's top experts, while still lacking Bach's true soul. In short, it's a most depressing thought, if the nested-circles image is accurate, that the innermost layer, though surely the most difficult of all layers to acquire, is also the smallest and perhaps, therefore, the least significant in terms of its effect upon listeners.

When Does a Beatles Song Sound Like a Bach Chorale?

In an email exchange with me, Bernie Greenberg was discussing his attempts to impart to others his ability to write Bach-like music, and he wrote this:

There are tricks of the trade, and you can teach chorale-writing such that anyone with a little talent can write a chorale that sounds like a Bach chorale *that you are not listening to closely.*

A little later in that same email exchange, in relating an episode in which he had helped an acquaintance who wrote four-part chorales and who wanted Bernie's advice on how to get them to sound more Bach-like, Bernie amplified his remarks as follows:

There is no question that by further refinement of style, I can make them sound more like Bach chorales than many other church hymns. Perhaps the right question is: "Do they sound more like Bach chorales *than what?*" rather than "Do they sound like Bach chorales?" After all, compared to jet takeoff noise, or even Balinese gamelan music, most Beatles songs "sound like Bach chorales," right?

A Portrait that "Looks Like" Its Intended Subject

Bernie's humorous point is right on the mark, and forces one to think carefully about what it means to say glibly "X *sounds like* Y." And further light is shed on the question by considering the analogous issue of what it means to say "X *looks like* Y." To make this issue vivid, let us take a standard "Smiley Face" image, as shown below. Presumably, the bland face shown in Figure 1.2 does not remind you of any individual you know, right? It would be surprising if it did. But if we now add to our bland, generic Smiley Face a tiny amount of "style"—just a few strategically placed parallel vertical lines—lo and behold (Figure 1.3)! All of a sudden, nearly everybody recognizes the familiar face of the Führer of the Third Reich. To be sure, nobody would say about this mustachioed inanity, "It looks very much

FIGURE 1.2
Bland face without any style.

FIGURE 1.3
Bland face with a tiny amount of style.

like Hitler"; perhaps nobody would even say, "It looks like Hitler"; but despite that, everybody sees Hitler in it. They can't help it. The point of this example, invented by David Moser (who grimly subtitled his ironic image "Have a Nice Holocaust!"), is that just a minimal gesture in the direction of a known style can, if well executed, have a stunning effect, summoning up much more than is really there.

So . . . How much are we being fooled when, on hearing a piece of music, we respond to some gestures that in the past we have come to associate with composer X, and then exclaim to ourselves, "This piece sounds like X"? Can we even distinguish clearly between responses at a shallow level and a deep level? Indeed, what *is* the difference, in music, between "shallow" levels and "deep" levels of style? Is it just a question of different levels of depth of syntactic pattern, or is it something more than that?

Lewis Rowell's "Bach Grammar"

Not long after I became a professor at Indiana University, I heard on the radio a very engaging piece for organ that to my ear sounded extremely Bach-like; when it was announced, however, I found out to my surprise, though not to my chagrin, that it had been composed by a music professor at IU—Lewis Rowell. I lost no time in contacting Rowell and suggested we have lunch together to talk over the idea of faking Bach. He was delighted that someone had taken an interest in his piece, and we soon met. Over lunch, I asked Rowell how he had composed such an authentic-sounding piece, and he said, "Oh, that's not hard—Bach developed a kind of grammar that I merely picked up, as could anyone who wished to. And then, armed with this grammar, I—just like anyone with a bit of musical talent—can easily compose any number of pieces in perfect Bach style. It takes no genius, believe me. It's all straightforward stuff. The only place where genius was involved was in coming up with the grammar."

I was astounded to hear how dismissively Rowell described his acquisition of "Bach grammar," and just as astounded to hear he thought that composing long, complex, and coherent new pieces in the full Bach style was basically merely a mechanical act, requiring no act of genius whatsoever. After all, I, a lifelong lover of Bach, had on several occasions tried composing pieces in the Bach style, and had found myself unbelievably stymied. Measures and short phrases, yes, perhaps—but a long movement? No way!

Rowell's claim, however, was that only Bach's own *creating* of his supposed "grammar" was hard, whereas *inducing* that grammar from Bach's output and then *exploiting* it was a piece of cake. A glib hack could create new works as deep and as great as any that had ever issued from the pen of the great baroque master—or from that of any other great master. Profundity becomes a snap, emerging at the drop of a hat. By contrast, my personal feeling, based on my own experience (and, I must say, based also on long observation of Bernie Greenberg), was that *extracting* a true and deep "Bach grammar" from Bach notes was itself an act that would require extraordinary insight—perhaps even genius. And even if such a grammar could be extracted (which struck me as highly implausible, Rowell's claims notwithstanding), I felt that to *exploit* it to make new pieces as great and as engaging as those of Bach himself would still be an act of enormous creativity.

Many years later, grappling mightily with the strange new world of Emmy and her algorithmically induced grammars, I remembered my stimulating lunch with Lew Rowell and wondered what Bernie Greenberg would think of our chat. So I sent Bernie the gist of Rowell's claims through email, to which he quickly responded with the following eloquent set of remarks in his own inimitable style (if I dare make such a claim!):

I'd be very interested in such a grammar. It would have to include a "syntactic description" of the theology of Paul as expressed in Romans, the innate intellectual tension between Christ's roles as Victim and Savior, and other emotional basis vectors of the space which is "Bach."

Anyone who has been moved by the St. John Passion, the St. Matthew Passion, or the Cross dialogue of Cantata 159 understands that the root of their emotional power is in the turgid psychodynamics of the Crucifixion, not in the seventh-chords, which are the mere paint that Bach has used to implement these canvases, incomparable paint though it be.

Although I sympathized with what Bernie was trying to say, I felt he had overstated the case. Does one really need to be a pious Christian to be able to compose deeply Bach-like music, or even to be powerfully moved by Bach's music? In point of fact, Bernie himself, a Jew by upbringing and an agnostic by credo, provided a counterexample. I argued that the essence of Bach's power comes not from his deep piety but from his deep humanity— from just those human experiences discussed in my Speculation (quoted from *Gödel, Escher, Bach,* previously) about a computational "music box" producing new Bach and Chopin pieces. Bernie, on hearing this objection, conceded that among the most important "emotional basis vectors of the space which is 'Bach'" are many that have nothing per se to do with religion, but that simply follow from being born into this crazy world, growing up in it, and living a full human life. And so Bernie closed his musings by saying this:

When the "grammar" is sufficient to cover such notions, the General AI problem will have been solved, I think.

Amen to that.

Emmy Tries Her Hand at Doing Chopin

In my lecture, I usually have a second musical interlude, this time involving two or three mazurkas, at least one by Chopin, and at least one by Emmy. Rather than describing what happens myself, I would like to quote here what one person who was in the audience of my most recent Emmy lecture at the University of Rochester wrote to Dave Cope and me afterwards.

From: kala pierson <kpi@ibm.net>
Subject: Emmy's big day at U. of Rochester . . .
Cc: dughof@indiana.edu

Hi, David! I heard Douglas Hofstadter's Emmy-demo at the U. of Rochester yesterday; and though you'll probably hear an account of it from him, I wanted to give you a report from the trenches too, since Emmy made such a dramatic impression on us.

As you know, Eastman School of Music is part of U.R.; much of the audience was made up of theorists and composers from Eastman (I'm a composer). DH gave us three listening tests: Bach inventions, live; Bach arias, on video; & Chopin mazurkas, live. It was easy for most of the audience to tell Emmy from Bach; there were a lot of knowing smirks among those around me during the not-Bach inventions. Okay, we concluded, those imitations are pretty remarkable on several levels but they just ain't the real thing, and we—Those In the Know—can tell.

When the pianist played the two "Chopin" mazurkas, we were similarly complacent. The first mazurka had grace and charm, but not "true-Chopin" degrees of invention and large-scale fluidity; there were very local-level, "shallow"-feeling modulations—just the type, I reasoned, that a computer program would generate based on more sophisticated examples of the real thing. The second was clearly the genuine Chopin, with a lyrical melody; large-scale, graceful chromatic modulations; and a natural, balanced form.

Although DH told us that the vote on this piece looked like "about 50/50" from his point of view, there was a definite preference among the theory/comp corner of the audience. I voted real-Chopin for the second piece, as did most of my friends. When DH announced that the first was Chopin and the second was Emmy, there was a collective gasp and an aftermath of what I can only describe as delighted horror. I've never seen so many theorists and composers shocked out of their smug complacency in one fell swoop [myself included]! It was truly a thing of beauty.

Cheers for now,

kala

"Truly a thing of beauty"! This is an amazingly refreshing and candid statement from someone at one of the most elite music schools in the United States. Perhaps only a student could have written it. But no, I take that back. There are professors who are just as honest, though certainly it is hard to swallow one's pride and admit having been taken in.

One stunning lesson from my Rochester lecture (and indeed, from all of the times I've lectured on Emmy) is that people with deep musical gifts and decades of training can, on occasion, mistake an Emmy product for "the genuine article." And remember—we are just embarking, we humans, on the pathway toward the realization of the dream of "preprogrammed mass-produced mail-order twenty-dollar desk-model music boxes"—those boxes on whose "sterile circuitry" I heaped so much scorn, back when I wrote *Gödel, Escher, Bach.*

Where will we have gotten in twenty more years of hard work? In fifty? What will be the state of the art in 2084? Who, if anyone, will *still* be able to tell "the right stuff" from rubbish? Who will know, who will care, who will loudly protest that the last (though tiniest) circle at the center of the style-target has *still* not been reached (and may never be reached)? What will such nitpicky details matter, when new Bach and Chopin masterpieces applauded by all come gushing out of silicon circuitry at a rate faster than H_2O pours over the edge of Niagara? Will that wondrous new golden age of music not be "truly a thing of beauty"?

COMPOSING IN YOUR SLEEP . . . OR IN YOUR GRAVE

Anyone who has composed a fair amount of music knows the exquisite joy of finding their own personal voice. One dreams of composing more and more, but of course time presses and one's finiteness constrains one's output. It is therefore natural to wonder what Emmy would do if fed one's own music as input. And I, given my close connection with Emmy's progenitor, could request this favor and actually find out. I submitted a diskette to Dave, containing 12 of my piano pieces (I've written around 40, all told), and he in turn fed my pieces into Emmy and started her churning. Promptly, out came pseudo-Hofstadter music!

And in the course of my Santa Cruz lecture, Mary Jane performed both a genuine Hofstadter piece and an Emmy-Hofstadter piece (called "Nope"), with me hearing myself aped for the very first time, in real time before the audience's eyes. It was delightful to listen as my own harmonies were spit back at me in new and unexpected combinations, although I have to admit that sometimes the "logic" of the flow, such as it was, sounded a bit incoherent.

IS LANGUAGE INTRINSICALLY DEEPER THAN MUSIC?

What would it take for a program, à la Emmy, to produce a spate of brand-new Hofstadter lectures or—let's go whole hog—books? (After all, if an opera by Mahler, who never wrote one, is in the planning stages, why not a novel by Hofstadter, who never wrote one?)

The answer, of course, is that it would fail ludicrously. Even if an Emmy-like text-imitation program could deal with global qualities of an input text, it would not come up with *new content* or *new ideas*. Who could have predicted, given my first few books, that I would next write an 800-page book on poetry translation (*Le Ton beau de Marot*)? There's nothing remotely resembling the manipulation and creation of new ideas in Emmy—and yet the crazy, undeniable truth of the matter is that Emmy's music does at least a decent job of creating "new Chopin" and "new Mozart," and so on. As Dave himself speculated in the journal entry that starts out his first book, "While never as good as the originals, they will be exciting, entertaining, and interesting."

Or consider "Prokofiev's tenth sonata," as Dave calls it. In the liner notes to his and Emmy's first compact disk ("Bach by Design"), he wrote the following:

This computer-composed Prokofiev *Sonata* was completed in 1989. Its composition was inspired by Prokofiev's own attempt to compose his tenth piano sonata, an attempt thwarted by his death. As such it represents another of the many potential uses of programs such as Emmy (i.e., the completion of unfinished works).

To me this comes close to blasphemy—and yet let me also add the following remark, to counterbalance that reaction. The first movement of this sonata by Emmy starts out with the actual 44 measures that Prokofiev himself had completed, and then continues with Emmy's own notes. What happens when measures 45, 46, and so on are encountered? Remarkably, there is no sudden drop in quality—indeed, it is as smooth a transition as one could possibly imagine, and all the way to the movement's end it sounds quite consistent with the way it started out.

Three Flavors of Pessimism

What worries me about computer simulations is not the idea that we ourselves might be machines; I have long been convinced of the truth of that. What troubles me is the notion that things that touch me at my deepest core—pieces of music most of all, which I have always taken as direct soul-to-soul messages—might be effectively produced by mechanisms thousands if not millions of times simpler than the intricate biological machinery that gives rise to a human soul. This prospect, rendered most vivid and perhaps even near-seeming by the development of Emmy, worries me enormously, and in my more gloomy moods, I have articulated three causes for pessimism, listed below:

1. *Chopin* (for example) is a lot shallower than I had ever thought
2. *Music* is a lot shallower than I had ever thought
3. *The human soul/mind* is a lot shallower than I had ever thought

To conclude, let me briefly comment on these. Pertaining to number 1, since I have been moved to the core for my entire life by pieces by Chopin, if it turns out that Emmy can churn out piece after piece that "speaks like Chopin" to me, then I would be thereby forced to retrospectively reassess all the meaning that I have been convinced of having detected in Chopin's music, because I could no longer have faith that it could only have come from a deep human source. I would have to accept the fact that Frédéric Chopin might have been merely a tremendously fluent artisan rather than the deeply feeling artist whose heart and soul I'd been sure I knew ever since I was a child. Indeed, I could no longer be sure of *anything* I'd felt about Frédéric Chopin, the human being, from hearing his music. That loss would be an inconceivable source of grief to me.

In a sense, the loss just described would not be worse than the loss incurred by number 2, since Chopin has always symbolized the power of music as a whole, to me. Nonetheless, I suppose that having to chuck *all* composers out the window is somehow a bit more troubling than having to chuck just *one* of them out.

The loss described in number 3, of course, would be the ultimate affront to human dignity. It would be the realization that all of the "computing power" that resides in a human brain's 100 billion neurons and its roughly ten quadrillion synaptic connections can be bypassed with a handful of state-of-the-art chips, and that all that is needed to produce the most powerful artistic outbursts of all time (and many more of equal power, if not greater) is a nanoscopic fraction thereof—*and* that it can all be accomplished, thank you very much, by an entity that knows nothing of knowing, seeing, hearing, tasting, living, dying, struggling, suffering, aging, yearning, singing, dancing, fighting, kissing, hoping, fearing, winning, losing, crying, laughing, loving, longing, or caring.

Playing the game of pattern and pattern alone will turn the whole trick—and, although Kala Pierson and many others may hail its coming as "truly a thing of beauty," the day when music is finally and irrevocably reduced to syntactic pattern and pattern alone will be, to my old-fashioned way of looking at things, a very dark day indeed.

APPENDIX: A FEW STANDARD QUESTIONS AND ANSWERS

Question: I'm a musician by training, and I remember how in undergraduate school my peers and I were required in various courses to copy many composers' styles. We all learned to do this without too much trouble, and some of the pieces we composed were pretty decent. It doesn't upset or worry me to think that stylistic imitation can result in pieces that are fairly effective, because I know that this can occur only *after* a composer has produced a body of material that establishes the style. The original, creative act must occur first. Indeed, I would propose that the most profound act of musical creation lies precisely in the invention of a novel and highly personal idiom or style. Thus I subscribe more or less to the Lew Rowell viewpoint—that the hard part, the only part requiring creative genius, is coming up with a new "grammar"; the easy part then is spinning off pieces that obey that grammar. Mastering musical mimicry may take a bit of talent, but it doesn't take creative genius.

Answer: First off, let me agree with you that coming up with a novel and highly personal idiom, as virtually all great composers have done, is definitely a greater achievement than writing one piece, or several pieces, even very high-quality pieces, that can pass for the composer's own but in fact are forgeries. Emmy apes previous styles, but she does not explore her very own stylistic worlds, nor was she ever intended to do so. In that sense, Emmy does not represent an assault on what I see as the very highest peak in the rugged mountain chain of musical achievement. So there is some agreement between our positions.

On the other hand, I would take issue with the imagery in your statement, which seems to suggest (although I doubt that you meant it this way) that a composer starts out spending a good deal of time devising a grammar, and then turns into a drone who spins off piece after piece using the rules of the grammar. Well, the composers whom I respect never did anything like create an explicit grammar. They just composed piece after piece, and as they composed, a set of statistical regularities emerged. Creating rules and then sticking to those rules was probably the furthest thing from their minds!

As a very minor composer, in fact, I might add a brief comment about my own feeling about remaining true to my own style, or staying within my own patterns. I almost always compose at the piano, and most of the time it is my fingers that guide me, in the sense that they are constantly trying out all sorts of small patterns on the keyboard, and after each such little unpremeditated motoric foray, I judge whether or not I like it, as well as whether or not it fits the piece's evolving and not-totally-stabilized mood. On the basis of such blurry considerations, I somehow decide whether or not to incorporate what my fingers just spontaneously came up with. What's interesting is that quite often my fingers will play a pattern that "I" would *never* have come up with, so to speak. Perhaps they stumble across a wrong note, or perhaps they just make a strange dissonance that I would never have thought of. At that point, my composer's mind enters the picture, and sometimes it says to me, "Hey, Doug—now *that* really was interesting, it was so unlike you—so why don't you incorporate it?" The logic of such a suggestion is that by using "un-Doug-like stuff" I sound more original than I really am, and I somehow break out of ruts. Per-haps over time I come to incorporate these un-Doug-like stylistic patterns and, somewhat ironically, they become Doug-like, at which point it is time for me to break out yet further. So much for a "Hofstadter grammar."

But I would like to answer this question in another way as well. Suppose that Lew Rowell really were able to distill a "Chopin grammar" from all of Chopin's *œuvre*, and that he then sat down to write new pieces using this grammar—say, a fifth bal-lade, for example (Chopin's four extant ballades being generally regarded as among his most powerful expressive efforts ever). The key question, in my mind, is the degree to which this new Rowell-Chopin ballade will sound like an equal sibling to the other four—something worthy of the name "Chopin's fifth ballade." Will lis-teners be moved to tears by it? Will pianists flock to perform it? Will audiences clamor for more—for a whole set of new "Chopin ballades"? Will this music move people, in short, with all the power with which the first four Chopin ballades move people?

The reason I raise this scenario is that my impression has always been that for Chopin himself to come up with each of his four ballades was itself a mighty cre-ative act, not anything even remotely like the spinning-off of a rule-bound piece from a fixed grammar. The four ballades are enormously different from each other, and not in any sense a bunch of pieces sharing an abstract skeletal structure.

If I might be excused for making the following rather presumptuous analogy, Chopin's four ballades are as different from each other as are, say, four of my most diverse articles, such as this one, an article on the subliminal connotations of the phrase "you guys," an article on a class of geometries related to projective geome-try, and a humorous article gently mocking John Cage's Zen attitude toward music. Such a collection of articles certainly does not seem to have been cast from the same mold. Likewise, one would hope that anything meriting the name "Chopin's fifth ballade," whether concocted by Lew Rowell or by Emmy (or whoever or whatever), would be just as different from its four progenitors as they are among themselves, and that the sixth and seventh and eighth ballades likewise would all differ among themselves in just as significant a way. *If* Emmy-Chopin ballades did pass this test, and *if* audiences clamored for more and more of them, then I would feel I would have to despondently throw in the towel as a researcher who is seeking the mechanisms of creativity, for everything that I could ever have imagined seeking would already have been found, and the book on the human mind's mysteries would be closed.

For a sharply contrasting case, though, consider the so-called "prairie houses" designed by the famous American architect Frank Lloyd Wright. He designed many houses in this family, and they all share a certain fairly clear set of properties—so much so that some years ago, a group of professors of architecture at the State University of New York, Buffalo distilled from them a "prairie-house grammar," which they conveyed to a computer, which then came up with dozens of new "Frank Lloyd Wright prairie houses." When I first saw this, I was quite astonished, but the more I thought about it, the more I realized that the original set of prairie houses itself was pretty formulaic, and therefore lent itself to "grammaticization." It would be entirely another matter, however, for a computer to come up with a Frank Lloyd Wright-style house that lay far outside the bounds of the prairie houses.

As this shows, even a great artistic mind can go into a temporary mode in which a certain fairly formulaic vein is explored for a while, and such explorations may lend themselves relatively easily to mechanical mimicking—but that is not the essence of being a great creator. For all I know—and though it pains me to say this—maybe some of Chopin's weaker mazurkas bear this kind of formulaic stamp. I certainly wouldn't hesitate for a moment to shout "Formulaic!" about many works of certain other hallowed names in music, such as Mozart and Beethoven, so why not Chopin as well? That might explain, at least in part, why an Emmy mazurka can sound better, in some ways, than a few Chopin mazurkas.

One last point about humans mimicking style and computers mimicking style. You say that you and your peers were pretty good at coming up with pieces in, say, "the Brahms style" or whatever. Well, part of what allowed you to do that is that *you all were human beings,* as Brahms himself was. Built into being human is the fact of living life and having all the sorts of experiences that—to my mind—underlie what musical expression is all about. And so, part of the power of *your* musical expressions came straight from your humanity. For an Emmy-type program to perform credibly at this type of task, however, is another matter entirely, because it does not have any human experience to draw on. So I don't buy into the viewpoint that says, "Stylistic imitation is a routine thing in music schools, ergo it's no big deal that we can get a computer program to do it too." To the contrary, it is indeed a big deal, because a program like Emmy, although I facetiously call it "she," is not a person.

The question that Emmy ultimately raises is whether people who come out of music schools and who become famous composers are really just masters of a difficult *craft,* people who have absorbed all sorts of complex traditions and styles, and who now practice their craft exactly in the way that a carpenter makes fine tables and bookcases and so forth—*or,* contrariwise, whether composers are constantly, though surely unconsciously, plumbing the furthest depths of their psyches, discovering mysterious yearnings and sighs, and putting a voice to them: making *art,* in short. These two images are unbelievably different pictures of what music is all about, and I must say, Emmy is forcing me personally to confront this question in a way that I never imagined I would have to—and making me squirm much more than I would like.

Question: Programs have been written that produce poetry based in rather simple ways on the poems of a human poet, and one can feel meaning in the output, but one realizes that such meaning is due to the input material. Thus if in a computer poem one finds the phrase "her haunting grace," it may be that this phrase was present as such in some poem, or if not, then its component words all were, and the machine stuck them together on the basis of some syntactic rules, maybe with a few rudimentary semantic guidelines as well. But a reader who feels depth in such phrases can also realize that it is basically *borrowed* depth, not *original* depth. It's just echoes and parrotings, not primordial screams from the depths of a feeling soul. Isn't that really what's going on in Emmy? If so, why worry?

Answer: If Emmy were just a plagiarizer or reshuffler at the simplistic level that you have suggested, then all over the place we would hear traces and echoes of the input pieces. But in many of her pieces, we do not hear where the elements are coming from. There is no wholesale borrowing of big phrases; rather, the elements of the composer's input have been chopped up into very fine-grained pieces, and those pieces have been reassembled in large structures in such a manner as to disguise their origins. And the reassembly process is faithful enough and subtle enough that at least some of the resulting compositions are good enough to fool excellent musicians— such as students and faculty at Eastman Rochester, for example. They cannot tell that the power has been borrowed.

Indeed, that's precisely the nub of the question: Is it fair to say that the power of a composer has been *borrowed* when Emmy dissects the input pieces into such tiny fragments that effectively, the accusation of plagiarism is no longer viable, in that even a sophisticated listener cannot put their finger on where the phrases and gestures in an output piece have come from? If the reshuffling is so fine-grained as to make it virtually untraceable, then in what sense is *borrowing* taking place?

Emmy is not a coarse-grained plagiarizer. If you hear a Mozart-style Emmy piano concerto, it will *remind* you all over the place of Mozart concertos, but you won't in general be able to point to a particular phrase and say, for example, "Ah!—*that* was borrowed from the A major concerto, Köchel 488, second movement!" Admittedly, there are episodes in some of Emmy's two-part inventions that clearly come from specific Bach inventions, but that is probably because only a couple of inventions were being drawn on, in those cases.

Analogously, I remember that when I first heard Mary Jane Cope perform "Nope" (Emmy's pseudo-Hofstadter piece) in front of me and the Santa Cruz audience, I had to try to suppress a smile at virtually every measure, because I could just hear its sources so easily. But the reason for that is very simple: it turns out that Dave was unable to use all twelve of the pieces I sent him as input to Emmy, but instead he selected just *two* of them, and it was on the basis of just those that Emmy composed "Nope." Well, obviously, if you have such a sparse data base on which to draw, your output is going to reek of its sources in a conspicuous manner.

I must add parenthetically that here we are forced to confront an amazing rigidity on Emmy's part, particularly when perceived in contrast to all her complexity and flexibility. Namely, Emmy cannot take a 3/4 piece and a 4/4 piece and use them both as inputs on which to base an output piece. All input pieces that are used together have to have the same time signature! Only if you convert your 3/4 piece into a 12/4 piece (putting four measures at a time into a "supermeasure") and also convert your 4/4 piece into a 12/4 piece (three measures making a supermeasure) will Emmy be able to deal with both of them at once. But you have to force-fit the pieces in this unnatural way for Emmy to be able to extract "style" from both at once.

It seems implausible in the extreme that a human musician would be stymied by the challenge of hearing stylistic similarities in a waltz and a 4/4 piece. But in any case it was this kind of rigidity that barred Dave from using all 12 pieces on my diskette as input to Emmy, and it was therefore clear as day to me, as a composer, where each tiny part of "Nope" was coming from. But, to take a contrasting case, I know all the Chopin mazurkas well, and yet I cannot pinpoint where the fragments of Emmy's mazurkas are coming from. It is too blurry, because the breakdown is too fine to allow easy traceability.

To recap, then, Emmy's power of course comes, in *some* sense, from borrowing, for by definition and by intention, that is all that Emmy is—a borrower. But the dissolving and recrystallization processes inside Emmy involve "musical molecules" at such a fine-grained level that how the emotions of the input pieces retain their power through it all is not in the slightest obvious.

Question: Having just heard a human perform music by Emmy and by human composers, and having myself just taken a pseudo-Bach piece for genuine Bach (for which I am not ashamed or crestfallen because I do not pride myself as a connoisseur of classical music), I am led to musing as to whether, rather than the composition itself, it is not its *performance* by a human with a heart and soul that gives meaning to the piece, whether that piece was composed by a person or by a machine. And thus the more sensitively performed a piece is, the greater will be its meaning, and conversely, the more mechanically performed it is, the less will be its meaning—no matter what its provenance might be.

Answer: To me, your suggestion seems analogous to claiming that unless, say, a short story is written out by hand by a human, what it says will be unable to convey any emotion. In other words, a story typeset by machine is empty, but the same story copied out by hand by someone will be rife with meaning. To me, that seems absurd. What contains the meaning is the set of *ideas* behind the notes or behind the words. How those notes or words are rendered is but a minor tweak in the story's effectiveness.

Let's shift back to music itself, rather than stories. I do not feel, as you seem to feel, that one needs a great performance of a piece in order to be able to hear its depths. Consider the first time I heard a mazurka by Emmy. Who was the performer? Myself—I was clumsily sight-reading it at my own piano, out of Cope's book. The notes were printed smaller than usual, which made it even more difficult to sight-read. Nonetheless, despite making mistakes left and right and playing it far too slowly and unevenly, I was able to discern a truly unexpected amount of "Chopinity" in that piece, and it was that experience—my own totally junky performance—that really made me feel something eerie was going on with this Emmy program. One might put it this way: since the performance was greatly lacking, whatever meaning I found in the piece could come from only one other source: the composer.

A few days later, I received in the mail from Dave a copy of *Bach by Design* (the first CD of Emmy's music), and on it there were very mechanical-sounding computer-produced performances of various Emmy pieces (including that same mazurka). I got a great deal out of hearing those pieces, even despite the wooden quality of the playing. Such awkwardness is mildly annoying, to be sure, but it makes me think of reading a great poem typed on a typewriter rather than in a beautifully typeset edition, and perhaps with a few typos in it to boot. What's the problem with that? It doesn't seem to me that beautiful typesetting makes the poem any better.

To me, adding the surface gloss of a virtuoso performer is not critical at all (in fact, confusing such glossiness with the depths conveyed by the notes alone is one big problem that plagues discussions of this sort).

Question: Why are you upset at the idea that Emmy can come up with great new pieces that sound as if they were by Chopin? There's no threat here to human dignity, for it was Chopin himself who created the database out of which these pieces are coming. The power and the genius reside, thus, entirely in the database, not in Emmy. Emmy can do no better than the data she is fed with. So you don't need to worry about threats to human dignity or human genius: after all, if wonderful new mazurkas emanate from Emmy, nearly all of the credit should go to Frédéric Chopin, and only a small portion of credit to Emmy—or perhaps to Dave Cope.

Answer: This amounts to saying "old genius in, new genius out," to which I certainly do not subscribe. Given a database that is filled with works produced by a genius, it would still take a fantastic program to come up with *new* works that exhibited flashes of that same genius.

Consider literary translation—something that I know quite a lot about, having just spent my past year quite obsessively translating Alexander Pushkin's celebrated novel-in-verse *Eugene Onegin* from Russian sonnets into English sonnets. Without doubt the database I was working on—the Russian original—was a work of genius. But does that guarantee that my output will also be a work of genius? Obviously not in the slightest. In fact, if you want to see genius turned into utter garbage, try running a stanza or two of *Eugene Onegin* through one of today's highly-touted machine-translation programs (an experiment I recently carried out with four state-of-the-art programs, by the way). The English that comes out is ludicrous and at times absolutely incomprehensible. It would be a mind-boggling achievement if a machine-translation program came up with so much as a *coherent* English-language rendition of *Eugene Onegin,* let alone a rhymed and metric version!

I might add that I devoted every ounce of my intellectual power for a full year to this translation effort, and I would say without hesitation that in so doing, I was constantly drawing on all that which makes me human: my life experiences in the fullest—my struggles, my yearnings, my triumphs, my defeats, and so forth and so on. It took all of that to *understand* the Russian deeply enough that I could fully internalize the ideas, reflect on them, turn them around in my head, and then slowly reinstantiate them in a new and alien linguistic medium. If my translation has any merit, it is precisely because I put my whole self—mind, heart, and soul—into it.

And now consider the fact that translation is a darn sight easier than creation *ab ovo.* We are not talking about Doug Hofstadter writing a *new* Pushkin novel—just about reconstructing the poetry of the original in a new medium. How much more would it take for me to write a brand new novel-in-verse "by Pushkin" (in the same sense that Emmy, given Prokofiev input, composed a brand-new piano sonata "by

Prokofiev")? Quite frankly, I wouldn't have the foggiest idea of how to even write the first sentence. The mere idea makes me laugh.

So what are we to conclude here? That although today's state-of-the-art machine translation programs can't come anywhere close to giving us a decent or even comprehensible Anglicization of a Pushkin novel, today's state-of-the-art pattern-recombination engines can quite handily produce for us any arbitrary number of new Prokofiev sonatas, Mozart concertos, Bach arias, Gershwin songs, and Chopin mazurkas? This would seem to suggest an astonishing and heretofore totally unsuspected discrepancy between the depths of the two different arts (music and literature). Does Pushkin's genius really tower above that of Chopin? Is music basically no more than suave pattern-play, whereas literature is something else altogether? I just can't buy into this view, for to me, throughout my entire life, music has always been just as deep as, indeed even deeper than, any kind of literature.

Question: As a composer, I find Cope's music composition program quite interesting, but frankly, I think your worry over it is a tempest in a teapot. Decades ago, John Cage taught us that music happens in the brain of the hearer; all a composer can do is create a situation in which music will happen in some of the audience members' minds. I, by some fluke, have the ability to hear music in my head and I've trained myself to put it into a reproducible form (a score). But I have no control over whether it is heard as music! A babbling brook, ocean waves breaking on boulders, or an oriole singing at dusk can create the same experience for the right listener. . . . So what if a machine's output pleases someone's mind through their auditory input channel? That's not the *machine's* doing! So don't worry—music is just as great as you've always thought—it's just that you've been looking to someone *else* (the composer) for the greatness, when in truth the wonder of it all happens in *you.*

Answer: Sorry, but I think this is a grotesque twist on the truth. I would agree that notes in the air can be thought of as vibrations drained of meaning, and the receiver's brain as adding the meaning back to them. But the phrases "drained of meaning" and "adding the meaning back" suggest that there once was meaning in them, and that it has been "sucked out" and requires the metaphorical "adding of water" to recreate it—namely, the processing by a listener's brain. And I will agree that as listeners, we find (or create) meaning in sequences of sounds in much the way that, as readers, we find (or create) meaning in a bunch of black splotches on white paper when we read a novel. However, to claim that the active involvement of our recipient brains transfers all credit for greatness and depth from the creator to the recipient is nonsense. Such a viewpoint would imply that we can find greatness in anything at all, simply by using our receiving brains' power.

Want to savor a great novel? Then pick up a Jacqueline Susann paperback at the grocery store, sit down, and just turn your mind on *real hard*—greatness will come oozing right out of it. For that matter, take anything at all and read it, and in your hands it will turn into great literature—merely provided that you can find it in *yourself* to make it so. Who cares what thoughts and ideas went into its mere *making*? There's really no need for deep and powerful insight at the creation end of things.

Leo Tolstoy, you are fully dispensable, because *my brain* is what makes you powerful and deep. (It will also make Erich Segal's banal *Love Story* powerful and deep.) Frédéric Chopin, you too are dispensable, because it is my great brain, yes, *my brain,* that gives your humble notes meaning. Moreover, my brain, in its infinite wisdom and power, will find (if I so choose) just as much meaning in Michael Jackson or Elvis Presley or Madonna—or for that matter, in random squawks.

Speaking of random squawks, I think it is sloppy thinking to equate babbling brooks and birds chirping at twilight with music (at least with traditional tonal music), which is produced deliberately by a human being in order to express or communicate something to other humans.

Given the absurdity of the notion that the creator/sender's role is irrelevant to the meaning produced in the receiver's brain, what is left but to shift the burden back to the creator/sender? *That* is where the power resides. It resides in the mysterious catalytic power of the sequence of notes that somehow that composer was able to find, and which other people had never stumbled across before. Yes, "catalytic"— yes, we *realize* the meaning (both in the sense of "come to understand" and in the sense of "manufacture") that lurks in the notes, but the true responsibility and credit redound to the *sender's* brain, not the *receiver's* brain.

Question: Mightn't it be the case that *composing* music is easier than *appreciating* music? Maybe you should only start to feel threatened if Emmy (or some cousin program) can listen to pieces and decide which ones are good and which ones are weak. Perhaps Cope's achievement can even be taken as constituting a proof that composition of music is, in some sense, relatively simple, compared to understanding music.

Answer: Whew! That's a bizarre claim. I'd start out by saying, "Composing is not a free lunch courtesy of a big database or a predefined grammar." By this, I mean that composing involves genuine musical intelligence, and in fact musical intelligence of the highest degree of refinement and subtlety. How could a composer know that a piece was coming along well without being able to make positive or negative judgments? How could listening, understanding, and judging be bypassed? Well, of course, your retort may be: "Just as in Emmy, that's how."

And to this retort, I guess I would have to say, "Emmy's compositions are precisely as deep as her capacity to listen to and understand music." Which forces us to ask, "Does Emmy listen to music, or understand music, at all?" Well, of course Emmy doesn't *hear* music, in the sense of having eardrums that vibrate in response to complex waveforms—Emmy's way of perceiving music involves just the ability to deal with numbers that represent pitches and times and so forth. This may seem a funny sensory modality to us, but in a sense, it is an abstract kind of "listening." After all, our eardrums also produce a set of numbers that then affect the neurons in our auditory cortex. And remember that there are highly trained musicians who can merely *look* at a score and "hear" the music in their heads.

Hearing music really means accepting some representation of pitches and timings and so forth, and producing the proper end result in the brain (or in the computer analogue thereof). Exactly which kind of representation kicks off the process is not crucial. In some sense, Emmy ingests notes (even though they don't have the rich timbres that we hear), and she makes sense of those notes by chunking them into larger and larger structures, labeling such structures with *SPEAC* labels, discovering signatures, detecting motif templates, and so forth. That's how Emmy "listens" to her databases. What Emmy *doesn't* do, as we know, is to associate the structures she finds with emotional experiences drawn from life. But in any case, Emmy's compositional ability is proportional to her ability to understand or find order in what she "hears." You can only be a composer to the extent that you are a good listener.

Once again, going back to literature, can you really imagine a writer who could churn out superlative short stories by the dozens, and yet who was at the same time incapable of reading a single story with comprehension? Give me a break! Reading is to writing as walking is to running, and the same goes for listening and composing. Don't put the horse before the cart, please!

Question: How does musical *meaning* differ from musical *style?*

Answer: Your question points straight at the heart of the issue raised so marvelously clearly by Cope's work—namely, *Is there such a thing as musical meaning?* Or is music just a set of elaborate, ornate gestures that for some reason please us esthetically but no more?

This reminds me of a wonderful but very rare book that I was lucky enough to get a copy of many years ago—the *Codex Seraphinianus* by Luigi Serafini. This book poses as an encyclopedia, but of a totally fantastic world. Every two-page spread has one page that is filled with delightfully curly squiggles that seem to form words, sentences, paragraphs, and full articles on subjects of every sort imaginable. But how do you know what the subject under discussion is? Because the facing page is an elaborate picture of some aspect of this bizarre world—flora, fauna, engineering, culture, science, the arts, clothes, foods, and so forth and so on. The question one naturally asks oneself, on looking at this wondrously idiosyncratic book, is: Do the complex arrays of symbols actually *mean* anything, or are they just curly squiggles, end of story?

Although I've looked through the entire book many dozens of times, I have no knowledge of whether Serafini's "language" actually means anything. My guess would be that, although it is very carefully and self-consistently structured, it is nonetheless just empty scribbling. But it's the question, not its answer, that interests me here. What would make us feel those arrays of squiggles were something *other* than just "empty scribbling"? What would make those squiggles "actually mean" something?

Presumably, we would have to figure out how to decode them. We would have to have some kind of objective way of finding meaning in them. If one notices a piece of paper in the gutter and picks the paper up and finds a series of roman letters on it that one cannot read, one can tackle the implicit challenge in various ways, such as asking people who know various foreign languages if they can read it, or trying to decode it by trying out various substitution ciphers (letter-to-letter codes), and so forth. Eventually, one may find the key and a message emerges clearly and unambiguously. Then you feel you have found the meaning. But what if you do not succeed? Have you thereby shown there is no meaning there? Obviously not—you may just not yet have hit on the right decipherment scheme.

I personally think that I hear meaning all over the place in music, but it is very hard for me to explain this meaningfulness in words. That's what makes music so important in my life. Were it just formal gestures, I would tire of it very quickly. But I cannot explain what it is, exactly, that I hear in a given piece, no matter how much I love that piece. I believe, as much as I believe anything, that musical semantics exists, but I don't think it is much like linguistic semantics. I think that when we understand musical semantics—and Dave's many years of hard work and loving devotion to Emmy, especially his *SPEAC* notions, may be a significant step in that direction—we will know a great deal more about how human emotionality is constituted. But I think that will be a long time in the coming.

Question: Why aren't you ecstatic, instead of very depressed, at the prospect of soon being able to have an unlimited new supply of great Chopin, whom you admire unboundedly?

Answer: If I believed Emmy's Chopin simulation would soon be capable of producing a raft of Chopin-style pieces that would make chills run up and down my spine, I would have to revise my entire opinion of what music is about, and that would destroy something profound inside me.

Consider this analogy. Suppose that my beloved father, who died some years ago, were to walk into my study right now as I sit here, typing. Would I not be overjoyed? Well, think of what that event would do to my belief system. Virtually everything that I have come to understand about the world would all go down the drain in one split second. Death would not exist. All the things I thought were true about biology would be instantly overturned. Pretty much all of science as I know it (and in fact as I learned it from my father) would be destroyed in a flash. Would I want to trade the joy of the return of my father for the destruction of my entire belief system?

There is, admittedly, one alternative reaction that I could have, were Emmy to spout forth new pieces that touched me to the core. Instead of revising my entire opinion of what music is about, I could conclude that I'm just a shallow listener. I could drastically downgrade my opinion of my own personal depth as a perceiver of music, thus coming up with a very different kind of pessimism from the three listed previously—namely, this one: "*I am a lot shallower than I had ever thought.*" Maybe that's the ultimate explanation of my Emmy perplexity. If so, I'd just as soon not know it.

ACKNOWLEDGMENT

An earlier version of this chapter appeared in David Cope, *Virtual Music: Computer Synthesis of Musical Style,* MIT Press, 2000. Thanks to Dave Cope for his kindness and encouragement.

DISCUSSION

TD: An article on Emmy in *New Scientist* (9 August 1997) says this:

Cope's experience turns out to be a crucial part of Emmy's success, because it is Cope who decides which examples Emmy should analyze before assembling a new piece—a choice that greatly affects the mood of the finished work. And when gathering signatures for a composition, Cope often tinkers with the pattern matcher for hours, tweaking one and then another of its 22 different controls until the signatures sound as though they were really written by Bach or Mozart.

"This is a very personal operation," says Cope. "I definitely want to take credit for most of the good work that Emmy has produced in the sense that I very much had a hand in developing the signatures."

And, most important of all, Cope decides which pieces are good enough to let out of his studio. Most of Emmy's music goes straight in the bin once Cope has picked over it. The small minority of pieces that survive are those that Cope finds pleasing—a judgment that Emmy cannot make for itself.

Ironically, the computer program that sometimes produces music as sublime as Mozart's can't tell the difference between a work of genius and a piece of lift music. In the end, that aesthetic judgment may prove to be the one thing that no programmer can code for.

The article (in which you feature prominently) says that Cope began tinkering with the idea of a computer composing music because he had composer's block, and he wondered whether he could devise a computer program that would look at other music he'd written and suggest what notes might come next to fill the void. So, at least to begin with, he wanted a tool, rather than an autonomous system. The article also says that in three months of continuous computing, Emmy turned out 5,000 of its own works, including 1,500 symphonies, 2,000 piano sonatas and 1,500 miscellaneous pieces.

This reminded me of what you say about Racter and AM (Automated Mathematician) in your Fluid Analogies Research Group (FARG) book (Hofstadter & FARG, 1995). You say, "Obviously, the passages by Racter . . . were culled by Chamberlain and friends from huge reams of output from Racter over a period of years." (p. 475) You ask at what point selection becomes direction, and you suggest that Lenat and Chamberlain both inadvertently directed the evolution of their programs.

Well, isn't it the same with Emmy? In fact, isn't it clearer in the case of Emmy? We don't know how many thousands of paragraphs Racter generated before it came up with the one that you quote, but we do know that Emmy produced 5,000 works (including 1,500 symphonies!) in a three month period. So the whole picture seems to be this. David Cope set out to produce a tool that would help him to compose. Sometimes he uses it for this purpose, so that at least sometimes it is only a tool. When he teaches it to compose in the fashion of a great composer, he decides which examples it should analyze. Some of these may be its own recent compositions, which would amplify the effect of his own earlier direction. He directs Emmy while it is composing a piece, by tinkering with the pattern matcher. And he decides which pieces are to be retained and which go in the bin.

So it seems that Emmy isn't autonomous. It seems that it is Emmy *and* David Cope, together, who produce the music, so that the question is: who contributes the most? how is the credit to be assigned? On the one hand, it's easy to see Emmy as a sophisticated tool, for the reasons I've just given—in which case Cope should get most of the credit. In fact he says: "I definitely want to take credit for most of the good work that Emmy has produced in the sense that I very much had a hand in developing the signatures." On the other hand, Emmy can produce 5,000 works in three months, which is something that no human could possibly do, and *this* suggests that Emmy might be the main contributor (even though Cope created Emmy).

Perhaps a way out of the impasse is this. In the FARG book you say that if a computer generated "a deeply moving new piece of music" (p. 481), you would not know how to assign credit (to the program or its author) unless you knew about the innards of the program. Well, you know about the innards of Emmy, and you believe that Emmy composes the music. And one of the things that worries you is that such relatively simple innards can produce such wonderful music (relative, that is, to the complexity of the human brain). Is there an inconsistency here? Isn't it inconsistent to say that the innards tell us how to assign credit, and then to be surprised that such simple innards can produce music that seems to come from the soul? If it's the innards that matter, and they're relatively simple, doesn't it follow that the credit doesn't lie with Emmy?

DH: Well, let me tell you the following anecdote. When I first was getting to know Dave Cope and Emmy, I had heard the first CD (*Bach by Design*) a number of times, and I commented to Dave, "I suppose that you chose some of Emmy's best pieces for this CD, right, since you presumably wanted to put your best foot forward, no?" Dave agreed with this, and then I said, "Maybe it would be interesting, for your next CD (which I knew was not too far off at that time), to include on it some of Emmy's less successful pieces, or perhaps just randomly chosen output instead of her best stuff." Dave thought this was a reasonable and an interesting idea. I then asked him how many Chopin-based Emmy mazurkas were in the "pile" from which he selected the single one on *Bach by Design*. He said, "Oh, I don't know—maybe a dozen, maybe two dozen—something on that order. I still have all of them on my hard disk." I said, "It would be interesting to hear a few randomly chosen ones from that set, instead of just hearing your very favorite one." Well, a few weeks later, I got in the mail a shipment from Dave, which was a piece of sheet music for an Emmy mazurka. He explained that this one had been chosen entirely at random from the batch of previously composed mazurkas. Dave had, in his usual highly impish manner, added a dedication of this second mazurka: "To Douglas Hofstadter." I was highly amused as well as delighted with this touch. I was also, needless to say, very curious as to how it sounded, so I instantly sat down to play it on the piano, just as I had played the original mazurka, whose sheet music was included in Dave's first book about Emmy. Well, some of this mazurka was really astonishingly good, and some of it was somewhat weak, and overall I felt that the first one was probably marginally superior to it, but on the other hand, this second one had some pretty amazing harmonic sequences that sounded *very* Chopin-like to my ear. And in fact—and this is perhaps important to point out—it was this *second* mazurka that fooled the Eastman Rochester crowd, not the first one (which was not played at all on that occasion). So it was the randomly chosen mazurka rather than Dave Cope's handpicked favorite that snowed the Rochester folks. Interesting, eh?

As for Dave continually twiddling Emmy's dials as she is working, I think that he has striven mightily to diminish his own role in her composition. After all, though his original goal (20 years ago, nearly!) was to have a program that could help him compose, by now the goal of making an autonomously composing program has far superseded that first goal. I can't tell you how much Dave participates in Emmy's compositional process, but my feeling is that it is less and less.

The 5,000 symphonies that Emmy composed in a short period of time, by the way, were not composed in order for Dave to listen to them all and select out the best one. That would have been, in fact, humanly impossible. They were an experiment of a totally different sort. Dave took some input from two or three composers (one of them being Stravinsky, as I recall, and maybe also some Bartok—I don't remember, exactly), and fed it into Emmy. Then he took Emmy's output and fed that back into Emmy as input, and around and around it went, in a loop. The idea was for Emmy to kind of stabilize in a feedback loop. Dave let it run this long just so he would be sure it reached stability. Then he randomly selected one of the symphonies and put it on the second CD, as I recall. He did not select "the best" from 5,000, since he probably only listened to a few of them at most! And in any case, they were probably all more or less of roughly the same level of quality.

After all, if you have a process that is good enough to produce a J. D. Salinger short story, you don't expect that among the rival pieces of output of the same program, you are going to find basically total garbage. The rejected stuff will be nearly of the same caliber as the best stuff. And in fact, that's what the randomly-chosen Emmy mazurka (the one dedicated to me) proves very effectively, especially in the way it fooled nearly all the theory and composition at the nation's number one ranked music school (usually the top three are Eastman, Juilliard, and Indiana, in some random order—but as luck had it, this year Eastman had come out on top in some poll).

NOTE

1. The epigram was actually stolen from David Cope, who himself had borrowed it from Pablo Picasso.

BIBLIOGRAPHY

Books and Articles

Bernstein, L. (1959). *The joy of music*. New York: Simon & Schuster.
Cope, D. (1991). *Computers and musical style*. (Volume 6 in the Computer Music and Digital Audio Series, John Strawn, Series Editor). Madison, WI: A-R Editions.
Hearst, E. (1977). Man and machine: Chess achievements and chess thinking. In P. W. Frey (Ed.), *Chess skill in man and machine*. New York: Springer-Verlag.
Hofstadter, D. R. (1979). *Gödel, Escher, Bach: An eternal golden braid*. New York: Basic Books.
Hofstadter, D. R. & the Fluid Analogies Research Group (FARG). (1995). *Fluid concepts and creative analogies: Computer models of the fundamental mechanisms of thought*. New York: Basic Books.
Serafini, L. (1981). *Codex seraphinianus*. Milano: Franco Maria Ricci.

Compact Disks

Cope, D. & Emmy. (1994). *Bach by design: Computer composed music*. Baton Rouge: Centaur Records, CRC 2184.
Emmy & Cope, D. (1997). *Classical music by computer*. Baton Rouge: Centaur Records, CRC 2329.

2

Acquisition and Productivity in Perceptual Symbol Systems: An Account of Mundane Creativity

Jesse J. Prinz and Lawrence W. Barsalou

Creativity is often portrayed as something exotic or peripheral. In this chapter, we hope to domesticate creativity. We think certain forms of creativity are not only common, but are actually among the most basic cognitive phenomena. We focus on two forms of creativity that fit into this category: concept acquisition and productivity. An adequate account of either form depends on an adequate account of the medium of thought. We must determine how our concepts are encoded, when they are acquired, and how those encodings can be productively combined to form thoughts. Thus, by insisting that central cognitive activities are creative, we uncover a close link between the analysis of creativity and more fundamental questions about how we think. As a result of this link, our project is inevitably twofold: we try to deepen our understanding of certain forms of creativity, and, in so doing, we discover a litmus for evaluating competing theories concerning the medium of thought. We avail ourselves of this litmus by comparing two such theories, which agree on a central point: thought is symbolic. The theories differ, however, in the way they construe symbols. According to the first, symbols are amodal and arbitrary. This view, which we outline in more detail below, is widely held by cognitive scientists. A less familiar account has it that the symbols used in thought are perceptually based. This is the view we will defend. Our approach is an extension of a theory of perceptual symbols that has been developed in a recent series of publications (Barsalou, 1993; Barsalou, Yeh, Luka, Olseth, Mix, & Wu; 1993; Olseth & Barsalou, 1995; Barsalou & Prinz, 1997; Barsalou, 1999; Barsalou, Solomon, & Wu, 1999; Prinz, 2001).[1]

The theory of perceptual symbols belongs to a larger project in cognitive science to ground cognition in perception. The project has a long history and is currently gaining momentum. Those involved in the current campaign involve linguists (Talmy, 1983; Langacker, 1987; Lakoff, 1987; Sweetser, 1990), philosophers (Johnson, 1987; McGinn, 1989; Prinz, 2002), psychologists (Mandler, 1992; Barsalou, 1993; Tomasello, Kruger, & Ratner, 1993; Gibbs, 1994; Glenberg, 1997), and researchers in Artificial Intelligence (AI) (Harnad, 1990; Edelman & Reeke, 1990; Stein, 1994; Regier, 1996). The theories developed by these researchers differ significantly, but they are united by the common conviction that perception plays an important role in cognition. We hope to contribute to the defense of that conviction by arguing that perceptual symbol systems offer a better account of concept acquisition and productivity than their amodal counterparts.

The present chapter is intended to complement and extend the discussion of creativity in Barsalou and Prinz (1997). In that paper, the authors discuss a number of features of perceptual symbol systems that constitute forms of mundane creativity. These include propositional construal, variable embodiment, and productivity. In this chapter, we extend the discussion of productivity and develop an account of concept acquisition. We also explore the prospects of constructing computational models of perceptual symbol systems using current strategies and technologies. We think an adequate account of creativity must exploit the creative potential of perceptual symbols. Correlatively, adequate computational models of creativity depend upon our ability to construct adequate models of perceptual symbol systems. We give a rough indication of some of the steps that must be taken before this goal can be realized.

We proceed as follows. First, we offer a general characterization of creativity. Then we will distinguish the two kinds of symbol systems, amodal and perceptual. Next we turn to our two examples of creativity. We argue that concept acquisition and productivity are both creative and that perceptual symbol systems offer a more promising account. Finally, we turn to the question of implementing perceptual symbol systems.

MUNDANE AND EXCEPTIONAL CREATIVITY

In order to domesticate the notion of creativity, we must provide a definition that does not advert to anything extraordinary, sublime, or otherwise exceptional. Once such a definition is established, it becomes apparent that creative acts are pervasive, and that all of us are creative individuals. We think creativity can be most accurately seen as the process by which cognitive systems generate or instigate the genesis of novelty.[2] The kinds of creative acts with which we will be concerned are representational. A representational act is the production of something that represents, designates, or "stands for" something else. The generation of a novel representation constitutes a creative act. A representation can be novel if it represents things that have not been represented or if it represents things in a new way.

As indicated, it is widely believed that creativity is something special, unusual, and exotic. Creative thinking is often thought to involve capacities possessed by a privileged few: artists, poets, inventors, scientists, and other individuals whose cognitive abilities transcend ordinary thinking. Creative acts are thought to be a rare commodity. We call creative acts with this privileged status *exceptionally creative*. Under the definition given above, many ordinary cognitive acts are also properly called creative. We call such acts *mundanely creative*. Bringing mundane creativity to the fore marks a shift in focus in the recent discussion of creativity. We do not in any way underestimate the value of inquiry into exceptional creativity; we merely want to suggest that mundane creativity is more rudimentary.

Exceptionally creative acts tend to involve original or groundbreaking forms of expression. They can be influential, leading to new ways of seeing or new ways of approaching problems. Sometimes exceptionally creative acts involve surprising combinations of elements from different domains. Exceptionally creative acts also tend to involve considerable effort, forethought, or deliberation. Mundanely creative acts are, in comparison, neither groundbreaking, influential, nor surprising. They are typically performed with little effort or deliberation. They can be important for the individual who is responsible for them, but they are rarely important from a social or historical perspective. Nevertheless, exceptional creativity and mundane creativity are in an important sense alike. Both involve the genesis of novelty.

SYMBOL SYSTEMS

Amodal Symbol Systems

In the most basic sense of the term, a symbol is something that represents something else.[3] Symbol systems are systems that govern the manipulation of symbols. At a minimum, a symbol system contains three things (cf. Goodman, 1968; Newell & Simon, 1976; Newell, 1980; Haugeland, 1985; Harnad, 1990): *primitive symbols*,[4] *formation rules* for combining symbols to form complex symbols or symbol structures, and *transformation rules* that alter symbols in systematic ways.

Many cognitive scientists believe that symbol systems are the medium of thought.[5] On this view, humans and many nonhuman animals think using symbols, which are governed by rules of formation and transformation. Within this consensus, there are deep disagreements about the details. What is the format of the symbols we use? How are they organized? How are they combined and transformed? How are they acquired? How do they represent?

Although there is little agreement about the answers to these questions, some opinions are widely shared. Among these, one stands out: most cognitive scientists assume (either tacitly or explicitly) that the symbols used in thought are amodal. Amodal symbols are symbols that bear no intrinsic relationship (e.g., identity or resemblance) to representations used in perceptual input systems. As a result, amodal symbols are arbitrary. They place no intrinsic constraints on their interpretation (Haugeland, 1985).

In natural languages, arbitrary symbols are the norm. The word "cow" could have referred to toads, boats, or quarks, if the history of English had been different. There is nothing about the word "cow" that prevents it from having any other meaning. Accordingly, similarities between words are not correlated with similarities in the things they represent. The word "goat" is more similar to "boat" than it is to "cow," even though goats are more similar in appearance to cows than to boats. When it is claimed that thought is symbolic, it is often assumed that the symbols used in thought have this arbitrary character. On this assumption, our mental symbol for cow is no less arbitrary than the word "cow." That both of these symbols refer to cows is simply a consequence of how they are used.

It is often assumed that symbols are arbitrary by definition (Newell & Simon, 1976; Haugeland, 1985; Harnad, 1990). On this view, "non-arbitrary symbol" is an oxymoron. Defining "symbol" in this way biases the case in favor of amodal symbols. We will not be party to this terminological chauvinism. On our view, symbols are representations that can be systematically combined and transformed. There is no reason to restrict these properties to representations that are arbitrary and amodal. We think that such restrictions derive from a failure to recognize that non-arbitrary representations can be systematically combined and transformed. Once this possibility is acknowledged, a more liberal interpretation of the term "symbol" should appear unobjectionable.

Perceptual Symbol Systems

A non-arbitrary symbol is one that places an intrinsic constraint on its interpretation. One class of non-arbitrary symbols is particularly interesting. We call these *perceptual symbols*. Perceptual symbols have been introduced and described at length elsewhere (Barsalou, 1993; Barsalou et al., 1993; Barsalou & Prinz, 1997; Barsalou, 1999). For the present discussion, we merely underscore a few of their important features.

First, perceptual symbols are derived from the representations generated in perceptual input systems (perceptual representations). By this we mean two things: they are *acquired* by performing operations on perceptual representations, and they are *similar* to those representations. At a minimum, perceptual symbols preserve some of the structure of the perceptual representations from which they were derived.

Second, as result of the first point, perceptual symbols are non-arbitrary. Unlike amodal symbols, they bear intrinsic similarity to perceptual representations, and similarity relations between perceptual symbols often correspond to similarity relations between (the observable features of) the objects they represent.

Third, perceptual symbols are multi-modal. Perception includes not only the classic five senses, but also neglected senses such as proprioception, kinesthesia, and introspection. Perceptual symbols are derived from representations in each of these modalities.

Fourth, perceptual symbols are schematic. On a naive view of perception, our input systems produce unstructured "snapshots" of the world. Unstructured representations would clearly be inadequate for perceptual recognition. Consequently, perceptual systems must abstract away the irrelevant details of incoming signals, separate aspects of a signal that are independent, and introduce a significant amount of structure. This kind of schematization is demanded by behavioral evidence that we can recognize commonality across very different inputs, which is a property presupposed by computational theories of perception (e.g., Marr, 1982; Biederman, 1987; Hummel & Biederman, 1992) and confirmed by neuroscience (e.g., Perrett, Harries, Mistlin, & Chitty, 1990; Zeki, 1992). Perceptual symbols can directly inherit schematic qualities from the perceptual representations from which they are derived.

Fifth, perceptual symbols should not be identified with mental images. Images are most likely representations in low-level perceptual subsystems (Kosslyn, 1994). Perceptual symbols are more like high-level perceptual representations in that they are highly structured and not accessible to consciousness.

This is not a complete characterization of perceptual symbols, but it suffices for now. The last two points are particularly important, because they distinguish the present account from its historical ancestors. Attempts to ground cognition in perceptually derived symbols have a long history (e.g., Aristotle, 1961; Hobbes, 1651; Locke, 1706; Berkeley, 1734; Hume, 1739; Russell, 1921; Price, 1953). It is widely believed that such accounts have failed (e.g., Geach, 1957; Dennett, 1969; Pylyshyn, 1984). We attribute the failure of historical accounts to a naiveté about the nature of perception. It was assumed by many that perceptually derived symbols must be relatively unstructured conscious images. In rejecting this claim, we believe that a defense of perceptual symbols can be successfully defended against the objections that cast historical views into ill repute. This case has been made more extensively elsewhere (Barsalou & Prinz, 1997; Barsalou, 1999; Prinz, 2002). Here, we have said just enough to explore the contribution of perceptual symbols to the explanation of mundane creativity.

MUNDANE CREATIVITY: CONCEPT ACQUISITION

Concept Acquisition as a Form of Creativity

As we use the term, a *concept* is a symbol structure used for representing objects, properties, relations, situations, or other things that populate our world. We will be primarily concerned with concepts representing categories, that is, collections of things typically united by the possession of similar features, functions, or capacities to serve goals. Concepts differ from individual symbols in that they can be highly complex or encyclopedic (Barsalou, 1987, 1989, 1992, 1993). They are, however, comprised of symbols. Humans acquire new concepts throughout the course of their lives. This may occur at an accelerated rate during development, but it continues as long as we are mentally capable. We constantly encounter unfamiliar things. To think about these things and to identify them in the future, we must represent them. The representations we form contribute to an ever-growing repertoire of concepts.

Concept acquisition is a creative act. Earlier, we defined creativity in terms of the genesis of novelty and discussed two kinds of novel representations: those that represent things that have not been represented, and those that represent familiar things in new ways. Concept acquisition can involve either form of novelty. First, consider a person who sees a hyena for the first time. After several encounters, she might generate a means of representing hyenas, that is, a hyena concept. This is a new concept for that individual. Now consider another individual who has seen hyenas before, but only during the daytime. Now she wants to learn how to identify hyenas at night. She already possesses a representation of hyenas, but it might not be adequate for night recognition. For that, she might need to form a representation that encodes information about how hyenas appear in the dark (e.g., information about their hunched silhouettes or glowing beady eyes). She might also augment her daytime hyena representation by encoding information about hyena attributes that can be detected in the darkness (e.g., information about the hyena's distinctive cry). In this case, the individual does not learn how to represent an unfamiliar class of objects. Instead, she learns new ways of representing a familiar class. These acts are not exceptionally creative, because their products are not groundbreaking or influential, but they are mundanely creative.

Concept Acquisition in Amodal Symbol Systems

To acquire a concept in an amodal symbol system, one must move from a perceptual representation of an object to an amodal symbol for the category that subsumes it. This move is far from trivial. Because amodal symbols do not resemble perceptual representations, we need to introduce some kind of mechanism that translates and correlates these perceptual and amodal states without exploiting intrinsic similarities.

The mechanisms that have been introduced to explain this translation process are called transducers. Transduction is often described as the process by which external objects and events generate internal symbols (Pylyshyn, 1984). Described in this way, transduction is largely the concern of those who study early levels of perception. To explain the move from perceptual representations to amodal symbols, one must postulate a second stage of transduction, which converts perceptual representations into the amodal symbols used in thought. This proposal leaves us with a number of puzzles (see also Barsalou & Prinz, 1997).

First, we must ask how arbitrary labels are chosen. If it is true that the interpretation of amodal symbols is not internally constrained, it is hard to understand why the cognitive system generates one amodal symbol rather than another. This we call the *Transduction Problem*.

Second, we must ask what purpose these amodal symbols serve. If one has already generated representations in perceptual input systems, why does one need to generate this other class of representations that are amodal? Why can't one get by with the representations it already has? We call this the *Parsimony Problem*.

Third, we must ask how amodal symbols and the internal transducers that produce them arose in evolution. Evolution explains the emergence of cognitive mechanisms by phylogenetic bootstrapping. The cognitive mechanisms at any stage of development must be explained as an outgrowth, extension, or enhancement of previously existing mechanisms. A spontaneous development of mechanisms that bear no deep relationship to previously existing mechanisms would be biologically implausible. The evolution of perceptual input systems is long and complex but not miraculous. For example, one can tell a fairly good story tracing mammalian visual systems back to rudimentary photosensitive cells (Mayr, 1982). Introducing amodal symbols seems to threaten this evolutionary continuity. It is hard to imagine how mechanisms that convert perceptual representations into amodal symbols might have emerged. We call this the *Evolution Problem* (see also Churchland, 1986; McGinn, 1989).

Cumulatively, these puzzles should sound some alarms. If a theory raises more questions than it answers, alternative theories should be sought. We think that this is the case with the hypothesis that thought is conducted using an amodal symbol system.

These puzzles do not threaten perceptual symbols. Perceptual symbols resemble the perceptual representations from which they are derived. They may filter or refine perceptual representations, but they retain the general structure and organization. Thus, the transition from perceptual representations to perceptual symbols does not require a mysterious or radical change in format. The Transduction Problem does not arise. Perceptual symbols are also more parsimonious than amodal symbols, because they are parasitic on representations that are independently motivated. They do not increase the number of representational types beyond necessity. Finally, perceptual symbols can be explained by evolution. Once perceptual representations have evolved, their exploitation in nonperceptual tasks can come about as the result of a gradual shift in our ability to store and invoke them at will (cf. Donald, 1991). Perceptual symbols do not appear as the result of the spontaneous emergence of an unprecedented system of representation. Instead, they are the result of a change in how a previously evolved system of representation is used. This kind of shift places a more manageable burden on natural selection.

Concept Acquisition in Perceptual Symbol Systems

On a perceptual symbols account, concepts are acquired by building complex symbol structures from more primitive perceptual symbols. To explain how such complexes are constructed, we must first explain how perceptual symbols are formed. Simply put, perceptual symbols are extracted from perceptual representations that are generated during experience. Extraction is a process by which we transfer information encoded in perceptual representations into long-term memory. In extraction, we do not redescribe perceptual representations in a dramatically different medium as in amodal symbol systems. Instead, we produce perceptual symbols, which preserve the structure, organization, and modal-specificity of perceptual representations.

Selective attention determines which symbols get extracted (Barsalou, 1993; Barsalou & Prinz, 1997). It is widely recognized that selective attention facilitates storage in memory (Craik & Lockhart, 1972; Craik & Tulving, 1975). When we focus attention on an object,[6] the perceptual representation of that object can be stored in the form of a perceptual symbol. The focus of selective attention can be determined in a number of different ways. Sometimes our attention is drawn by objects that are naturally salient. Moving objects or objects that stand out from their backgrounds in some other way can "pop out" by triggering preattentive mechanisms. Once these objects have been brought into focus by our sense organs, they can be scrutinized and thereby encoded in memory. Other times, attention is more voluntary or goal driven. By using attention strategically, we can exercise some control over the symbols we acquire during perception. Attention can also be driven by social factors. Members of a society can use language to make objects and relations perceptually salient to one another. For example, in learning words, we are often shown samples of the objects that those words designate.

The flexibility of selective attention makes it an ideal mechanism for acquiring concepts. Natural, strategic, and social factors allow us to focus on many different aspects of perceptual experience. We can focus on objects, parts of objects, properties, relations, activities, internal states, and so on. When we do this, we can ignore extraneous information that is present in a signal. For example, we can focus on the basic form of an object without taking note of its color, size, or location (Ungerleider & Mishkin, 1982; Zeki, 1992). Likewise, we can focus on an object's pattern of movement, for example, the trajectory it is following or the pattern in which it moves its legs, without storing more specific information about its form. We can even focus on a relation between two objects, for example, the fact that one is above the other, without storing information about the identity of the objects in those relations.

To form complex concepts, we must organize more primitive perceptual symbols into complex symbol structures. There are at least two ways in which this is done. On the one hand, there are concepts whose genesis is directed largely by external or environmental factors. These *taxonomic* concepts come about as a natural consequence of perceiving objects in the world. On the other hand, there are concepts that are generated more effortfully to classify objects that satisfy certain conditions, constraints, or goals. We explore how both of these are generated within a perceptual symbol system.

Taxonomic concepts come as a result of attending to different features of perceived members of a category. Representations of different features are then clustered together to form a complex representation. We believe that concepts are symbol structures that are used to simulate members of a category (Barsalou & Prinz, 1997). Concept possession involves the ability to simulate competently. To achieve simulation competence, we must know what members of a category look like from different vantage points, how they vary from one another, how they relate to things around them, and how they behave. This information can often be attained only if we use our senses to attend to different exemplars and different aspects of individual exemplars. For example, to acquire simulation competence with a *hyena* concept, one must attend to hyenas' hunched backs, their beady eyes, their round ears, their awkward gait, their hideous laughter, and their savanna habitat. Because these features are observed together in individual exemplars or in groups of similar exemplar, they are grouped together to form a complex database of information. The correlation of features in a taxonomic concept is dictated by the environment. We group a beady eye symbol with a round ear symbol, because these features are co-instantiated on the same objects. Their correlation is given to us, not imposed by us.

This should not be taken to imply that the way in which we acquire taxonomic concepts is completely out of our control. Their acquisition depends on attending to different features and correlating them. By willfully attending to different features given to us in the environment, we can exercise control over our concepts. This insight reveals how the mundanely creative activity of acquiring concepts from the environment can become exceptionally creative. By attending to features or relations between features that are given in nature but often ignored, we can discover new things and arrive at unprecedented ways of conceptualizing our world.

The second class of concepts we discuss are goal-derived. These have been extensively studied by one of the authors of this chapter (e.g., Barsalou, 1983, 1991). The symbols that comprise goal-derived concepts are correlated by us, not nature. Consider the category of objects that can be used to prop open a door. These objects differ significantly in physical appearance, but they all serve a common goal. Goal-derived concepts can be represented using perceptual symbols. In order to prop open a door, an object must satisfy certain constraints of size, weight, and mobility (Barsalou, 1991). To determine the requisite size, we can form a perceptual symbol representing an open door and "carve out" a region in that symbol corresponding to the maximum size of the door holder. Any object larger than that region would obstruct the entranceway. Next, we can approximate the weight that would be required to prop a door open, by recalling perceptual symbols derived from kinesthetic experiences with doors. When we open doors, we have an experience of resistance that can be stored in memory in the form of perceptual symbols. We invoke these symbols as a second constraint on the concept we are constructing. An object can prop open the door only if it is heavy enough to overcome a door's resistance. At the same time, the desired objects must be light and mobile enough to be lifted. Again, kinesthetic experience gives us an idea of how much weight we can lift. In sum, we want an object that is heavy enough to prop the door without being too heavy to lift or move and without being too large to obstruct the entranceway. Perceptual symbols representing objects with which we have had sufficient interaction will encode information about their size, weight, and mobility. We can compare these object representations against the criteria established by our goals. This comparison process yields a scaled set of perceptual symbols representing objects that can be used to prop open doors. This process can be carried out using perceptual symbols because goals can be represented by constraints along perceptible dimensions.

Goal-derived concepts carve up the world in novel ways, by grouping items together on the basis of their ability to serve a common function. As our example illustrates, these concepts are often mundanely creative. They play a critical role in day-to-day planning and problem solving. But, they can also be exceptionally creative. For example, technological developments often involve setting goals and bringing together, or organizing independent elements to realize those goals. The mechanisms underlying artistic expression might also have some kinship with goal-derived concepts. Artists bring together surprising combinations of elements in order evoke a reaction in their audience. For instance, painters choose color schemes and composers choose chords with the intention of manipulating our emotions. "Colors and sounds which make us sad" constitutes a paradigmatic goal-derived concept.

These examples are intended to reinforce our claim that concept acquisition is fundamentally creative. They also provide a rough sketch of how perceptual symbol systems can explain concept acquisition. If we are right, perceptual symbols lie at the heart of this important form of creativity.

MUNDANE CREATIVITY: PRODUCTIVITY

Productivity as a Form of Creativity

The concept of mundane creativity owes much to Noam Chomsky. Throughout his work, Chomsky refers to creativity (Chomsky, 1957) or, more recently, the creative use of language (Chomsky, 1968; see also Kasher, 1991). What Chomsky has in mind is our ability to form expressions of arbitrary complexity from finite means during linguistic communication. This ability qualifies as creative by our definition, because it involves the genesis of novelty. When we utter a sentence, we construct something new, a combination of words that has probably never been formed before. Sometimes these sentences represent facts that have never been described; sometimes they describe familiar facts in new ways. In either case, we are producing something new.

The creative use of language is closely related to and dependent upon the creative use of thought. As with language, it seems that we can spontaneously generate novel thoughts of arbitrary complexity. Both the creative use of language and the creative use of thought can be explained by appeal to productivity. We are capable of generating novel sentences and thoughts in virtue of the fact that sentences and thoughts are comprised of symbols that are governed by productive symbol systems. A productive symbol system is one that allows for a boundless number of distinct, arbitrarily complex symbol structures to be formed from a finite set of rules and representations. Unbounded productivity is purchased by using formation rules that are combinatorial and recursive. In this section, we compare the combinatorial properties of amodal and perceptual symbols. We argue that perceptual symbols provide a more psychologically realistic account of productivity.

Productivity in Amodal Symbol Systems

Amodal symbol systems are often described by analogy to languages. For example, Fodor (1975) refers to the amodal symbol system he advocates as "the language of thought," and Pylyshyn (1984) refers to symbol structures in his preferred amodal symbol system as "sentence analogues." We have already observed that amodal symbol systems share with languages the characteristic of using arbitrary symbols. They also account for productivity in a way that closely parallels explanations of productivity in language.

Linguistic productivity is explained by appeal to combinatorial, recursive formation rules. Linguistic expressions or "strings" are formed by spatial or temporal concatenation. Primitive symbols are placed next to each other in space or time. One interesting feature of these concatenative formation rules is that they are largely insensitive to context. The syntactic form of a symbol is usually unaffected by the contents of the symbols with which it is concatenated. The verb in the sentence, "the human runs" is syntactically equivalent to the verb in the sentence, "the lion runs." This is the model on which amodal symbol systems are conceived.

Context-insensitivity contributes to productivity. Rules that are overly sensitive to context cannot be used to construct novel combinations. In the extreme case, a rule will cause a symbol to be modified in a different way for every symbol with which it can be combined and each of these different modifications will have to be learned separately. If the rule for combining a symbol changes with each potential combination, we will not be able to generate new combinations productively. Each combination must be learned in advance. If rules are insensitive to context, productivity can easily be achieved. Completely new combinations can be generated on the basis of a few familiar patterns.

Context-insensitivity also has some hidden costs. In formal languages, symbols are unaffected by the symbols with which they are combined. In thought, this does not seem to be the case. In the literature on concepts, context-sensitivity is widely recognized and discussed (e.g., Barsalou, 1982, 1987; Barsalou et al., 1999). Context-sensitivity can be modeled using amodal symbols (Smith, Medin, Rips, & Keane, 1988), but amodal symbols do not predict the kinds of context sensitivity found in thought. One important kind of context sensitivity is discussed by Langacker (1987). He argues that symbols "accommodate" each other. For example, the way we represent a human being running differs from the way we represent a lion running. In both formal and natural languages, the predicate representing running remains unchanged when combined with symbols representing different kinds of objects. It seems unlikely that this is true in thought. If someone has never seen a quadruped running, it might be harder for her to think about a lion running than a human running. If amodal symbols are truly language-like, they are not ideally suited for explaining this asymmetry.

Formation rules that are completely insensitive to context run the danger of being *overly* productive. In such systems, there are not enough constraints on what combinations can be formed. In actuality, the thoughts we can form are semantically constrained. Combinations of symbols that are semantically anomalous are difficult, if not impossible to think (except, perhaps, metaphorically). For example, we cannot form a (literal) thought with the content of, "truth runs." Our inability does not seem to stem from rules that advert only to syntactic categories. Instead, the problem with the sentence is semantic. Truth just cannot run. The challenge is to find a way of constructing formation rules that respect these semantic constraints. We should find a way to make the syntax of thought (the rules that manipulate symbols) coincide with the semantics of thought (the things that thoughts are about).

There are two basic strategies for meeting this challenge. We can build constraints directly into the symbols, or we can impose constraints on symbols through beliefs and knowledge (cf. Pylyshyn, 1984). Call these the intrinsic and extrinsic strategies respectively. If amodal symbols are truly language-like, it is hard to imagine how their combinations could be intrinsically constrained. Advocates of amodal symbols opt for the extrinsic strategy. There are a number of problems with this. First, once it is conceded that conceptual combination is context-sensitive, the analogy with language is broken, and the amodal symbols account loses some of its impetus. Second, extrinsic constraints are too weak. Our inability to conceive of truth running seems to stem from something deeper than our beliefs. No matter what beliefs one possesses, it is impossible to literally imagine truth running. Finally, the appeal to extrinsic constraints is ad hoc. It would be more satisfying if we could demonstrate that our inability to combine certain concepts is a direct, that is, intrinsic, consequence of the way those concepts are represented.

These difficulties are not fatal. An amodal symbol system with extrinsically constrained formation rules could probably produce the right behavior. Nevertheless, these difficulties should raise some doubts. We began by saying that amodal symbol systems seem to have an easy time explaining productivity, because they can exploit context-insensitive formation rules. We then discovered that these rules are too powerful. To compensate, external constraints must be introduced. Once this concession is made, the nature of formation rules in amodal systems can no longer be advertised as an advantage. The elegance of these rules is overshadowed by cumbersome external constraints. This observation should lead us to consider how other kinds of symbol systems handle productivity.

Productivity in Perceptual Symbol Systems

We think that perceptual symbol systems offer a more psychologically realistic explanation of productivity. As with amodal symbol systems, perceptual symbol systems achieve productivity by means of combinatorial, recursive formation rules. It has often been assumed without argument that non-arbitrary symbols cannot be combined in a productive way (e.g., Haugeland, 1985). This assumption derives from the fact that the most familiar form of non-arbitrary symbols, ordinary pictures, do not have obvious parts or principles of combination. Fortunately, other non-arbitrary symbols help dispel the assumption. Maps, diagrams, and architectural figures readily lend themselves to productive combination (Schwartz, 1981; Rollins, 1989; Haugeland, 1991; Barwise and Etchemendy, 1991; Mitchell, 1990). Similarly, Biederman (1987) proposes a theory of visual object representations in which complex representations are constructed from a very small set of volumetric primitives (geons). We think perceptual symbol systems can be productive as well (Barsalou, 1993; Barsalou et al., 1993; Barsalou & Prinz, 1997).

To demonstrate that a system of non-arbitrary symbols can be productive, consider the symbol system pictured in Figure 2.1. The system includes a set of primitive symbols (a) for objects (table, chair, box, cup) and spatial relations (left-of, right-of; inside, outside). We follow Langacker (1987) in using dark lines to represent the locus of focal attention. A shift of focus distinguishes extensionally equivalent relation symbols in a non-arbitrary way. We also follow Langacker in representing spatial relations using empty regions. These regions function like argument places in that they can be "filled" by different object symbols. Formation rules that combine relations with objects are displayed in (b). For convenience, we used variable symbols (standing for either objects or relations) in representing these rules. Explicit variable representations would not be necessary in an implementation of this system, because the formation rules could be implicit in the operation of the system. Finally, (c) illustrates some transformation rules. The first two license focal shifts, and the third is an instance of transitivity.

This example illustrates the potential productivity of non-arbitrary symbol systems. By combining object symbols with spatial relation symbols, we get combinatorics, and by embedding spatial relation symbols in other spatial relation symbols, we get recursion. This system is simpler than anything we use in thought, but it functions as an existence proof for the productivity of non-arbitrary symbols.

It should already be apparent that the formation rules in perceptual symbol systems are quite different from the formation rules in language-like, amodal symbol systems. In language-like systems, the spatial or temporal sequence in which symbols are arranged remains constant across large classes of expressions. For example, there may be rules that say that all symbols representing objects should be placed to the right of symbols representing properties regardless of what objects or properties are being represented. This kind of general formation pattern is common in notational systems for predicate calculus. In perceptual symbol systems, the arrangement of symbols can vary significantly. The way an object symbol combines with a spatial relation symbol, for example, depends on the conceptual structure of that symbol. The perceptual symbols representing "the box is left-of the chair" are ordered differently than the perceptual symbols representing "the box is right-of the chair," despite the fact that the sentences are ordered in the same sequence. The arrangements correspond more faithfully to the semantics.

FIGURE 2.1
A symbol system with non-arbitrary symbols. (a) Primitive object and relation symbols; (b) formation rules; (c) transformation rules.

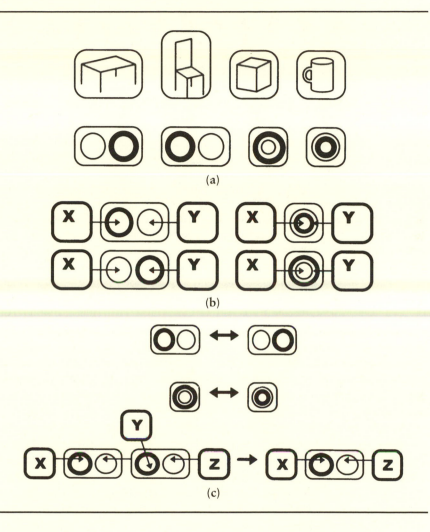

(a)

(b)

(c)

Perceptual symbols are also context-sensitive. This becomes more apparent when we consider perceptual symbols representing physical activities. We believe that such symbols are dynamic. For example, the verb *to run* can be represented by a sequence of perceptual symbols representing the sequence of leg movements that comprise the activity of running. The perceptual symbol for running is quite different from the perceptual symbols representing spatial relations. Spatial relation symbols are combined with

FIGURE 2.2
Schematic bipedal and quadrupedal running symbols.

object symbols via a fairly simple role-filling operation. When an object symbol is assigned to an empty region in a spatial relation symbol, it does not need to be modified.[7] In contrast, symbols representing physical activities can only be combined with object symbols by accommodation. For example, the way we represent a human running differs from the way we represent a lion running.

Consider a person who has never seen a quadruped running. Our theory predicts that it will be hard for her to accurately conceive of running lions, because her running symbol is extracted from perceptual states representing running bipeds. She will have to adapt her bipedal running symbol to accommodate a lion symbol by making four legs move instead of two. If she attempts this merger, she may be able to extract a new schematic symbol for representing running quadrupeds (see Figure 2.2). This symbol can be embellished and improved if she later observes actual instances of running quadrupeds.

Physical activity symbols also place strict semantic constraints on the symbols with which they can be combined. For example, the running symbol represents the activity of running using a sequence of leg representations. An object symbol is applicable for combination only if it has components that can conform to the pattern of movements specified by the running symbol. It must have components that are leg-like. Many object symbols fail to meet this requirement. Symbols representing rocks, fish, and eggplants lack leg-like components. Consequently, they cannot be combined with the running symbol (unless they are supplemented with prosthetic leg symbols). A more extreme case involves the perceptual symbol representing truth. The perceptual symbol for truth does not include any leg-like components (Barsalou & Prinz, 1997). Therefore, the perceptual symbol for truth cannot be combined with the perceptual symbol for running. This gives us an explanation for why "truth runs" is an unthinkable thought.

Following Chomsky's usage, we have already claimed that productive symbol combination constitutes a form of mundane creativity. Context-sensitivity illustrates one way in which mundane creativity can lead to something more exceptional. When non-arbitrary symbols modify or accommodate each other in combination, new things can be discovered. This possibility has been explored in recent work on image combination (Finke, Pinker, & Farah, 1989). It also may illuminate the creativity found in domain transfer and metaphor. When we combine concepts that are not usually brought together, they can accommodate each other in fruitful and surprising ways.

There is a potential concern to be raised. If rules were overly sensitive to context, we would have to learn each symbol combination in advance. We would not be able to predict context effects in an unfamiliar combination on the basis of earlier examples, because each combination will be completely distinct.

Fortunately, formation rules in perceptual symbol systems are not *overly* context-sensitive. Similar context effects can apply to large classes of symbols. Consider the perceptual symbol for the verb to run. Above, we said that this verb affects the symbol for human and the symbol for lion in different ways. If would be a mistake to infer from this claim that the symbol for run will affect all object symbols differently. It is likely to affect the symbol for lion in much the same way as it affects the symbol for tiger. If perceptual symbols are sufficiently schematic, the perceptual symbol for run might apply in the same way to all perceptual symbols representing quadrupeds. Thus, one can form a symbol structure representing running wombats or running armadillos based on the example of running lions. Moreover, even if the symbol for run does affect all object symbols differently, there is a kernel of commonality. In each of the cases we have considered, running involves rapid movement of legs. Any differences between the representation of a lion running and an armadillo running might be extrapolated from knowledge about differences in the anatomies of these two animals (e.g., knowledge about the length of their legs). In other words, knowledge of a simple rule for modifying leg positions sequentially, coupled with specific information about the length and number of an animal's legs, can be sufficient for representing an animal running, even if one has never seen that animal run. Context-sensitivity does not require that every symbol combination be learned in advance.

The combinatorial properties of perceptual symbol systems have yet to be investigated in detail. The discussion in this section was designed to pump the intuition that perceptual symbols lend themselves to systematic combination. The ways in which perceptual symbols are combined differ from the ways in which language—like amodal symbols are combined, but this is not cause for alarm. First, the context-sensitivity exhibited by perceptual symbol formation rules is consonant with what we know about the constraints on symbol combination in thought. Second, and more importantly, moderate context-sensitivity does not preclude productivity. Perceptual symbols seem to be ideally suited for explaining this kind of mundane creativity.

CONSTRUCTING PERCEPTUAL SYMBOL SYSTEMS

We have been arguing that perceptual symbol systems comprise one of the most promising avenues for explaining mundane creativity. If we want to develop computational models of mundane creativity, we must first determine how perceptual symbol systems should be implemented computationally. Currently, two kinds of architectures, classical and connectionist, are widely used. We cannot provide a detailed comparison of these architectures here. However, in the next two sections we briefly discuss and compare their prospects for implementing perceptual symbol systems. We discover that classical and connectionist architectures both have features that are advantageous and disadvantageous. This suggests that the best model of a perceptual symbol system would exploit an architecture that lies somewhere between classical and connectionist architectures. This does not mean that perceptual symbol systems cannot be implemented using existing technologies. The key to constructing a perceptual symbol system is embodiment. Both connectionist and classical architectures could be used to construct perceptual symbol systems if they were hooked up to models of perceptual systems that grounded them in the world. Nevertheless, we still seem to be far away from the goal of constructing perceptual symbol systems that have all the features discussed in the preceding sections.

Classical Models

Perceptual symbol systems are combinatorial. They generate symbol structures by combining primitive symbols in accordance with rules. Combinatorial syntax is at home in classical models. Historically, the development of classical models is intertwined with the study of formal languages. Formal languages constitute symbol systems in the sense defined earlier. The same is true of classical models: they are comprised by primitive symbols, formation rules, and transformation rules. Moreover, classical models can exploit recursive rules. As a result, they are capable of exhibiting productivity (Fodor & Pylyshyn, 1988).

All this might lead one to suspect that perceptual symbols should be implemented using a classical architecture. Our use of the term "symbol system" seems to push us in that direction. This conclusion, however, would be too hasty. There are reasons to believe that classical architectures are not ideally suited for implementing perceptual symbol systems. The primary difficulty derives from the fact that classical models are notoriously bad at modeling input systems. They have a very hard time recognizing patterns efficiently. An input system that is inefficient at pattern recognition would not be capable of generating a rich vocabulary of perceptual symbols. To remedy this problem, we might construct a perceptual symbol system that extracts symbols from a more efficient *non-classical* input system. The problem with this proposal is that it would force us to correlate states of a nonclassical model with symbols in a classical model. It is difficult to see how this could be done in a non-arbitrary way. In perceptual symbol systems, symbols bear a similarity relation to perceptual representations. If input systems are architecturally distinct from symbol systems, it is difficult to establish similarity relations between the two. Hybrid systems are vulnerable to the Transduction Problem. We can summarize in the form of a dilemma: if we were to use a model that is classical all the way down, we can establish non-arbitrary relations between perceptual representations and perceptual symbols, but the number of perceptual symbols would be limited, because classical systems are bad at recognizing patterns; if we were to use a hybrid model, we could achieve superior pattern recognition, but the correlation between perceptual representations and perceptual symbols would run the danger of becoming arbitrary. If purely classical models and hybrid models are both unsuccessful, then we might consider the possibility of implementing perceptual symbol systems using a purely nonclassical model.

Connectionist Models

In many ways, connectionist models seem to offer a more suitable method for implementing perceptual symbol systems. They have a number of advantageous features. First, they are good at acquiring symbols. Their symbols emerge during training rather than being "innately" specified by programmers. In training, programmers expose a network to a set of inputs or desired input/output pairs, and the network adjusts its connection weights in responses. Algorithms for making these adjustments are innately specified, but the weights themselves can be randomly set at the beginning.

Second, connectionist architectures can be used to model perceptual input systems more successfully than their classical counterparts. For example, Hummel and Biederman (1992) have developed an impressive connectionist model based on Biederman's (1987) theory of shape recognition.

Third, connectionist models address information semantically. Semantic addressing allows for more flexibility in recall. Information can be accessed along many different dimensions. If a concept encodes information about different features, each of these features can be used to index the concept simultaneously. This facilitates the construction of goal-derived concepts (Bechtel & Abrahamsen, 1991). For example, in constructing a concept for things that can be used to prop open a door, it is necessary to access information about the size and weight of objects. If stored information is semantically addressed, applicable concepts can be called up by their size and weight, even if these features are usually not very salient. In a classical filing system memory, such peripheral information might be more difficult to access.

Fourth, in connectionist models, syntactic similarities between symbols (i.e., activation patterns) often corresponds to semantic similarities. This is often brought out by post hoc analyses in which the state space of a network is partitioned. Units mediating between similar inputs and outputs typically occupy similar regions of state space. As we saw above, this feature is shared by perceptual symbols. Similar perceptual symbols are produced by similar perceptual representations, and similar perceptual representations are produced by perceptual encounters with similar objects. Therefore, similarities between perceptual symbols are often semantically relevant.

Finally, symbol combination in connectionist systems is context-sensitive. The way a symbol is represented will depend on the symbols with which it is combined (e.g., Smolensky, 1988; Elman, 1992). This recalls the context-sensitivity of perceptual symbols. Elman (1992) explicitly relates connectionist context-sensitivity to Langacker's notion of accommodation, and Langacker (1991) has expressed his enthusiasm for connectionism.

In spite of these features, connectionist models suffer from some shortcomings. Unlike classical models, connectionist models have difficulty achieving the kind of combinatorial behavior that we attributed to perceptual symbol systems. Since the re-emergence of connectionism, there has been a tremendous effort to construct productive, combinatorial systems using connectionist architectures (e.g., Smolensky, 1988; Pollack, 1990; van Gelder, 1990; Hinton, 1991). At this stage, however, the combinatorial behavior of connectionist networks seems to differ from the combinatorial behavior one would expect to see in a perceptual symbol system. The problem involves constituent structure. Intuitively, one would expect a perceptual representation of a chair left-of the box to contain an element in common with a perception of the chair in isolation. By extension, one would expect a perceptual symbol representing a chair left-of the box to contain a representation of the chair. That embedded representation should be similar to the representation that would be invoked if we were to represent the chair in isolation. It is not obvious that this requirement is met by current connectionist analogues of compositionality. In connectionist architectures, the activation pattern corresponding to a symbol combination can be very different from the activation pattern corresponding to its constituents. In classical architectures, a symbol representing the lamp can be a real constituent of a symbol structure representing the lamp above the table. If connectionist architectures cannot be designed to preserve constituents to a greater degree, they might not provide an adequate account of perceptual symbol combination.

Another problem stems from the fact that connectionist models often rely on supervised learning to acquire symbols. In this process, they are presented with correct pairings of inputs and outputs. In acquiring symbols through perception, real organisms do not have the luxury of such explicit instruction. Our cognitive systems must figure out what symbols to form in response to perceptual inputs without external assistance. Thus, training methods that rely on explicit specification of desired outputs lack psychological plausibility (see Edelman & Reeke, 1990, for a related criticism).

A third problem is that connectionist symbols tend to be less versatile than classical symbols. Connectionist models tend to simulate specific tasks within specific domains; their representations mediate between fixed kinds of inputs and outputs. Perceptual symbol systems require representations that are not task bound. The representations used in high-level cognitive processes (perceptual symbols) are essentially the same as the representations used in perception (perceptual representations). Similar or identical representations are exploited in very different ways. Connectionist models must master this ability to exploit representations in multiple ways before they can be used to model perceptual symbol systems (for a good discussion of connectionist approaches to multiple exploitability, see Clark, 1993).

A final problem reveals a limitation of one of the virtues of connectionist architectures. We noted that similarity relations between representations in a connectionist system are often semantically relevant. This is true only of complex representations. Primitives (e.g., the nodes in a connectionist net) are often arbitrarily related to each other. The same is true in classical architectures. Complex data structures might reflect semantic similarities by shared features or structural properties, but similarity relations between primitive symbols are generally semantically irrelevant. In perceptual symbol systems, we believe that non-arbitrary similarity relations can hold between primitives.

Embodied Systems

It is quite possible that the worries we have raised can be answered, but there is another worry that is even more significant. The major shortcoming of most classical and connectionist models is their lack of embodiment (Johnson, 1987; Glenberg, 1997). Perceptual symbol systems are embodied. Their representations depend on states of perceptual input systems that depend, in turn, on states of the body. The constituents of perceptual symbol structures are generated through interaction with the world. An adequate model of a perceptual symbol system must contain models of input systems. Something is a perceptual symbol only if it has been extracted from an input system. This requirement places extraordinary demands on the modeler. It is not sufficient to model a single task or even a single system. At least three things are necessary: we need adequate models of perceptual input systems, adequate models of high-level cognitive systems that can exploit non-arbitrary symbols, and mechanisms for integrating these two.[8]

Consider the input systems that ground perceptual symbol systems. These must satisfy important requirements. First, they must be designed to produce representations that are suitable for combinatorial manipulation in higher level systems. Second, they must be directed towards both an external environment and internal states. Perceptual symbol systems cannot have adequate expressive power if they are incapable of generating symbols through both introspective experience and experience of the external world (Barsalou & Prinz, 1997). At the same time, input systems cannot be under complete control of the environment. They must allow top-down effects such as the strategic allocation of attention. These requirements are necessary for explaining the acquisition of perceptual symbols and the concepts they comprise. Constructing input systems that meet these requirements is a challenge.

Mechanisms for integrating input systems with higher level systems (hereafter, integration mechanisms) also pose a challenge. They convert perceptual representations into perceptual symbols by encoding idealized facsimiles or perceptual representations in memory. They also play an important role in concept acquisition. As we saw, concept acquisition often involves our ability to coordinate information garnered from different sense modalities. A model of a perceptual symbol system must include mechanisms for grouping together multi-modal symbols. Integration mechanisms can play this role. Perceptual symbol systems yield multiple perceptual representations concurrently. Integration mechanisms convert these perceptual representations into symbols and group them together to form concepts that can be accessed by higher level systems. Constructing mechanisms that play this role is far from trivial. To form idealized facsimiles of perceptual representations, integration mechanisms must be able to determine which aspects of a high-level perceptual representation are unnecessary for future categorization. To group together symbols from different modalities, integration mechanisms must determine which symbols are being generated by the same object. If a system receives visual and haptic stimulation simultaneously, it must decide whether they derive from a common source.

Challenging demands are also placed on the high-level cognitive systems that manipulate perceptual symbols. These must be able to perform sophisticated cognitive tasks such as planning, reasoning, and problem solving using symbols derived from perception. Theories of these high-level tasks are still deeply invested in amodal symbols. Accounts of reasoning, for example, are often based on formal calculi in which symbols are arbitrarily related to their referents. Attempts to ground reasoning in less arbitrary media are not uncommon (e.g., Johnson-Laird, 1983), but these accounts rarely exploit symbols that are as rich and perceptually based as those we have been advertising. We must develop accounts and, ultimately, models that can explain reasoning using perceptual symbols. In addition, we must develop ways of implementing a system capable of context-sensitive productivity. As we have argued, formation rules that are overly sensitive to context impede productivity. It is a challenge to construct a system that allows for accommodation without sacrificing this important form of mundane creativity (see Prinz, 2001: chapter 11).

Using existing technologies and techniques, we could probably construct extremely primitive perceptual symbol systems. For example, we can construct an input system by attaching a video camera to a sophisticated analog-to-digital converter; we can construct an integration mechanism by introducing a system that filters the digital outputs of the input system and writes them to memory; and, finally, we can construct a high-level system that can access and manipulate the representations stored by the integration mechanism. In a trivial sense, this would qualify as a perceptual symbol system, but it would lack sophistication. Constructing a model that approximates the complexity of the symbol systems used by real organisms is still far out of reach. The challenges mentioned in the last three paragraphs must be met. This requires a change in strategy. All too often, researchers limit their attention to either perception or cognition without exploring their relationship. In arguing that cognition exploits perceptual symbols, we hope to motivate the reconsideration of this methodological myopia. We suspect that a broader perspective that acknowledges the perceptual basis of cognition will prove more fruitful. At this stage it is probably too early to predict what kind of architecture will be needed. An adequate model of a perceptual symbol system might require some technological advances. Nevertheless, we strongly encourage attempts to model perceptual symbol systems using existing technologies. We strongly believe that analysis of creativity will benefit significantly from the exploration of systems that integrate perception and cognition.

ACKNOWLEDGMENT

The research reported in this chapter was supported by National Science Foundation Grant SBR-9421326 to the first author. The authors would like to thank the editor, Terry Dartnall, for his many valuable comments.

DISCUSSION

TD: You provide an account of cognition that emphasizes the importance of perception, and that tells a story of how we acquire concepts from perceptual symbols, which are "idealized facsimiles of perceptual representations." As you say, this story has much in keeping with a tradition that originates in Aristotle, but which is most obviously associated with Classical Empiricism—and which is commonly believed to have failed. You attribute this failure to naive beliefs about the nature of perception: the historical account sees perceptually derived symbols as relatively unstructured, conscious images, whereas you believe that they are structured but inaccessible to consciousness, and you set out to rehabilitate the traditional account by equipping it with a more sophisticated theory of perception.

JP/LB: That's right. Classical Empiricism fell into disfavor for several reasons. One was an inadequate theory of perception. Another problem we don't address is an inadequate theory of learning. Hume's associationism fueled the idea that empiricists are committed to very simplistic theories of learning. This forged an alliance between empiricism and behaviorism, which has contributed to anti-empiricist sentiments in cognitive science. Locke also did a disservice by focusing on nativism in the first book of his Essay. This has led people to believe that empiricists must deny the innateness of everything. Actually, Locke was primarily concerned with the innateness of principles, especially principles of religion and logic. Here his interest was partially political: Locke was a crusader for tolerance and was impressed by increased European awareness of human cultural diversity. Delimiting innateness is an important part of the empiricist platform, but this can be taken too far. Empiricism is first and foremost a positive thesis about the perceptual origins of mental representation. There can be significant innate biases built into our senses. Empiricism should be divorced from implausibly extreme forms of anti-nativism, from simplistic theories of learning, and from inadequate theories of perception.

TD: My first question is this. How does talk about idealization or schematization help you? Isn't the problem with the traditional account *just* that idealization won't deliver the goods? What I mean is this. The Classical Empiricists said that we derive our concepts (they called them "ideas") from corresponding impressions, or percepts (roughly, experiences). Impressions give rise to simple ideas, and simple ideas are combined to form complex ones. But how do we form the *general* concept "dog"? According to Classical Empiricism this has to be some sort of visual image, but it's difficult to see what kind of an image it could be. It would have to cover the properties of everything from a Great Dane to a Chihuahua, but exclude similar things, such as rats, cats and possums. You say that perceptual systems "must abstract away the irrelevant details of incoming signals, separate aspects of a signal that are independent, and introduce a significant amount of structure." This schematization is demanded by "behavioral evidence that we can recognize commonality across very different inputs." You say that we can recognize commonality across different inputs because we have highly structured, schematized inner symbols. But how can *any* symbols be flexible enough to pick out the relevant commonalities? How can we have a "general idea" of a dog (in the sense of some kind of inner copy of a percept, whether schematized or not), which picks out Great Danes and Chihuahuas, but doesn't pick out rats, cats, and possums?

JP/LB: There are several things to say here. First of all, there is absolutely no question that we succeed in reliably identifying dogs and distinguishing them from other quadrupeds. There is no question that we can do this on the basis of information garnered through the senses. Now it may be that we have to learn some of this through explicit instruction; we might have to be taught that Great Danes and Chihuahuas go together. But, then again, we may not. Eimas and Quinn (1994) have shown basic level categorization in three-month-olds, and every parent knows how successfully their toddlers extend categories. All the publicized instances of over extension are counter-balanced by remarkable success, when, for instance, young children effortlessly identify cartoon dogs as belonging to the same category as their pet Spot. Our perceptual systems are great at this kind of pattern recognition, and schematized representations may play a role in that.

Second, we don't want to stop with schematization. We fear that our discussion has left the misleading impression that all categories can be represented using a single perceptual symbol. This is quite wrong. In most cases, we rely on multiple category representations. We may have a family of different dog representations stored in memory corresponding to dogs we have experienced. One might have one perceptual symbol for Cujo and another for Benji. These exemplars may be similar enough to co-classify in memory, but distinct enough to warrant storage of separate symbols. In addition, we can spontaneously create new category representations during online processing. Contextual demands can be met by mixing and combining parts of existing perceptual symbols. Relatedly, we must underscore our conviction that individual perceptual symbols can be modified online to fit contextual demands. This is partially achieved through the structure introduced in the process of schematization. For example, schematization might generate a decomposable representation of a normal, four-legged dog, which can be used to identify or simulate a three-legged dog, by simply removing a part. In sum, we believe that categories generally have multiple representations and that each of these representations can be modified to achieve a high degree of flexibility.

Third, there is a general question of how we ever have mental representations that refer to dogs and only dogs. Empiricists are sometimes saddled with the view that reference depends on resemblance. On that view, a perceptual representation could not refer to all and only dogs, because, no matter how schematized, no representation could resemble all and only dogs. We think resemblance, or structural isomorphism, does contribute to our ability to plan, categorize, and reason, but it is insufficient for reference. A dog representation refers to dogs partially in virtue of the fact that it has certain causal relations to dogs. Simplifying a bit, one can say that representations of dogs refer to dogs in virtue of the fact that they were initially created as a result of dog encounters or in virtue of their ability to reliably (though not infallibly) detect dogs when they are present. This explanation of the reference relation enjoys support across the empiricist and non-empiricist divide.

TD: Another notorious problem for Classical Empiricism is what we might call the "problem of the representational veil." Locke believed that what we are directly aware of are ideas in our minds and he believed that some of these ideas represent properties of things in the world, whereas others do not. Locke's problem now is that his ideas cut him off from the world. He has no independent access to the world, so that he can't know which ideas correspond to properties of things in the world and which do not. This leads to a dilemma for you, I think. Either we have independent access to the world (other than through our ideas or representations or symbols) or we do not. If we do not, we are trapped inside our own representations. If we do, then we must know about the world *already,* and in this case it is difficult to see why we need representations, or perceptual symbols, at all. In order to know that a representation is a representation of a lion or an antelope we *already* need to know about lions and antelopes, and if this is the case, why do we need representations? Maybe the situation is a bit like using a road map. A road map is useful, but a driver who doesn't have independent access to the road isn't going to survive for very long!

I think we can see this problem fairly clearly if we look at your Figure 2.2, of the running legs. You present these as examples of perceptual symbols. You say they have been derived from perceptual representations by a process of idealization, so that they are non-arbitrary; and they are schematic, so that they capture commonalities in the inputs.

It seems to me that we can only know that these symbols are symbols of legs if we already know about legs. And we can only know that they are symbols of people or lions or antelopes, if we already know about people and lions and antelopes. We can flesh them out and see them as representations of people or lions or antelopes, but this is because we already know much more about these things than we find in their representations. The symbols could be different, and we would still be able to recognize them as symbols of people or lions or antelopes, just so long as we already knew about these things, and knew that the symbols are meant to represent them. It seems that the cognitive load in these cases is carried, not by the symbols, but by our *knowledge about* the symbols and what they represent. I think this was Wittgenstein's point when he rejected his picture theory of meaning: representations don't inherently picture or represent. They do so by virtue of the conventions that we use to map them onto the world. It's also the gist of traditional rationalism, which emphasizes the active, constructive role of the knowledge that we bring to experience, and which downplays the importance of manipulating and combining stored copies of experience.

That's more of a statement than a question, but would you like to comment?

JP/LB: These are interesting issues, which could take us on a ride through the history of philosophy. There is a long-standing debate about whether Locke held a veil of perception view. Like much in Locke, you can find textual support for various interpretations. Historically, there have been two primary alternatives to the veil of perception. One denies the existence of mental representations entirely. Somehow, we directly experience the world. We are not convinced that this is a serious possibility. First, planning, adaptive response, complexly structured performance, and creativity all seem to depend on inner mental representations. Traditional rationalists and empiricists all agreed about this, but the lesson had to be rediscovered again and again in cognitive science. The arguments are too famous to rehearse. Second, representations are not mysterious or ontologically expensive. On our view, they are just neural events, typically elicited by external impingement on the senses, or by inner mechanisms that reactivate sensory states. If we embrace representations, we must opt for the second alternative to a veil of perception. The second alternative says that there is no veil, because inner representations are not themselves the objects of perception. Perceiving isn't a matter of seeing an inner image and inferring the world. Rather, it is a matter of seeing the world by having an inner representation of it. Likewise, it doesn't make sense to talk about understanding our mental representations. They are not the objects of understanding, but the vehicles of understanding. What we understand is the world. In that sense, internal symbols are utterly distinct from external symbols. To know that the word "antelope" refers to antelopes, one needs to learn a convention, which requires an independent handle on what antelopes are. A mental representation of an antelope, in contrast, represents antelopes in virtue of being a neural state caused in some way by interactions between antelopes and our sensory transducers. We never need to figure out what that neural state means. Its meaning stems from the way it was formed and from the way it allows us to respond to antelopes when we encounter them. We are not trapped looking at our own representations and we are not capable of accessing the world without representations. There is a middle way: representations give us the world.

TD: So far we've talked about cognition, so here's a question about creativity (although it is really a continuation of my previous questions). I agree that creativity is a litmus for cognition. In Dartnall (1994) I call it the "acid test" for the claim that machines can be intelligent. But my suspicion is that your account of cognition fails the test. A key factor in creativity is *cognitive flexibility* (see the chapters in this collection by McGraw & Hofstadter and Partridge & Rowe). The fact is that we can imagine pretty much anything. We can imagine our favorite politician riding a donkey, we can imagine him with a green face, with red hair and horns, and so on. An active, constructive, account of cognition, couched in terms of our knowledge about representations and the world, can account for this ability. It can say that we construct representations in the imagination, deploying our knowledge about things in the world, and that we modify them by using our general knowledge of the properties of things in the world (for instance, that shapes and colors can vary). This is a different story to yours, which talks in terms of making copies of experience— schematized copies, but copies nonetheless. Now you can either stick with your copy-and-schematize account as it is, *or* you can amplify it by introducing knowledge-about, as generalized, nonperceptual knowledge. If you stick with it, you will be stuck with a fixed representational repertoire that will give you very little cognitive flexibility. And such an account flies in the face of our everyday experience, which is that we modify things in the imagination all the time (as in the case of the politician and the donkey). In fact you don't stick with this account. You amplify it with *knowledge about:*

> Any differences between the representation of a lion running and an armadillo running might be extrapolated from *knowledge about* differences in the anatomies of these two animals (e.g., *knowledge about* the length of their legs). In other words, knowledge of a simple rule for modifying leg positions sequentially, coupled with specific information about the length and number of an animal's legs, can be sufficient for representing an animal running, even if a cognizer has never seen the animal run." (my emphasis.)

You say that we have a *general* symbol for running, plus *knowledge about* the anatomy of the two animals (such as the length of their legs). Now it seems to me that you have two problems. You have the problem about general symbols (in this case, "running") *and* you have to provide an account of what it is to know about something (in this case, the anatomy of the two animals). Since you have to provide an account of knowing-about anyway, why not let it do *all* the work? Look at the running case. We know a great deal about running. We know about bodies and legs, and how we move them to get from one place to another. And we also know (and this isn't allowed by your symbols) that we can run on our hands and arms, or with our fingers ("he ran his fingers up her arm"); we know that we can run downhill in a car, and that if we are in freefall and "running" with our legs, we aren't really running at all. Since knowing-about can provide us with all this general knowledge, why do we need general perceptual symbols at all? They are problematic anyway.

Of course, I could say the same thing about representations or inner images, and we certainly have these, so isn't this an existence proof of representations and inner images, and aren't these at least *similar* to perceptual symbols? Well, the fact that we have representations and inner images doesn't mean that they are extracted from experience. I believe that we *construct* them in the imagination, using our knowledge about things in the world. And the fact that we construct them, and can vary them at will, accounts for the flexibility and fecundity of our imagination.

JP/LB: Here, again, we may not have been sufficiently clear. The worry may stem from the false impression that each category is represented by a single, static symbol on our view. It is very much part of our story that we have multiple representations of categories and that we can freely recombine perceptual symbols to form representations of novel objects and events. We can imagine a politician with a green face and horns riding a donkey. This is a forte of perceptual symbols as a matter of fact. Here we borrow a page from Hume, who talked about representing golden mountains by combining an idea of gold with an idea of a mountain, both construed perceptually. By saying symbols are perceptual, we mean that they are neural states in our input systems. But states in these systems have complex parts. The visual system, for example, processes color, motion, and form separately. Our view is that the brain can generate combinations of perceptual features not found together in experience. We typically do this by taking features that are found in experience (say, the color red and a person's face) and putting them together. Putting perceptual symbols together exploits the same binding mechanisms that are found in ordinary perception. When we see a face that is pink or brown, color centers and face-shape centers coordinate their activity in some way (perhaps through oscillation synchrony and receptive field coincidence). When we imagine a red face, we call up a face-shape from memory by reactivating a pattern in the face-shape center in our visual system, then we reactivate the neural pattern for red in our color system, and finally we bind these in the usual way. Accumulating perceptual symbols can be a passive process in the first instance, but, once acquired they can be creatively and constructively recombined.

The second worry you raised concerns our suggestion that we have general symbols and knowledge about various properties of objects. If we have this knowledge about properties, why have the general symbols? For example, why do we have both knowledge of armadillo leg length and a general symbol for quadrupedal running? If we don't need both, we might as well do away with the running symbol and stick to the knowledge of armadillo properties. The answer to this worry is related to the last point. Our ability to creatively recombine symbols allows us to imagine many things we have never seen or even thought of imagining. Suppose I have never seen an armadillo run. I might have never stored explicit knowledge of what that would look like. But I do have knowledge of what other creatures look like when they run and knowledge of what armadillos look like. I can combine these two, to predict what a running armadillo will look like. This kind of recombination is invaluable. Police can identify a culprit who has been described as being an albino in an orange jump suit, by combining perceptual symbols, even if they have never seen such a combination. Having general knowledge of what running looks like, or of what jumpsuits, or orange, or albinos look like, is useful because it can be creatively recombined. There is another reason for such knowledge. We often benefit from our ability to detect commonalities across distinct entities. We benefit from our ability to see that a running lion and a running armadillo are both engaged in the same kind of activity, running. Having a schematized symbol for running may help in this. Finally, we should point out that the contrast between general symbols and knowledge about properties is not intended to be sharp. Knowledge about properties is general in that it can apply to many individual objects. Knowledge of armadillo anatomy applies to many armadillos. More importantly, we fear that we have left the impression that such knowledge is not contained in perceptual symbols. To the contrary. Knowledge of armadillo anatomy and knowledge of the dynamic forms involved in running are both represented perceptually. Likewise for other kinds of knowledge we have. Knowledge about different ways one can run can be presented perceptually. It isn't obvious that one can run with one's hands. The fact that some might not count this as running can be explained by the fact that it departs from a typical perceptual representation of running; the fact that others would count it as running can be explained by the fact that the dynamic symbol for rapidly moving legs might be similar to the symbol for rapidly moving arms. Freefall leg movements are also a borderline case, but they might be excluded because typical perceptual representations of running depict leg-forms contacting a surface. Our appeal to knowledge does not require representations that lie outside of the perceptual symbols view.

TD: One last thing. I don't see how an account of cognition that's based on reassembling and rearranging the contents of experience, however idealized and schematized, can account for "abstract" cognition. I take this to include not only thinking that involves abstract concepts such as truth and beauty, but counterfactual and highly relational cognition, and any cognition that can't be cashed out in terms of something like inner images. How do you account for our ability to have abstracts ideas, and to realize that if Attila the Hun was alive today he wouldn't be in favor of the welfare state? I think we have to provide a "knowledge-about" account of things such as this.

JP/LB: Abstract concepts are actually everyone's problem. Opponents of perceptual symbols sometimes say, "Aha, you can't explain beauty, virtue, and truth, but we can." How do they explain these concepts? Well, they say we have symbols in the head for beauty, virtue, and truth. But how do these symbols represent anything? How can an abstract symbol, a mere squiggle in the head, have any meaning? Merely appealing to such symbols is a cheat, until you have given a theory of meaning. The best theories of meaning often turn out to involve our ability to recognize instances of a concept or to engage in verbal behavior ("language games"). Both of these can be explained by perceptual symbols. Language games can be explained by appeal to perceptual representations of words and sentences, stored in lexical networks. Knowledge of what a welfare state is may consist, partially, in being able to produce certain sentences. These, in turn, get their meaning by associations with other perceptual symbols or by complex patterns of social interaction and deference. Language allows us to track properties whose perceivable manifestations are too distributed to be verified by a single individual. Instance recognition, which turns out to be pivotal for abstract conceptualization, involves our ability to perceptually identify instances by their appearance and by the internal states (including emotional states) that they produce in us. Beauty is an obvious example. We reiterate, once more, that a single category can have multiple representations on our view. Abstract concepts may each be associated with a variety of verbal information and an ability to simulate multiple different instances. We do not think there is a single image corresponding to virtue, for example.

You focus on another problem, however, which deserves to be addressed. How do we represent counterfactuals and other abstract relations? These can be regarded as ways of manipulating perceptual symbols. Consider counterfactuals. A counterfactual thought may involve a way of forming perceptual simulations. Simplifying a bit, you can be said to have a counterfactual thought if you form a simulation representing some nonactual state of affairs, P, and you are disposed, upon doing so, to add a representation of another state of affairs, Q, to your representation. This is a way of representing the fact that Q would have occurred if P had been the case. The point is that such abstract relations need not be pictured themselves. We don't need an image of the counterfactual relation to be an empiricist. Instead, such relations are methods of constructing perceptual simulations. The suggestion has been one of the great contributions of Johnson-Laird's work on mental models. Johnson-Laird is less obviously committed to perceptual representations than we are, but he heroically shows how such representations might participate in patterns of reasoning that have been presumed to undermine empiricism.

In closing, we would like to suggest that the interesting problem in cognitive science is not, "How is abstract thought possible?" but rather, "How is thought possible at all?" We must explain how our minds come to carry information in a way that allows us to successfully negotiate the world. There seem to be three possibilities. One is that we think using internal symbols that are entirely unrelated to perceptual states. Another is that we think using nonperceptual symbols that are grounded by links to perceptual states. The final view is that we think using perceptual states. The first view can be rejected, because, short of magic, there is no way to explain how symbols dissociated from perception could ever convey world knowledge or allow for environmentally adaptive behavior. The second view can also be rejected. If we have perceptual states connecting our minds to the world, there is no reason to add on an extra layer of nonperceptual symbols. This, of course, depends on showing that perceptual states can serve as symbols that can do all the work of alleged nonperceptual symbols. There is increasing evidence that people do, in fact, think using perceptual symbols. We have been trying to uncover more evidence and to demonstrate that well designed perceptual symbol systems can actually outperform their nonperceptual competitors. We are very grateful for all the challenging questions that help us explore, sharpen, and improve on this empiricist vision.

NOTES

1. The reader is encouraged to consult these papers for a more detailed comparison of amodal and perceptual symbol systems.

2. Cases in which genesis is instigated by cognitive systems are those in which the product of a creative act is external to the cognitive system. For example, a painting is created by hands whose activities are instigated by cognitive systems.

3. Some philosophers and computer scientists do not define symbols as representations. They define symbols by their formal or syntactic properties alone. In contrast, we think representation is the primary function of symbols.

4. Primitive symbols need not be innate or unstructured. Compare Mandler (1992).

5. Though, see, for example, Churchland (1986) and Dartnall (1996a; 1996b; 2000; this volume).

6. We will use the term "object" loosely here. The "objects of perception" can include aspects, properties, situations, events, and so on.

7. Spatial relation symbols may be modified by the objects that fill them, however. Filling might occur by replacing empty regions with object symbols, and the distance between empty regions may be affected by the identity of the object symbols that fill them.

8. Edelman & Reeke (1990) argue further that we need to endow our models with means of manipulating their environments.

REFERENCES

Aristotle (1961). *De Anima, Books II and III* (D. W. Hamlyn, Trans.). Oxford: Oxford University Press.

Barsalou, L. W. (1982). Context-independent and context-dependent information in concepts. *Memory & Cognition, 10,* 82–93.

Barsalou, L. W. (1983). Ad hoc categories. *Memory and Cognition, 11,* 211–227.

Barsalou, L. W. (1987). The instability of graded structure: Implications for the nature of concepts. In U. Neisser (Ed.), *Concepts and conceptual development: Ecological and intellectual factors in categorization.* Cambridge: Cambridge University Press.

Barsalou, L. W. (1989). Intra-concept similarity and its consequences for inter-concept similarity. In S. Vosniadou & A. Ortony (Eds.), *Similarity and analogical reasoning.* Cambridge: Cambridge University Press.

Barsalou, L. W. (1991). Deriving categories to achieve goals. In G. H. Bower (Ed.), *The psychology of learning and motivation: Advances in research and theory.* Stanford, CA: Stanford University Press.

Barsalou, L. W. (1992). Frames, concepts, and conceptual fields. In A. Lehrer & E. F. Kittay (Eds.), *Frames, fields and contrasts: New essays in semantic and lexical organization.* Hillsdale, NJ: Lawrence Erlbaum and Associates.

Barsalou, L. W. (1993). Flexibility, structure, and linguistic vagary in concepts: Manifestations of a compositional system of perceptual symbols. In A. Collins, S. Gathercole, M. Conway, & P. Morris (Eds.), *Theories of memory.* Hillsdale, NJ: Lawrence Erlbaum and Associates.

Barsalou, L. W. (1999). Perceptual symbol systems. *Behavioral and Brain Sciences, 22,* 577–660.

Barsalou, L. W., & Prinz, J. J. (1997). Mundane creativity in perceptual symbol systems. In T. B. Ward, S. M. Smith, & J. Vaid (Eds.), *Conceptual structures and processes: Emergence, discovery, and change.* Washington, DC: American Psychological Association.

Barsalou, L. W., Solomon, K. O., & Wu, L.-L. (1999). Perceptual simulation in conceptual tasks. In M. K. Hiraga, C. Sinha, & S. Wilcox (Eds.), *Cultural, typological, and psychological perspectives in cognitive linguistics: The proceedings of the fourth conference of the International Cognitive Linguistics Association, Vol. 3,* pp. 209–228. Amsterdam: John Benjamins.

Barsalou, L. W., Yeh, W., Luka, B. J., Olseth, K. L., Mix, K. S., & Wu, L.-L. (1993). Concepts and meaning. *Chicago Linguistics Society, 29,* 23–61.

Barwise, J., & Etchemendy, J. (1991). Visual information and valid reasoning. In W. Zimmerman & S. Cunningham (Eds.), *Visualization in mathematics.* Washington, DC: Mathematical Association of America.

Bechtel, W., & Abrahamsen, A. (1991). *Connectionism and the mind: An introduction to parallel processing in networks.* Oxford: Blackwell.

Berkeley, G. (1734). *A treatise concerning the principles of human knowledge* (2d ed.). Dublin.

Biederman, I. (1987). Recognition-by-components: A theory of human image understanding. *Psychological Review, 94,* 115–147.

Chomsky, N. (1957). *Semantic structures.* The Hague: Mouton.

Chomsky, N. (1968). *Language and mind.* New York: Harcourt.

Churchland, P. S. (1986). *Neurophilosophy: Toward a unified science of the mind/brain.* Cambridge, MA: MIT Press.

Clark, A. (1993). *Associative engines.* Cambridge, MA: MIT Press.

Craik, F. I. M., & Lockhart, R. S. (1972). Levels of processing: A framework for memory research. *Journal of Verbal Learning and Verbal Behavior, 11,* 671–684.

Craik, F. I. M., & Tulving, E. (1975). Depth of processing and the retention of words in episodic memory. *Journal of Experimental Psychology: General, 104,* 268–294.

Dartnall, T. H. (Ed.). (1994). *Artificial Intelligence and creativity: An interdisciplinary approach.* Dordrecht: Kluwer.

Dartnall, T. H. (1996a). Redescription, information and access. In D. Peterson (Ed.), *Forms of representation: An interdisciplinary theme for cognitive science.* Exeter: Intellect Books.

Dartnall, T. H. (1996b). Retelling the representational story: An anti-representationalist's agenda. *Communication & Cognition, 29,* 479–500.

Dartnall, T. H. (2000). Reverse psychologism, cognition and content. *Minds and Machines, 10,* 31–52.

Dennett, D. C. (1969). *Content and consciousness.* London: Routledge.

Donald, M. (1991). *Origins of the modern mind: Three stages in the evolution of culture and cognition.* Cambridge, MA: Harvard University Press.

Edelman G. M., & Reeke, G. N. (1990). Is it possible to construct a perception machine? *Proceedings of the American Philosophical Society, 134,* 36–73.

Eimas, P. D., & Quinn, P. C. (1994). Studies on the formation of perceptually based basic-level categories in young infants. *Child Development, 65,* 903–917.

Elman, J. L. (1992). Grammatical structure and distributed representations. In S. Davis (Ed.), *Connectionism: Theory and practice.* Oxford: Oxford University Press.

Finke, R. A., Pinker, S., & Farah, M. J. (1989). Reinterpreting visual patterns in mental imagery. *Cognitive Science, 13,* 51–78.

Fodor, J. A. (1975). *The language of thought.* Cambridge, MA: Harvard University Press.

Fodor, J. A., & Pylyshyn, Z. (1988). Connectionism and cognitive architecture: A critical analysis. In S. Pinker, & J. Mehler (Eds.), *Connections and symbols.* Cambridge, MA: MIT Press.

Geach, P. T. (1957). *Mental acts.* London: Routledge.

Gibbs, R. W. (1994). *The poetics of mind: Figurative thought, language, and understanding.* Cambridge: Cambridge University Press.

Glenberg, A. M. (1997). What memory is for. *Behavioral and Brain Sciences, 20,* 1–55.

Goodman, N. (1968). *Languages of art: An approach to a theory of symbols.* New York: Bobbs-Merrill.

Harnad, S. (1990). The symbol grounding problem. *Physica, D 42,* 335–346.

Haugeland, J. (1985). *Artificial intelligence: The very idea.* Cambridge, MA: MIT Press.

Haugeland, J. (1991). Representational genera. In W. Ramsey, S. P. Stich, & D. E. Rumelhart (Eds.), *Philosophy and connectionist theory.* Hillsdale, NJ: Lawrence Erlbaum and Associates.

Hinton, G. E. (1991). Representing part-whole hierarchies in connectionist networks. In G. Hinton (Ed.), *Connectionist symbol processing.* Cambridge, MA: MIT Press.

Hobbes, (1651). *Leviathan: Or the matter, forme and power of a commonwealth ecclesiaticall and civil.* London.

Hume, D. (1739). *A treatise on human nature.* London.

Hummel J. E., & Biederman, I. (1992). Dynamic binding in a neural network for shape recognition. *Psychological Review, 99,* 480–517.

Johnson, M. (1987). *The body in the mind: The bodily basis of meaning, imagination, and reason.* Chicago: University of Chicago Press.

Johnson-Laird, P. N. (1983). *Mental models.* Cambridge, MA: Harvard University Press.

Kasher, A. (1991). Pragmatics and Chomsky's research program. In A. Kasher (Ed.), *The Chomskyan turn.* Oxford: Blackwell.

Kosslyn, S. M. (1994). *Image and brain: The resolution of the imagery debate.* Cambridge, MA: Harvard University Press.

Lakoff, G. (1987). *Women, fire, and dangerous things.* Chicago: University of Chicago Press.

Langacker, R. W. (1987). *Foundations of cognitive grammar, volume I: Theoretical perspectives.* Stanford, CA: Stanford University Press.

Langacker, R. W. (1991). *Foundations of cognitive grammar, volume II: Descriptive application.* Stanford, CA: Stanford University Press.

Locke, J. (1706). *An essay concerning human understanding* (5th edition). London.

Mandler, J. M. (1992). How to build a baby: II. Conceptual primitives. *Psychological Review, 99,* 587–604.

Marr, D. (1982). *Vision: A computational investigation into the human representation and processing of visual information.* San Francisco: W. H. Freeman.

Mayr, E. (1982). *The growth of biological thought.* Cambridge, MA: Harvard University Press.

McGinn, C. (1989). *Mental content*. Oxford: Basil Blackwell.

Mitchell, W. T. (1990). *The logic of architecture: Design, computation, and cognition*. Cambridge, MA: MIT Press.

Newell, A. (1980). Physical symbol systems. *Cognitive Science, 4,* 135–183.

Newell, A., & Simon, H. A. (1976). Computer science as empirical inquiry: Symbols and search. *Communications of the Association for Computing Machinery, 19,* 113–126.

Olseth, K. L., & Barsalou, L. W. (1995). The spontaneous use of perceptual representations during conceptual processing. *Proceedings of the seventeenth annual meeting of the Cognitive Science Society,* 310–315. Hillsdale, NJ: Lawrence Erlbaum and Associates.

Perrett D., Harries, M., Mistlin, A. J., & Chitty, A. J. (1990). Three stages in the classification of body movements by visual neurons. In H. Barlow, C. Blakemore, & M. Weston-Smith (Eds.), *Images and understanding*. Cambridge: Cambridge University Press.

Pollack, J. (1990). Recursive distributed representations. *Artificial Intelligence, 46,* 77–105.

Price, H. H. (1953). *Thinking and experience*. Cambridge, MA: Harvard University Press.

Prinz, J. J. (2002). *Furnishing the mind: Concepts and their perceptual basis*. Cambridge, MA: MIT Press.

Pylyshyn, Z. W. (1984). *Computation and cognition*. Cambridge, MA: MIT Press.

Regier, T. (1996). *The human semantic potential: Spatial language and constrained connectionism*. Cambridge, MA: MIT Press.

Rollins, M. (1989). *Mental imagery: On the limits of cognitive science*. New Haven, CT: Yale.

Russell, B. (1921). *The analysis of mind*. New York: Macmillan.

Schwartz, R. (1981). Imagery—There's more to it than meets the eye. In N. Block (Ed.), *Imagery*. Cambridge, MA: MIT Press.

Smith, E. E., Medin, D. L., Rips, L. J., & Keane, M. (1988). Combining prototypes: A selective modification model. *Cognitive Science, 12,* 485–527.

Smolensky, P. (1988). On the proper treatment of connectionism. *Behavioral and Brain Sciences, 11,* 1–74.

Stein, L. A. (1994). Imagination and situated cognition. *Journal of Experimental and Theoretical Artificial Intelligence, 6,* 393–407.

Sweetser, E. E. (1990). *From etymology to pragmatics: Metaphorical and cultural aspects of semantic structure*. Cambridge: Cambridge University Press.

Talmy, L. (1983). How language structures space. In H. Pick & L. Acredolo (Eds.), *Spatial orientation: Theory, research, and application*. New York: Plenum.

Tomasello, M., Kruger, A. C., & Ratner, H. H. (1993). Cultural learning. *Behavioral and Brain Sciences, 16,* 495–552.

Ungerleider, L. G., & Mishkin, M. (1982). Two cortical visual systems. In D. J. Ingle, M. A. Goodale, & R. J. W. Mansfield (Eds.), *Analysis of visual behavior*. Cambridge, MA: MIT Press.

van Gelder, T. J. (1990). Compositionality: A connectionist variation on a classical theme. *Cognitive Science, 14,* 355–384.

Zeki, S. (1992). The visual image in mind and brain. *Scientific American, 267,* 3, 68–76.

3

Creativity and the Varieties of Explicitation

Donald M. Peterson

The phenomenon of creativity poses a challenge to our understanding of the knowledge and performance of cognitive systems, whether human or artificial. In particular, an apparent paradox attaches to the issue of novelty in creativity, as noted by Boden (1990). On the one hand, we expect something creative to be new and unforeseen; and yet on the other hand, we expect it to have origins and antecedents, and so we expect it not to be entirely new. Thus, the type or types of novelty involved in creativity require explanation and analysis.

The range of phenomena we call "creative" is very broad, and in this chapter I shall concentrate on those which involve "re-representation": cases in which we increase our knowledge by reconfiguring knowledge which we already possess. The internal, cognitive processes involved in such knowledge-expanding re-representation have been examined by Karmiloff-Smith (e.g., 1990, 1992, 1996), who has considered cases such as children's drawing, in which children become able to depart from known reality, and rearrange the elements of objects they know in order to draw imaginary objects. Other authors have focused on increases in problem-solving performance resulting from changes in external representations, such as formalisms and diagrams (see e.g., Amarel, 1968; Newell & Simon, 1972; Peterson, 1996). These may involve replacing the original notation, as in the case where Arabic numerical notation replaced Roman, or they may involve re-representation within the original notation, as performed in deductive logic. Such cases belong to the minor rather than to the dramatic end of the creative spectrum, but they have the advantage of being relatively tractable to analysis and experiment.

Examples of these phenomena will be considered below. In each case, we find one or another variety of "explicitation" in which new system output (the production of an imaginary drawing, the solution to a problem, etc.) becomes available. Such system output may previously have been available in principle, and so was implicit, but is now available in practice, and so has been made explicit. The etymology of the terms "implicit" and "explicit" may suggest a simple model. "Implicit" comes from the Latin *implicare,* and suggests something "enfolded" or "entangled," and "explicit" comes from *explicare,* and suggests something "unfolded" or "laid open." We might thus think of explicitation as revealing something that already exists, fully formed but hidden, so that what is involved is simply the process of uncovering it. We might call this the "Rabbit Model," since it is reminiscent of a real, live rabbit hiding in a hutch and then being induced to jump out.

This chapter will make three main points. First, following Dartnall (1996), re-representation crucially involves the issue of *access* to knowledge, and the types of explicitation examined below reveal not one but several types of such access. Second, however, the Rabbit Model oversimplifies the ways in which a procedure or part of the cognitive system gains applicability or access to internal or external representations. Third, for the minor cases of creativity considered here, analysis of the nature of the explicitation involved reveals that the apparent paradox of novelty, mentioned above, dissolves.

INTERNAL RE-REPRESENTATION

I turn first to explicitation as it has been investigated by Karmiloff-Smith. On the basis of a wide range of empirical evidence, primarily in developmental psychology, Karmiloff-Smith argues that we have the ability to explicitate knowledge held in our cognitive structures (internal representations) through a process of internal transformation that she calls "representational redescription." What begins as a structure *in* the system becomes available *to* the system: it becomes manipulable, flexible, and open to consciousness and verbal report.

Two of Karmiloff-Smith's cases are the general illustrative example of piano playing and the experimentally investigated case of children's drawing. In piano playing (Karmiloff-Smith, 1990; 1992), a point of behavioral mastery comes when the person can play a piece, but with distinct limitations. He or she cannot start in the middle, cannot insert parts from other pieces, cannot perform variations on what is written, cannot change the order of parts, and so on. If the pianist progresses, he or she will retain behavioral mastery, but will become free of some of these limitations, with a resulting increase in flexibility.

Now the case of children's drawing. By the age of 4–5 years, children have behavioral mastery in drawing such things as a man, a house or an animal. In a series of experiments, children were asked to draw a house, a man or an animal (which almost all could do), and then to draw one "which does not exist" (which most could do) (Karmiloff-Smith, 1990). That is, the children were verbally instructed to depart in their drawings from known reality. Children aged 4–6 were able to execute some moderate changes (shape of elements changed, shape of whole changed and deletion of elements), while those aged 8–10 were able in addition to execute more radical changes, such as inserting new elements, changing position or orientation, and inserting items from other categories (Karmiloff-Smith, 1990). Whereas deletions performed by the younger group were limited to the end of a drawing sequence, the older group was not so constrained. Karmiloff-Smith sees the ability of the older group as evidence of a developmental reduction in the "mechanical" nature of the relevant sequential procedures (though see Karmiloff-Smith, 1992). She describes this phenomenon by saying that the representations of the younger group were more implicit, while those of the older group, through re-representation, had become more explicit, with a resulting increase in flexibility.

Karmiloff-Smith's account of these phenomena goes beyond a simple implicit/explicit distinction and appeals to four levels of explicitness. Internal representations at the I (implicit) level are procedures which are available as a whole to the rest of the cognitive system, but which cannot be decomposed or manipulated by the rest of the system. Those at the E1 (explicit 1) level lack this bracketed quality, those at the E2 (explicit 2) level are available to consciousness, and those at the E3 (explicit 3) level are available to verbal report.

Karmiloff-Smith's re-representation is an "endogenously driven" propensity to "spontaneous" re-representation after what she calls "behavioral mastery" has been achieved. Re-representation is not driven by failure alone, but by a natural tendency to go beyond adequate proficiency. The success and stability of behavioral mastery is consistent with re-representation which can be stimulated by an "internal drive" that does not require external pressures, thus contrasting with Piagetian and behaviorist views of change. Karmiloff-Smith argues for a domain-specific "phase model" rather than a Piagetian "stage model": while the process of re-representation is the same in all domains, its actual occurrence in different domains is not developmentally synchronized. A child's representations may therefore be of one type in one domain and of another type in another domain.

For present purposes, two main points stand out here. First, this sort of explicitation involves the creation of new cognitive structures. A structure in I-format acquires a counterpart in E1-format, another in E2-format, and yet another in E3-format. Lower level structures are retained, but are supplemented by more accessible ones; and as one becomes four, the population of the cognitive system expands. Second, on this account explicitation involves three main elements: (a) the original structure, (b) a more explicit counterpart of that structure, and (c) other parts of the cognitive system.

An alternative account of explicitation, of the sort explored in Dartnall (1996), would speak, not of generating new structures, but of one and the same structure becoming increasingly accessible to the cognitive system. Viewed in this light, the I-level is characterized by a set of constraints which are increasingly shed at higher levels of explicitation. At the E1 level the structure loses its procedural, sequential character and its impenetrability to the rest of the cognitive system. At the E2 level it loses its unavailability to consciousness, and at the E3 level it loses its unavailability to verbal report. This model supposes less load on the cognitive system than the previous one, since it does not require multiplied counterpart representations, and the system does not have to maintain consistency between these counterparts.

On either of the above interpretations of internal explicitation, we have procedures with outputs: the piano-playing procedures produce musical performances, and the drawing procedures produce drawings. In both cases explicitation is a matter of another part of the cognitive system gaining access to a procedure so as to intervene and modify that output. Here, then, explicitation involves (a) the original procedure, (b) an "unbracketed" version of that procedure, (c) the part of the cognitive system which modulates the behavior of the unbracketed procedure, and (d) a new output resulting from this intervention. An output (for example, a modified performance or a fantasy-drawing) is "implicit" in the sense that it is merely potential, since the required modulation has not been or cannot be applied, and it becomes "explicit" or actualized when this happens. And it is clear that the Rabbit Model is inadequate here: we do not simply have a cognitive structure which comes out of hiding, but in addition some part of the cognitive system which, having gained access to that structure, is able to intervene and produce new system output.

NOTATIONAL RE-REPRESENTATION

I turn now to explicitation as it appears in the re-representation of externally notated inscriptions. Human beings have the capacity to extend their cognitive systems through the creation of inscriptions, written in one or other notation on paper, computer screens, and so on. These are not only means of communication with others but also a form of working memory which is used as an extension to the cognitive system. In the case of external inscriptions as in the case of internal cognitive structures, our knowledge may be amplified through restructuring: the introduction of a new notation for what we had already written down may increase our abilities to answer questions and solve problems (see Peterson, 1996). Arithmetic calculation, for example, was facilitated by the transition from Roman to

Arabic numerals, mathematical calculation was facilitated by the introduction of algebraic notations, logical proof was facilitated by the introduction of the predicate calculus, and navigation of the London Underground system was facilitated by the introduction of the well-known topological Underground Map.

Taking the case of numerical notation, the modern system of Arabic decimal numerals uses a positional notation, the base 10, and the numeral zero. In this system a numeral signifies a sum of products of powers of the base, the power being indicated by position: a numeral ABCD signifies $(A \times 10^3)$ + $(B \times 10^2)$ + $(C \times 10^1)$ + $(D \times 10^0)$. There have been a great many numeral systems. The Babylonians had a positional system with base 60 but without a zero. The Mayans had a positional system with zero and base 20, although here the third digit indicates not multiples of 20^2 but of 20×18 in order to give the days in their year a simpler representation. The system of Roman numerals has several variants, but generally few primary symbols are used (e.g., I, V, X, L and C), and these are arranged according to additive and subtractive principles. Different systems suit different purposes. "Grouping systems" are useful for keeping incremental tallies, and Roman numerals have the advantage that few primary symbols have to be remembered. But the overwhelming advantage of a positional system with zero is that it makes possible a divide-and-conquer strategy for the basic arithmetic operations of addition, subtraction, multiplication and division. This is achieved by a simple operation of "carrying" that is iterated over the columns of numerals. It is not the expressive power of the notation which is at issue here, but its syntactic consistency, its lack of superfluous structure, and the facilitating effect which these have on the application of arithmetic procedures.

In positional notation, each digit has an associated multiplier (a power of the base), and this multiplier is "built into" the syntax in the form of the digit's position. If two numerals are "lined up," so are their digits' multipliers, and arithmetic operations can proceed in a simple iterative way. We can contrast this with Roman notation, where lining up two numerals does not produce such a concordance. The numeral "XVII" is built on additive principles, whereas "XIV" is built on additive and subtractive principles. The positions of the digits cannot be straightforwardly interpreted as with "17" and "14." The advantage of positional over Roman numerical notation, then, is not "representational": it is not a matter of expressive power over a domain, since both systems can denote numbers adequately. Rather, it is due to the fact that numerical structures in a positional notation are *accessible* to simple, efficient, and uniform arithmetic procedures which facilitate calculation.

Generally speaking, then, such explicitation involves (a) a task, (b) features of a domain, (c) a procedure to which these features are made accessible, (d) a notation in which these features are made salient, and (e) a user for whom the procedure is tractable. In short, domain features are made accessible to a user-tractable procedure through salience in a notation. And as in the previous cases, issues of access and procedure are prominent, and the Rabbit Model over-simplifies what is involved.

WEAK NOTATIONAL RE-REPRESENTATION

The previous section looked at the general issue of re-representation through notational change. We now look at re-representation *within* a given notation. We will define "weak notational re-representation" as the transition from one inscription to another *within the same notational language,* where the new inscription expresses all or part of what is expressed by the first. One example of this is source-to-source program transformation in computing, in which a program is transformed into a more efficient counterpart in the same programming language. Another example is to be found in deductive logic.

Consider the set of premises {A → B, ~B, A v C} and the question "Does C follow?" Even in such a simple case, we do not usually have a procedure (an inference rule) for immediately deriving an answer. But we can make a start by employing the inference rule *modus tollens,* "given X → Y and ~Y, infer ~X." We then get the set {~A, A v C}. In absolute, informational terms, this constitutes a reduction in information, rather than something new. But in terms of accessibility, it does introduce something new: we can now apply the rule of "disjunctive syllogism" which says "given X v Y and ~X, infer Y," and so derive the set {C}, and hence we can answer the original question "Does C follow?" in the affirmative. The point here is that the first weak re-representation, effected by *modus tollens,* produces a result that is accessible or tractable to the further operation of disjunctive syllogism, which in turn solves the problem. The application of *modus tollens* is therefore ampliative (knowledge expanding) in the sense that it makes the following stage possible.

This variety of explicitation involves (a) a first set of sentences, (b) a second set of sentences, (c) a rule which gets us from the first to the second, and (d) a further rule which can be applied to the second set but not the first, and which solves a problem. The key notion, as in the previously examined cases, is that of *access,* since the explicitation achieved through the first rule allows the second rule to be applied.

In logical theory, an apparent paradox attaches to the issue of whether deductive reasoning is ampliative. The first arm of the paradox says that deduction cannot be ampliative, since in a valid deductive argument the sense of the premises "contains" the sense of the conclusion. That is, the conclusion of a valid deduction does not express new information, but only draws out what is already there in the premises, and this is why the conclusion follows with necessity from the premises (see Peterson, 1990;

Salmon, 1966). The second arm of the paradox says that deduction *is* ampliative since in fact it enables us to work out answers to questions, and without it our knowledge would be impoverished (cf. Frege, 1884/1978; Dummett, 1973/1978).

The apparent paradox is worth mentioning because its two arms are the products of two different views of the processing of information. The conception behind the first arm, if it considers a mind at all, assumes a cognitive system of absolute power that is indifferent to the format in which information is presented to it. The conception behind the second arm is that adopted here, and assumes a cognitive system of limited and particular processing powers, for which representational format will affect which of its limited set of procedures can be applied, and hence what output can be produced.

STRONG NOTATIONAL RE-REPRESENTATION

We now turn to the case of "strong notational re-representation," in which an epistemic advance is achieved through transition from one inscription to another, where the second does not belong to the same notational language as the first (cf. Amarel, 1968; Boden, 1987; Larkin & Simon, 1987; Peterson, 1994; Peterson, 1996). I shall take as an example the game of Number Scrabble, and its re-representation as presented by Newell and Simon (1972). Nine cards, each bearing a different numeral between 1 and 9, are placed face-up between the two players. The players draw cards alternately, and the first player to acquire three cards which sum to 15 wins. (If the cards are exhausted without either player acquiring a winning triplet, then the result is a draw.) This is not the world's most difficult game, but it is quite hard, especially at speed, to pick cards which will: (a) produce a winning triplet, (b) prevent one's opponent from gaining a winning triplet, and (c) create a "fork" situation in which either of two cards will produce a winning triplet (so that whatever the opponent chooses, one still wins on the next draw).

The key to re-representing the problem is that it has a structure which can be presented in a diagram so that it is accessible to (of all things!) the procedures of the game of tic-tac-toe. There are 8 triples that add up to 15: {{2,7,6}, {2,9,4}, {2,5,8}, {9,5,1}, {4,3,8}, {6,5,4}, {7,5,3}, {6,1,8}}. These triples have an intersection pattern, in that various triples share a common element. The nature of the game requires us to navigate our way through this pattern, and so it will be advantageous to make this pattern accessible to appropriate and pre-existing reasoning procedures. Newell and Simon's re-representation does this by employing a 3-by-3 magic square that places the numerals 1 to 9 in a matrix so that each row, column and diagonal sums to 15 (see Figure 3.1). We now play tic-tac-toe on this square. The ampliativity of this re-representation is evident. The initial representation of the game requires us to proceed by using arithmetic calculation and memory. In

FIGURE 3.1
3-by-3 magic square.

2	7	6
9	5	1
4	3	8

---

the magic square re-representation, we can proceed by using our capacities of spatial reasoning and visual pattern recognition. Instead of using our memories we can mark off both players' moves by drawing in Os and Xs, and the crucial configurations such as winning triples and forks are easily recognized. Moreover, the required procedures are familiar to anyone who already knows how to play tic-tac-toe. And if the re-representation were known to only one player (for example, if the game were played at speed over the telephone), this would put that player at a significant advantage.

In the present process of explicitation, we start with an initial representation in ordinary language. We then apply concepts from elementary set theory to it, which do not appear in the representation. We then calculate, either by hand or by using a computer program, to discover the intersection pattern. This information is *emergent* relative to the initial representation, since it is not provided in that representation (cf. Peterson, 1994). We then incorporate this into a diagram, with the advantages described above. This sort of explicitation involves several factors: (a) the initial representation of the problem, (b) new concepts, (c) calculation, (d) emergent information, (e) a diagram, and (f) the cognitive capacities of the user of the diagram. To state the obvious, the Rabbit Model of explicitness is insufficient to explain this case. We are not dealing simply with a hidden object that is made "visible" in some absolute sense, but with all of the above factors.

EXPLICITATION AND CREATIVITY

I have taken a systemic approach to knowledge, which acknowledges not only the things we say and think (our beliefs, our system output) but also the cognitive processes and changes which allow us to say and think these things. And the change with which I have been concerned is explicitation (rearrangement, re-representation) which produces new output from old structures. The cases identified differ in detail as indicated by the different relations of explicitness described, but each involves an increase in some sort of cognitive access.

This allows us to characterize the *creativity* of explicitation. Explicitation is creative where its new access allows new system output (answers to questions, responses to problems, etc.) to be produced. That is: a particular procedure or process becomes applicable, and new system-output can be produced as a result. Thus both the access and the system output at issue are new (at least to the particular cognitive system), but the knowledge or procedure accessed is not.

This can be seen in the examples discussed above. In Karmiloff-Smith's cases, the children's drawing procedures are not new: what is new is that they become accessible and manipulable, and so new drawings become possible. Likewise, the procedure for playing a piano piece is not new: what is new is again that it becomes accessible and manipulable, with the result that the performance can be altered in a flexible manner. In the case of numerical notation, our knowledge of numerical facts need not change: what changes is that the new representational format makes this knowledge tractable to simple and effective procedures which enhance calculation. In the case of logical deduction, what is asserted in our conclusion does not go beyond what is asserted in the premises (as is revealed by analysis in terms of truth-conditions): what changes is its tractability to further procedures. In the case of Number Scrabble, the game remains the same and we do not change the basic rules: what is new is tractability to effective and pre-existing procedures for visual reasoning.

This bears on the apparent paradox of creativity mentioned previously. We have something new and something not new, but this is no paradox, since cause and effect operate at different levels. In creative explicitation, the cause is that a procedure or part of the cognitive system gains applicability or access to internal or external representations, and the effect is an amplification of system-output. Thus the effect is an emergent phenomenon: it has a cause, but this is not of its own type (it does not itself constitute an item of system-output). Hence the result of explicitation may be *new* without its lacking antecedents, history and cause; and the explicitation itself may, without paradox, be creative.

ACKNOWLEDGMENT

I am grateful to Terry Dartnall and Antoni Diller for helpful comments on previous drafts. Address for correspondence: D. M. Peterson, Cognitive Science Research Centre, School of Computer Science, University of Birmingham, Edgbaston, Birmingham, B15 2TT, U.K. Email: d.m.peterson @cs.bham.ac.uk.

DISCUSSION

TD: Do you think that explicitation gives us *new knowledge,* or does it make old knowledge available, more tractable, easier to understand? It's tempting to say that explicitation gives us knowledge through an epistemological third route: knowledge can be learned, or it can be innate, or we can acquire it by accessing what we might call "informational states" (states that we are in by virtue of being situated in the world, but which we have not yet articulated to ourselves as *knowledge*). As you say, I argue in Dartnall (1996) that information becomes knowledge when we gain access to it, so that knowledge is information plus access. In that paper I was concerned with cognitive structures and processes, but we can probably apply the idea to external notations as well. Information that is couched in a representation that I don't understand does not constitute *knowledge* for me. The representation contains the information, but I cannot access it. It becomes knowledge for me when it is reformulated in a notation that I do understand. An obvious example of this is translating from one language to another. If I understand one language but not the other, the situation is cut and dried. The more interesting cases are where I have some facility with a notation but I'm not very adept with it, and it's then re-expressed in a format I can handle more easily. List handling is a good example, where the information is reformulated as a tree. Anyway, that's one possibility, that explicitation actually gives us new knowledge. The other possibility is inherent in the notion of explicitation: explicitation does not give us new knowledge, but explicitates knowledge that we already have. Do you think that explicitation gives us new knowledge, or does it make previously existing knowledge *accessible?*

DP: I've been emphasizing new system output resulting from the new applicability of a pre-existing procedure. An analogy would be the new utility which results when we manage to apply an effective tool to a task. We had the tool already, and we had the task, but only when they fit together do we get our new effectiveness in doing whatever it is. So I am assuming a constructivist account of knowledge according to which at least some of what we know is constructed *on the spot* in response to problems and questions, and does not have the status of permanent, resident knowledge-items stored in memory. Thus there is no problem in calling some system output a form of knowledge, and where system output is enhanced, knowledge may be enhanced too. So, yes, I do think that explicitation gives us new knowledge in the sense that it gives us new system output. This output may have been available in principle all along. For example, Number Scrabble can be played without the re-representation I discuss. But to a cognitive system of realistically limited resources, what is available in principle may not be available in practice, and the new representation may allow new output to be produced. In particular I want to avoid the simple Rabbit Model which says that in explicitation we simply uncover something. The further question is "uncovered to what?" And here we need to identify the external procedure and so on which becomes applicable and produces the new output.

TD: Do you think that the re-representation of Number Scrabble as tic-tac-toe is creative in itself, or does it just facilitate creative behavior?

DP: I think that it is creative in itself, but the justification for this is that it allows new or better system output without new empirical knowledge. That is, we have coordinated two things we already knew (Number Scrabble and tic-tac-toe), rather than learning something afresh. So what is creative is a productive rearrangement of what we already knew: this is a rather general notion, and I've tried to give it more specific form in my characterization of the varieties of explicitation. The rearrangement is creative, and the resulting new system output is creative too, though I think the second point is the criterial one: the rearrangement is only creative *because* it results in new system output.

TD: Number Scrabble is a funny example in some ways, because it doesn't obviously help us to be *creative*, simply because we don't associate creativity with such simple games. It would be nice if we could do the same thing for a complex game, such as chess. Suppose we could develop a more perspicuous representation for chess, which enabled us to see series of forced moves—series of moves which you initiate and control, and which leave you at an advantage. Your Number Scrabble re-representation as a tic-tac-toe game makes this possible for Number Scrabble. It's not inconceivable that we could do the same thing with chess.

DP: I agree that re-representation of Number Scrabble, like all the examples I discuss, is at the non-dramatic end of the creative spectrum. The advantage of examining such cases is their relative tractability to analysis. It would be nice to address, head on, the issue of how Beethoven, Newton and Virginia Woolf did it; but I think the issue is very big and woolly, and I think there is a role for more minute analyses. With regard to chess: yes, a productive re-representation would be a more significant achievement than the re-representation of Number Scrabble. All I can say is that I'm not aware that such a re-representation exists!

TD: Let me ask you about *access*. You want to cash out explicitation in terms of increased access to knowledge, but isn't there a tension between explicitation and access? When we *access* something, we, well, we access it—we don't change it. It's *there* to be accessed. Explicitation, on the other hand, suggests that we make something more accessible by changing it. We *change* it in order to get better access to it. Actually your talk of access sounds a bit like the Rabbit Model: the knowledge is there, and just needs to be coaxed into the light of day. So is there a tension between access talk and explicitation talk?

DP: We can make the point by saying that knowledge gets accessed. Or we can make it by saying that a procedure becomes applicable (to that knowledge). So what I've proposed is not "access" in the sense of the Rabbit Model of uncovering something. It might be called the "possibility of engagement" which exists between a procedure and knowledge. And this is consistent with the requirement that the cognitive knowledge-structure needs to change in order to make this possible.

TD: We both talk, in various ways, about getting better access to our knowledge in a way that does not require a change of inner representational format. But does this work when we go from one type of notation to another? It seems to me that we really do have a *different form of representation* in these cases, and not just better access to the same representation, or better access to the knowledge that it expresses.

DP: In the case of external representations, I agree that the presentational format evidently changes when we convert to a new notation. However, not everything changes, since (if the translation is correct) the truth-conditions of what we have notated remain constant. That is: the new and the old representations will be true or false (or more generally, right or wrong) under the same conditions. In the case of internal representations, we are dealing with mysterious and nebulous objects. We don't know where they are or what they are: all we know is that the cognitive system has output, and that this must come from somewhere. Also, we have no identity conditions for internal representations: we have no way of deciding whether a cognitive system is employing one or two of them. So I think this makes it hard to say with any certainty that the cases of internal and external representations are different in the way you mention.

TD: That anticipates my next question. You talk about re-representing internal cognitive structures, on the one hand, and changing the form of the external notation, on the other, and this is the principal difference you draw between the varieties of explicitation. But these things are so different that I wonder if they even belong to the same family. Redescription, as discussed by Karmiloff-Smith, is an endogenous process that happens whether we like it or not. We're *driven from within* to go beyond behavioral mastery, and to articulate implicit knowledge as explicit knowledge that we can reflect upon and change. But changing representational format is different, isn't it? When we change the notational format of knowledge—when we change its form of representation, to use your phrase—we do so wittingly and consciously. We quite intentionally change the format of Number Scrabble, for instance. So do you think that Karmiloff-Smith's representational redescription and your notion of changing the forms of representation even belong to the same family?

DP: Well, as I've said, I'm not so sure that the cases divide clearly. According to Karmiloff-Smith, internal re-representation happens "spontaneously." But are we sure that it can't happen, or be encouraged, deliberately? Likewise, external re-representation can happen deliberately, but can't it also just "come to us"? The notion of Cartesian Coordinates came to Descartes as he was lying in bed, and the notion of the benzene ring came to Kekulé as he was gazing at the fire. In any case, my main point concerns the "logic" of creative re-representation, rather than the issue of whether it is deliberate.

TD: We often re-represent or explicitate something so that we can visualize it. Word Scrabble is a good example—so are truth trees. We can bring the processing power of the visual cortex to bear on something when we can see it, and the language of understanding is shot through with visual terminology—we "see the point of something," "gain an insight," and so on. Do you think that re-representing something in visual format is just one case of explicitation, or redescription, or is there something especially important about the role of vision in understanding and creativity?

DP: I don't think visualization is crucial to the account I've given of explicitation. However, it can provide dramatic cases, since our powers of visual and spatial reasoning are considerable, and if re-representation makes them applicable to a problem (where they were not applicable before), the result may be a dramatic facilitation of calculation and problem solving.

REFERENCES

Amarel, S. (1968). On representations of problems of reasoning about actions. In D. Michie (Ed.), *Machine Intelligence 3*. Edinburgh: University Press.

Boden, M. (1987). *Artificial intelligence and natural man* (2nd ed.). London: MIT.

Boden, M. (1990). *The creative mind: Myths and mechanisms*. London: Weidenfeld and Nicolson.

Dartnall, T. H. (Ed.). (1994). *Artificial Intelligence and creativity: An interdisciplinary approach*. Dordrecht: Kluwer.

Dartnall, T. H. (1996). Redescription, information and access. In D. M. Peterson (Ed.), *Forms of representation: An interdisciplinary theme for cognitive science*. Oxford: Intellect Books.

Dummett, M. (1973/1978). The justification of deduction. In *Truth and other enigmas*. London: Duckworth.

Frege, G. (1884/1978). *The foundations of arithmetic* (J. L. Austin, Trans.). Oxford: Blackwell.

Karmiloff-Smith, A. (1990). Constraints on representational change: Evidence from children's drawing. *Cognition, 34,* 57–83.

Karmiloff-Smith, A. (1992). *Beyond modularity: A developmental perspective on cognitive science*. Cambridge, MA: MIT Press.

Karmiloff-Smith, A. (1996). Internal representations and external notations: A developmental perspective. In D. M. Peterson (Ed.), *Forms of Representation: An interdisciplinary theme for cognitive science*. Oxford: Intellect Books.

Larkin, S., & Simon, H. (1987). Why a diagram is (sometimes) worth ten thousand words. *Cognitive Science, 11* (1), 65–100.

Newell, A., & Simon, A. (1972). *Human problem solving*. Englewood Cliffs, NJ: Prentice Hall.

Peterson, D. M. (1990). *Wittgenstein's early philosophy: Three sides of the mirror*. Hemel Hempstead: Harvester.

Peterson, D. M. (1994). Re-representation and emergent information in three cases of problem solving. In T. H. Dartnall (Ed.), *Artificial Intelligence and creativity: An interdisciplinary approach*. Dordrecht: Kluwer.

Peterson, D. M. (Ed.). (1996). *Forms of representation: An interdisciplinary theme for cognitive science*. Oxford: Intellect Books.

Salmon, W. C. (1966). *The foundations of scientific inference*. Pittsburgh: University of Pittsburgh Press.

4

Creativity, Relational Knowledge, and Capacity: Why Are Humans So Creative?

Graeme S. Halford and William H. Wilson

Creativity depends on using our mental processes to create novelty. However, for novelty to be creative it must be effective, either in some practical sense, or in that it establishes a coherent set of relations where no relations, or a less coherent set of relations, existed before. Creativity may be defined therefore as the production of effective novelty through the operation of our mental processes. It is a truism that human beings are the most creative systems that we know. They are more creative than any machines invented so far. They are also more creative than other animals, and they become more creative as they develop. This is not to say that children are not creative, as they may well be less afraid of novelty than most adults, but the power of creative processes generally increases with development. Our problem then is to ask what it is about adult humans that confers on them such unique creative power.

An answer is suggested by Dartnall (1994), who draws attention to the fact that creativity depends on explicit representation. He points out that creativity depends on more than being able to do things. It is also necessary to represent what has been done. In a similar way Clark and Karmiloff-Smith (1993) distinguish between implicit and explicit knowledge. Implicit knowledge is sufficient to perform a task but the performance cannot be modified solely by the operation of mental processes. A person who has learned a particular skill may perform well without being able to describe how the performance is executed, just as an animal that has learned how to find food is evidently not aware of what it does. Both cases depend on procedural knowledge, but there is no declarative knowledge (Anderson, 1983), meaning that the performer is unable to describe, or declare, what is done. Such performances can only be changed by further experience. Components of the skill can be modified or rearranged, or the animal can learn to run in a different direction. However, such modification requires further experience, with external input, including feedback, and mental processes alone cannot achieve it. The golfer cannot perfect his swing solely by thinking about it, and there is solid experimental evidence that lower animals cannot reverse their habits on the basis of a single signal. They only change their performances incrementally, a little at a time, under the continued influence of concrete experience. Such automatic, inaccessible, unmodifiable performance is generally termed "implicit" (Clark & Karmiloff-Smith, 1993).

Explicit processes on the other hand are mentally accessible and modifiable (Clark & Karmiloff-Smith, 1993). The transition from implicit to explicit cognitive processes has been explained in terms of representational redescription (Karmiloff-Smith, 1990). This means that implicit knowledge is represented in a progressively more abstract manner, thereby becoming more accessible to other cognitive processes. For example, a young child might say and comprehend both "a dog" and "the dog," but not recognize that "a" and "the" are related, or have the grammatical concept of the article (Karmiloff-Smith, 1990). Similarly, young children might be able to draw houses, but if asked to draw a "funny" house they make only superficial changes, leaving the essential structure of the drawing unchanged. Karmiloff-Smith interprets this as indicating that the child has drawing skills that are not accessible and cannot be modified by the operation of internal cognitive processes alone.

Boden (1990) proposes that creativity entails "breaking out" of old conceptual frameworks and creating new ones. Dartnall (1994) interprets this as breaking out of one rule set, and creating a new one. For this to happen we need explicit knowledge of the rules under which we operate. At the implicit level we are subject to the rules, but at the explicit level we can articulate the rules and modify them. Animals that are phylogenetically more primitive lack this ability. For example, a beaver can build a dam, but has no explicit knowledge of dam building, so a beaver is not an engineer. Even if a beaver and an engineer were to build precisely the same dam on some occasion, their mental processes would be very different. The differences would become apparent if modifications had to be made to the dam-building procedure, and the more fundamental the modifications, the more the difference would become apparent. We will present empirical evidence of comparative performances of various animals and humans later.

We can conclude, then, that creativity requires explicit representation, in the sense that it is accessible to, and modifiable by, other cognitive processes, without the necessity of external input. However, the argument so far has been essentially descriptive, but now we want to consider how the differences we have been discussing can be defined at a more theoretical level. For this purpose we will apply the theory of representational ranks (Halford, Wilson, & Phillips, 1998b; Halford, Wilson & Phillips, 1998a; Halford, Phillips & Wilson, 2001) which is an extension of relational complexity theory (Halford et al., 1998b). Representational rank theory provides a complexity metric in which different levels of cognitive functioning are distinguished. It also provides a way of identifying the essential properties of higher cognitive processes. We will consider how effective each of these levels of cognitive processing will be in mediating creativity. Then we will attempt to provide at least a rudimentary explanation for differences in creativity between animals and humans, between children and adults, and between humans and machines.

TYPES OF REPRESENTATIONS

To develop our argument we first need to summarize the levels of representation, defined by Halford et al. (1998b) and the extension by Halford et al. (2001). These are shown schematically in Figure 4.1, together with possible implementations in neural nets based on the STAR model (Halford, Wilson, Guo, Gayler, Wiles, Stewart, 1994; Wilson, Halford, Gray, & Phillips, in press). The ranks correspond to levels of conceptual complexity, and new psychological processes emerge at each level. Ranks 0 and 1 are restricted to the associative mode, and embody mechanisms traditionally identified with associationist psychology. Ranks 2–6 permit processing of explicit relations, and the higher cognitive processes depend on these levels.

Rank 0: Performance Without Representations

This level includes reflexes, stimulus-response associations, and perceptuo-motor skills, insofar as they are not guided by a representation of the task. These processes can be captured in neural net models by pattern associators, or two-layered nets, as shown in Figure 4.1. That is, there is an association between input and output, without internal representation, and the association is either acquired incrementally through the operation of a learning algorithm, or is hard-wired. The acquisition is not influenced by other cognitive processes, and is not under strategic control in the way that higher cognitive processes are.

Psychologically, Rank 0 corresponds to *elemental association*, which is a link between two entities, without intervening representation. For example, a two-object discrimination might consist of the following two associations:

Element triangle   →   R+   (respond)
Element square   →   R−   (don't respond, avoid)

FIGURE 4.1
Representations of six different ranks, with possible Parallel Distributed
Processing (PDP) representation.

Rank	Representation	Neural Net Specification
0	No representation	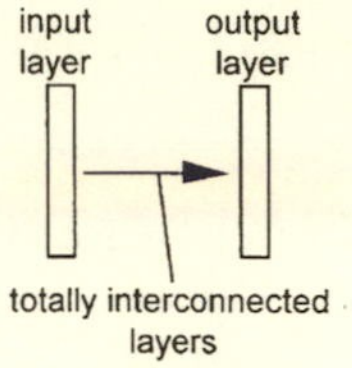
1	Wholistic representation (no explicit relations)	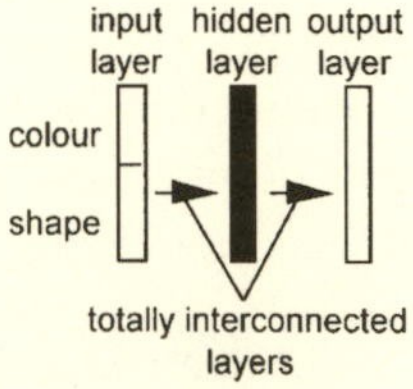
2	Unary relation	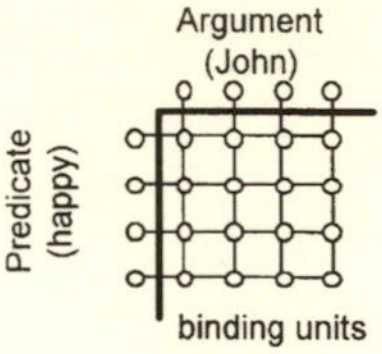
3	Binary relation	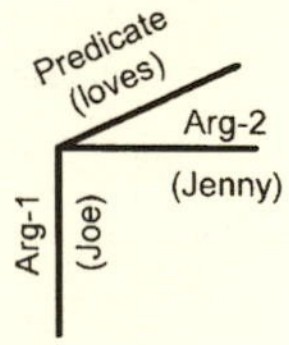
4	Ternary relation	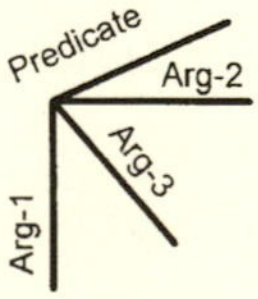
5	Quaternary relation	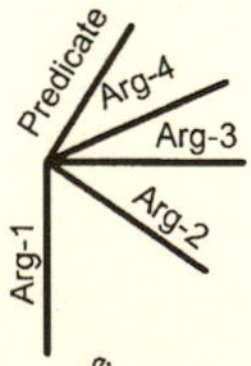
6	Quinary relation	

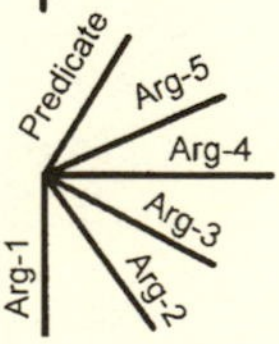

This is the most primitive level of functioning, and presumably occurs in all animals. However, the term "elemental" should not be confused with the everyday meaning of "elementary," and this level can produce some quite complex performances, such as transitivity of choice (McGonigle & Chalmers, 1984; Wynne, 1995). However, it does not have the properties of higher cognitive processes, and it would not support creativity, in the sense that we have defined the term.

Rank 1: Computed, Nonstructural Representations

At this level there is internal representation, but it is undifferentiated, and is unrelated to other representations. Many features, and quite a large amount of information, can be represented, but no relations with semantic interpretations are defined between components of the representation.

Psychologically, this level corresponds to configural association, in which the link between cue and response is not direct, but is modified by another entity. One example would be conditional discrimination tasks. Participants, either animals or humans, might be trained to choose a circle and avoid a triangle on a white background, and this might be reversed on a striped background (i.e., triangle becomes positive and circle negative). The contingencies that must be learned can be expressed this way:

$$
\begin{array}{ll}
\text{circle, white} & \rightarrow \quad + \\
\text{triangle, white} & \rightarrow \quad - \\
\text{circle, striped} & \rightarrow \quad - \\
\text{triangle, striped} & \rightarrow \quad +
\end{array}
$$

Each stimulus (circle, triangle, white, striped), taken singly, is equally associated with positive or negative responses, so the task cannot be acquired through elemental association (Halford, 1993; Rudy, 1991). Consequently the discrimination must be based on configurations, such as "circle&white," "circle&striped," and so on. This performance requires internal representation of the configurations, and there is evidence that rats are capable of it, although it depends on maturation of the hippocampus (Rudy, 1991). Conditional discrimination is isomorphic to the exclusive-OR (XOR).

Another example of this level of performance would be the representation of objects in space in the manner that has been observed in five-month-old infants by Baillargeon (1995; but see also Rivera, Wakeley, & Langer, 1999). Infants represent features of objects, such as height, and their distance from other objects, but there is no evidence that they can relate such representations to other representations. They can represent perceptible features, but presumably have no explicit representations of relations. Other examples of computed nonstructural representations are prototypes and image schemas. Prototypes (Rosch & Mervis, 1975) are the basis of natural categories, and can be learned by infants of a few months of age (Quinn, Eimas, & Rosenkrantz, 1993). They can be modeled by three-layered nets (McClelland & Rumelhart, 1985; Quinn & Johnson, 1997). Image schemas, such as self-motion, animate-motion, support and containment (Mandler, 1992) are also examples of this level of cognition.

Performances at this level can be captured by three-layered nets, comprising input, output, and hidden layers, as shown in Figure 4.1. Configural learning tasks such as conditional discrimination can be performed by using units in the hidden layer which represent conjunctions of features such as "circle&white" (Schmajuk & DiCarlo, 1992), just as hidden units can be used to represent conjunctions in the exclusive-OR task. In spatial tasks, hidden units could represent various features of objects such as height and distance from other objects.

These features are represented by activations in one or more of the hidden units. They do not have a relational structure, such as conjunction (circle,white), so it is not possible to answer a query such as "what is combined with circle?" They are therefore more primitive, and less accessible, than the relational representations at Ranks 2–6.

Ranks 2–6: Relational Representations

Phillips, Halford and Wilson (1995) have argued, on the basis of the work of Codd (1990), that essential properties of higher cognitive processes, including data structures such as lists and trees, can be captured by a model based on the processing of relations. Relational representations have properties such as explicit representation and accessibility to other cognitive processes which enable them to be processed recursively. Phillips et al. (1995) have argued that representational redescription can be explained at least in part by the transition from associative to relational representations.

This argument was developed further by Halford et al. (2001) who defined the properties of relational knowledge that are essential to higher cognitive processes. We will summarize this argument here to provide a basis for our account of creativity.

In general, an n-ary relation $R(a_1,a_2,...,a_n)$ is a subset of the Cartesian product $S_1 \times S_2 \times ... \times S_n$. Representation of a relation requires a set of bindings between a relation symbol, R, and the arguments $(a_1,a_2,...,a_n)$. The binary relation BIGGER-THAN(whale,dolphin) is a binding between the relation symbol BIGGER-THAN and the arguments "whale" and "dolphin." Relational representations have the following properties:

Symbolization means that the link between the arguments of a relation is explicitly symbolized (e.g., the link between "whale" and "dolphin" is explicitly symbolized by the relation symbol LARGER-THAN), whereas associative links are all the same and do not carry a label. This makes a relation accessible to other cognitive processes, so that a relational instance can be an argument to another relation. For example:

BECAUSE(LARGER-THAN(whale,dolphin), AVOIDS(dolphin,whale)).

Higher-order relations have relations as arguments, whereas first order relations have objects as arguments.

Omni-directional access means that, given all but one of the components of a relation, we can access (i.e., retrieve) the remaining component. For example, given the relational schema R(a,b), any of the following can be performed:

$$R(a,-) \rightarrow b$$
$$R(-,b) \rightarrow a$$
$$-(a,b) \rightarrow R$$

Given a relational instance such as MOTHER-OF(woman,child), and given MOTHER-OF(woman,–) we can access "child," whereas given MOTHER-OF(–,child) we can access "woman," and given –(woman,child) we can access "MOTHER-OF." When we are dealing with more than one relational instance, the answers will not always be unique. For example, MOTHER-OF(woman,–) may yield child, toddler, infant, baby, teenager, and so on. Because omni-directional access seems to be inherent in relations they have more flexible access than elemental and configural associations, which are not inherently bi-directional.

Role representation means that relational knowledge entails representation of argument roles or slots, independent of specific instances. Thus BIGGERTHAN(–,–) entails representation of slots for a larger and a smaller entity.

Decomposability of relations means that relations can be composed of simpler relations. A decomposable relation is one that can be written as a conjunct of instances of relations of lower arities. For example, the ternary relation MONOTONICALLY-LARGER(*a,b,c*) can be decomposed into >(*a,b*) & >(*b,c*) & >(*a,c*). Not all relations are decomposable (Halford et al., 1998b, Sections 3.4.3 and 4.2.8).

Relational systematicity means that certain relations imply other relations. For example, >(*a,b*) → <(*b,a*), and sells (seller,buyer,object) → buys (buyer,seller,object). This is really a case of higher-order relation; for example implies (>(*a,b*), <(*b,a*)).

Dimensionality of relations means that each argument of R can be instantiated in more than one way, and therefore represents a source of variation, or dimension. An *n*-ary relation may be thought of as a set of points in N-dimensional space. The number of arguments, N, corresponds to the number of dimensions in the space defined by the relation. In terms of sets, a unary relation R on a set S is a subset of S. It is the set of objects $\{x \in S \mid R(x) \text{ is true}\}$. Similarly, a binary relation on a set S is a subset of the Cartesian product $S \times S$ of elements of S, a ternary relation is a subset of $S \times S \times S$ of elements of S, and so on. Each set contributes a dimension of the Cartesian product. This is the basis for our complexity metric (Halford et al., 1998b). The relation symbol can contribute an extra dimension if it is a variable (i.e., the relation changes) within the task.

Relational representations can represent the knowledge structures that are important to higher cognition, as follows.

Proposition. A *proposition* is defined as the smallest unit of knowledge that can have a truth value. Let $\{R_1, R_2 \ldots\}$ be the collection of all valid relations. Each R_i is a subset of some Cartesian product, which we refer to as C_i. A true proposition, then, is a relational instance, that is, a member of one of the relations R_i. A false proposition is an "expressible non-fact"—that is, a member of one of the complements $C_i \backslash R_I$ of the relations R_i, and not a member of any of the R_i. For example, the true proposition bigger-than(dog, mouse) is an instance of the "bigger-than" relation. We choose to regard "bigger-than" as a subset of the Cartesian product animals × animals. The false proposition bigger-than(mouse, dog) has the property that (mouse, dog) belongs to animals × animals \ bigger-than. Each proposition is a point in the space defined by union of the Cartesian products C_i.

An *attribute* is a relation symbol with one argument. An attribute value is an instance of a unary relation. An attribute is therefore distinct from a feature as defined earlier, because an attribute has the properties of relational knowledge, whereas a feature does not. Thus the attribute wags-tail(dog) is a unary relational instance, and has the properties of relational knowledge, including omni-directional access. If we ask "what is (an) attribute of dog"(i.e., ?(dog)) we can answer "wags-tail" and if we ask "what wags its tail?"(i.e., wags-tail(?)) an answer is "dog." Features are distinct from attributes in this respect. Representation of features plays a role in determination of responses, but the representation is not accessible to other cognitive processes. A good model for this is the representation of features in the hidden layer of three-layered nets. The representation consists of an activation in one or more hidden units, and is a variable that determines the activations in the output layer. However, the structure of the representations in the hidden layer is not typically accessible to other cognitive processes of the performer. It might be accessible to researchers (e.g., by performing cluster analyses of hidden-layer activations [Elman, 1990]) but it is not accessible to the participant.

Operations on relations. *Operations on relations* are adapted from those defined in the theory of relational databases (Codd, 1990). They include select, project, join, add, delete, union, intersect, and difference

(Halford et al., 2001; Phillips et al., 1995). A model of relational knowledge that includes these operations can capture important properties of higher cognitive (Halford et al., 2001). These operations permit information stored in relational knowledge structures to be accessed and manipulated in flexible and powerful ways.

Planning and analogy. Relational representations are essential to planning, or the organization of a sequence of actions to achieve a goal, and to analogy. Planning, which has been explicitly modeled by VanLehn and Brown (1980), Greeno, Riley and Gelman (1984) and Halford, Smith, Dickson, Maybery, Kelly, Bain, and Stewart (1995), entails representing relations between components of a task. Analogy entails mapping relations between a base or source and a target (Gentner, 1983; Gick & Holyoak, 1983; Holyoak & Thagard, 1989). Both of these will be considered in more detail later.

We can now consider the specific properties of Ranks 2–6.

Rank 2: Representations with Two Components

At this level of representation there are two components that can be related to one another. This is the lowest level at which propositions can be represented. The simplest proposition requires representation of a relation-symbol and one argument, which is a Rank 2 representation. Where a relation-symbol represents a state, such as happy(John), the proposition corresponds to a unary relation.

Unary relations, $R(x)$, have one argument. The proposition big(dog) is a binding between the unary relation "big" and one argument. The relation can be interpreted as expressing a state or an attribute. Other cases of propositions with one argument can be interpreted as class membership, for example, dog(fido). A binding between a variable and a constant can also be expressed as a unary relation, for example, HEIGHT(1 meter). This proposition represents a binding between a variable, height, and an argument, which can take a range of values (Halford, Wiles, Humphreys, & Wilson, 1993; Smolensky, 1990).

Halford et al. (1994) and Halford et al. (1998b) have shown that relation symbol-argument bindings can be modeled using tensor product networks. Each tensor product representation comprises a vector representing the relation symbol, and a vector representing each argument, as shown in Figure 4.1. The binding units (whose values correspond to the computation of the tensor product) are interpreted as activations or as weights. Where they are interpreted as activations, bindings can be changed dynamically and the relation may be changed in all-or-none fashion without external input. For example, we can change happy(John) to sad(John). One component of the representation (John) remains the same, but when the other component is changed a new binding is formed. This means representations can be changed in the course of reasoning tasks. They are not dependent on incremental change as a function of experience. Where activation units are interpreted as weights, the only change mechanism is incremental adjustment of weights under the influence of environmental input. In memory models (Humphreys, Bain, & Pike, 1989), binding units are interpreted as weights, implying that the change is incremental rather than dynamic.

Several important new properties emerge at Rank 2 that are not possible with lower rank representations. These include ability to represent propositions, relations, and variables. This is a sizeable step towards explicit, conceptual thought. There is also increased content independence, because a relation symbol expresses an idea that is independent of its argument to some extent: large(x) means the same irrespective of what x is. Further properties emerge at each of the higher ranks, as we will see.

Rank 3: Representations with Three Components

Representations of this rank have three components. With associative binding this level is exemplified by the three-way associations between cue, target and context which have been important in memory retrieval theories (Humphreys et al., 1989); for example. What did you have for breakfast (cue) on Sunday (context)? Bacon and eggs (target).

Binary relations, or relations with two arguments, can be represented, with one component representing the relation symbol and two components representing the arguments. For example, bigger(–,–) has two arguments, which can represent any pair of objects such that the first is bigger than the second. Univariate functions, $f(a) = b$, and unary operators, such as change-sign$\{(x,-x)\}$, can also be represented at this level.

At Rank 3, more complex variations between components can be represented. The binary relation R(x,y) represents the way x varies as a function of y, and vice versa, neither of which is possible with Rank 2 representations. Propositions with two arguments can be represented: for example, loves(Joe, Jenny).

Rank 4: Representations with Four Components

At this level, concepts based on ternary relations can be represented. These include the "love-triangle," in which two persons, x and y, both love a third person, z. Concepts such as transitivity and class inclusion entail core representations that are ternary relations (Andrews & Halford, 1998; Halford, 1993; Halford et al., 1998b). This level requires one component of the representation for the relation symbol and three to represent arguments.

The number of possible relations between elements increases again with ternary relations: R(x,y,z) represents three binary relations, R1(x,y), R2(y,z)

and R3(x,z), as well as the three-way relation, R(x,y,z), which is not defined in a binary relation. This means that with a ternary relation, but not with unary or binary relations, it is possible to compare x with $y,z,$ and y with $x,z,$ and z with x,y. It thus becomes possible to compute the effects on x of variations in $y,z,$ and so on. More complex interactions can be represented than at the lower levels, which increases the flexibility and power of thought.

Bivariate functions and binary operations may also be represented at this level. A binary operation is a special case of a bivariate function. A binary operation on a set S is a function from the set S×S of ordered pairs of elements of S into S, that is S×S → S. For example, the binary operation of arithmetic addition consists of the set of ordered pairs of $\{..(3,2,5),..$ $(5,3,8),..\}$.

Rank 5: Representations with Five Components

At this level, quaternary relations, R(w,x,y,z), may be represented, with one component representing the relation symbol and the other four the arguments. An example would be proportion; $a/b = c/d$ expresses a relation between the four variables $a,b,c,$ and d. It is possible to compute how any element will vary as a function of one or more of the others. With a quaternary relation all the comparisons that are possible with ternary relations can be made, as well as four-way comparisons; the effect on w of variations in $x,y,z,$ the effects on x of variations in $w,y,z,$ and so on. Quaternary relations can also be interpreted as functions or as operations. A trivariate function is a special case of a quaternary relation. It is a set of ordered 4-tuples (a,b,c,d) such that for each (a,b,c) there is precisely one d such that $(a,b,c,d \in f)$. Quaternary relations may be interpreted as a composition of binary operations. For example, $(a + b) \times c = d$ is a quaternary relation. As with Rank 4 there do not appear to be any concepts using associative representations.

Rank 6: Representations with Six Components

At this level there would be a relation symbol and five arguments. The psychological existence of this level is speculative, and if it exists, it is probably available only for a minority of adults, which makes evidence about it difficult to obtain. It would permit processing of quinary relations that would enable people to reason about relations between systems, each of which is composed of compositions of binary operations. If we assume that theories are composed of mathematical expressions each of which integrates a set of binary operations, then representation of the relation between theories amounts to representing the relation between structures defined by a composition of binary operations. This means that the ability to work within a theory would require Rank 5 reasoning, whereas ability to deal with relations between theories would require Rank 6.

There is no mathematical limit to the number of arguments that a relation can have, but there may be psychological limits to the complexity of relations that can be computed. There is evidence that normal human cognition entails representations only up to Rank 5 (Halford, 1993; Halford et al., 1998b). That is, adult humans appear to be limited to processing one quaternary relation in parallel, though a minority of adults can process quinary relations under optimal conditions.

Concepts more complex than Rank 5 are handled by *segmentation* and *chunking* (Halford et al., 1994; Halford et al., 1998b). Segmentation means that complex tasks can be decomposed into smaller segments that can be processed serially. The development of serial processing strategies permits complex tasks to be performed without exceeding limits on the amount of information that can be processed in parallel. Chunking means that representations of high dimensionality, represented by tensor products of high rank, are recoded into fewer dimensions, with tensor products of lower rank. An example would be velocity, defined as $v=s/t$ (velocity = distance/time). This is three-dimensional, but it can be recoded into one dimension (as occurs when we think of speed as the position of a pointer on a dial). However, this does not mean that all processing loads can ultimately be reduced to that for a one-dimensional concept, because conceptual chunking results in loss of representation of some relationships. For example, when velocity is chunked as one dimension, the three-way relation between v, s, and t is no longer represented, so that changes in v as a function of s and/or t cannot be computed without returning to the three-dimensional representation, which entails the higher processing load.

The arguments of chunked relational representations can be unpacked, to provide lower level relations. Consider, for example, a moderately complex concept such as that temperature difference is the cause of heat flow. We can represent this as cause(temperature difference,heat flow). However, this is really a higher-order relation, and the arguments *temperature difference* and *heat flow* are chunked representations of lower-order relations. Thus temperature difference can be unchunked to greater(temperature1,temperature2) and heat-flow can be unchunked to flow(heat,conductor,high temperature,low temperature), that is, heat flows along a conductor from high to low temperature. Thus the concept can be represented as a higher-order binary relation, one argument of which is a lower-order binary relation, and the other is a lower-order quaternary relation. This hierarchical structure can be modeled within the tensor product formalism mentioned earlier (Halford et al., 1994; Halford et al., 1998b; Wilson et al., 2001).

A major component of expertise is to have knowledge organized into efficient hierarchical structures in this way. This enables humans to operate within the limitation that no more than one quaternary (or, in some cases, quinary) relation can be processed in parallel. Thus the expert may not process relations more complex than those processed by the novice. A person with a knowledge of physics can understand heat flow without processing anything more complex than a quaternary relation at one time, as illustrated above. A novice might experience a higher processing load by attempting, unsuccessfully, to consider relations between all variables at once. One function of expertise is to maintain processing load at manageable levels.

However, there are limits to the decomposability of relations in this way. Chunked relations become inaccessible, as noted above, some relations cannot be decomposed without loss of information (Halford et al., 1998b, Section 3.4.3) and individuals may not have appropriate chunking and unchunking or segmentation strategies available. A more subtle, but in some ways more serious, problem is that some representation of the structure of the concept is needed for strategies to be developed. This notion is incorporated into the TRIM model (Halford et al., 1995) to be considered later.

THOUGHT AND RANK OF REPRESENTATION

Rank of representation is a measure of the power and flexibility of thought. Higher rank representations permit higher levels of relations to be represented, and permit more of the structure of a concept or situation to be processed in thought. Rank is analogous to the number of facets of a situation that can be viewed simultaneously.

Rank of representation has been associated with phylogenetic and ontogenetic development. We will briefly review evidence of the type of representation that is within the capacity of each level in the evolutionary scale, and at each age range in human development.

Representational Rank of Animals and Children

Levels of representation equivalent to those defined here have been related to species differences by Holyoak and Thagard (1995) and by Halford et al. (1998b). Rank 0, equivalent to simple associations, appear to be possible for all species of animals, albeit with varying degrees of efficiency. Mammals appear capable of Rank 1, as indicated by the fact that rats are capable of configural learning (Rudy, 1991). Rank 2 appears to be possible for monkeys, because they can recognize the binding between attributes and objects. For example, they can learn to choose which of two objects is like a sample. If they are shown, say, an apple as sample object, and required to choose between an apple and, say, a hammer, they can learn to choose the apple. This could be done of course by associative learning, which is Rank 0. However, they can transfer to a new task in which, say, the sample is a hammer, and the choices are a banana and a hammer. Transfer of the principle implies they can represent a binding between an attribute (hammer-like) and a specific object. This can be interpreted as a Rank 2 representation. They can represent a dynamic binding between an attribute and an object.

Chimpanzees appear capable of representing a binary relation between objects, which implies Rank 3 representations (Halford et al., 1998b; Halford et al., 2001; Premack, 1983). For example, they can learn that if the sample is XX, they should choose AA rather than BC. If the sample is XY, they should choose BC rather than AA. They learn to choose a pair of objects that has the same relation as the sample. This implies they can represent binary relations, a Rank 3 representation.

As Holyoak and Thagard (1995) have shown, such performances are really a form of analogical reasoning. The animals are sensitive to the fact that an attribute, or a relation, in the sample is the same as in the correct choice item. Analogical reasoning entails dynamic binding (Halford et al., 1993), so these performances indicate that monkeys and apes are capable of relational representations with dynamic binding. This interpretation is born out by studies of what has been called "reversal learning" (Bitterman, 1960). Suppose an animal is trained in a discrimination in which, say, circle is positive, and triangle is negative. Then, without any warning, the contingency is reversed, so triangle is now positive and circle negative. Then when that discrimination is learned the reversal process is repeated, so circle becomes positive again, and triangle negative, and so on. The question of interest is whether animals learn to make successive reversals more and more quickly, indicating that they "catch on" to the reversal principle. Species differ considerably in the rate at which they learn to do this. Apes will learn to make a reversal immediately after the contingency is reversed, and monkeys also learn, but at a slower rate, while other mammals learn more slowly still. Birds, reptiles and amphibians show less benefit from training with successive reversals, while fish show no benefit at all. This performance clearly differentiates between species at different levels of the phylogenetic scale. As with other tasks that make this differentiation, it requires representation of the relations in the task, together with dynamic binding. That is, it requires recognition that there is always one positive and one negative stimulus, together with the ability to change the mapping of positive/negative into the stimuli dynamically. The higher animals can do this, but the lower animals can only relearn the discrimination incrementally. They are not capable of dynamic change. This paradigm is a subset of so-called "learning set" acquisition (Harlow, 1949, 1959) in which the structure underlying a set of isomorphic discrimination tasks is acquired. It can be interpreted as acquisition of relational knowledge, combined with analogical mapping of a problem into the relational representation (Halford, 1993; Halford, Bain, Maybery, & Andrews, 1998).

It appears then that ability to represent relations and to change the representation dynamically is a fact or which differentiates species at different points in the phylogenetic scale. Putting it another way, the capacity for creative thought is a recent evolutionary development, which is present only in the highest non-human animals, and then in rudimentary form.

Children's representational abilities have been reviewed elsewhere (Halford, 1993; Halford et al., 2001; Halford et al., 1998b). Neonates are capable of Rank 0 associative learning, but there is evidence that Rank 1 representations are possible at five months. This is indicated by infants' awareness of properties of recently vanished objects (Baillargeon, 1995) and ability to form prototypes (Quinn et al., 1993; Quinn & Johnson, 1997). Rank 2 representations are possible at approximately one year, when infants become capable of treating the hiding place of an object as a variable, and recognizing category memberships explicitly, which in turn leads to their understanding referents of words; for example "Doggy gone" can be represented as GONE(doggy), which is a relation symbol with one argument.

Rank 3 representations appear to be possible at age two, because children of this age can make discriminations based on explicit representation of binary relations. One consequence is that they can perform proportional analogies of the form A:B::C:D, provided the content is familiar to them.

Rank 4 representations become possible at a median age of five years, and they open up a wide range of new performances, including transitive inference, hierarchical classification and inclusion, certain kinds of hypothesis testing, concept of mind, and many others. Transitivity entails a ternary relation, because premises $R(a,b)$ and $R(b,c)$ are integrated into the ordered triple, monotonic-$R(a,b,c)$. Twenty percent of four-year-olds and 40 percent of five-year-olds can perform it (Andrews & Halford, 1998). Class inclusion and the part-whole hierarchy are essentially ternary relations. A class inclusion hierarchy has three components: a superordinate class, a subclass and a complementary class (e.g., fruit, divided into apples and non-apples). Part-whole hierarchies are similar, and comprise a whole divided into a part and a complementary part. Though the age of attainment of these concepts has been controversial, it appears that children have difficulty processing tasks that entail ternary relations until approximately five years. This issue has been discussed in greater detail elsewhere (Halford, 1992, 1993; Halford & Leitch, 1989; Hodkin, 1987).

Representations of Rank 5 are typically understood at about age 11, as evidenced by understanding of proportion and a number of other concepts, including understanding of the balance scale. This entails representing the interaction of four factors: weight and distance on the left and weight and distance on the right.

Capacity to represent relational concepts increases with phylogenetic level, and also with age. There is evidence that processing load is a function of the complexity of relations being processed (Halford, Maybery, & Bain, 1986; Maybery, Bain, & Halford, 1986; Posner & Boies, 1971). The reason becomes apparent from distributed representation models, and it is due to the number of binding units being an exponential function of the number of arguments (Halford, 1993; Halford et al., 1998b).

Relational Complexity and Creativity

As we saw earlier, creativity depends partly on more explicit representation of the relational structure of a task. It is a matter of being able to change the structure, rather than being subject to the structure. This can be achieved using the higher rank representations, because of three factors: dynamic binding, higher-order relations, and ability to change strategies. We will consider these in turn.

Dynamic binding means that relational representations can be changed without incremental learning. Consider a representation of the proposition likes(John,Tom). We can change that to hates(John,Tom). Under the tensor product and similar models of relation symbol argument bindings mentioned earlier, this can be done by changing the vector on the relation symbol units. The result is a different pattern of activation on the binding units, while the argument vectors remain unchanged. The representations of John and Tom have remained constant, but the relation between them has been changed. This is a simple example of a principle that applies to all relational representations with dynamic bindings, and it can have quite spectacular effects. We have shown how it can be employed in analogical and other forms of reasoning (Halford, 1993; Halford et al., 1993; Wilson et al., 2001).

Representations of Rank 3 and above can support *higher-order relations*. The sentence "It's good that Peter returned" can be expressed as GOOD(RETURNED(Peter)), and includes the higher-order relation symbol GOOD, which has one argument, the relation symbol RETURNED which itself has one argument. It is a Rank 3 representation, because it requires three vectors, representing GOOD, RETURNED, and Peter. It is not possible to represent higher-order relations below Rank 3. They can of course be represented by higher rank representation. For example, "Tom hit Peter because he kissed Wendy" can be expressed as CAUSE(kiss(Peter,Wendy), hit(Tom,Peter)). In this case CAUSE is a higher-order relation symbol whose arguments are two, two-valued relation symbols. It can be represented by the higher-order binary relation CAUSE(kiss/Peter/Wendy,hit/Tom/Peter). The arguments of this higher-order relation can be unchunked to the first-order binary relations kiss(Peter,Wendy) and hit(Tom,Peter).

Higher-order relations permit more abstract correspondences to be recognized. For example CAUSE(LOVE(Jane,Mark),JEALOUS(Michael, Mark)) is structurally identical to the example in the previous paragraph, and one can be mapped into the other solely on the basis of structural correspondence (Holyoak & Thagard, 1989). The mapping can be made independently of similarity of lower-order relations or arguments. Thus the level of abstraction, or content-independence increases with higher structural complexity, and higher rank, because higher-order relations can be represented. This enables analogies to be formed between situations that are structurally similar but are very different in content, and this is an important component of creativity.

Finally, ability to represent the structure of a task permits *strategies to be developed*. A computational model of this process has been developed in the domain of transitive inference. The implication is that understanding, which entails ability to represent the structure of a task, can guide the development of efficient skills, strategies, and procedures.

The Transitive Inference Mapping Model (TRIM) (Halford et al., 1995) simulates the acquisition of transitive inference strategies in children and adults. It is a self-modifying production system model using the PRISM (Ohlsson & Langley, 1986) modeling language. The base language is LISP.

The development of adequate strategies depends on ability to represent an ordered set of three elements. Without this ability, inadequate strategies result. To acquire such a strategy spontaneously, as most children do, is undoubtedly creative, but it depends on ability to represent ternary relations. The development of a strategy depends on a representation of a concept of an ordered set, which has the following components:

- Understanding of one or more antisymmetric binary relations (e.g., larger than, better than). The child need not, and would not, know that they are asymmetric and binary. The child just needs to know examples of relations that have this property.
- Each element in the set occurs once and only once in an ordered set.
- End elements have the same relation to all other elements; for example, $a>b$, $a>c$, $a>d$ in the string a,b,c,d.
- The position of an internal element is defined by relations to elements on either side of it; for example, $b<a$, $b>c$.
- The same relation must exist between all pairs, both adjacent and nonadjacent; for example, $a>b$, $b>c$,..., $a>c$, and so on.

Any ordered set of at least three elements instantiates these properties. It is sufficient therefore for the child to know any concrete instance of an ordered set of three or more elements. The three bears, the three billygoats gruff, or a set of blocks ordered for size, would suffice. An "abstract" representation is not required.

Transitive inference strategies develop under the dual constraints of the concept of order and problem solving experience. When the child is presented with the problem of ordering elements, he or she first compares the known relations to the ordered set, which provides a "template" or concept of order. The comparison process is performed by analogical mapping. The correct order is determined by a valid and consistent mapping. No other criterion is required. Once this is determined, means-end analysis is used to determine an operator that will produce the correct ordering of the problem elements. Then a production is devised that incorporates the current problem situation in its condition side, and the correct operator in its action side. The production then fires and an ordering results.

If a production already exists that has the current situation in its condition side, and if the production is above threshold strength, it fires. There is then no need to build a new production. If more than one production has conditions that match the current situation, the strongest production fires. Feedback is provided about the correctness of the ordering. Positive feedback increases the strength of the production, while negative feedback weakens it.

The model shows how procedural knowledge, in the form of a transitive inference or ordering strategy, develops under the guidance of relational knowledge. There is creativity in the development of the strategy, because the model begins without any strategy. It is equipped initially with basic cognitive processes such as memory storage and retrieval, means-end analysis, and analogical mapping. From these basic tools, under the stimulus of problem solving experience with feedback, it develops new strategies. To do this however it requires relational knowledge, in the form of a representation of an ordered set. This ordered set provides a template for the strategies that are developed.

To summarize this section, creative reasoning depends on ability to form dynamic representations of relations. This ability appears to have evolved relatively recently, and continues to develop throughout childhood. The complexity of relations that can be represented influences the conceptual power of creative reasoning, but is obtained at the cost of higher processing loads for more complex relations. In the next section we will examine more specific models of creativity using representations of this type.

REPRESENTATIONS IN COMPUTERS

Given that we can define the representations of biological intelligence in terms of the complexity of relations represented, we should be able to apply the same metric to computers.

Models of Creative Processing

One aspect of creativity is the retrieval of an idea that relates formerly unrelated things. This can be illustrated using one of the practice items from the Remote Associates Test for creativity (Mednick, 1962). What word relates "rat," "blue," and "cottage"? (cheese). These words are not normally seen as related, but all have a common association with cheese. Another example is supplied by Rubin and Wallace (1989), as analyzed by Humphreys, Wiles, and Bain (1993), and Wiles, Halford, Stewart, Humphreys, Bain, and Wilson

(1994): name a mythical being that rhymes with post (ghost). Here the target element, ghost, is weakly associated with either the cue "mythical being" or the cue "rhymes with post," but is quite strongly retrievable to the two cues. These examples may not meet the effectiveness criterion, because the set of relations created by the retrieval of cheese, or ghost, is not particularly coherent. Nevertheless the memory processes entailed in these tasks probably have much in common with those used by a painter producing new juxtapositions of colors and forms, a poet composing images, or a scientist seeing a connection between apparently unrelated ideas. The memory model of Humphreys et al. (1989) has been demonstrated to handle this type of memory retrieval using Rank 3 tensor product representations.

Transfer of a relation from one domain to another is another aspect of creativity. Analogy is fundamental to creative thought in many domains (Holyoak & Thagard, 1995) and recent work has documented its use in scientific creativity (Dunbar, 2001). The scientific use of analogy is well illustrated by the Rutherford analogy between the structure of the hydrogen atom and the structure of the solar system, as analyzed by Gentner (1983). Here the essential insight was recognizing that the structure of the atom entailed the principles of orbital motion, as exemplified in the solar system. This entails transferring the system of relations between solar and planetary bodies to the nucleus and electron. This can be modeled using the Structured Tensor Analogical Reasoning (STAR) model (Halford et al., 1995; Wilson et al., in press).

In the STAR model relation symbol-argument bindings are represented as tensor products, as shown in Figure 4.2. The proposition MOTHER-OF(woman,baby) is represented as a Rank 3 tensor product. The three vectors represent the relation symbol MOTHER-OF and its arguments, "woman" and "baby." As with the memory model of Humphreys et al. (1989), representations are superimposed. Therefore the bindings MOTHER-OF(mare,foal), MOTHER-OF(cat,kitten), as well as LOVES (mother,baby), . . . , LARGER-THAN(mare,foal) are all superimposed on the same tensor product.

Simple proportional analogies, such as woman:baby::mare:? can be solved by entering the base arguments, "woman" and "baby" into the representation, and the output is a relation symbol bundle representing "MOTHER-OF," "FEEDS," "LARGER-THAN," and so on. That is, it is a vector equivalent to the linear sum of vectors representing each of these outputs. In the next step this relation symbol bundle is the input, together with the first argument of the target, "mare," as shown in Figure 4.2. The output is an argument bundle that includes "foal." Possible solutions can be recognized by one or more cleanup processes, the simplest of which entails computing the inner product of vectors representing candidate solutions with this output. There is also an auto-associative clean-up process that performs the task in parallel (Chappell & Humphreys, 1993).

FIGURE 4.2
Simple proportional analogies performed by the Structured Tensor Analogical Reasoning model.

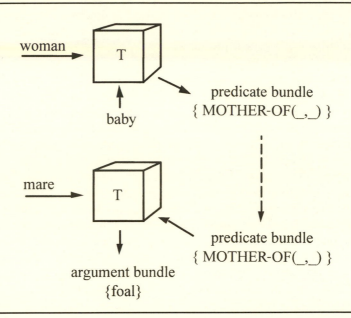

This model can solve all the major classes of analogies (Halford et al., 1994; Wilson et al., in press), but we will consider how the model would solve a simplified and idealized version of the Rutherford analogy.

We will assume that the structure of the base, the solar system, is known completely, but that the structure of the atom is incompletely known. We will further assume that the atom was known to comprise two major components, a nucleus and an electron, that there was a mutual attraction relation between them, and a size difference (the nucleus was known to be of larger mass). Most important of all, we assume that the correspondence between the atom and the solar system had not been previously recognized. This recognition was at the core of the creative contribution. The simulation of the analogy in the STAR model begins with this information coded in a tensor product.

The discrepancies between this hypothetical situation and the actual state of Rutherford's knowledge at the time are less relevant than the idea of starting with an incomplete representation of a target domain, finding a base domain to which it is analogous, transferring relations from the base to the target, then making candidate inferences about the target. It is this creative use of analogy that we want to simulate, the Rutherford analogy being a convenient and well-known example.

Recognition of the solar system as a potential base is a memory retrieval process in the model. The relation symbols ATTRACTS and DIFFERENT-SIZE in the representation of the target serve as retrieval cues. If these are used as input to the representation of the task, the output is a tensor product of vectors representing all sets of arguments of these relation symbols. For example, when ATTRACTS is used as input, the output will include the tensor product of vectors representing "sun" and "planet," plus other pairs of arguments of ATTRACTS.

When arguments of a potential base are recognized, they can be used as input. If the input is "sun" and "planet" the output will include ATTRACTS, LESS-MASSIVE-THAN, ORBITS-AROUND, and so on. These relation symbols become candidate inferences for the target, leading to the hypothesis that the electron orbits around the nucleus.

This simplified account of how analogical reasoning is simulated in the STAR model was designed to illustrate the main argument of this section, that a computational process can produce an output which is inherently creative, using representations of relations of the kind defined earlier. In this case a computational model has been constructed which can retrieve a base, the solar system, which is a potential analog of the target. Relations in the base are transferred to the target, and become candidate inferences for the target. The higher rank representations permit more powerful and more flexible reasoning, and also permit representations to be changed dynamically in the course of cognitive processing.

The Rutherford analogy illustrates the point that creativity can depend on representation of complex relations in an explicit form, that is accessible to other cognitive processes. Expertise brings with it the ability to make the best use of processing capacity, so that a physicist can represent complex relations such as orbital motion efficiently as chunks, using minimum processing capacity. However, the processes of chunking and segmentation do not remove the need to represent complex relations. The recognition of the analogy between the atom and the solar system would have necessitated representation of some complex relations in parallel. In our simulation, it depends on representing quaternary relations in parallel.

Much less exalted cases of creativity require representation of relations in a similar way. When a four-year-old child is first working out how to cope with monotonic series, he has to use his representations creatively to develop efficient, reliable strategies and skills. If, for example, he notices that not only is his next oldest sibling taller than he is, but the oldest sibling is taller still, he has to work out some strategy or procedure for making reliable inferences about who is taller than whom. There is definite creativity in this performance, the fact that all normal human beings go through it notwithstanding. It is what Boden (1990) calls "P-creative." Our research (Halford et al., 1992; Halford et al., 1995) shows that such creativity depends on ability to represent relations with an appropriate degree of complexity. We suggest that development of strategies for transitive inference and serial order tasks requires ability to represent ternary relations in parallel. If the child can only represent binary relations, inadequate strategies result.

ACQUISITION OF RELATIONAL KNOWLEDGE

Perhaps the most intriguing question of all is how relational knowledge develops. Unfortunately comparatively little is known about acquisition of relational knowledge, as distinct from associative knowledge. However, there have been attempts to model and investigate this process (Halford et al., 1998a; Holland, Holyoak, Nisbett, & Thagard, 1986; Holyoak, Koh, & Nisbett, 1989). There are two ways of formulating the question, which we will briefly consider.

The first is to consider the transition from Rank 1 neural nets to Rank 2 neural nets. This is basically to change from a three-layered net to a tensor net. So far we know of no published algorithm that could make that transition. It is possible that some extension of cascade correlation, in which new hidden units are recruited as required to handle extra dimensions of the task, might be worth exploring in relation to this question. Another possibility would be the use of genetic algorithms. There are hybrid models, such as the tensor recurrent net of Phillips (1994), that certainly show promise. Then there have been interesting attempts to extend three-layered nets to handle relational information (Hinton, 1990; Phillips, 1994; but see also Halford et al., in preparation). But research so far has been more concerned with modeling phenomena that belong to particular levels (ranks), than with making the transition between levels. In our work we have been attempting to define the levels with more precision, using the concepts of relational complexity and representational rank. We believe this is a prerequisite to understanding the transition process.

The second approach would be to take advantage of the transition as it occurs in nature. Actually this phenomenon is well established, but the literature has been curiously reluctant to recognize its significance. We refer here to so-called "learning set" acquisition, discussed earlier. In this paradigm a series of isomorphic discrimination tasks are learned. Learning becomes progressively faster as more problems are experienced. Thus the participants, humans or (other) animals, learn something more general, more "abstract" than the properties of individual stimuli. This is often called "learning to learn" or "learning set." Yet, despite the fact that the phenomenon goes back to Harlow (1949) and a few attempts at modeling notwithstanding (e.g., Levine, 1975; Restle, 1958) there is almost no understanding of how improvement across problems occurs. It is standardly attributed to "rule learning" (e.g., Kendler, 1995), which explains nothing. As mentioned previously, we have proffered the explanation that learning set entails acquisition of relational knowledge, together with analogical mapping of the relational representation from one problem to another (Halford, 1993; Halford et al., 1998a). If this interpretation is correct, it means that so-called learning set acquisition actually amounts to relational knowledge acquisition occurring in nature, right before our eyes! So why not study it? The only reason that occurs to us is the inhibitory effect of neo-behaviorist attitudes, together with the rather uninformative label "learning set," that stand in the way of cognitive analyses of the phenomenon. Whatever the cause, the inhibition of work on this problem is very regrettable, because it means we lose the opportunity to study the formation of abstract, relational processes as they occur.

CONCLUSION

We suggest that human creativity depends on our ability to represent complex relations in parallel, in a way that is explicit and accessible to other cognitive processes. The kinds of relations required are defined in terms of the number of arguments, or number of separately varying, interacting components, that are related. The representations required are defined in terms of rank. The model can be neatly implemented in a PDP architecture, using tensor products, which enables many of the properties of each rank to be simulated.

In less technical terms, creativity depends on having an adequate cognitive "window" on sets of interacting processes. If a person or, more generally, a system cannot represent the relations between the relevant interacting processes, creative, non-routine, or non-algorithmic thought is not possible.

DISCUSSION

TD: You've already incorporated new material into the chapter in response to some of my earlier questions, but I do have one more question for you.

You say that creativity requires *explicit representations* that are accessible to other cognitive processes. More specifically, you say that it requires the ability to represent and recursively modify explicit, complex relations in parallel. You discuss this in the context of your theory of representational ranks and provide a hierarchy of cognitive processes that is defined in terms of the complexity of the relations that can be handled at each level.

Your main model of these ranks is a connectionist one—and here I have problems. The inner states of connectionist systems are notoriously hard to access and explicitate, so I wonder how explicit and accessible your representations really are. You say that they are explicit in the sense that they are *explicitly symbolized*. Your example is LARGER-THAN(whale,dolphin). Here the relation is explicitly symbolized by "LARGER-THAN," which you say is accessible to other cognitive processes, as in

BECAUSE(LARGER-THAN(whale,dolphin), AVOIDS(dolphin, whale))

But these are symbolisms that *you have given to the system*. To what extent are they, or the relations that they express, explicitly represented in the states of the system? And so, to what extent are they accessible to the system and to other systems running other cognitive processes?

GH/WW: We agree that accessibility is an issue in neural net models. Thus the representations in the hidden layer of a lot of three-layered nets are not semantically interpretable, as Smolensky (1988) has pointed out. Entities that are represented do not retain their identity in the representation, and the components are not recoverable, so the representation is not compositional. Consider, for example, the configural discrimination task discussed earlier. A neural net model might include hidden units that represent the configurations circle/white, triangle/white, and so on. The activations on these units are important for computing the output, but they are only accessible to the net by means of the inputs. That is, activation of a set of inputs is transmitted, via variable connections, to the hidden units, the activations on which are transmitted via another set of variable weights, to the output units. But, as we mentioned previously, the net cannot query the hidden units to ask questions such as "what is combined with circle when the output is positive?" Researchers may be able to study hidden unit activations by techniques such as clustering analysis, but this information is not accessible to the organism whose cognitions are being modeled by the net, as we all seem to agree.

However our contention is that representations in tensor product nets are more accessible than those in the hidden unit of a three-layered net of the kind that might be used to model conditional discrimination. Thus the binary relational instance MOTHER-OF(woman,baby) is represented by the tensor product of three vectors, representing MOTHER-OF, woman, and baby. The three components are each represented by a vector, that corresponds to activations on a set of neural units. Their composition into the relational instance is represented by the three-dimensional matrix or tensor product, corresponding to activation of units representing both the components and their binding. Thus the components, MOTHER-OF, woman, and baby retain their identity in the composite representation. Furthermore they are accessible to the system, because the model includes operations for recovering the components from the tensor product representation. As illustrated in Figure 4.2, if the input is "woman" and "baby" the output will be MOTHER-OF plus other predicates bound to these arguments. Or again, if the input were MOTHER-OF and "woman" the output would be "baby." The STAR model routinely accesses tensor product representations in this way. The representations are also modifiable, by changing the vector on the predicate units, as indicated earlier. Thus tensor product representations of relations, as used in the STAR model, are accessible in a way that, say, representations in a three-layered net model of conditional discrimination are not.

What makes our representations accessible is that they are symbols, whereas representations in a typical three-layered net model are inaccessible because they are not symbols. To avoid confusion here, it is important to note that accessibility of cognitive processes does not depend on whether they are modeled by neural nets, but on whether they are symbolic. Cognitive processes modeled by neural nets are not inherently inaccessible. Neural nets can be used to model symbols, and processes for accessing them, which we have done with our tensor product formalism. It is important not to confuse the cognitive processes modeled, in this case symbols and processes for operating on them, with the architecture of the model, in this case neural nets. To illustrate, people can be aware of symbols like "whale." When this occurs, the neurophysical reality underlying their awareness of the symbol "whale" is a pattern of neural activity in (parts of) their brain. The fact that we are unable to interpret the neural patterns directly does not invalidate their awareness of and access to the symbol "whale." In our, much simpler, model of some aspects of cognition, similarly, the fact that symbols are encoded as binding unit patterns in tensor product networks does not invalidate our view that these structures encode accessible symbols. It is not the neural patterns, or the neural net patterns, that people are aware of, but the symbols they represent. To argue otherwise is to confuse different levels of description.

While we would certainly not contend that tensor product models have solved all the problems of modeling symbolic processes in neural nets, we do believe that they have taken a significant step in that direction. It is true of course that in achieving this we have sacrificed the learning functions of three-layered nets. Consequently, we have to agree that in our model the representations are supplied to the net by the modelers. Therefore representations are not emergent properties of tensor product nets, as they are with three-layered nets. So at the present time the two types of neural net architectures are most appropriately seen as complementary.

REFERENCES

Anderson, J. R. (1983). *The architecture of cognition*. Cambridge, MA: Harvard University Press.

Andrews, G., & Halford, G. S. (1998). Children's ability to make transitive inferences: The importance of premise integration and structural complexity. *Cognitive Development, 13*, 479–513.

Baillargeon, R. (1995). A model of physical reasoning in infancy. In C. Rovee-Collier & L. P. Lipsitt (Eds.), *Advances in infancy research* (Vol. 9, pp. 305–371). Norwood, NJ: Ablex.

Bitterman, M. E. (1960). Toward a comparative psychology of learning. *American Psychologist, 15*, 704–712.

Boden, M. A. (1990). *The creative mind: Myths and mechanisms*. London: Weidenfeld and Nicholson.

Chappell, M., & Humphreys, M. S. (1993). *Analysis of a neural network with application to human memory modelling*. Fourth Australian Conference on Neural Networks.

Clark, A., & Karmiloff-Smith, A. (1993). The cognizer's innards: A psychological and philosophical perspective on the development of thought. *Mind and Language, 8*, 487–519.

Codd, E. F. (1990). *The relational model for database management: Version 2*: Reading, MA.: Addison-Wesley.

Dartnall, T. H. (1994). Creativity, thought and representational redescription. In T. H. Dartnall (Ed.), *Artificial Intelligence and creativity: An interdisciplinary approach*. Dordrecht, Netherlands: Kluwer Academic Publishers.

Dunbar, K. (2001). The analogical paradox: Why analogy is so easy in naturalistic settings, yet so difficult in the psychological laboratory. In D. Gentner,

K. J. Holyoak, & B. Kokinov (Eds.), *The analogical mind: Perspectives from cognitive science* (pp. 313–334). Cambridge, MA: MIT Press.

Elman, J. L. (1990). Finding structure in time. *Cognitive Science, 14,* 179–211.

Gentner, D. (1983). Structure-mapping: A theoretical framework for analogy. *Cognitive Science, 7,* 155–170.

Gick, M. L., & Holyoak, K. J. (1983). Schema induction and analogical transfer. *Cognitive Psychology, 15,* 1–38.

Greeno, J. G., Riley, M. S., & Gelman, R. (1984). Conceptual competence and children's counting. *Cognitive Psychology, 16,* 94–143.

Halford, G. S. (1992). Analogical reasoning and conceptual complexity in cognitive development. *Human Development, 35,* 193–217.

Halford, G. S. (1993). *Children's understanding: The development of mental models.* Hillsdale, NJ: Erlbaum.

Halford, G. S., Bain, J. D., Maybery, M., & Andrews, G. (1998). Induction of relational schemas: Common processes in reasoning and complex learning. *Cognitive Psychology, 35,* 201–245.

Halford, G. S., & Leitch, E. (1989). Processing load constraints: A structure-mapping approach. In M. A. Luszcz & T. Nettelbeck (Eds.), *Psychological development: Perspectives across the life-span* (pp. 151–159). Amsterdam: North-Holland.

Halford, G. S., Maybery, M. T., & Bain, J. D. (1986). Capacity limitations in children's reasoning: A dual task approach. *Child Development, 57,* 616–627.

Halford, G. S., Maybery, M. T., Smith, S. B., Bain, J. D., Dickson, J. C., Kelly, M. E., & Stewart, J. E. M. (1992). *Acquisition of reasoning: A computational model of strategy development in transitive inference.* University of Queensland, Australia: Department of Psychology, Centre for Human Information Processing and Problem Solving.

Halford, G. S., Phillips, S., & Wilson, W. H. (2001). Structural complexity in cognitive processes: The concept of representational rank. Manuscript in preparation.

Halford, G. S., Smith, S. B., Dickson, J. C., Maybery, M. T., Kelly, M. E., Bain, J. D., & Stewart, J. E. M. (1995). Modeling the development of reasoning strategies: The roles of analogy, knowledge, and capacity. In T. Simon & G. S. Halford (Eds.), *Developing cognitive competence: New approaches to cognitive modelling* (pp. 77–156). Hillsdale, NJ: Erlbaum.

Halford, G. S., Wiles, J., Humphreys, M. S., & Wilson, W. H. (Eds.). (1993). Parallel distributed processing approaches to creative reasoning: Tensor models of memory and analogy. In T. H. Dartnall, S. Kim, R. Levinson, F. Sudweeks, D. Subramanian (Eds.), *Artificial Intelligence and creativity, papers from the 1993 Spring Symposium Technical Report.* Menlo Park, CA: AAAI Press.

Halford, G. S., Wilson, W. H., Guo, J., Gayler, R. W., Wiles, J., & Stewart, J. E. M. (1994). Connectionist implications for processing capacity limitations in analogies. In K. J. Holyoak & J. Barnden (Eds.), *Advances in connectionist and neural computation theory, Vol. 2: Analogical connections* (pp. 363–415). Norwood, NJ: Ablex.

Halford, G. S., Wilson, W. H., & Phillips, S. (1998a). Processing capacity defined by relational complexity: Implications for comparative, developmental, and cognitive psychology. *Behaviorial and Brain Sciences, 21,* 803–831.

Halford, G. S., Wilson, W. H., & Phillips, S. (1998b). Relational processing in higher cognition: Implications for analogy, capacity and cognitive development. In K. Holyoak, D. Gentner, & B. Kokinov (Eds.), *Advances in analogy research: Integration of theory and data from the cognitive, computational, and neural sciences* (pp. 57–73). Sofia, Culgaria: New Bulgarian University.

Harlow, H. F. (1949). The formation of learning sets. *Psychological Review, 42,* 51–65.

Harlow, H. F. (1959). Learning set and error factor theory. In S. Koch (Ed.), *Psychology: A study of a science: Vol. 2. General systematic formulations, learning, and special processes* (pp. 492–537). New York: McGraw-Hill.

Hinton, G. E. (1990). Mapping part-whole hierarchies into connectionist networks. *Artificial Intelligence, 46,* 47–75.

Hodkin, B. (1987). Performance model analysis in class inclusion: An illustration with two language conditions. *Developmental Psychology, 23,* 683–689.

Holland, J. H., Holyoak, K. J., Nisbett, R. E., & Thagard, P. R. (1986). *Induction: Processes of inference, learning and discovery.* Cambridge, MA: Bradford Books/MIT Press.

Holyoak, K. J., Koh, K., & Nisbett, R. E. (1989). A theory of conditioning: Inductive learning within rule-based hierarchies. *Psychological Review, 96,* 315–340.

Holyoak, K. J., & Thagard, P. (1989). Analogical mapping by constraint satisfaction. *Cognitive Science, 13,* 295–355.

Holyoak, K. J., & Thagard, P. (1995). *Mental leaps.* Cambridge, MA: MIT Press.

Humphreys, M. S., Bain, J. D., & Pike, R. (1989). Different ways to cue a coherent memory system: A theory for episodic, semantic and procedural tasks. *Psychological Review, 96,* 208–233.

Humphreys, M. S., Wiles, J., & Bain, J. D. (1993). Memory retrieval with two cues: Think of intersecting sets. In D. E. Meyer & S. Kornblum (Eds.), *Attention and performance XIV: A silver jubilee.* Hillsdale, NJ: Erlbaum.

Karmiloff-Smith, A. (1990). Constraints on representational change: Evidence from children's drawing. *Cognition, 34*(1), 57–83.

Kendler, T. S. (1995). *Levels of cognitive development.* Mahwah, NJ: Erlbaum.

Levine, M. (1975). *A cognitive theory of learning.* Hillsdale, NJ: Erlbaum.

Mandler, J. M. (1992). How to build a baby: II. Conceptual primitives. *Psychological Review, 99,* 587–604.

Maybery, M. T., Bain, J. D., & Halford, G. S. (1986). Information processing demands of transitive inference. *Journal of Experimental Psychology: Learning, Memory and Cognition, 12,* 600–613.

McClelland, J. L., & Rumelhart, D. E. (1985). Distributed memory and the representation of general and specific information. *Journal of Experimental Psychology: General, 114,* 159–188.

McGonigle, B., & Chalmers, M. (1984). The selective impact of question form and input mode on the symbolic distance effect in children. *Journal of Experimental Child Psychology, 37,* 525–554.

Mednick, S. A. (1962). The associative basis of the creative process. *Psychological Review, 69,* 220–232.

Ohlsson, S., & Langley, P. (1986). *PRISM tutorial and manual.* Irvine, CA: University of California.

Phillips, S. (1994). *Strong systematicity within connectionism: The tensor-recurrent network.* Sixteenth Annual Conference of the Cognitive Science Society.

Phillips, S., Halford, G. S., & Wilson, W. H. (1995, July). *The processing of associations versus the processing of relations and symbols: A systematic comparison.* Seventeenth Annual Conference of the Cognitive Science Society, Pittsburgh, PA.

Posner, M. I., & Boies, S. J. (1971). Components of attention. *Psychological Review, 78,* 391–408.

Premack, D. (1983). The codes of man and beasts. *Behavioral and Brain Sciences, 6,* 125–167.

Quinn, P. C., Eimas, P. D., & Rosenkrantz, S. L. (1993). Evidence for representations of perceptually similar natural categories by 3-month-old and 4-month-old infants. *Perception, 22,* 463–475.

Quinn, P. C., & Johnson, M. H. (1997). The emergence of perceptual category representations in young infants: A connectionist analysis. *Journal of Experimental Child Psychology, 66,* 236–263.

Restle, F. (1958). Towards a quantative description of learning set data. *Psychological Review, 65,* 77–91.

Rivera, S. M., Wakeley, A., & Langer, J. (1999). The drawbridge phenomenon: Representational reasoning or peceptual preference? *Developmental Psychology, 35,* 427–435.

Rosch, E., & Mervis, C. B. (1975). Family resemblences: Studies in the internal structure of categories. *Cognitive Psychology, 7,* 573–605.

Rubin, D. C., & Wallace, W. T. (1989). Rhyme and reason: Analysis of dual retrieval cues. *Journal of Experimental Psychology: Learning, Memory and Cognition, 15,* 698–709.

Rudy, J. W. (1991). Elemental and configural associations, the hippocampus and development. *Developmental Psychobiology, 24,* 221–236.

Schmajuk, N. A., & DiCarlo, J. J. (1992). Stimulus configuration, classical conditioning, and hippocampal function. *Psychological Review, 99,* 268–305.

Smolensky, P. (1988). On the proper treatment of connectionism. *Behavioral and Brain Sciences, 11,* 1–74.

Smolensky, P. (1990). Tensor product variable binding and the representation of symbolic structures in connectionist systems. *Artificial Intelligence, 46,* 159–216.

VanLehn, K., & Brown, J. S. (1980). Planning nets: A representation for formalizing analogies and semantic models of procedural skills. In R. E. Snow, P. A. Federico, & W. E. Montague (Eds.), *Aptitude learning and instruction. Vol. 2. Cognitive process analyses of learning and problem solving* (pp. 95–137). Hillsdale, NJ: Erlbaum.

Wiles, J., Halford, G. S., Stewart, J. E. M., Humphreys, M. S., Bain, J. D., & Wilson, W. H. (1994). Tensor models: A creative basis for memory retrieval and analogical mapping. In T. H. Dartnall (Ed.), *Artificial Intelligence and creativity: An interdisciplinary approach* (pp. 147–161). Dordrecht: Kluwer.

Wilson, W. H., Halford, G. S., Gray, B., & Phillips, S. (2001). The STAR-2 model for mapping hierarchically structured analogs. In D. Gentner, K. Holyoak, & B. Kokinov (Eds.), *The analogical mind: Perspectives from cognitive science* (pp. 125–159). Cambridge, MA: MIT Press.

Wynne, C. D. L. (1995). Reinforcement accounts for transitive inference performance. *Animal Learning and Behavior, 23,* 207–217.

5

Analogy and Creativity: Schema Induction in a Structure-Sensitive Connectionist Model

John E. Hummel and Keith J. Holyoak

Even though a comprehensive account of human creativity remains elusive, some of its necessary requirements can be stated unequivocally. A prominent requirement for creativity is that the cognitive system, functioning with a high degree of autonomy, must generate new representations from experience. The generation of new representations—new ways to describe things and their relationships—is a cornerstone of creative accomplishment. New representational elements can take many forms, including what cognitive scientists have termed features, categories, concepts, predicates, propositions, rules, and schemas. We shall refer to the autonomous generation of such elements as *induction*, in the very general sense of Holland, Holyoak, Nisbett and Thagard (1986): "all inferential processes that expand knowledge in the face of uncertainty" (p. 1).

As Holland et al. emphasized, induction (like creativity in general) does not proceed by blind search. Rather, a central part of induction is the discovery of systematic correspondences among existing elements and using those correspondences to guide inference. In addition to driving "mundane" inferences, the discovered correspondences can change the representation of the elements themselves, revealing regularities that apply across elements (i.e., driving the induction of a schema describing a more general class), or filling gaps in the representation of one entity based on elements in the other. In either case, relationships between objects or events become explicit: induction is a process whereby knowledge is modified by its use (Holland et al., 1986).

Particularly in its more creative manifestations, induction depends on mechanisms that access and use relevant prior knowledge from outside the immediate domain of the problem at hand. A prominent example of such a mechanism is reasoning by analogy. It has often been noted that the use of analogies to draw inferences and learn new abstractions likely plays an important role in creative thinking (e.g., Gentner, 1989; Hofstadter & Mitchell, 1994; Holyoak & Thagard, 1995). Analogical reasoning generally involves the use of a relatively well-understood *source* analog to guide inferences about a less familiar *target* analog. This process has four major components: (a) accessing a potentially useful source analog; (b) mapping the source to the target to identify systematic correspondences; (c) using the mapping to draw new inferences about the target; and (d) inducing a generalized schema that captures the commonalities between the source and target (e.g., Carbonell, 1983; Gentner, 1989; Gick & Holyoak, 1980). Each of these components can contribute to creative thinking. The access stage may lead to the concurrent activation of information that had not previously been connected; mapping may reveal systematic correspondences that go beyond preexisting similarities; inference may generate novel propositions that constitute plausible conjectures about the target; and schema induction may create useful new abstractions.

In recent years a large number of computational models of analogy have been developed (e.g., Falkenhainer, Forbus & Gentner, 1989; Forbus, Gentner & Law, 1995; Halford et al., 1994; Hofstadter & Mitchell, 1994; Holyoak & Thagard, 1989; Keane, Ledgeway & Duff, 1994; Kokinov, 1994; Thagard, Holyoak, Nelson & Gochfeld, 1990). These models collectively address the stages of analogical access, mapping and inference. On the face of it, such models provide a key prerequisite for modeling complex relational schema induction: structure-based correspondences between elements of the source and target analogs (the output of analogical mapping) play a central role in schema induction, providing essential information about what elements to generalize over.

However, this apparent connection between analogy and schema induction, while widely recognized, has generally not been computationally realized. Rather, the leap from analogical correspondences to the induction of abstract schemas has been left as a promissory note. This deficit is problematic because schema induction is a key component in the link between analogy and creativity. Induction is not simply a nicety that follows from analogical thinking; rather, it is a primary reason for being interested in analogy in the first place. But it is by no means clear that all mechanisms for analogy are also suitable as mechanisms for induction. As we shall see, there is reason to believe that most extant mechanisms for analogy are *not* suitable as mechanisms for induction. Studies of human problem solving strongly indicate that analogical mapping and inference lead quite directly to schema induction (Gick & Holyoak, 1983; Novick & Holyoak, 1991;

Ross & Kennedy, 1990). In contrast to current models, which treat mapping and schema induction as fundamentally separate processes (i.e., by performing one without performing the other), the human apparently performs both as components of the same mental operations.

There are reasons to suspect that the failure of current analogy models to provide an account of schema induction may be symptomatic of important limitations in their core representational assumptions (Hummel & Holyoak, 1997). Analogical mapping is an inherently structural business, so a mapping engine must represent knowledge in a form that makes structure explicit (Falkenhainer et al., 1989; Gentner, 1989; Holyoak & Thagard, 1989). At the same time, mapping requires the simultaneous satisfaction of multiple, often contradictory constraints (Holyoak & Thagard, 1989). The dual requirements of structure sensitivity and multiple constraint satisfaction can be jointly satisfied by a mapping engine that (a) uses localist units to represent analog elements (predicates, objects, and propositions) and/or their correspondences, and (b) uses an algorithm that in one way or another enforces multiple constraints. It is not surprising, therefore, that most models of analogical mapping are based on variants of this approach [for example, ACME (Holyoak & Thagard, 1989), SME (Falkenhainer et al., 1989), IAM (Keane et al., 1994), AMBR (Kokinov, 1994)].* But although a purely localist representation of meaning is useful for analogical mapping, it is inadequate for generalization and building abstractions (basic components of schema induction). This limitation is problematic because it is not straightforward to adapt current mapping algorithms to operate on distributed representations. Thus, the representational requirements of most current mapping models may be fundamentally incompatible with the representational requirements of schema induction.

We have recently developed a computational model of analogy based on very different assumptions about the representation of analog elements and, therefore, the operations that discover correspondences between them (Hummel & Holyoak, 1997; for earlier versions of the model see Hummel, Burns & Holyoak, 1994; Hummel & Holyoak, 1992). This model, called LISA (*Learning and Inference with Schemas and Analogies*), is designed to provide an integrated account of all four major components of analogy use, from access to schema induction. Hummel and Holyoak (1997) describe LISA's account of analogical access and mapping in detail, and show that the model accounts for 14 major phenomena in human analogical access and mapping. Kubose, Holyoak and Hummel (2001) and Waltz, Lau, Grewal and Holyoak (2001) report additional empirical tests of LISA's mapping predictions, and Holyoak and Hummel (2001) report simulations that demonstrate LISA's ability to map analogies as large as any that have been

---

*ACME = Analogical Constraint Mapping Engine, SME = Structure Mapping Engine, IAM = Incremental Analogy Machine, AMBR = Associative Memory-Based Reasoning.

shown to be within human limits. Recent theoretical work has focused on the development of a general architecture for cognition (Holyoak & Hummel, 2000), the interface between reasoning and perception (Hummel & Holyoak, 2001b), and inference and schema induction (Hummel & Holyoak, 1996, 2001). The LISA system provides a natural platform for simulating aspects of induction and other forms of creativity.

LISA integrates analogical mapping with a representation of the semantic content of propositions. Predicates and objects are represented as patterns of activation distributed over units representing semantic primitives, giving the model the flexibility and automatic generalization capacities associated with distributed connectionist models. But LISA departs from traditional connectionist models in that it actively binds these representations into propositional structures. The benefit of this type of representation is that it has both the systematicity (structure-sensitivity) of a localist or symbolic representation and the flexibility of a distributed representation; the cost is that it is subject to inherent capacity limits (cf. Halford et al., 1994; Hummel & Holyoak, 1992, 1993). As we will see, both the benefits and the costs of this approach have important implications for LISA as a model of analogy, induction, and creativity. In particular, the capacity limits can be alleviated by—and hence serve to motivate—inductive mechanisms that "compress" representations, resulting in a form of predicate discovery.

The remainder of this chapter will sketch the LISA model and describe how its approach to analog retrieval and mapping can be used to induce new schemas and other structures. In brief, the approach is the following. Analog retrieval is viewed as a form of guided pattern matching whereby distributed, structured representations of propositions in working memory (WM) excite one or more propositions in long term memory (LTM). Augmented with the capacity to learn which propositions respond to which active patterns, this retrieval mechanism serves as the basis for analogical mapping. And augmented further with a capacity to (a) highlight elements that are common to both active and recipient propositions, and (b) encode those elements into memory as new propositions, the retrieval and mapping operations form the basis of inference and schema induction.

ANALOGICAL ACCESS AND MAPPING IN LISA

Basic Architecture

The access and mapping components of LISA, along with detailed simulation results, are described in Hummel and Holyoak (1997). Here we will only sketch the basic architecture and operation of the model. The fundamental representational principles in LISA are motivated by the problem (forcefully posed by Fodor & Pylyshyn, 1988) of using distributed representations of meaning to capture the structural relations in propositions.

Solving this problem entails *dynamically* (i.e., actively) binding independent representations of predicate case roles to their fillers (e.g., objects) (see Hummel & Holyoak, 1992; Shastri & Ajjanagadde, 1993). The core of LISA's architecture is a system for representing dynamic role-filler bindings in WM and encoding those bindings in LTM. LISA uses synchrony of firing for dynamic binding in WM. Case roles and objects are represented in WM as patterns of activation distributed over a collection of *semantic units* (see Figure 5.1); case roles and objects fire in synchrony when they are bound together and out of synchrony when they are not.

Every proposition is encoded in LTM by a hierarchy of *structure units* that store, recreate, and respond to synchronized patterns on the semantic units (Figure 5.1a). At the bottom of the hierarchy are *predicate* and *object* units. Each predicate unit locally codes the semantic primitives of one case role of one predicate. For example, the predicate unit *own1* represents the first (agent) role of the predicate "own," and has bi-directional excitatory connections to all the semantic units representing that role (e.g., units for *state1, possess1, legal1,* etc.); *own2* represents the second case role of the "own" relation and is connected to the semantic units representing that role (e.g., *state2, possess2, legal2,* etc.). We generally distinguish semantic primitives for predicates by place: *possess1,* representing possession in the first role of a possession predicate, and *possess2,* representing possession in the second role, are separate units. (As discussed later in the context of the "*n*-ary restriction," this convention is not inviolable, and there are times when it is useful to violate it.) Semantically-related predicates share units in corresponding roles (e.g., the units *own1* and *has1* will be connected to many of the same semantic units). In this way, the semantic similarity of different predicates is made explicit.

Object units are just like predicate units except that they are connected to semantic units describing things rather than roles (and, of course, they are not distinguished according to place). For example, the object unit *Mary* might be connected to semantic units such as *human, adult, female,* and so on, whereas *book* might be connected to *artifact, information,* and *paper.*

Sub-proposition (SP) units are structure units that bind case roles to objects in LTM. For example, "Mary owns the book" would be represented by two SP units: One representing Mary as agent of owning, and the other representing book as patient of owning. The Mary-agent SP would share bi-directional excitatory connections with *Mary* and *own1,* and the book-patient SP would share connections with *book* and *own2.* Proposition (P) units reside at the top of the hierarchy. Each P unit shares bi-directional excitatory connections with the corresponding SP units. P units serve a dual role for the purposes of representing hierarchical structures, such as "Sam knows Mary owns the book" (see Figure 5.1b). In their role as binding units for a proposition, they are connected to SPs representing their constituent role-filler bindings (see Figure 5.1a). When a proposition serves as the filler

FIGURE 5.1

a. The encoding of the proposition *own(Mary,book)* in LISA's LTM. Structure units are depicted as ovals (P units), rectangles (SP units), triangles (predicate units), and large circles (object units). Semantic primitive units are depicted as small circles. (Although the structure units are labeled according to their "meaning"—for example, "own1," "Mary"—all semantic content is coded in the semantic units; structure units serve only the purpose of binding that content in LTM.) Lines depict excitatory connections between units; inhibitory connections are not shown. See text for details.

b. The encoding of the hierarchical proposition *know(Sam,own(Mary,book))*.

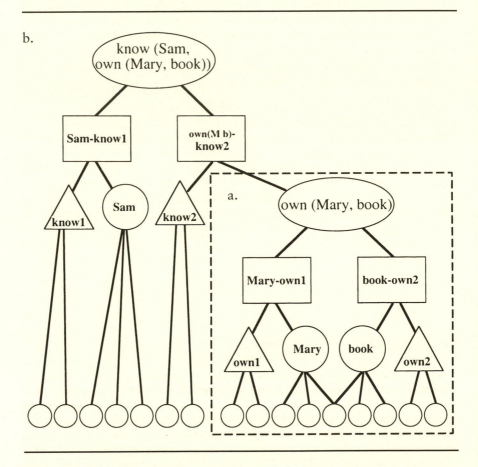

of a role in another proposition, the lower-level P unit serves in the place of an object unit under the appropriate SP. For example, the P unit for "Mary owns the book" is connected (in the place of an object) to the second SP of the proposition "Sam knows [X]," making the binding of "Mary owns the book" to the patient role of "knows" explicit in LTM. It is important to emphasize that P units do not encode semantic content in any direct way.

Rather, they serve only as "pointers" to a hierarchy of SP, predicate, and object units that are collectively capable of generating this content on the semantic units.

The final component of LISA's architecture is a set of *mapping connections* between structure units of the same type in different analogs. Every P unit in one analog shares a mapping connection with every P unit in every other analog; likewise, SPs share connections across analogs, as do objects and predicates. Mapping connections have both *buffers,* which accumulate evidence that two units do or do not represent corresponding elements, and *weights,* which are periodically updated on the basis of the buffers, and which allow the units to directly excite and inhibit one another. At the beginning of a simulation run, the buffers and weights are initialized to zero. The weight on a mapping connection grows larger whenever the units it links are active simultaneously, and more negative whenever the one unit is active and the other is inactive. In this way, the model keeps track of what corresponds to what across the analogs and uses known mappings to constrain future mappings. By the end of a run, corresponding units will have large positive weights on their mapping connections, and non-corresponding units will have large negative weights.

For the purposes of mapping and retrieval, analogs are divided into two mutually exclusive sets: a *driver* and one or more *recipients*. Mapping and retrieval are controlled by the driver. There is no necessary linkage between the driver/recipient distinction and the more familiar source/target distinction. However, a canonical flow of control would involve initially using a target analog (the unfamiliar situation) as the driver to access a familiar source analog in long term memory. Once a source is in active memory, mapping can be performed in either direction. After a stable mapping is established, the source is used to drive inference generation in the target and schema induction.

Basic Operation

LISA performs structured comparisons as a form of guided pattern matching. One at a time, propositions in the driver are chosen to become active. When a proposition becomes active, it generates a series of patterns (one pattern for each role-argument binding) on the semantic units. The semantic units are shared by all propositions, so the patterns generated by one proposition will drive the activation of one or more similar propositions in LTM (analogical access) or in an active subset of LTM (analogical mapping). By keeping track of which propositions become active in response to which patterns, the model learns the correspondences between the elements that generated a pattern and the elements that responded to it. These correspondences then serve to constrain subsequent memory access. Over the course of several activated propositions, the result is a representation of the correspondences between the elements of the analogs.

These correspondences are monitored (learned) only in the course of analogical mapping. For the purposes of analog access, propositions in one analog activate propositions in other analogs, but the model does not keep track of which propositions activate which. (The number of correspondences that would have to be monitored would be prohibitive given the number of propositions in all of LTM.) Hummel and Holyoak (1997) show that this single difference between access and mapping allows LISA to simulate observed differences in human sensitivity to various types of similarity in these two component process (e.g., Ross, 1989).

The structural comparison process (i.e., access plus mapping) can be subdivided into three levels at increasingly fine-grained time scales, each related to a different aspect of working memory. *Active memory* can be viewed as the largest subset of long-term memory that is currently the focus of attention—namely, the driver and recipient analogs, along with whatever additional units are involved in learning a schema from the driver and recipient. We also assume that the buffers on the cross-analog mapping connections reside in active memory. Active memory is assumed to be relatively stable over a time range of several seconds to minutes.

Within active memory, a very small number of propositions in one analog can enter a state of phase-locked activity that represents their variable bindings. This dynamic WM, which is the most significant bottleneck in the system, is termed the *phase set,* and consists of the set of mutually desynchronized role-argument bindings (SPs). We assume that adult humans can maintain an upper bound of about four to six non-overlapping phases (see Hummel & Biederman, 1992; Shastri & Ajjanaggade, 1993). The phase set is assumed to be relatively stable over a range of a few seconds, and intuitively corresponds to the system's "current thought."

The boundaries of a phase set are defined by updating the weights on the mapping connections: updating the weights (and "flushing" the buffers) terminates one phase set and initiates the next. "Space" in the phase set is occupied by role-argument bindings (i.e., SPs). For example, the proposition "Mary owns the book" requires two role-argument bindings, and would therefore fill a phase set of size two. "Mary gave the book to John" has three role-argument bindings, and would fill a phase set of size three. Propositions are placed into the phase set one at a time, but as a whole, a set may contain more than one proposition. For example, with a set of size five, LISA could activate "Mary owns the book" (occupying two phases), then activate "Mary gave the book to John" (occupying three), and *then* update the mapping connections, converting the buffer values to weights. With a maximum set size of three, LISA would have to update the weights *between* selecting the propositions (i.e., selecting the *owns* proposition, then updating the weights, then selecting the *gave* proposition and updating the weights again). With a set size of two, it could not reliably represent the three-argument *gives* proposition at all.

The theoretical claims motivating these conventions are the following:

1. The phase set corresponds to the current contents of "awareness."

2. The maximum size of the phase set is given by the number of role-filler bindings that can be explicitly entertained simultaneously (i.e., be kept simultaneously active but out of synchrony).

3. The mapping hypotheses generated during a given phase set (as embodied in the connection buffers) must be consolidated (i.e., converted to weights so the buffers may be flushed) before moving on to the next phase set.

The main computational significance of the phase set for LISA is that mappings for information within a single phase set mutually constrain each other to a greater extent than do mappings in different phase sets. This is a consequence of two properties of the LISA algorithm. First, the information in a single role-filler binding is the basic unit for matching the driver to the recipient (due in part to between-proposition inhibition and within-proposition excitation in the recipient). And second, updating the weights on the mapping connections represents a kind of commitment, in the sense that those weights then serve to influence (for better or worse) future mappings. Prior to this updating, potential mappings within a phase set constrain one another in an order-independent fashion. Because the weights are not updated until the end of the phase set, mappings entertained early in the set do not influence mappings entertained later in the set. As a result, LISA's algorithm behaves much more like parallel constraint satisfaction within a phase set than between phase sets. The size of the available phase set therefore places an upper bound on the formal complexity of the analogies that LISA can map (see Hummel & Holyoak, 1997).

At the most microscopic level (on the order of 25 milliseconds; Gray, Konig, Engel, & Singer, 1989), each role-filler binding in the phase set becomes active serially. A proposition is selected by setting the activation of its P unit to 1.0, causing that unit to excite the SP units below itself. SPs under the same P unit represent separate role-filler bindings, so they must fire *out* of synchrony with one another. To this end, SPs inhibit one another, competing to respond to the input from the P unit. Due to random noise in their excitatory inputs, one SP will win the initial competition, becoming highly active and inhibiting all others to inactivity. Active SPs excite the predicate and object units under them, which in turn excite the semantic units to which they are connected. The result is a pattern of activity on the semantic units representing the semantic content of the object and case role connected to the winning SP (see Figure 5.2a). SPs "take turns" firing due to the operation of an inhibitory unit associated with each SP. In combination with SP-SP inhibition (and SP-to-predicate and SP-to-object excitation), this arrangement causes SPs, predicates, and objects to oscillate in SP-based groups. For example, when "Mary owns the book" is selected, the

FIGURE 5.2
The active representation of the proposition *own(Mary,book)*. Active ("firing")
units are depicted in dark gray and inactive ("resting") units are depicted in white.
Units representing separate case roles fire out of synchrony with one another.
a. The structure and semantic units firing represent the binding of Mary to the
agent role of owns.
b. The structure and semantic units firing represent the binding of book to the
patient role of owns.

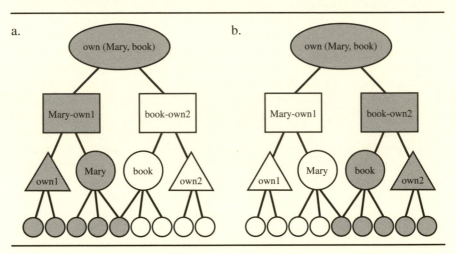

Mary-as-owner group fires out of synchrony with the book-as-owned
group, alternating between the patterns depicted in Figure 5.2a and Figure
5.2b, respectively.

Dynamics of Mapping

Distributed patterns of activation are produced on the semantic units in
response to the sequential selection of propositions in the driver. These patterns are arranged hierarchically in time. At a coarse time scale patterns correspond to propositions: one proposition is selected to fire, followed by
another. At a finer time scale, patterns correspond to role-filler bindings: the
SPs under a common P unit fire out of synchrony with one another.

The job of a recipient analog is to respond to these patterns. Object, predicate, and SP units in the recipient (and in dormant analogs in LTM) compete
to respond to patterns varying over the fine time scale, and P units compete
to respond to patterns varying over the coarse time scale. That is, the recipient analog treats patterns on the semantic units as inputs to be "classified"—
a task for which connectionist networks are well suited. In the recipient, units
of the same type are competitive (mutually inhibiting one another) and
units within a proposition are cooperative (mutually exciting one another).

Consider mapping "Mary owns the book" in the driver onto "Bill has an apple" versus "Peter fears mathematics" in the recipient (see Figure 5.3). When the SP for Mary-as-owner fires in the driver, it will activate *Mary* and *own1*, which will activate their semantic units (e.g., *human, female, adult*, and *state1, possess1, legal1*). This pattern will excite object and predicate units in the recipient, which will compete to become active. *Human* and *adult* will excite both *Bill* and *Peter*, which will become equally active and inhibit *apple* and *mathematics*. Based on their semantic overlap alone, LISA begins to act as if *Mary* corresponds to either *Bill* or *Peter*. At the same time, *state1*, and *possess1* will excite the predicate unit *has1*, but only *state1* will excite *fear1*. *Has1* will inhibit *fear1*: LISA begins to act as if *own1* in the driver corresponds to *has1* in the recipient. Because *has1* is more active than *fear1*, the SP *Bill-has1* will receive more bottom-up input—and therefore become more active—than the SP *Peter-fear1*. SPs excite the P units to which they belong, so the P unit for "Bill has an apple" will become more active than the P unit for "Peter fears mathematics"; hence LISA concludes that "Mary owns the book" corresponds to "Bill has an apple" rather than "Peter fears mathematics." The SP mappings also allow LISA to resolve the semantically ambiguous *Mary-to-Bill* versus *Mary-to-Peter* mappings. SPs feed activation back to their predicate and object units, giving *Bill* an edge over *Peter*. Now, LISA concludes that *Mary* corresponds to *Bill* rather than *Peter*. Analogous operations will cause LISA to conclude that *book* corresponds to *apple* rather than *mathematics*, and that *own2* corresponds to *has2*.

As these operations run, the cross-analog mapping connections keep track of which structure units are coactive across the analogs. When structure unit *i* is active at the same time as structure unit *j* (where *i* and *j* are units of the same type in different analogs), the buffer on the connection from *j* to *i* is incremented; when *i* is active while *j* is inactive, the buffer from *j* to *i* is decremented. At the end of each phase set, the values accumulated on the buffers are used to update the weights on the mapping connection. Weights are incremented or decremented in proportion to the value of the corresponding buffer, with the result that structure units develop positive mapping weights to the extent that they are active simultaneously, and negative weights to the extent that one is active while the other is inactive. The weights are then normalized to enforce the constraint of one-to-one mapping (see Hummel & Holyoak, 1997). In the preceding example, the weights from *Mary* to *Bill*, *book* to *apple*, *own1* to *has1*, and *own2* to *has2* (as well as the associated SP and P weights) will all develop positive values. All other mapping weights will develop negative values. The resulting weights serve as LISA's representation of the mapping, with positive weights between corresponding elements.

The emerging cross-analog mapping weights serve to enforce structural consistency, both with hierarchical and non-hierarchical propositions. First

FIGURE 5.3
Two simple analogs, one consisting of the proposition *own(Mary,book)*, and the other consisting of *has(Bill,apple)* and *fear(Peter,math)*. The small circles between the analogs depict the shared semantic units. When the analog at top of figure acts as driver, *own(Mary,book)* will map onto *has(Bill,apple)* (along with their constituent elements) rather than *fears(Peter,math)*. See text for details.

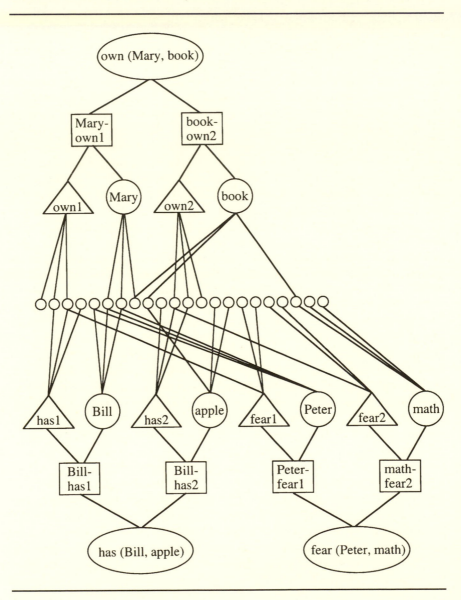

consider the non-hierarchical case. Imagine that LISA learns to map *Mary* to *Bill* and *book* to *apple,* and let us add some additional propositions to the driver and recipient analogs: "Mary gave John the book" in the driver, and "Bill gave Susan the apple" and "Robert gave Beth a flower" in the recipient. If we assume that *book* shares as much semantic content with *apple* as it does with *flower,* then in isolation the "give" mapping is ambiguous: "Mary gave John the book" maps equally well to both "Bill gave Susan the apple" and "Robert gave Beth a flower." But if "Mary owns the book" has already mapped to "Bill has an apple," then "Mary gave John the book" will tend to map to "Bill gave Susan an apple" because of the positive weights from *Mary* to *Bill* and *book* to *apple.* As a result, LISA will also map *John* to *Susan* rather than *Beth.*

The same biasing allows LISA to map hierarchical propositions. Suppose the driver consists of the proposition "Sam knows Mary owns the book," and the recipient consists of "Joe knows Bill has an apple," and "Robert has a flower." At the lowest level of hierarchy, the mapping of Mary to Bill versus Robert is completely ambiguous: "Mary owns a book" maps equally well to both "Bill has an apple" and "Robert has a flower." But in the context of the higher-level propositions, "Sam knows [X]" and "Joe knows [Y]," the mapping is unambiguous. The Mary and Bill propositions serve as arguments of corresponding higher-level propositions (and therefore correspond to one another), so the correct mapping places *Mary* into correspondence with *Bill* rather than *Robert.* The weights on the mapping connections allow LISA to discover this mapping. When "Sam knows [X]" is selected in the driver, "Joe knows [Y]" will become active in the recipient, establishing the correspondence between *Sam* and *Joe* and—more importantly—between [X] ("Mary owns the book") and [Y] ("Bill has an apple"). This latter mapping will be stored as a positive weight on the connection from the P unit for "Mary owns the book" to the P unit for "Bill has an apple." When "Mary owns the book" is selected, this positive weight will give "Bill has an apple" an advantage over "Robert has a flower," causing *Mary* to map to *Bill* rather than *Robert.*

Capacity Limits on Mapping in LISA

As noted previously, LISA's mapping ability is inherently limited by the size of the available phase set, which determines how many SPs can be activated prior to updating the mapping weights. It follows that increases in the size of the phase set will be accompanied by increases in the maximal complexity of the analogical mappings that can be computed (as shown in simulations; Hummel & Holyoak, 1997). This capacity limit is non-arbitrary. It has important manifestations in the context of LISA's account of human mapping limitations (including issues in cognitive development and phylogenetic differences in mapping ability; see Hummel & Holyoak, 1997), and it can be related to a dimensional analysis proposed by Halford and his colleagues (Halford, 1992, 1993; Halford, et al., 1994; Halford & Wilson, 1980). But interestingly, the direct equivalence of LISA's phase set size and the number of independent dimensions in Halford's taxonomy breaks down at a certain complexity level (system mapping and beyond). The point at which this breakdown occurs warrants consideration, both because it distinguishes LISA from all other mapping algorithms, and because it serves to motivate LISA's most basic mechanism for predicate discovery.

In Halford et al.'s (1994) taxonomy, the complexity of a mapping problem corresponds to the number of independent dimensions that must be considered simultaneously in order to correctly solve the problem. For small numbers (one or two), the number of dimensions maps directly onto the number of role-object bindings (i.e., phase set size in LISA). But for more complex problems, the number of dimensions can be less than the number of overt role bindings. Transitive inference provides a good example. It has often been argued that people represent transitive orderings by mapping relational premises onto a mental array (e.g., DeSoto, London & Handel, 1965). For example, a person may map binary ordered pairs from a set of three objects onto a three-place array. A mapping problem of this sort would have a form such as:

Target   *Source*

taller-than (Abe, Bill)   top-to-bottom (Top, Middle, Bottom)
taller-than (Bill, Charles)

According to Halford's analysis, the source and target analogs have the same fundamental complexity. However, the number of overt SPs (i.e., the phase set sizes) required by LISA differ (four for the target, three for the source). As discussed shortly, discovering a structure like that of the source, given a structure like that of the target, can be seen as a kind of creative induction. But even prior to discovering one structure given the other, a system must be able to map one onto the other (otherwise, once discovered, the "compressed" three-role structure of the source would be useless for interpreting future four-role targets).

As Hummel and Holyoak (1997) have noted, this kind of mapping problem poses an insurmountable difficulty for all computational models of mapping prior to LISA. Previous models operate under an inviolable "n-ary restriction": a predicate with n arguments can only map to another predicate with n arguments. This restriction is sensible to a first approximation, and serves a critical role in models that incorporate it (see Hummel & Holyoak, 1997). But honoring this restriction renders mapping problems such as the example above unsolvable. In contrast to most previous models, which represent predicate-argument structures essentially as list elements (for an exception see Kokinov, 1994), LISA represents predicate-argument structures as collections of activation patterns distributed over units representing semantic features. The "list position" of an argument has no meaning in this type of representation. Role-argument bindings are multiplexed over time rather than vector (list) elements, so the dimensionality of the representation (vector or list) is independent of the number of case roles (Hummel & Holyoak, 1993, 1997).

One consequence of this fundamentally different approach is that LISA is able to map examples that violate the n-ary restriction. To let LISA map the above example, we defined the semantic features of the "Top" role to include three of four features representing the first role of "taller"; the features for the "Bottom" role to include three of four features representing the second role of "taller"; and the features of the "Middle" role to include the union of the above features. (The "middle" person is both taller than someone and shorter than someone.) Using the two binary relations jointly in the phase set, LISA successfully mapped the two binary propositions onto the single trinary proposition, generating mappings of Abe to Top, Bill to Middle, and Charles to Bottom. These simulations revealed that LISA can find sensible mappings that violate the n-ary restriction. (For a more sophisticated account of such transitive inferences, see Hummel & Holyoak, 2001b.) Thus even though in some respects LISA's mapping ability is less powerful than that of some previous models (because of its limited working memory), in other respects LISA has greater mapping ability because of the flexibility afforded by its distributed representations of meaning and its ability to dissociate list/vector elements from case roles. It is interesting to note that this very same property allows models of object recognition based on dynamic binding (e.g., Hummel & Biederman, 1992; Hummel & Stankiewicz, 1996) to recognize objects with occluded features or parts. (Missing features or parts constitute the visual analog of "missing" case roles.) A natural consequence of dissociating structural elements (parts, features, or case roles) from vector elements is that it gives robustness to incomplete or missing structure elements. As discussed below, LISA's ability to map structures with different numbers of overt SPs also enables it to learn new "compressed" structures, thereby reducing the number of overt SPs required to represent a given set of information.

INFERENCE AND SCHEMA INDUCTION IN LISA

As we have seen, LISA treats mapping as a form of learning (i.e., updating mapping connections). However, to cash out the promissory note of analogy as a mechanism for creativity, it is necessary to augment the model with additional learning mechanisms that make use of the learned mapping to generate inferences and new abstractions. The key additional element is a self-supervised learning algorithm for encoding structured information

FIGURE 5.4
The LISA architecture for schema induction.

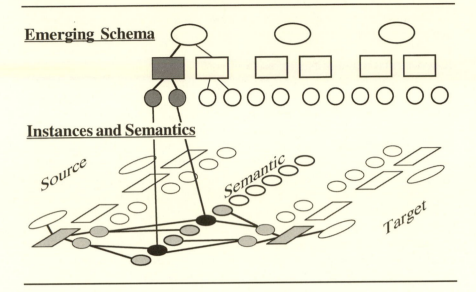

into LTM. With this extension, LISA's approach to representing and mapping structured knowledge provides a natural approach to the problems of automatic inference generation and schema induction (Hummel & Holyoak, 1996, 2001).

We will first describe the learning algorithm as it applies to schema induction. Consider the architecture illustrated in Figure 5.4. On the horizontal plane (labeled "Instances and Semantics") is a highly schematized depiction of a mapped analogy as it would be represented in LISA. The structure units encoding a source are on the left of the plane, those encoding a target are on the right, and the semantic units are in the middle. Above this plane are units (labeled "Emerging Schema") that will learn, in a self-supervised fashion, to extract and encode a schema from these two analogs.

To understand the extension of LISA to schema induction, first consider what will happen when an SP in the source (depicted in gray) fires. In the usual way, it will generate a synchronized pattern of activation on the semantic units, which will selectively activate some SPs in the target (also depicted in gray). Now consider the problem of schema induction in the context of this representation. For the purposes of illustration, imagine that the active source proposition is *owns* (*Mary, book*) and the target proposition it activates is *has* (*Bill, apple*). Recall that a schema should specify what is common to the instances from which it is derived. In this example, the specific people and objects differ, but common to both propositions is the fact that a person possesses an object. A simple schema that might naturally be induced from these propositions is the relation *possess (person, object)*.

Let us assume that the source and target SPs depicted as firing in Figure 5.4 encode the role-object bindings *own-agent = Mary* (in the source) and *have-agent = Bill* (in the target). To encode this small piece of the schema, a schema induction engine must (a) discover what is common to the case roles, and (b) encode those common elements into memory. As discussed below, solving (a) is relatively straightforward in a connectionist architecture. Solving (b) is more challenging, and entails satisfying two very important constraints: The schema induction mechanism must preserve the structure of the information it encodes, and it must be able to operate without detailed feedback.

Self-Supervised Encoding of Structure

A schema in memory, like the instances from which it is generated, must preserve the structure of the information it encodes. It is this aspect of the problem that poses the greatest challenge to traditional connectionist models. In the context of this example, preserving structure means encoding each element of the schema in such a way that it can be kept separate from—but still be integrated with—both the rest of the individual proposition of which it is a part, and the rest of the schema as a whole. This requirement motivates, and is satisfied by, the architecture of LISA's structure units. The second constraint on encoding is that it must be done in a self-supervised fashion. It is unreasonable to expect a schema induction engine to have access to "advice" from an external teacher that will tell it exactly what to learn when (as in supervised learning by error back-propagation; Rumelhart, Hinton & Williams, 1986). Accordingly, what is required to encode schema elements (and, therefore, entire schemas) from small numbers of examples, without external error correction, is a self-supervised learning algorithm for generating the architecture of LISA's LTM (i.e., its structure units).

There are a variety of known algorithms for learning without error correction in neural networks (e.g., Grossberg, 1971; von der Malsburg, 1973). To adapt such algorithms to LISA's architecture, it is first necessary to generalize them to operate on multiple layers of connections in parallel. Object and predicate units must learn to respond to specific combinations of semantic units. Simultaneously, SP units must learn to respond to specific conjunctions of predicate, object, and (in the case of hierarchical propositions) P units, and P units must learn to respond to specific combinations of SP units. The second requirement for self-supervised learning in a LISA-like architecture is that different units must learn to respond to patterns at different time scales: object, predicate, and SP units must encode rapidly changing patterns, whereas P units must integrate their inputs over longer intervals to encode multiple, desynchronized SPs. Hummel and Saiki (1993) developed an algorithm that satisfies these joint requirements. (Although the Hummel and Saiki model learns object structural descriptions rather than propositions, the problems are formally equivalent.) The learning algorithm in LISA is similar to that of Hummel and Saiki (except in some relatively incidental details), so we shall not discuss it at length here. In essence, the algorithm works to recruit a hierarchy of object, predicate, SP and P units in response to the semantic representation of any sufficiently novel proposition. In combination with a set of routines for choosing *what* should be encoded into a schema, this algorithm provides an ideal vehicle for encoding a schema into LTM in a completely automatic, self-supervised fashion.

What to Encode: Discovering the Schema in the Instances

To a first approximation, the problem of deciding what to encode into a schema (given a set of specific instances) is relatively straightforward: it is the problem of discovering what is common to the instances. The LISA architecture exploits a natural way to discover these common elements. In the example shown in Figure 5.4, two semantic units (depicted in black rather than gray) are shared by (common to) the active SPs in the source *and* target. In the case of the above example, one of these shared semantic units might code the meaning of *human* and the other might encode *possess1*. Given this representation, one way to tag these units as "shared" and the others as "not shared" is to allow the target to feed activation back from its predicate and object units to the semantic units. With an appropriate activation function, semantic units receiving input from both the source and target will be substantially more active than those receiving input from only one analog. Those that are shared by two analogs will thus be tagged as such by their activation values.

LISA exploits these tags by means of an input threshold on the learning function for the schema units. The maximum connection weight between a structure unit and a semantic unit (and, therefore, the maximum input to any semantic unit from any single structure unit) is 1.0, and a semantic unit's activation is a linear function of its input. As a result, semantic units receiving input from both analogs tend to be twice as active as those receiving input from only one. Structure units representing known instances (i.e., "recruited" structure units) have an input threshold of zero: they can receive input from any active semantic unit with which they share a connection. By contrast, unrecruited schema units (i.e., predicate and object units that are "waiting" to encode new schemas into LTM) have an input threshold of 1.5: they receive no input whatsoever from any semantic unit with an activation less than 1.5. As a result, an unrecruited structure unit can only "see" semantic units that receive input from (i.e., are common to) both the source and the target. Effectively, the input threshold forces unre-cruited schema units to perform a kind of intersection discovery on the patterns generated by the source and target. In the case of the now familiar "Mary owns the book" example, the schema induced by this intersection discovery procedure would specify what is common to "Mary owns the book" and "Bill has an apple" examples from which it was induced—namely, something along the lines of "human1 owns inanimate object" and "human1 gives inanimate object to human2."

For clarity, we have illustrated the basic LISA account of schema induction using only simple, first-order propositions. However, just as LISA can map hierarchical propositions, it also can learn hierarchical schemas. For example, consider a set of hierarchical propositions of the general form *cause (P1, P2)* where P1 states that human1 loves human2, and P2 states that human1 gave human2 a gift. The schema to be learned from these instances might be *cause (love (X, Y)), give (X, Y, gift))*. This problem is directly analogous to the problem of learning schemas based on first-order propositions. In response to specific instances of people loving one another causing them to give one another gifts, the model must learn propositions describing the causal relationship between non-specific people loving non-specific other people, and the former non-specific people giving the latter non-specific gifts. Given the intersection discovery mechanism described above, the only additional problems are (a) to encode *P1* = love *(X, Y)* and *P2* = give *(X, Y, gift)* as arguments of the higher-level proposition *cause (P1, P2)*, and (b) to ensure that the values of X and Y are the same in both cases (e.g., the agent of loving is also the agent of giving gifts). LISA solves this problem by using P units in the source as pointers that, via the mapping connections, constrain the hierarchical structure of the source-to-target mapping.

Extensions of Schema Induction

The induction mechanism discussed so far uses intersection discovery to induce general schemas from specific instances. A result of this operation is a simplified kind of predicate and object discovery wherein general predicates and objects (e.g., "possess" or "human") are induced from specific examples ("own" and "have," or "man" and "woman," respectively). A different inductive mechanism can form new "compressed" predicates from combinations of existing predicates. This form of predicate discovery is more sophisticated than simple intersection discovery. Although intersection discovery can abstract out the common, ignoring the specific, it cannot combine semantic primitives in novel ways (i.e., nothing new is added to the induced elements). By contrast, predicate compression can combine semantic primitives in completely novel ways, generating fundamentally new predicates. Importantly, compression is not unconstrained. Rather, predicates are compressed only when they refer to the same object. Just as analogical mapping uses common relations (predicates, or higher-order structural relations) to make explicit previously unnoticed similarities between objects (e.g., between Mary and Bill in the previous examples), compression uses common objects to generate new predicates from combinations of familiar ones. This capacity is at its richest when it results in the compression of otherwise incompatible case roles. An example will serve to make these principles clear.

Consider the "taller-than" analog presented earlier: *taller-than (Abe, Bill)* and *taller-than (Bill, Charles)*. In LISA's "normal" mode of operation synchrony is controlled by the SPs, so this analog would be represented by four distinct patterns of activation on the semantic units: Abe-taller1, Bill-taller2, Bill-taller1, and Charles-taller2. Each pattern would contain the semantic primitives for one person (Abe, Bill, or Charles) and one case role (taller1 or taller2). In "compression mode," synchrony is controlled by object units rather than by SPs. Operating in this mode, LISA would generate three patterns on the semantic units: Abe-taller1, Bill-taller1-taller2, and Charles-taller-2. In the Bill group, the first and second roles of the taller relation are "compressed" into a single pattern containing the semantic primitives of both roles. Neither a taller1 nor a taller2 predicate unit is suited to respond to this pattern (it contains elements extraneous to both), so the pattern presents an opportunity for the learning algorithm to recruit a new predicate unit. In combination with compression by object-controlled synchrony, the learning algorithm will thus induce a brand new case role. In this way, LISA can use a representation based on multiple propositions (such as the target in the previous "taller-than" example) to generate a new representation with fewer propositions (such as the source analog in the example).

We have discussed these processes in the context of compressing two roles of the same predicate into one group. More interesting is the possibility of compressing the roles of different predicates. In terms of LISA's operation in compression mode, there is no difference between these cases: Synchrony is controlled by the objects without regard for the predicates to which they are bound in LTM, so it is just as easy to compress case roles of different predicates as to compress roles of the same predicate. For example, LISA could compress *own (Mary, book)* and *give (Mary, book, John)* into a predicate such as *own-give (Mary, book, John)*. Once compressed, *own-give*—which would now have its own representation in LTM—can be expressed in a phase set of size three, rather than requiring the full five-group set that *own* and *give* (represented individually) would require together.

We have yet to fully explore LISA's behavior in compression mode, so it is necessary to be cautious in speculating on its properties. But a few properties of this mechanism are suggestive and warrant mention. First, although a compressed predicate such as *own-give* can operate more efficiently than separate *own* and *give* predicates, operating in this mode makes it impossible to map (or otherwise operate on) *own* and *give* separately. This property is reminiscent of automaticity and chunking: efficiency is purchased at the price of the capacity to treat the individual elements independently (Halford et al., 1994). Second, in combination with the intersection discovery mechanisms discussed previously, the capacity to invent new predicates by combining familiar ones gives LISA tremendous (indeed, unbounded) generative capacity: working together, these operations can combine a finite set of semantic primitives representing predicates in any fashion (with compression putting novel combinations together and intersection discovery taking them apart). Importantly, the specific set of combinations generated will depend entirely on the population of examples used and the modes of operation to which they are subjected. As such, these operations may ultimately speak to the joint roles of experience (i.e., exposure to instances) and strategic processing (i.e., which instances are subjected to which operations) in creative discovery.

Analogical Inferences from Source to Target

So far we have described inductive mechanisms that form new abstractions by structure-based intersection discovery and by object-based predicate compression. Both these operations are involved in the induction of whole new schemas from specific examples. We have yet to describe the process by which specific inferences can be made about the target based on its analogical mapping with the source—that is, the processes whereby knowledge about a specific instance may be augmented on the basis of mapping to a schema or another instance.

In typical uses of analogy, such as problem solving, the most immediate form of transfer involves the use of the better-understood source as a model to fill in "gaps" in the less-understood target (e.g., to generate an analogous solution to the target problem). Previous models of analogical transfer have modeled the generation of inferences by some form of a "copy with substitution and generation" ("CWSG") algorithm (Falkenhainer et al., 1989; Holyoak, Novick & Melz, 1994). The basic idea of CWSG is to identify source propositions that lack a corresponding proposition in the target; and for each such unmapped source proposition, create a new target proposition by (a) copying the elements (i.e., predicate and role fillers) of the source propositions, (b) substituting mapped target elements wherever possible, and (c) generating new target elements if no mapped element is available. Previous models implement CWSG as a separate symbolic procedure that is allowed to directly inspect the source propositions and the mapping between the source and target. That is, CWSG, like schema induction, is treated as a process separate from analogical mapping.

Like other models, LISA implements analogical inference by CWSG, but it does so using a much more implicit mechanism based on self-supervised learning (Hummel & Holyoak, 1996, 2001a). In LISA, CWSG is performed by the same self-supervised learning algorithm that performs schema induction, except that the unrecruited units reside not in a completely separate analog (the to-be-induced schema), but in the target itself. The processes of mapping and CWSG are performed in two phases, distinguished only by which analog (source or target) serves as driver. As an example, consider a simulation in which LISA inferred the *uncle* relation in a target by analogy to a source. The source and target analogs both specify the relations among three male members of a family:

Target	*Source*
father (Abe, Bill)	father (Adam, Bob)
brother (Charles, Abe)	brother (Cary, Adam)
	uncle (Cary, Bob)

In the first phase of the simulation, LISA was run with the target as the driver. During this phase, the relations in the source and target establish mappings (i.e., positive mapping weights) between Abe and Adam, Bill and Bob, and Charles and Cary. As all the people in both analogs share an identical amount of semantic overlap (e.g., semantically, Abe is as similar to Bob as to Adam), LISA must discover the correspondences between them based strictly on their common relations. For example, when the father proposition in the target is selected, father1 (in the target) will activate father1 (in the source), thereby establishing a mapping between Abe and Adam; likewise, father2 establishes the mapping between Bill and Bob, and the two roles of the brother relation establish the mapping between Charles and Cary, and reinforce the Bill-Bob mapping, respectively.

Armed with these mappings, LISA enters the second phase of the simulation, during which the source serves as the driver. When *father (Adam, Bob)* is selected, the father roles map to one another, Adam maps to Abe, and Bob maps to Bill, mirroring and reinforcing the mappings established during the first phase. Similarly, when *brother (Cary, Adam)* is selected, earlier mappings are reinforced. But when *uncle (Cary, Bob)* is selected, the semantic patterns representing uncle1 and uncle2 cannot activate any existing (recruited) predicate units in the target. Similarly, no existing P units in the target are prepared to respond to Charles in one role and Bill in another (activated via the mapping connections by Cary and Bob, respectively). That is, the activation of *uncle (Cary, Bob)* in the source generates a novel pattern in the target. Because no structure units in the target yet exist to respond to this pattern, new units are recruited. Two new predicate units are recruited to respond to the first and second roles of the *uncle* pattern. These units will become active in synchrony with Charles and Bill, respectively. (Charles is activated by Cary, which is firing in synchrony with uncle1, and Bill is activated by Bob, which is firing in synchrony with uncle2.) These novel role-object bindings will recruit new SP units to encode them; and because the SPs are new, a new P unit will be recruited to respond to them. Based on the *uncle* relation in the source and the source-target mappings established earlier, LISA has inferred that Charles is the uncle of Bill. Importantly, this inference results from the same mapping and learning operations that support analogical mapping and schema induction.

CONCLUSION

Although we are far from achieving a full computational account of creativity, we believe that the LISA model constitutes a significant advance in fulfilling the promise of analogy as a driving force in creative induction. The model unifies analogical access and mapping, treating each as a process of guided pattern matching. The sole difference between the two processes is that mapping is able to construct new structural connections. These new connections then provide critical inputs that feed into a mechanism for self-supervised learning, which is able to form both new specific inferences about the target and new abstractions based on the commonalities between the source and target. The new structures generated by analogy will in turn change future analogical processing. For example, a schema will be accessed in long-term memory more readily than a distant analog (Hummel & Holyoak, 1997), and new compressed predicates can allow more information to be considered together in active memory, thereby alleviating the impact of the model's inherent capacity limits. LISA thus has begun to provide a computational realization of the power of the creative human mind to bootstrap itself beyond its limited inputs and processing capacity.

ACKNOWLEDGMENT

Preparation of this chapter was supported by NSF Grant SBR-9729023. Correspondence should be directed to John Hummel, Department of Psychology, UCLA, Los Angeles, CA 90095-1563 (jhummel@lifesci.ucla. edu).

DISCUSSION

TD: Do you think that LISA is creative, or does she reason in a way that satisfies some, but not all, of the requirements for creativity? For instance, is the derivation of the schema "Somebody possesses an object" creative, or does it demonstrate a generalizing, abstracting ability that could be deployed creatively if other conditions were satisfied?

JH/KH: LISA's present capabilities are clearly only one part of the complex constellation of activities that constitute creative thinking. Arguably, they are only a small part; but also arguably, they are an essential part. Structure mapping and schema induction involve the ability to appreciate abstract, relational similarities between situations (even in the absence of any obvious perceptual or semantic similarity), and the ability to induce a more general principle (schema or rule) from those relational similarities. We believe these are necessary first steps to creative thinking.

TD: You say that analogical mapping is an inherently structural business. This is true in the cases you talk about, but what about cases like "hot is to cold as hard is to soft," or "hay is to horses as seeds are to birds"? Suppose a child looks at an analogy quiz book that shows hay and horses and a pile of seeds. The book asks what corresponds to the seeds. There's no structure in the pictures (in fact there's *nothing* in the pictures) that provides the answer. The child just has to *know about* hay and horses, and seeds and birds. We can map hay onto horses and seeds onto birds but, of course, this isn't mapping structures or components of the situation, is it? How would LISA handle these situations? In the case of the hot:cold::heavy:? analogy, wouldn't you have to give "hot," "cold," "heavy," and so on, internal structure, so that LISA can map them?

JH/KH: It is what the child *knows about* hay, horses, seeds and birds, and what it must do with that knowledge, that is structural. What hay has to do with seeds in the context of horses and birds is that hay stands in the same *relation* to horses that seeds stand in to birds, namely "eat (horses, hay)" and "eat (birds, seed)." To solve the hay:horses::seeds:X analogy, the child must recognize the relation that holds between hay and horses, and find the missing argument, X, such that the same relation holds between seeds and X. This problem is inherently structural in the sense that it requires the child to understand and process (among other things) the correct role bindings in the two instantiations of the "eats" relation (i.e., that both horses and birds are bound to the agent role of eat, while hay and seeds are bound to the patient role).

The essential nature of the role bindings is even more transparent if we change the analogy slightly to hay:horses::worms:X. In this case, as in the previous analogy, one correct answer is birds (some birds eat worms). Moreover, if the child answered "dirt" on the grounds that worms eat dirt, we would say that he or she made an error, because the answer to the analogy must be something that eats worms, rather than something that worms eat. That is, as adults, we understand that the analogy requires us to respect the proper role bindings.

In the case of the hot:cold::heavy:X analogy, it is perhaps more accurate to say that LISA would need to embed "hot," "cold," and "heavy" in a richer *external* structure, than to say that it would need to give them a richer *internal* structure. Specifically, hot and cold are opposite ends of a single continuum (temperature), just as heavy and light are opposite ends of the continuum of weight. Just as hay:horse is analogous to seed:bird because both pairs are arguments of the same relation, hot:cold and heavy:light are both arguments of the three-place relation opposite-ends (X, Y, Z), where X and Y are ends of continuum Z. That is, hot:cold is analogous to heavy:light because there is a single relation that describes both pairs in corresponding roles. Just as the "eats" relation is in an important sense "external" to hay and horses (it links the two, rather than being an internal "feature" of either), opposite-ends is "external" to hot:cold and heavy:light.

TD: LISA can induce commonalities between situations. Given "Mary owns a book" she can retrieve "Bill has an apple," and she can then induce the schema "Somebody possesses an object." But she can only do this because you've given her a set of primitives, such as "adult," "female," and "human." How did you derive these primitives? Presumably (because they're abstractions) you derived them by a process of inductive generalization—by finding commonalities between situations. So in the big picture, primitives are derived by finding commonalities between situations, and these primitives are then used to find new commonalities between situations. (This sets the scene for a computational model of analogy that finds analogs by searching through a space of formally specified features using guided pattern matching.)

Maybe this *is* how analogical thinking operates: we have to *already* know the basic components of the problem. If we look at the standard examples of water and electricity, or atoms and the solar system, we seem to find something like this. But isn't there a problem about how we could have derived the primitives, or any kind of basic commonalities, in the first place? We can't have derived them by using a method that assumes that we already knew them! At the end of the chapter you talk about our ability to bootstrap ourselves beyond our limited inputs and processing capacity. Do you have any thoughts about how such analogical bootstrapping might get off the ground in the first place? Do we need some other process to enable us to pick out some basic structure? Maybe we need something like representational redescription, which is supposed to give us structured thoughts out of skills and abilities. (See Chapter 3 in this volume.)

JH/KH: The problem of how we derive the primitives of mental representation in the first place is indeed a huge problem—not just for LISA, but for all models of higher cognitive function. All such models must assume a set of primitive features or symbols. (To our knowledge, only models of very basic perceptual functions—e.g., models of primary visual cortex—are currently well-constrained by any detailed understanding of the nature of the primitives on which the simulated processes operate.) Ultimately, cognitive science will have to grapple seriously with the question of where the primitives of mental representation come from. Philosophers have worried about this problem for centuries, and there are some preliminary proposals in the more recent literature. For example, Barsalou (1999; Prinz & Barsalou, this volume) argues that all mental primitives are ultimately derived from perception; and some of our recent work (Hummel & Choplin, in press) makes some early steps toward understanding how primitives describing simple relations (grounded ultimately, perhaps, in perception) may be combined into semantic primitives that describe the basic features of objects and more complex relations (see also Kellman, Burke & Hummel, 1999). However, all this work is preliminary, and a great deal remains to be done. In the mean time, LISA is by no means unique in being limited to operating on a set of semantic primitives chosen largely by intuition.

TD: A recurring theme in this collection is the way in which we acquire concepts and mechanisms in the course of input creativity, and redeploy them in output creativity. The distinction between input and output creativity is intuitively pretty clear, I think. We are input creative when we solve puzzles, listen to music or poetry, and make sense of the world (generally, when we analyze) and we are output creative when we write music or poetry, and when we imagine things (generally, when we synthesize). This kind of creativity seems to use the concepts and mechanisms acquired during input creativity, and redeploy them, either in the world or off-line in the imagination. I wonder if this distinction has any bearing on the origins of our analogical abilities. LISA can retrieve analogs and induce schema but to do this she needs a set of semantic primitives, and there seem to be problems in explaining how these could have been derived in the first place. Could it be that the primitives are derived through analysis, during input creativity, and that they are then synthesized to give us output creativity? There is a sense in which schemas are abstract constructions that are *put together,* rather than *analyzed out* of analogs. I admit that this idea is a bit forced. Analogy can be used constructively ("My love is like a red red rose") but just as often it is used analytically. Rutherford used it to throw light on the properties of the atom, for instance. But then again, maybe our intuitions about input and output creativity are incorrect. Maybe all cognition involves analysis and synthesis to some extent. Do you have any thoughts about this?

JH/KH: Probably not very satisfying or illuminating ones. LISA can indeed put ideas together, as when the system uses known facts in one analog to infer unknown facts in another (analogical inference), and take them apart, as when it induces a general schema from specific instances by intersection discovery. But as you observed in your previous question, both these processes operate on primitives that already exist in LISA's repertoire. The problem of discovering genuinely new primitives and relations is of course a different matter, and lies outside the scope of LISA's current abilities (although we are actively working on it: for some early progress on relation discovery in the domain of visual perception, see Kellman et al., 1999).

TD: I mentioned representational redescription earlier on. Representational redescription apparently articulates implicit, procedural knowledge as explicit, declarative knowledge that we can reflect upon and change. Explicitation is the more general process of articulating implicit knowledge as explicit structure. (Donald Peterson explains this distinction in his chapter.) Explicitation is a theme that recurs throughout your chapter. You talk about "revealing regularities that apply across elements" and you say that "relationships between objects or events *become explicit*" (my emphasis). You say that P units don't encode semantic content in any direct way, but serve as pointers to a hierarchy of SP, predicate, and object units that are collectively capable of generating this content on the semantic units. So propositional content isn't explicitly represented.

I think that representational redescription and explicitation are vital for our understanding of creativity. A working model of representational redescription would show us how we are able to articulate our domain-specific skills as accessible structures that we can reflect upon and change (and map onto structures in other domains). This would explain how we can get out of procedural ruts, how we can come up with structured thoughts in the first place, and how we can cross-pollinate our concepts across domains—which might lay the foundations for analogical thinking. The trouble is that we *don't* have a working model and we don't know how the brain turns the trick. To some extent we can model our procedural knowledge using neural networks, and our symbol-handling abilities using traditional architectures, but there seems to be an unbridgeable gulf between the two types of system. We would expect the answer to lie in some sort of connectionist/symbolic hybrid. One possibility might be to sit a symbol-handler on top of a connectionist system, train up the connectionist system, and get the symbol-handler to articulate the knowledge implicit in the connectionist system's trained-up states as explicit rules and representations. But again, we don't know how to do this, because we don't know how to systematically analyze the way in which knowledge is stored in neural networks.

Now enter LISA, who combines the generalizing abilities of a neural network with the systematicity of a symbol-handler. LISA certainly seems to be able to explicitate her implicit knowledge as accessible symbolic structures. But how implicit *is* her "implicit" knowledge? Is it really just stored propositional knowledge, in which synchronous firing stands in for syntactic structure? Her stored knowledge is far more structured than that of a standard network, isn't it? (Compare LISA's stored knowledge with that of NETtalk [Sejnowski & Rosenberg, 1987], for instance.) And do her semantic primitives and dynamic binding hinder her connectionist capabilities? To what extent does she behave like a standard connectionist system? How much plasticity does she have with respect to local context, for instance? And—the $64,000 question—can she give us anything at all like representational redescription?

JH/KH: We agree whole-heartedly that the answers to many important questions about human cognition lie in discovering the nature of the symbolic/connectionist "hybrid" underlying the human cognitive architecture (see Holyoak & Hummel, 2000). However, we doubt the correct approach is to ". . . sit a symbol-handler on top of a connectionist system. . . ." Rather, we argue that the human cognitive architecture is essentially a connectionist architecture at base (artificial neural networks arguably more closely approximate the architecture of the brain than do von Neumann machines), but one that is explicitly configured to form and manipulate symbolic representations and functions (namely, by solving the dynamic binding problem, among others). Indeed, LISA is an explicit attempt to characterize the symbolic/connectionist nature of the human cognitive architecture. And as you observe, its architecture is decidedly more structured than those of "traditional" connectionist models.

We do not know whether the particular symbolic connectionist architecture embodied in LISA can give rise to representational redescription. In its current state, LISA cannot do this (but see Hummel & Choplin, in press, for progress in this direction), but this problem seems well within the domain of the approach. And as noted in the response to the previous question, this is the kind of problem to which we have turned our recent attention.

One more minor note: at the end of the first paragraph (of this question), you stated "So propositional content isn't explicitly represented," in the context of our statement that P units do not, themselves, make the semantic content of propositions explicit. From this, it does not follow that LISA does not make propositional content explicit: we would argue that it does indeed! But it does so in *working memory* (i.e., in the synchronized distributed patterns of activation over semantic units that represent an active proposition). These patterns make both the semantic content and the structure (i.e., role bindings) of a proposition explicit. Our claim is only that—by contrast to the distributed semantic patterns that represent an active proposition in working memory—the P, SP, object, and predicate units that store a proposition in long-term memory do not make its semantic content explicit.

TD: Yes, of course. What I meant to say was that propositional content isn't explicitly represented *at the level of P units*. But the P units point towards a hierarchy of SP, predicate, and object units that are collectively capable of generating this content on the semantic units—and this looks like explicitation to me.

REFERENCES

Barsalou, L. W. (1999). Perceptual symbol systems. *Behavioral and Brain Sciences, 22,* 577–660.

Carbonell, J. G. (1983). Learning by analogy: Formulating and generalizing plans from past experience. In R. S. Michalski, J. G. Carbonell, & T. M. Mitchell (Eds.), *Machine learning: An artificial intelligence approach* (pp. 137–161). Palo Alto, CA: Tioga Press.

DeSoto, L. B., London, M., & Handel, L. S. (1965). Social reasoning and spatial paralogic. *Journal of Personality and Social Psychology, 2,* 513–521.

Falkenhainer, B., Forbus, K. D., & Gentner, D. (1989). The structure-mapping engine: Algorithm and examples. *Artificial Intelligence, 41,* 1–63.

Fodor, J. A., & Pylyshyn, Z. W. (1988). Connectionism and cognitive architecture: A critical analysis. In S. Pinker & J. Mehler (Eds.), *Connections and symbols* (pp. 3–71). Cambridge, MA: MIT Press.

Forbus, K. D., Gentner, D., & Law, K. (1995). MAC/FAC: A model of similarity-based retrieval. *Cognitive Science, 19,* 141–205.

Gentner, D. (1989). The mechanisms of analogical learning. In S. Vosniadou & A. Ortony (Eds.), *Similarity and analogical reasoning* (pp. 199–241). New York: Cambridge University Press.

Gick, M. L., & Holyoak, K. J. (1980). Analogical problem solving. *Cognitive Psychology, 12,* 36–355.

Gick, M. L., & Holyoak, K. J. (1983). Schema induction and analogical transfer. *Cognitive Psychology, 15,* 1–38.

Gray, C. M., Konig, P., Engel, A. E., & Singer, W. (1989). Oscillatory responses in cat visual cortex exhibit inter-column synchronization which reflects global stimulus properties. *Nature, 338,* 334–337.

Grossberg, S. (1971). Pavlovian pattern learning by nonlinear neural networks. *Proceedings of the National Academy of Science, USA, 68,* 828–831.

Halford, G. S. (1992). Analogical reasoning and conceptual complexity in cognitive development. *Human Development, 35,* 193–217.

Halford, G. S. (1993). *Children's understanding: The development of mental models.* Hillsdale, NJ: Erlbaum.

Halford, G. S., & Wilson, W. H. (1980). A category theory approach to cognitive development. *Cognitive Psychology, 12,* 356–411.

Halford, G. S., Wilson, W. H., Guo, J., Gayler, R. W., Wiles, J., & Stewart, J. E. M. (1994). Connectionist implications for processing capacity limitations in analogies. In K. J. Holyoak & J. A. Barnden (Eds.), *Advances in connectionist and neural computation theory, Vol. 2: Analogical connections* (pp. 363–415). Norwood, NJ: Ablex.

Hofstadter, D. R., & Mitchell, M. (1994). An overview of the Copycat project. In K. J. Holyoak & J. A. Barnden (Eds.), *Advances in connectionist and neural computation theory, Vol. 2: Analogical connections* (pp. 31–112). Norwood, NJ: Erlbaum.

Holland, J. H., Holyoak, K. J., Nisbett, R. E., & Thagard, P. (1986). *Induction: Processes of inference, learning, and discovery.* Cambridge, MA: MIT Press.

Holyoak, K. J., & Hummel, J. E. (2000). The proper treatment of symbols in a connectionist architecture. In E. Deitrich & A. Markman (Eds.), *Cognitive dynamics: Conceptual change in humans and machines* (pp. 229–263). Mahwah, NJ: Erlbaum.

Holyoak, K. J., & Hummel, J. E. (2001). Toward an understanding of analogy within a biological symbol system. In D. Gentner, K. J. Holyoak, & B. N. Kokinov (Eds.), *The analogical mind: Perspectives from cognitive science* (pp. 161–195). Cambridge, MA: MIT Press.

Holyoak, K. J., Novick, L. R., & Melz, E. R. (1994). Component processes in analogical transfer: Mapping, pattern completion, and adaptation. In K. J. Holyoak & J. A. Barnden (Eds.), *Advances in connectionist and neural computation theory, Vol. 2: Analogical connections* (pp. 130–180). Norwood, NJ: Ablex.

Holyoak, K. J., & Thagard, P. (1989). Analogical mapping by constraint satisfaction. *Cognitive Science, 13,* 295–355.

Holyoak, K. J., & Thagard, P. (1995). *Mental leaps: Analogy in creative thought.* Cambridge, MA: MIT Press.

Hummel, J. E., & Biederman, I. (1992). Dynamic binding in a neural network for shape recognition. *Psychological Review, 99,* 480–517.

Hummel, J. E., Burns, B., & Holyoak, K. J. (1994). Analogical mapping by dynamic binding: Preliminary investigations. In K. J. Holyoak & J. A. Barnden (Eds.), *Advances in connectionist and neural computation theory, Vol. 2: Analogical connections* (pp. 416–445). Norwood, NJ: Ablex.

Hummel, J. E., & Choplin, J. M. (in press). Toward an integrated account of reflexive and reflective reasoning. To appear in the *Proceedings of the Twenty Second Annual Conference of the Cognitive Science Society.* Mahwah, NJ: Erlbaum.

Hummel, J. E., & Holyoak, K. J. (1992). Indirect analogical mapping. In *Proceedings of the Fourteenth Annual Conference of the Cognitive Science Society* (pp. 516–521). Hillsdale, NJ: Erlbaum.

Hummel, J. E., & Holyoak, K. J. (1993). Distributing structure over time. *Behavioral and Brain Sciences, 16,* 464.

Hummel, J. E., & Holyoak, K. J. (1996). LISA: A computational model of analogical inference and schema induction. In G. W. Cottrell (Ed.), *Proceedings of the Eighteenth Annual Conference of the Cognitive Science Society* (pp. 352–357). Hillsdale, NJ: Erlbaum.

Hummel, J. E., & Holyoak, K. J. (1997). Distributed representations of structure: A theory of analogical access and mapping. *Psychological Review, 104,* 427–466.

Hummel, J. E., & Holyoak, K. J. (2001a). A symbolic-connectionist theory of relational inference and generalization. Manuscript in preparation. Department of Psychology, UCLA.

Hummel, J. E., & Holyoak, K. J. (2001b). A process model of human transitive inference. In M. L. Gattis (Ed.), *Spatial schemas in abstract thought* (pp. 279–305). Cambridge, MA: MIT Press.

Hummel, J. E., & Saiki, J. (1993). Rapid unsupervised learning of object structural descriptions. *Proceedings of the Fifteenth Annual Conference of the Cognitive Science Society* (pp. 569–574). Hillsdale, NJ: Erlbaum.

Hummel, J. E., & Stankiewicz, B. J. (1996). An architecture for rapid, hierarchical structural description. In T. Inui and J. McClelland (Eds.), *Attention and Performance XVI*, in press.

Keane, M. T., Ledgeway, T., & Duff, S. (1994). Constraints on analogical mapping: A comparison of three models. *Cognitive Science, 18*, 387–438.

Kellman, P. J., Burke, T., & Hummel, J. E. (1999). Modeling perceptual learning of abstract invariants. *Proceedings of the Twenty First Annual Conference of the Cognitive Science Society* (pp. 264–269). Mahwah, NJ: Erlbaum.

Kokinov, B. N. (1994). A hybrid model of reasoning by analogy. In K. J. Holyoak, & J. A. Barnden, (Eds.), *Advances in connectionist and neural computation theory, Vol. 2: Analogical connections* (pp. 247–318). Norwood, NJ: Ablex Publishing Corp.

Kubose, T. T., Holyoak, K. J., & Hummel, J. E. (2001). Strategic use of working memory in analogical mapping. Manuscript in preparation. Department of Psychology, UCLA.

Novick, L. R., & Holyoak, K. J. (1991). Mathematical problem solving by analogy. *Journal of Experimental Psychology: Learning, Memory, and Cognition, 17*, 398–415.

Ross, B. (1989). Distinguishing types of superficial similarities: Different effects on the access and use of earlier problems. *Journal of Experimental Psychology: Learning, Memory, and Cognition, 15*, 456–468.

Ross, B. H., & Kennedy, P. T. (1990). Generalizing from the use of earlier examples in problem solving. *Journal of Experimental Psychology: Learning, Memory, and Cognition, 16*, 42–55.

Rumelhart, D. E., Hinton, G. E., & Williams, R. J. (1986). Learning internal representations by error propagation. In D. E. Rumelhart, J. L. McClelland, & the PDP Research Group (Eds.), *Parallel distributed processing: Explorations in the microstructure of cognition* (Vol. 1) (pp. 318–362). Cambridge, MA: MIT Press.

Sejnowski, T., & Rosenberg, C. (1987). Parallel networks that learn to pronounce English text. *Complex Systems, 1*, 145–168.

Shastri, L., & Ajjanagadde, V. (1993). From simple associations to systematic reasoning: A connectionist representation of rules, variables, and dynamic bindings using temporal synchrony. *Behavioral and Brain Sciences, 16*, 417–494.

Thagard, P., Holyoak, K. J., Nelson, G., & Gochfeld, D. (1990). Analog retrieval by constraint satisfaction. *Artificial Intelligence, 46*, 259–310.

von der Malsburg, C. (1973). Self-organization of orientation sensitive cells in the striate cortex. *Kybernetik, 14*, 85–100.

Waltz, J. A., Lau, A., Grewal, S. K., & Holyoak, K. J. (2001). The role of working memory in analogical mapping. *Memory & Cognition, 28*, 1205–1212.

6

Creativity: A Computational Modeling Approach

Derek Partridge and Jon Rowe

There is a rapidly growing history of computational models of creativity. On the positive side, the use of computational models to explore creativity can add precision and specificity to the more nebulous theories that are sometimes proposed. These models can be used to expose weaknesses in the theories about the underlying mechanisms that might account for creativity. On the negative side, computational models can force an unhelpful overprecision on the modeler: in order to obtain a working computer program (a computational model) it is necessary to make precise decisions about how each part of the mechanism operates, and often there is no better basis for this than inspired guesswork. The motivation behind many of the earlier computational models was to reproduce creative behavior rather than to model human creative mechanisms proposed by psychologists. These earlier models are often called "discovery" or "rediscovery" programs, and we have been surveyed and evaluated them elsewhere (Partridge & Rowe, 1993).

In this chapter we focus on psychological theories of human creativity, and on programmed models of these theories. As Margaret Boden (1990) says, there may be no general agreement on what we mean by creativity, but we cannot deny that it exists (Boden, 1990). Boden adopts the view, claiming support from recent psychological research, that "creativity requires no specific power, but is an aspect of intelligence in general—which, in turn, involves many different capacities" (p. 24). She sees computational concepts and theories as crucial to the development of psychology, and in particular as an important source of help in developing an explanation of creativity.

Indeed, she believes that computational psychology "even helps us to see how creative understanding is possible at all" (p. 278).

An attempt to give a fixed definition of creativity is probably misguided, since definitions tend to be biased towards a particular theory. In accord with many earlier studies, we follow the line that creativity involves producing something *novel* and *appropriate* (see, for example, Martindale, 1981). However, the degree to which something is novel is a relative matter, depending on the thinker's culture. Findlay and Lumsden (1988) further define "discovery" as the product of the creative process and "innovation" as a discovery that is accepted by the creator's society. This last definition seems a little strange when we consider that many great artists are only recognized some time after their deaths. However, the social aspect of creativity is accidental as far as the psychological mechanisms are concerned. Cohen (1988) distinguishes between "percipience," which is the production of an idea that is novel with respect to the thinker, and "originality," which is novel with respect to the culture. Margaret Boden (1990) draws a similar distinction between "P-creativity," which is novel for the individual, and "H-creativity," which is novel with respect to the whole of human history.

The model that we describe is chiefly concerned with the personal aspect of creativity and the mental processes involved. That is, it is about the mechanisms of "percipience" in the above sense—Boden's "P-creativity." A further constraint is that we restrict the study to explanation in terms of computational mechanism. This distances our approach from others, such as Arieti (1976), who believe that real progress into an understanding of creativity must be based on the "methods of deep psychology"—by which he means psychoanalysis and psychiatry. It is similarly difficult to relate our study directly to the broader issues raised in Sternberg's (1988) collection of articles on creativity. This is because Sternberg maintains that a "complete model of creativity would have to take into account the environmental as well as the personal variables that facilitate as well as impede the manifestation of creativity" (p. 146). We have no pretensions about presenting a complete model of creativity. We aim merely to shed some light on the relative merits of several computational mechanisms as accounts of the personal aspects of human creativity.

We draw a further distinction between *input* and *output* creativity. Input creativity involves the analysis of incoming data, whereas output creativity involves the production of something new, unconstrained by external influence. In some cases (for example, portrait painting) it is a matter of degree, depending on how objective a representation is sought. Our model can account for both types of creativity, and is evaluated within an application domain that requires the use of both types.

The implemented models are expected to demonstrate creative behavior, but not just as an end in itself. The idea is to provide a basis for comparing and evaluating two rival psychological theories of creativity: the cortical arousal, or "special mechanism," theory, and the theory that creativity does not involve a special mechanism, and that it is just normal problem solving.

THE CORTICAL AROUSAL THEORY

An early account of the creative process is provided by the French mathematician Poincaré (1924). He asks how it is possible that many rational people do not understand mathematics. A proof consists of a series of logical steps whose reasoning no sane person could deny. How then can anyone fail to appreciate it? According to Poincaré, it is not the individual steps that matter so much as the overall structure of the proof. The question is how such patterns can be created and perceived. Poincaré accounts for his own experiences as follows. During a period of concentrated work a number of ideas are activated, though without forming any appropriate combinations. While the mind is occupied with other things, these ideas are still being processed unconsciously. When a good combination is made it is reported to consciousness. The fact that sensible new ideas are made is explained by the early, concentrated period of work which sets the right kind of ideas into action. While these ideas are in full swing there is no sense of having achieved a solution, but eventually they combine in the hoped-for manner.

On the basis of such accounts as Poincaré's, Wallas formulated an analysis of creative thinking. He suggests that there are four stages to be considered: preparation, incubation, illumination and verification (Wallas, 1926).

Preparation is the stage of concentrated work, accumulating data and trying out various approaches. Occasionally this gives rise to a solution but often, as Poincaré noted, nothing is achieved. Incubation is the time when the mind is relaxed or working on a different problem. This corresponds to Poincaré's notion of ideas floating about in the unconscious, occasionally interlocking, while consciousness is focused elsewhere. The third stage, illumination, is the moment of insight when the solution is presented to consciousness. This stage seems impossible to predict or control. Verification consists of a further period of conscious work when results can be checked out, for example, against new data.

A modern theory based on the four-stage model is put forward by Martindale (1981), based on various theories and experiments connecting creative problem-solving with levels of *cortical arousal* and *focus of attention*. Measures of cortical arousal can be displayed, for example, as an electroencephalogram (EEG) which depicts brain-wave patterns picked up as voltage changes in various parts of the head. The focus of attention is the extent to which short-term memory and consciousness are concentrated. In low states of cortical arousal, attention is unfocused. This corresponds to primary processing: the low-level activation of a large number of cognitive units. At high levels of arousal, attention is highly focused, corresponding to secondary processing (high-level activation of a small number of units).

FIGURE 6.1
Differing responses to stimuli in creative and uncreative people.

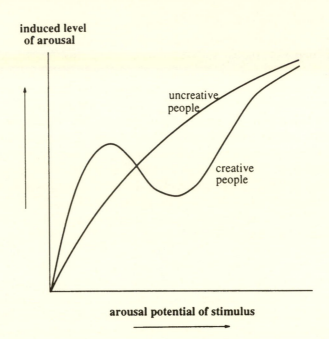

It has been shown that creative people exhibit a marked decrease in cortical arousal while solving problems creatively (Martindale & Hines, 1975).
However, when given uncreative tasks, or when elaborating an idea, creative people do not show this distinctive pattern of arousal.

Martindale (1981) also suggests that creative people respond to stimuli
of medium arousal potential by a decrease in arousal (see Figure 6.1). Thus
for sufficiently interesting stimuli, the focus of attention is widened and
more cognitive units are active in working memory. This would explain
why the regression from secondary (or "conscious") processing to primary
("subconscious") processing is not entirely within the control of creative
people. It is "built-in."

It is reasonable to suppose that creativity occurs in varying degrees in
people. People with high levels of creativity would have the pronounced dip
in arousal shown in the graph. The less creative a person is, the more the
graph will tend to the straighter curve.

Martindale's four-stage model is as follows. Initially, information is gathered and various approaches to the problem are tried. This requires secondary processing, which involves a high level of cortical arousal and a small

focus of attention: only strictly relevant concepts are activated in working memory. As the amount of information increases, two things can happen. In less creative people, the arousal level keeps rising, so they try the same attacks on the problem again and again: they have fallen into a rut. Eventually they will reach panic levels of arousal. However, for creative people, there comes a point when their arousal starts to decrease, primary processes come into play and the focus of attention is widened. This means that a larger number of representations become active in working memory. Given a suitable semantic organization, a discovery will be made connecting the problem situation with a seemingly disparate concept. This is the third stage, the moment of insight. Now that a link has been forged, the focus of attention can narrow and still maintain these two schemata, now indexed by a new representation. Ideas associated with the second schema can be called into play, to help resolve the problem. As these resources are applied in a straightforward, logical manner, secondary processing is necessary. This is the verification (or elaboration) stage.

CREATIVITY AS NORMAL PROBLEM SOLVING

The four-stage model has been challenged by Weisberg, who argues that it is not supported by experimental evidence and that its continued acceptance is due to the propagation of myths about the creative process in psychological folklore (Weisberg, 1986).

Weisberg's criticism of the idea of an incubation stage rests on the results of a number of experiments that have tried to isolate incubation in laboratory conditions. One such experiment, conducted by Olton, involved observing expert chess players solving chess problems (Olton, 1979). One group was allowed to take a break (to encourage incubation) while the second worked continuously. There was no significant difference between the performance of the two groups.

In a second experiment, by Read and Bruce, subjects were shown pictures of actors from the 1960s whose names were not easy to recall (Read & Bruce, 1982). During the following week, subjects kept a diary of their attempts to recall these names. Only about four percent of successful recalls involved spontaneous remembering of the names and most of these incidents were reported from only four of the thirty subjects. All other cases involved conscious effort of remembering, showing that incubation (unconscious processing) and illumination are not necessary for insight to take place.

Weisberg claims that creativity is merely a part of normal problem solving, and that there is no special creative process. It is intelligence combined with a large amount of domain knowledge that enables a person to have creative insights, but the mechanisms are the same as those used in everyday problem solving.

The main weakness of Weisberg's theory is that it fails to account for the peculiar experience of illumination that occurs on some occasions. This is explicitly accounted for in the cortical arousal theory as a return from low to higher levels of arousal. We will return to this later on.

A THEORY OF EMERGENT MEMORY:
A COMPUTATIONAL MODEL

Both of the psychological theories outlined above can be described in terms of a set of *cognitive units*. These correspond to the representation of concepts in the mind. A cognitive unit has a certain degree of activation depending on how significant it is to the current problem. The computational equivalent of a cognitive unit is an *agent*. This is a self-contained piece of programming that reacts in certain ways to certain situations. It can have a numerical activation that determines whether or not it is allowed to run in the current problem-solving situation. According to the arousal theory, under high levels of arousal only the most active agents will run (those most relevant to the task at hand) but at low levels, there are no such distinguished agents. There are many agents with a similar activation. Under such circumstances, many agents, even unrelated ones, have a chance to operate. According to Weisberg's "no special mechanism" theory, creativity is normal problem solving with lots of knowledge, so that only relevant agents will ever run.

Different types of agent perform different tasks. One type of agent builds representations of perceptions. Memory agents recognize certain mental states (configurations of representational elements) and activate other agents, according to recorded patterns. Motor agents drive the output, if there is a mechanical interface with the world.

A fundamental paradox of creativity is the question of the source of novelty. If a result has been derived from previous experience, then it is hard to see how it can be novel. If on the other hand a creative act contains something new, that is not derived from experience, then it is difficult to see where it could have come from. To address this problem, we distinguish between two types of creativity. First, there is creativity in perception and problem solving. This is the analysis and representation of given information which we call *input creativity*. Second, there is the production of something new, that originates within the creator. We call this *output creativity*. An example of input creativity is solving a chess problem. An example of output creativity is *devising* a chess problem. Listening to music requires input creativity, whereas composing music requires output creativity.

These two forms of creativity are related, and we suggest that this provides an answer to the paradox. In both cases mental representations are constructed. In order to analyze an input, a representation has to be built. When creating a new structure, a representation is formed. The difference is that constraints in the latter case are internal, whereas the constraints on problem solving are external: they are inherent in the structure of the problem. It may be argued that output creativity is really input creativity on a higher level, where we try to find a solution to a problem, such as "create a chess problem." But there are much less rigid constraints on output creation than on solving a particular problem.

Since both forms of creativity involve the creation of a representation, it is plausible that they share the same building mechanisms. The novelty paradox may then be resolved by considering output creativity to consist of new combinations of elements of previously constructed representations. Suppose there is a class of agents that build these representations. When solving a problem (for example, analyzing a given structure) these agents cooperate to provide an appropriate solution. Their action is continuously constrained by the problem at hand. Later, in the absence of this information, these agents could repeat this action, reproducing the representation achieved. This would be a *memory* of the solution. However, suppose that the action of several agents from another solution were involved. In this case a representation would be built which contained elements of two previous experiences and would be in some ways analogous to each. But the representation itself would be new and could be used, by motor agents, to construct a novel external object. This is output creativity.

The combinations of memories cannot be merely random. There has to be some way of appropriately linking the ideas, and of doing it efficiently. Some aspects of one situation should provide a reminder of the other, which enables part of the other to be built onto the first. Thus creativity is related to the way in which memory works, and this is related to the way in which experiences are learned.

If memory is organized in a rigid fashion, by storing learned concepts whole with some pointers, then it will be difficult to break them down into meaningful units for recombination. The alternative is to create memory links between agents as they create parts of representations. These parts may then be used to fit into any other appropriate representations under construction. Notice that this method assists with both kinds of creativity. As previously described, output creativity may be the result of a novel combination of memories without external constraints. However, it is also possible for pieces of previous solutions to be used in an input situation. This would happen when the structure of a problem is sufficiently similar to an earlier one, in which case part of the solution may be added on directly by analogy.

This kind of mechanism is an *emergent memory*. Instead of concepts or categories being recalled whole, because they match a certain input, concepts are *reconstructed* in appropriate situations. If the same situation is encountered again and again, eventually one memory link may come to represent the whole, but the partial memories would still exist to be used in combination with others. This provides flexibility, as often an experience is similar, but not identical, to a previous one. In such a case, a substantial part of the previous representation may be constructed (in as far as it conforms to the external constraints of the new situation) and then smaller memories and the construction agents themselves, may be used to fill in the gaps.

In his "Society of Mind" theory, Minsky proposes the idea of agents that form links between other agents, to create memories (Minsky, 1985). He calls these agents *k-lines,* but gives no details as to how such agents might operate. We have developed a formal theory of learning based on this idea (Rowe, 1991; Partridge & Rowe, 1994), which provides the basis for modeling the psychological theories of creativity we discussed earlier.

Cognitive units are thought to have *activation levels,* which determine how active they currently are, that is, how much attention is focused on them. This corresponds to the notion of *bidding.* An agent's bid represents its claim to be processed. The higher the bid, the greater the chance of it cooperating in solving the current problem. Thus the process of agent selection is a theory of attention. A theory along these lines has much in common with the principles of Artificial Life (Langton, 1989).

We have implemented the emergent-memory model in a program called "GENESIS" (Generation and Exploration of Novel Emergent Structures in Sequences). In GENESIS, there are two kinds of agents: *builders* that construct representations, and *k-lines,* which group together successful agents. A k-line is created when a subgoal has been reached in the current problem situation. The k-line collects together all the agents which have worked towards this subgoal and becomes an agent in its own right. It may be activated in the future if half (or some other proportion) of its component agents are used together. It responds by activating the remaining agents. In this way, memories are reconstructed in a bottom-up fashion but with higher-level representations able to guide the process. Agents have *weights* which help determine which potentially relevant agents are activated. These weights are altered according to the *bucket-brigade* algorithm used in classifier systems (Holland, 1986). Following this algorithm, successful sequences of agent activity are rewarded by a pay-off, which increases their weights, whereas unsuccessful sequences have their weights reduced.

AGENT SELECTION STRATEGY: THE POINT OF COMPARISON

The crucial element of difference between the two psychological theories is the arousal mechanism proposed by Martindale. The alternative view is that no special mechanism is required for creative thinking.

To model the arousal theory, we used a search method based on what Hofstadter calls a *terraced scan* (Hofstadter & FARG, 1995). (Hofstadter explains the concept of a terraced scan in the discussion at the end of Chapter 8.) Cortical arousal is represented by the *temperature* parameter. This parameter varies according to the state of the problem-solving process. When little order is discovered, the temperature is high. This corresponds to a *low* level of arousal. This is because a high temperature increases the amount of randomness in the task selection process. In other words, it flattens the gradient of activation across agents. This is precisely what low cortical arousal is hypothesized as doing. At times when little progress has been made on a problem, arousal is low and attention defocused. This means that weak cognitive units may receive some attention. A low temperature arises as the system converges on a solution. At low temperatures, only the strongest bidding agent is likely to run. This corresponds to attention being highly focused on one or two units under high levels of cortical arousal. If a representation is found to be incorrect it is abandoned. Temperature increases after such an event. This corresponds to a regression from secondary processing (focused attention) to primary processing (unfocused attention), which, Martindale suggests, is a key mechanism for creative thought.

The terraced-scan method of agent-selection is based on using the range of bids as a probability distribution, where an agent $a \in A$ (the set of all agents) has the probability of being picked given by:

$$p(a) = \frac{bid(a)}{\sum_{i \in a} bid(i)}$$

The terraced scan modifies the bid distribution using the temperature parameter, T. This measures the order discovered in the system so far, that is, the extent to which the current solution successfully accounts for the current input information. If there is little order, then the temperature is high. Lots of order means a low temperature ($T \to 1$). When T is high ($T \to \infty$) then the bids are unaffected. As ($T \to 1$) so the selection process becomes more like the best-first process. Thus while there is little order in the system, T is high and weak contenders have a chance to act. However, in the finishing stages of the process, only strong agents will be chosen—the ones most frequently encountered in such situations. A formula for adjusting the bids in this fashion is:

$$bid(a)' = bid(a)e^{\frac{bid(a)-m}{T}}$$

where

$$m = \max_{i \in A}\{bid(i)\}$$

Figure 6.2 shows this process at work on a set of bids ranging from 0 to 200. With the temperature at 100, the adjusted bids are virtually the same as the originals. As the temperature lowers, however, the distribution becomes more skewed. With a temperature of 1, only the highest bid still

FIGURE 6.2
Adjusted bids from the set {1, 2, 3, ..., 200} at various temperatures according to the "terraced scan."

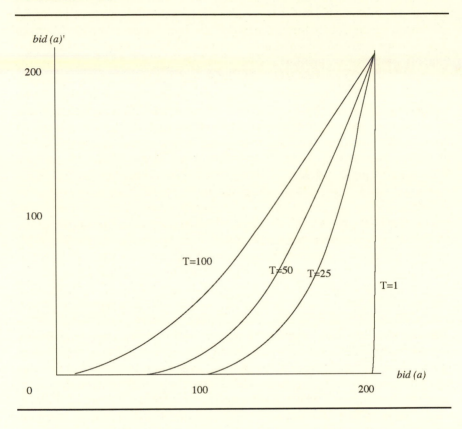

has significance, once adjusted. At this temperature, the search would proceed as a best-first search.

One way of measuring the order in the system is to define T as the ratio of the amount of data currently under consideration to the amount that can be accounted for by the current partial theory representation. In the card sequence domain, which we describe in the next section, T is the number of cards in the sequence divided by the number of cards currently accounted for.

The terraced-scan algorithm can be made to model the way in which, according to Martindale, different levels of cortical arousal affect the focus of attention in a creative thinker. By raising and lowering the temperature as a function of the success of problem-solving behavior we can extend and contract the scope of likely problem-solving agents and thereby shadow the four stages hypothesized in the cortical-arousal theory.

Weisberg, on the other hand, claims that there is no special mechanism, and that creative thinking is just a part of normal thinking. Normal problem solving involves trying out the most likely ideas first and correcting them if they prove inadequate. If an idea is completely wrong, it will be replaced by a competing one. In the computational theory, this corresponds to agent selection being a *best-first* process. The highest bidding agent is the one that runs. If a representation is wrong then it is abandoned. The bucket-brigade credit-assignment scheme means that agents on the chain that led to this representation are all eventually weakened if the same mistake is repeated. This means that an alternative move will be stronger, leading to the building of a different representation. The difference between the two theories is a difference in the method used for selecting between competing agents.

COMPUTATIONAL BEHAVIOR

We chose the card game *Eleusis* as the application domain for our models. Gardner selected this game as one which models the classic creative act: theory discovery in science (Gardner, 1977). In this game the dealer thinks up a card-sequence rule (e.g., red-odd follows black-even, etc.). This is output creativity. The individual players then try to discover the rule, on the basis of evidence collected by playing cards which the dealer declares to be correctly following the rule or not. This process of discovery is input creativity. The scoring is such that overly complex rules are counterproductive. The best score for the dealer is obtained from a rule that is quickly discovered by just one of the players. We used a simplification of Eleusis, called *Micro-Eleusis*, in which a card is either red or black, and either odd or even, so that there are effectively only four distinct cards in the pack: red-even, red-odd, black-even, and black-odd.

In a number of experiments, the two programs (one for each selection strategy) were compared with one another and with some other programs. GENESIS with the best-first strategy (GENESIS-BF) models Weisberg's "normal problem-solving" theory, whereas the terraced-scan version (GENESIS-TS) models the cortical-arousal theory. Both programs took turns as dealers and players.

The GENESIS programs construct and store memories of successful problem-solving activity (memories about sequences correctly interpreted), which can then be reused. These memorized, problem-solving chunks are Minsky's "k-lines." The long-term outcome is the creation of a dynamic "society" of interrelated meaningful chunks, and hence a "fluid" potential for representation in both analytic and synthetic roles. The reconstructive nature of the k-line theory means that the representations are flexible: there is no a priori commitment to particular models. A k-line may be used in future problem solving whenever it recognizes a new problem-solving situation that is sufficiently similar to the one that led to its creation. The notion of "sufficiently similar" is implemented as some fixed proportion (we used one half) of its component agents occurring in the current problem-solving task. This, together with the fact that the components of k-lines are not specific agents but abstractions from them, enables k-lines to be activated in partially matching situations. The competition between alternative partial solutions, governed by the bucket-brigade algorithm, provides a controlled relaxation of constraints. The terraced-scan version goes further in allowing memories that are only partially relevant a chance to be activated. Both versions allow multiple representations of the notational and structural kinds. The best-first selection method favors staying with one theory until it is sufficiently weakened for another to take over. The terraced-scan method encourages the creation of multiple problem-solving memories, and allows them opportunities to be used without the risk of their being penalized because of short-term problems. However, it also allows many useless or over-complex memories to be produced. The terraced scan tries to control the randomness, but does not direct the combination process (beyond the requirements of the external situation, that is). The best-first method, on the other hand, always has a reason for its combinations. There is still room for further self-criticism, however. It has a method of elaboration in the bucket-brigade algorithm which can be harsh, but prevents the build up of useless k-lines. The terraced-scan version of the bucket-brigade algorithm tends to upset the k-line organization.

As can be seen from the two graphs of average scores obtained by the two programs (Figures 6.3 and 6.4), they both settled down to play reasonable games as both dealers and players.

The most negative observation from this data is that the terraced-scan program, GENESIS-TS, gets progressively worse as a dealer. This is because it produces rules that look complex but which are, in fact, so full of non-determinism that they are trivial. The best-first program, GENESIS-BF, on the other hand, does seem to learn an appropriate output creativity.

The two programs also played a number of games against two human players, and although the humans beat them, their overall performance was quite creditable. GENESIS-TS scored just over half the human scores (the two human players scored almost exactly the same totals). GENESIS-BF was less impressive at just one quarter of the average human score. The programs scored the same as each other as dealers, and the same as one of the humans, whereas the other human scored twice as much. From these trials we conclude that the programs exhibit significant creative behavior, both input creativity as players, and output creativity as dealers.

THE "AHA!" PHENOMENON: CAUSE OR EFFECT?

One of the most important results is the behavior of GENESIS-BF in its analysis of Micro-Eleusis sequences. As commitment to one theory is weakened

FIGURE 6.3
Average *play* score per hand over 35 rounds.

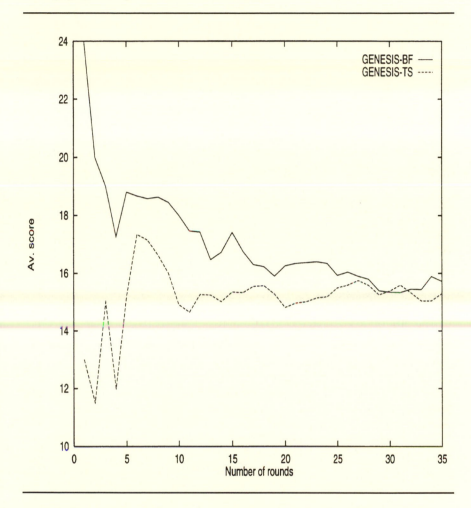

by the bucket-brigade algorithm, another, possibly completely different, theory has a chance to take over. The effect is an "aha!" experience as an unfruitful path is suddenly replaced by a more profitable one, possibly of a quite different sort. Consequently, best-first search can give rise to behavior reminiscent of the *illumination* stage of creativity. One of the chief objections to Weisberg's theory, which is modeled by GENESIS-BF, is that it does not account for this illumination phenomenon. It now turns out that the "normal problem-solving mechanism," he suggests, can in fact give rise to this kind of behavior. This strengthens the position of his theory.

FIGURE 6.4
Average *deal* score per hand over 35 rounds.

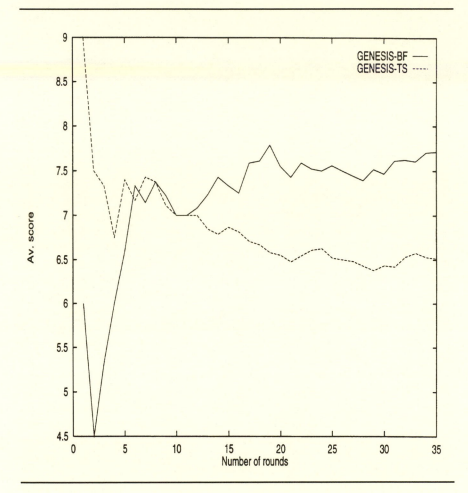

Martindale found that changes in cortical arousal occur during creative problem solving, and this finding is often taken as evidence in favor of a special-mechanism theory. However, one way to explain this is that it may be an *effect* of the problem solving process, and not a *cause*. In support of this theory, work on evoked brain potentials has concluded that unexpected, high-value stimuli and the registration of semantic mismatch when processing metaphorical sentences, can both cause cortical arousal (results surveyed in Partridge, 1985). So recognition of a creative insight, which is in some ways quite similar to the stimuli used in evoked-potential research, might *cause* cortical arousal. Cortical arousal, in other words, might indicate the mental registration of a creative breakthrough, rather than being associated with the mechanism that caused the breakthrough. It might occur *after* the moment of insight, and not before it.

CHUNKING AND MAGIC NUMBERS

A second goal was to evaluate the use of k-lines and the terraced scan as AI learning and search techniques. The advantages of the k-line theory come from the fact that it implements an *emergent memory*. This means that the system is flexible in its behavior and representations. An important consequence is that *analogies* are an emergent property of such memory systems. The main weaknesses are the deterioration in analysis performance, occasional trivia in output creativity, and the lack of feature selection. The first two could be tackled by some self-criticism method. The feature selection problem may be susceptible to using a learning method along the same lines as the structural k-lines.

The k-line idea is a manifestation of the repeatedly explored notion (from the "memo functions" of Michie, 1968) in the sixties to the Soar architecture of the late eighties (e.g., Rosenbloom & Newell, 1986) of caching successful behavior for more efficient and effective performance in the future. The general effectiveness of this strategy relies on the future bearing a sufficient resemblance to the past. In the short run this similarity requirement may hold good, but there is also likely to be long-term drift. To properly capitalize on the similarity factor, the learned chunks (the k-lines) must be abstractions from the successful behavior so that they will be applicable in a range of similar situations, and not just in identical ones. We implemented this abstraction by chunking *contexts* rather than the specific builder agents to form k-lines. An unfortunate consequence of this continual chunking was that it introduced a good deal of clutter. It might be better to create k-lines less frequently and on the basis of a clear-cut problem-solving success rather than on the achievement of every tentative success (such as subgoal achievement in the current implementation).

It is just possible that there is an optimal number of learned chunks, as in Miller's "magic number," 7 ± 2, the number of pieces of information that we can hold in short-term memory. It does, however, seem unlikely that there is such a domain-independent number. It is more likely that we maintain larger stores of learned chunks for more important tasks. More mental effort expended on a particular domain can probably lead to a larger store of learned chunks through better organization, or indexing, of what is stored. Currently we have little idea of what size of look-up store to associate with a given task. The machine learning community has not seriously addressed this sort of boundary condition for learning mechanisms.

CONTROLLED RANDOMNESS

The terraced scan has advantages as a search method incorporating a random element, that is, a mechanism of controlled randomness. These advantages include the ability to avoid ruts and the use of unusual methods without severely punishing them when they go wrong. However, the terraced scan is generally slow, and it can be unreliable. This might be an inevitable consequence of its random element, and, of course, nobody expects creativity to guarantee results. The terraced-scan method does not mix well with the k-line theory as the two methods for guiding the search interfere with each other's actions. This is not surprising—the k-line theory will capitalize on situations where each new problem resembles the last—a steady accumulation of appropriate problem-solving expertise will be the best strategy. The terraced scan with its "randomizing" potential provides the essential means of dealing with the occurrence of "odd" problems (that are not just like the previous ones). An appropriate rut is a good place to be in the former problem-solving context, but it needs to be vacated quickly in the latter. It might be possible to devise a learning algorithm that cooperates with the terraced scan, and to improve the terraced scan itself. However, we suspect this incompatibility problem is far more wide-ranging than merely a question of two specific mechanisms that are sometimes mutually obstructive.

The reader should recall Hofstadter's claim (Hofstadter & FARG, 1995) about the human role in artistic creativity of certain famous programs: the human "selects" from amongst the wealth of output or, in the case of the Automatic Mathematician (AM) system, the human guides the development of the final output. It would appear that a case can be made for control at both ends: at the front end, we need rules and constraints on the initial random productions, to ensure that the system has a manageable number of "likely" options to work with. At the back end, we need some sort of "quality control" on the final product.

The mechanism of evolution seems to involve what we are calling "controlled randomness." In gene mutation there seems to be a significant random element, but the many examples of convergent evolution (separate evolutionary paths ending up with similar solutions, e.g., within marsupial and placental mammals) suggest that the constraints on the expression of these genetic mutations as viable phenotypes closely control the basic randomness of the process. Is this what a mechanism of creativity requires? Does it require a complex hierarchy of interlocked constraints filtering a randomizing element at the bottom level, enough control to almost cancel out the random element, but not quite? Unfortunately, the attractiveness of the evolutionary metaphor diminishes when we realize how long the mechanism takes to generate novel solutions to its problems. This problem is echoed in our experiments with a genetic-algorithm model (Partridge & Rowe, 1994).

Even the historical record of scientific discovery seems strangely peppered with instances of duplicate, independent creative acts. We might term this "convergent discovery," and again it suggests that the random element in creativity is under tight control. The overall result is that the breakouts (if that is what they are) are almost predetermined, almost inevitable for a mind that is sufficiently steeped in the relevant information. Of course, the idea of a "scheduled breakout" does not sit easily with the notion of creativity as one-off flashes of insight.

Dartnall (1994) outlines two general ways in which machines might be creative: a *compatibilist* view, which maintains that creativity is a deterministic process based on "rich internal processes that stamp a distinctive hallmark on their products"; and a *libertarian* view which admits indeterminism via a "randomizing element at a low-level of description." Dartnall sketches out the latter possibility in terms of a two-stage, cyclic model based on generation of ideas followed by evaluation of their worth. A low-level randomizer is a crucial part of the generative stage of such a model—low-level, because we want the outcome to be creative rather than chaotic.

Dennett favors the libertarian approach in his earlier work (Dennett, 1978), but more recently has advocated a "Society of Mind" scenario. His (1991) "Thumbnail Sketch" of the architecture of the human mind dismisses the notion of a "central Headquarters." Instead he posits a system "in which specialist circuits try, in parallel pandemoniums [i.e., autonomous agents], to do their various things, creating multiple drafts as they go," with the result that the "seriality of this machine [is] the upshot of a succession of coalitions of these specialists" (p. 254).

Use of the terms "chaotic" or "random" is sometimes an easy substitute for an unknown or too complex mechanism. Typically, as understanding of a phenomenon advances, the scope of the postulated random component tends to shrink. Elements of the currently emerging conglomerate of activities known as *chaos theory* (e.g., Gleick, 1987) vividly illustrate this. There are many examples of discoveries of systematic fine structure in what at first sight seem to be random patterns—from fluctuations in the price of cotton in the United States to life-threatening fibrillations of the heart.

In some cases, it is now clear that chaos has a structure, sometimes quite a simple structure, but often wrapped in a periodic system which obscures the underlying simplicity. Michael Arbib, a long-time champion of computational modeling of the brain at a neuroanatomical level, seems to have foreseen this type of advance. In 1967 he wrote:

We have nothing approaching an adequate theory for what I term "the structured chaos," in which a large population of elements are subject to a small number of laws, the elements themselves being grouped in local structures of some regularity, be they random or deterministic. I believe that the exploration of different models of a "structured chaos" will be a major challenge . . . and may well prove to be of great importance to the study of the brain. (Arbid, 1967, p. 97)

Edward de Bono, in his popular introduction to *lateral thinking* (de Bono, 1969), seems to have hit upon a similar idea in his efforts to describe how a creative problem solver (a lateral thinker) must break out of fixed and rigid thought paths, and yet not fall into formlessness:

Flexible-rigidity is perhaps an ideal state. Enough rigidity to give context, meaning, and security. Enough flexibility to give change, improvement, adventure, and hope. . . . Controlled-chaos means that by design chaos is allowed, in order that material may come together in unexpected ways which can then be harvested and developed further. (p. 205)

There is a broad consensus concerning the need for the flexibility that, apparently, only randomness can supply, and a similarly pressing requirement for a rigidity of structure upon which real creativity must apparently be based. Too much of the former, and we get chaos. Too much of the latter, and we lose the creativity. There are many ways of combining non-deterministic elements with a rigidly structured framework of constraints. How we should do so to get a mechanism that mimics human creative ability is still an open question.

BREAKING OUT AND GOING WRONG

There is a persistent belief among theoreticians that a creative act derives from the system transcending normal problem-solving behavior, breaking out of its usual conceptual spaces, ignoring rules instead of slavishly following them, and so on. We think this is a difficult notion to accommodate within the computational modeling paradigm (which may be an argument against computational models of creativity, but we do not believe that this is the case). We are uneasy with this notion because any computer model must follow deterministic rules. If the model is to break out of its basic rules, there must be higher-level rules that determine how and when it should do so. These meta-rules may be heuristic or they may have a pseudo-random element in them, but they are rules nonetheless.

The game of chess provides a clear example of creative behavior as the exploration of unexplored regions of the space, rather than as breaking out into a new conceptual space. Chess is a well-defined game. Its space of moves is well defined, yet creative problem solving is a hallmark of the best chess players. The space of possible moves is so vast that there will always be virgin territory to explore. Perhaps the breakout theorist will say that the conceptual space is the space of strategies for thinking about moves, and not the moves themselves.

The perception of a need for a breakout mechanism may be a misperception due to our inability to accurately predict the outcome of a simple but extended sequence of interactions. In mathematics, for example, generating and proving the correctness of theorems is an important creative activity. A true theorem is, however, a well-defined extension from what is already known, and the proof is an explicit demonstration of this. But no one believes that theorems therefore ought to be *obviously* true. We know that they are often not (and sometimes appear, at first, to be patently false). We readily accept this sort of demonstration of our inability to accurately follow long, but simple, sequences of well-defined steps. An innovative and creative insight, which is subsequently shown to be an inevitable consequence of following the rules, does not, for that reason, become relegated to a non-creative act. The four-color conjecture, which was recently elevated to the status of a theorem, is a nice example of this.

Another good source of examples of misperceptions of breakouts is to be found in the craft of programming. Surprising, and at times quite unbelievable, program behavior is not an uncommon occurrence. When faced with this situation, the novice programmer is sometimes tempted to attribute it to some malfunction within the computer system, that is to say that the rules must have been broken. Either the programming language instructions are not obeying the rules of the language or the basic computer system itself is failing to observe its rules of operation. This is almost never the correct diagnosis. The more experienced programmer soon learns that, however "impossible" the observed output appears to be, it will turn out to be a straightforward consequence of the rules embodied in the program. Even for quite small programs the intricacies of all the alternative computational pathways can quickly elude the conceptual grasp of the programmer. The lesson to be learned by the novice is that what seems to be impossible is in fact completely predictable.

The emergent approach that we have taken in this chapter emphasizes the importance of a set of primitive representational elements. The implication is that one important determinant of creative potential is the size and variety of this set, in other words, the depth and breadth of the thinker's knowledge. Fortune, as usual, favors the prepared mind.

This last observation is appropriate for two reasons. First, creative achievement is based upon being steeped in the domain (the "preparation" and "incubation" steps of the four-stage model). Second, it begins to account for the phenomenon of convergent discovery, where there are two or more virtually simultaneous, independent discoveries of a creative solution to a problem. Within the scope of a mechanism of emergent creative thinking, the statement that the discovery was "in the air" can be realized in terms of common concerns and shared knowledge inducing a focus on similar combinations of representational primitives, and hence similar creative solutions.

It would seem more difficult to account for the simultaneous occurrence of similar *breakouts*.

The idea of a mechanism that supports human creativity in terms of breaking rules and developing new conceptual spaces stems, we think, from the classical notions of AI and cognitive science. These fields have tended to work with complex representations very much at the problem-solving level, which is like building a house from prefabricated units. This can be contrasted with the emergent approach, which is based on the interaction of populations of primitive representational units, rather like building a house from a pile of bricks or rocks. Using prefabricated units results in faster houses but of a limited number of types, whereas cementing bricks together presents the builder with an almost unlimited number of options. The resultant "representational fluidity" eliminates the need to posit the discontinuity of a "breakout." This still leaves us with the problem of selecting representational primitives, and in the previous section we addressed this in terms of the notion of controlled randomness.

CONCLUSION

This chapter has presented a computational study of the nature and process of creativity. It has looked at both psychological factors and computational mechanisms. Using non-classical AI techniques, based on the models of Artificial Life, an *emergent memory* model was developed, in terms of which rival psychological theories were compared.

The most significant psychological implication arises from the "aha" behavior of the best-first search. This repairs the chief weakness of Weisberg's theory, which says that there is no special mechanism for creativity, even though a distinctive brain-wave pattern is sometimes observed. We suggest that this is an effect, rather than the cause, of the emergence of an insight. The "no special mechanism" viewpoint now seems to be stronger than the cortical arousal theory.

There are two main implications for AI. First, Minsky's k-line theory can be made to work reasonably well. But there is room for improvement, especially in the areas of feature selection and self-criticism. The second result is that the terraced scan is a useful search algorithm in some cases. It can avoid local optima, but it needs to be made more stable and efficient. It also tends to interfere with learning strategies. It remains to be seen whether it can cooperate with a learning algorithm.

The main result, on which these others rest, is that the notion of representational fluidity, implemented within a multi-agent system as an emergent-memory mechanism, exhibits behavior that is both input and output creative. Emergent memory does not so much permit a system to "break out" of a representational space. Rather, it provides an effectively infinite virtual space, so that novelty can always be found in unexplored regions.

ACKNOWLEDGMENT

This chapter is based on work reported in D. Partridge and J. Rowe (1994), *Computers and Creativity,* Oxford: Intellect Books.

DISCUSSION

TD: How did you implement GENESIS?

DP: In the case of a GENESIS program acting as a player in the Eleusis card game, its task is to discover the card-sequence pattern devised by the dealer. It has an example sequence (perhaps partial) to guide it as well as some information on illegal cards at various positions, and it has the opportunity to experiment by playing a card when it's seen the example sequence. A solution will be a finite-state automator (FSA) that correctly encodes the card-sequence rule.

A central data structure is the FSA currently under construction. This is represented as a list of arcs which may include labeled arcs and not-yet-labeled arcs, called *templates* (which are set up by k-lines—abstractions of previously successful subsequence rules). This partial theory is called the *box*. A typical theory under construction is:

[[1 2 [red-even]] [template 2 1] [2 3 [black-odd]]]

[1 2 [red-even]] says "transition from State 1 to State 2 if the card is red-even," and [template 2 1] says "transition back from State 2 to State 1, but with no card characteristics yet specified." This arc remains to be completed with, say, activation of the builder [2 1 red-odd] which would result in this arc being labeled "red-odd." In this case the box would be completed, to give:

[[1 2 [red-even]] [2 1 [red-odd]] [2 3 [black-odd]]]

which specifies the rule "Alternate red-even red-odd red-even as many times as you like. Finish with black-odd."

But this rule leads to a dead end with black-odd, and is thus unacceptable. It would either be extended (by means of a further agent) with a fourth arc from State 3 to State 1 or to State 2, or it would be "trimmed" to remove the dangling arc, that is [2 3 [black-odd]] would be deleted from the box. If this latter trimming action were taken the final rule would be:

[[1 2 [red-even]] [2 1 [red-odd]]]

In order to analyze a card sequence, the program processes the given sequence one card at a time. Starting with the initial State 1, arcs from the box are selected until there are no acceptable arcs. If there is an arc in the box that enables an illegal card to be played, the box is scrapped and the process begins again. Otherwise, an agent must be selected for activation. All agents which fit the current state and which allow the appropriate card to be played are put forward for selection (see "relevant" builders and k-lines, in the next response).

TD: So in the final box given, if red-odd is appropriately played after red-even, this allows the FSA to transition from State 2 back to State 1, at which point red-even may be played again, and so on. The box would now be a complete FSA, a complete theory.

DP: Right! In general, an incomplete theory (box) may be changed by either a simple builder or by a k-line (these are composite builders that have been memorized from previously successful builder, and k-line, combinations). A relevant builder is one that can operate on the box's incomplete features (such as specify the card features for the unlabelled transition [template 2 1] in the incomplete theory given previously). A relevant k-line is any one that matches the "context" of the current theory under development. This context is determined by the list of agents (simple builders and k-lines) that have been used successfully on the current box so far— we call this the *events list*. Any k-line that has at least half its elements (simple builders and simpler k-lines) as the last entries of the events list is deemed relevant. All simple builders and k-lines that are relevant will be put forward for selection as the next agent to apply. The appropriate selection procedure now chooses a *task*, that is, an agent to activate. The list of possible tasks is formed by joining the list of relevant k-lines to the front of the list of relevant builders. This ensures that a k-line has priority over a builder in the event of them having equal weights in the best-first selection procedure. Further, if the agent selected is a builder, it is moved to the end of the list of builders. This enables other equally valid builders a chance of execution next time.

The two selection procedures are *best-first* and *terraced scan* which give rise to the two models GENESIS-BF and GENESIS-TS, respectively.

If a GENESIS model is acting as dealer then there are a few differences in the action. There is no priority for agents that have already contributed to the box over other agents. Only if the task selected constructs an arc already in the box is it used to move through the sequence (by one card) and the state changed accordingly. A sequence of length five is to be derived in this fashion before the program will finish. There are no external constraints, though. Only the current state and events list constrain the relevance of tasks. The length of five is also used in determining the temperature. In this case, it is defined as five divided by one more than the number of cards already generated (the one being added to prevent division by zero).

If the chosen task is a builder, then its corresponding arc is added to the box. If this builder was reinforced by the presence of a template in the box, then this template is removed. Otherwise the builder is a "new" agent and a template (indicating the context) is added to the events list.

If the chosen task is a k-line, then the first action is to form a list of all its elements that have not been recognized from the events list. Further, any censored elements are excluded (censored elements are ones that were not used in the previously successful actions that led to the creation of the k-line). The remaining agents are then recursively activated. If a component agent is a builder, it works as usual (unless censored). If it is a k-line, it is again evaluated and executed. Notice that k-lines within the main k-line will not have elements on the events list to be deleted. They may well have censored elements, however, from any k-line within which they are contained. While this activation is being executed recursively, censors are accumulated and passed down to more deeply embedded k-lines.

There are two final results of a k-line being executed. First, the events list is updated, replacing recognized events with the k-line. Second, a number of templates may have been added to the box. These will then reinforce the bid of builders with the corresponding contexts (by doubling the bid).

A solution is found (and a subgoal achieved) when the end of the sequence is reached, since each task involves moving one card along the sequence. The arcs within the box form a theory explaining the sequence so far.

Once a solution has been found to the current sequence, there is some response to be made. If GENESIS is the dealer, then the box is returned as its created theory. The box may require some *trimming*. This is the removal of any state that has no outgoing arcs. It is necessary to trim the box so that only infinite sequences can be generated, and the players won't get stuck at a dead end. Recall the trimming of [2 3 [black-odd]] in the example given.

If GENESIS is a player, it should play a card that fits according to the theory developed. If it has no such card in its hand then it will declare "No Play."

A limit must be set on the amount of time that GENESIS can spend on a problem, if it is to play in a game situation. Thus, after 2,000 new tasks have been tried, it gives up and simply plays any legal card in its hand, that is, any that are not already known to be illegal (by being in the sideline of the last correct card). Naturally, if it holds no legal card, it declares "No Play." This task counting considers only new agents that are tried. Actions that come from the box, or that are inspired by k-lines are not counted. There is a trade-off in efficiency between the number of tasks and the number of k-lines allowed. The balance reached in GENESIS is fairly arbitrary, but gives a reasonable response time for playing in a game situation.

TD: You say that the main result is that representational fluidity, implemented with a multi-agent system as an emergent-memory mechanism, exhibits behavior that is both input and output creative. Can you give us an example of this?

DP: The experimental context that we chose presented the opportunity to explore both input and output creativity (which was, of course, one of the reasons for choosing it). In the Eleusis card game the players exercise input creativity when they must discover the dealer's rule, and the dealer must exhibit output creativity when he devises a rule that is tricky enough to elude most of the players but simple enough for one player to discover it relatively quickly. Our programmed models were tested as both dealers and players.

Examples of analytical problem solving (and therefore candidates for input creativity), which will also serve to illustrate the later point of analogy in problem solving, are provided by the two different solutions found by the programs to the rule "Alternate reds and blacks."

GENESIS-BF found the succinct representation when it constructed the following box:

[[1 2 [red-even]] [1 2 [red-odd]] [2 1 [black-even]] [2 1 [black-odd]]]

But GENESIS-TS found an altogether more elaborate solution:

[[4 2 [red-even]] [1 2 [red-even]] [2 1 [black-even]]
[4 2 [red-odd]] [2 4 [black-odd]] [1 2 [red-odd]]]

which is not obviously a solution at all. But on close inspection it is possible to see that "reds" can only be played from States 1 or 4, and in all cases they cause a transition to State 2. From State 2 only "blacks" can be played, and "black-even" leads to State 1, while "black-odd" leads to State 4. It is, of course, debatable whether this ability to find obscure ways to express simple things is a characteristic of creativity.

This tendency to construct complex solutions exhibited by GENESIS-TS counted heavily against it when acting as a dealer. It tended to invent rules that looked complex but were so full of non-determinism that they were trivial. GENESIS-BF, however, often seemed to strike the necessary balance between complexity and simplicity in its rules invention—it produced some good candidates for output creativity. In one game when it was the dealer it invented the "switch" rule composed of two sub-rules "play red-odds only" and "play anything but a red-odd" where a "black-even" switches from the first sub-rule to the second and a "black-odd" switches back.

TD: In Chapter 8, McGraw and Hofstadter also talk about representational fluidity. The main source of fluidity in Letter Spirit is in the conceptual haloes that allow slippage from one concept to another. I think you say that the fluidity of GENESIS is due to its fine-grained, low-level representations, but it's not clear to me how this fine granularity, just by itself, gives us fluidity.

DP: Fine granularity, just by itself, does not give representational fluidity. Coupled with the fine granularity must be a uniform non-restrictive set of "associations," the glue if you like, for sticking the representational "atoms" together in very many different combinations. It is almost a truism that the finer grained, or more low-level, the representational "atoms" with respect to the macro-structures to be represented, the greater the representational freedom and apparent fluidity of construction and destruction (provided the "glue" is available) from the macro-level perspective. A good analogy may be the endless diversity of physical compounds that can be constructed from the 92 natural elements (which are no more than minor variants of each other—one proton and perhaps a few neutrons more or less) using electromagnetic forces.

TD: Do you think that representational fluidity is just necessary for creativity, or is it sufficient as well? (I think we are tempted to ask, "Where does the creativity come from?" But this is probably a misleading question. It suggests that there is a "source" of creativity, and that we can turn it on like a tap.)

DP: Of course, no one knows, but we can hypothesize. Under our non-breakout theory, representational fluidity would seem to be necessary to account for creative insights as part of normal problem solving (the "aha!" sensation, you will recall, we view as an after-the-event phenomenon). If nothing mechanistically different is involved with a creative breakthrough, then the process of constructing the representation that amounts to a novel solution (to some knotty problem) must be the very same process that produces mundane solutions and non-solutions. The novel solution is not a different sort of solution. It is, we suggest, no more than a solution that has been plucked from previously unexplored solution space, perhaps a region in the space of representational possibilities that has not been explored because it had been thought to be unproductive. A powerful manifestation of a representationally fluid scheme would seem to be needed to permit fast and "smooth" access to all the odd corners of potential solution space.

Where does the creativity come from? It comes from being the first to look in an unlikely region of the representational space and finding a neat solution there. What drives the looking? It is, we believe, a mechanism that embodies an adaptive feedback-influenced combination of randomness and constraints. But what exactly? That's the million-dollar question.

TD: You say that an important consequence is that analogies are an emergent property of such memory systems. Can you give us an example of this?

DP: Syntactic and semantic similarities between problem-solving representations are a further consequence of representational fluidity. If all representations are constructed from the same primitive units using the same "glue," then similarity is unavoidable. Of course, the implementation details of the deceptively easy term "similarity" forms the meat of this question. We implemented two different aspects of "similarity":

1. Successful problem-solving representations were not cached explicitly. Only the abstract framework of the solution was stored. The system "memorized" only the structure, the syntax, of the successful solution. As solutions were finite-state machines (FSAs), the specific transitions on the arcs were removed so that the stored "k-line" would be analogous to any structurally similar problem.

2. K-lines were activated for problem solving when only a proportion (we used one half) of their structure matched the problem at hand.

In summary, only partial structural similarity was required to bring an "analogous" problem-solving representation to bear on the current problem.

As an example we can consider the solution given previously that GENESIS-BF produced to discover the rule "Alternate reds and blacks." The specific solution:

[[1 2 [red-even]] [1 2 [red-odd]] [2 1 [black-even]] [2 1 [black-odd]]]

became memorized as the k-line:

[[template 1 2] [template 1 2] [template 2 1] [template 2 1]]

This k-line then provided the basis for solution of several subsequent rules: "Play the same parity or color (but not both) as the preceding card," and "Alternate red-even and red-odd with black-odds wild." In both cases the simplest solution is alternating two-state FSA, and in both cases GENESIS-BF used the above k-line to discover the correct rule efficiently. We would say that the system exploited the analogy between these new problems and the one that it had solved earlier.

TD: You say that you get an "aha!" situation when GENESIS-BF suddenly replaces an unfruitful path with a more profitable one, possibly of a quite different sort. How does this phenomenon manifest itself? What does GENESIS-BF actually do when this happens?

DP: GENESIS-BF uses the very simple technique of choosing the agent that is offering the highest bid (an agent's bid is simply some constant times the agent's weight) when it is in need of a potential problem-solving action (or set of actions). The agents, primitive builders and k-lines, have their weights increased whenever they contribute to a successful problem-solving exercise, and decreased whenever they are selected to contribute to problem solving. Thus the highest bidding agent will be selected repeatedly (remember that the same agent, if it is a k-line, can be used repeatedly in a number of different but analogous ways) while it remains the highest bidding agent. But with each lack of success, its weight, and hence its subsequent bid, will decrease. Eventually, it will no longer be the highest bidding agent and suddenly after repeated analogous attempts to use a previously very successful agent (hence its very high weight and bids) a totally different agent will be selected and may prove successful.

The behavioral result of this series of problem-solving attempts is the sudden switch from a series of unproductive problem-solving attempts to a new and different approach which succeeds—apparently a snap change to try something novel, and it works.

TD: How well do you think your models capture the psychological theories? How well does the terraced-scan version of GENESIS model the Cortical Arousal Theory, and how well does best-first search model the No Special Mechanism Theory?

DP: We would claim no more than that our two variants of the GENESIS model implement plausible analogues of the two psychological theories mentioned. It is of interest and significance for the purposes of comparison that the theoretical differences become manifest in the models purely as differences in the task selection procedure, the mechanism by which potential problem-solving agents are chosen. This offers the great advantage that differences in model behavior must emanate from this focus of implementational difference. But in broad-brush terms our two mechanisms do seem to possess appropriate functionality, although the no-special-mechanism theory is really no more than a catch-all for the opposition to cortical arousal theory. The best-first selection process struck us as a reasonable candidate for no special mechanism. This is, however, a far cry from claiming to have accurately modeled the two psychological theories.

TD: I'm not sure why you think that representational fluidity eliminates the need for "breaking-out," in Boden's sense (she calls it "impossibilist creativity"). Your analogy is that it's like building a house from a pile of bricks, rather than from prefabricated units: smaller units give us more flexibility in terms of what we can build. Now let's apply this to Boden's example of Kekulé's discovery of ring molecules. Kekulé gazes into the fire and thinks he sees images of twisting, turning serpents. Suddenly he sees one with its tail in its mouth, and he hits on the idea of a ring molecule, which the rules of chemistry at that time didn't allow. Boden says that this enabled him to break out of the conceptual space of standard chemistry and open up the space of aromatic chemistry. How does your idea of *smaller building blocks* affect this story?

DP: It is of course dangerous to argue science on the basis of a single data point (and an anecdotal one at that), but we won't let that hinder us. Some years prior to his benzene-ring insight, Kekulé proposed that carbon atoms could link one to another to form carbon chains. The representational "atom" is a carbon atom with four hands, and the "glue" is the holding of hands between any two atoms. The fact that any two carbon atoms can hold one, two, or even three hands in common with another carbon atom (as well as with numerous other sorts of atom) makes for a very large (effectively infinite) and intricate representational space—it is the vast world of organic chemistry.

A representation-building mechanism with a small random element would soon start to produce closed-loop structures alongside the linear chains. No breakout seems to be needed, merely the possibility that the two carbon atoms that join hands happen to be at the ends of the same chain (for benzene that chain happens to be six atoms long). This latter requirement was in fact inferred by Kekulé based on his six-atom ring creative insight and the known details of the hitherto problematic "aromatic" substances. It served to confirm the discovery by fitting in with the four-fold valency of carbon and resolving puzzles about the general composition of the aromatic compounds. It also happened to be wrong (at least, according to currently accepted theories of distributed electron bonding—the discrete holding-hands view of atomic bonding is an oversimplification that works well most of the time, but throws up "puzzles" with benzene, curiously).

Under this sort of interpretation, the surprise would seem to reside more in the fact that it took chemists so long to hit upon this possibility. And the answer to that may be found in the fact that "structural" theories of chemistry were not well accepted in the early 1860s. So for many chemists of the day, the space of carbon-chain structures did not have a reality. Indeed, far from rule breaking, we might view Kekulé's insight as based on the fact that he was one of the few structural theory advocates, and so he simply followed his rules.

Breakout theory may be no more than an artifact of the classical cognitive modeling paradigm (and its ready realization in Good Old-Fashioned Artificial Intelligence—GOFAI). A Parallel Distributed Processing (PDP) model, for example, would appear to offer no opportunity for a breakout hypothesis.

REFERENCES

Arbib, M. (1967). Models of the brain. *Science Journal,* May, 95–99.

Arieti, S. (1976). *Creativity, The Magic Synthesis.* New York: Basic Books.

Boden, M. A. (1990). *The creative mind: Myths and mechanisms.* London: Weidenfeld and Nicolson.

Cohen, J. L. (1988). Creativity: Some ambiguities in the issue. *Journal of Social and Biological Structures, 11,* 77–79.

Dartnall, T. (Ed.) (1994). *Artificial Intelligence and creativity: An interdisciplinary approach.* Dordrecht: Kluwer.

de Bono, E. (1969). *The mechanism of mind.* Harmondsworth, UK: Penguin.

Dennett, D. C. (1978). *Brainstorms: Philosophical essays on mind and psychology.* Cambridge, MA: MIT Press.

Dennett, D. C. (1991). *Consciousness Explained.* London: Penguin.

Findlay C. S., & Lumsden, C. J. (1988). The creative mind: Toward an evolutionary theory of discovery and innovation. *Journal of Social and Biological Structures, 11,* 3–55.

Gardner, M. (1977). On playing the new Eleusis, the game that simulates the search for truth. *Scientific American, 237,* 18–25.

Gleick, J. (1987). *Chaos: Making a new science.* New York: Viking.

Hofstadter, D. R., & FARG (Fluid Analogies Research Group) (1995). *Fluid concepts and creative analogies: Computer models of the fundamental mechanisms of thought.* New York: Basic Books.

Holland, J. H. (1986). Escaping brittleness: The possibilities of general-purpose learning algorithms applied to parallel rule-based systems. In R. S. Michalski, J. G. Carbonell, & T. M. Mitchell (Eds.), *Machine learning: An artificial intelligence approach* (Vol. 2, pp. 593–623). San Mateo, CA: Morgan Kaufmann Publishers Inc.

Langton, C. (Ed.). (1989). *Artificial life.* Redwood City, CA: Addison-Wesley.

Martindale, C. (1981). *Cognition and consciousness.* Homewood, IL: Dorsey Press.

Martindale C., & Hines, D. (1975). Creativity and cortical activation during creative, intellectual and EEG feedback tasks. *Biological Psychology, 3,* 71–80.

Michie, D. (1968). Memo functions and machine learning. *Nature, 218,* 19–22.

Minsky, M. (1985). *The society of mind.* New York: Simon and Schuster.

Olton, R. M. (1979). Experimental studies of incubation: Searching for the elusive. *Journal of Creative Behaviour, 13,* 9–22.

Partridge, D. (1985). Input-expectation discrepancy reduction: A ubiquitous mechanism. In *Proceedings of the Ninth International Joint Conference of Artificial Intelligence,* 267–273.

Partridge, D., & Rowe, J. (1993). Creativity: A survey of AI approaches. *Artificial Intelligence Review, 7,* 43–70.

Partridge, D., & Rowe, J. (1994). *Computers and creativity.* Oxford: Intellect Books.

Poincaré, H. (1924). Mathematical creation. In P. E. Vernon (Ed.), (1970). *Creativity.* Penguin.

Read, J. D., & Bruce, D. (1982). Longitudinal tracking of difficult memory retrievals. *Cognitive Psychology, 14,* 280–300.

Rosenbloom, P., & Newell A. (1986). The chunking of goal hierarchies. In R. S. Michalski, J. G. Carbonell, & T. M. Mitchell (Eds.), *Machine Learning II.* Los Angeles: Morgan Kaufmann.

Rowe, J. (1991). *Emergent creativity: A computational study.* Ph.D. thesis, Computer Science Department, University of Exeter, UK.

Sternberg, R. J. (Ed.). (1988). *The nature of creativity: Contemporary psychological perspectives.* Cambridge: Cambridge University Press.

Vernon, P. E. (Ed.). (1970). *Creativity: Selected readings.* Harmondsworth, UK: Penguin.

Wallas, G. (1926). The art of thought. In P. E. Vernon (Ed.), (1970). *Creativity: selected readings.* Harmondsworth, UK: Penguin.

Weisberg, R. W. (1986). *Creativity, genius, and other myths.* New York: Freeman.

7

Creativity and Runaway Learning

Chris Thornton

This chapter adopts a strictly *non-empirical* approach to the study of creativity. Rather than offering a model of the experimental data, such as it exists, the aim will be to carry out a logical analysis of the operational characteristics of basic learning procedures, and to use this analysis to tease out some interesting facts about the relationship between learning and some types of creativity.

The key idea to be worked out is that our ability to be creative might be partly founded on our ability to *learn*. I shall argue that certain creative processes may be viewed as learning processes *running away out of control*. The notion of a connection between learning and creativity is nothing new, of course. Many authors have identified close relationships between creativity, abduction, and analogy (e.g., Koestler, 1964; Schaffer, 1994; Langley, Zytkow, Simon, & Bradshaw, 1986; Hummel & Holyoak, this volume). But this chapter will try to put some new flesh on the relationship by showing that the generative aspect of creativity may be understood in terms of a particular type of learning. The aim will be to show that what one might term "intellectual" or "scientific" creativity can plausibly be viewed as a form of empirical learning extended beyond the normal boundaries of objectivity.

What I mean by "the normal bounds of objectivity" is this. When we talk about "learning" we tend to think of a process which seeks to identify *objective* features of the world. But when the learning is concerned with very abstract phenomena, such as "reactionary politics," the process teeters on the boundary between objectivity and subjectivity. Is reactionary politics really an objective feature of the world? Probably not, since it depends so much on individual judgment. This suggests that a learning process that generates this concept is at least partially subjective. I shall argue that if this subjective element in the learning is pushed a few stages further (e.g., to the point where it generates the hitherto unknown concept of "reactionary expressionist politics") we might want to say that its outputs have become *creative*.

As I said, the argument will be based, not on any empirical model, but on a logical analysis of the learning task. The reliability of the conclusions will be primarily a function of their analytical coherence.

LEARNING ANALYZED AS A TASK

Definitions and characterizations of the process we call "learning" vary a good deal. There are many different forms of the process, each of which may operate on a characteristically distinct basis. We can cut away some of the complexity by focusing our attention, not on the process itself, but on the *task* that it addresses.

All forms of learning involve some form of behavior acquisition. In any given behavior—which may range from a simple motor skill to an abstract cognitive transition—certain "actions" must be produced in certain "situations." And it is these contingency relationships which give the behavior its distinct character. The problem that is solved in a learning event, therefore, is the establishment of a set of contingency relationships, or, in computational terms, the implementation of a set of *if-then* associations. For example, the result of learning the concept "reactionary politics" may be thought of as an if-then rule which says that *if* the statements made by some politician have certain properties *then* the politician may be classified as pursuing reactionary politics.

At this level of abstraction, no judgments need to be made about the objects involved in the contingency relationships. In the case of human learning, behaviorists will say that the antecedent objects are sensory stimuli and the consequent objects are motor outputs. Cognitivists will say that the antecedent objects are elements of inner, mental states and the consequent objects are representational constructs. Whichever way we look at it, any particular contingency relates to some particular set of antecedent objects. But it can do so in two different ways. The contingency may relate to an *absolute* property of the antecedents or to a *relative* property. Putting it another way, the if-then rules may test for absolute properties ("does antecedent A have property P?") or they may test for relative properties ("do antecedents A and B have relationship R?"). In the reactionary politics example, an if-then rule might require that the politician's views are both "backwards-looking" and "knee-jerk." This would be a non-relational rule.

Or the rule might require that the "backwards-looking" views are expressed more strongly than the "knee-jerk" views. This would be a relational rule.

What this tells us is that learners may follow two different strategies. They may pursue a *relational learning* strategy, in which case the identified contingencies are tagged to relational properties of antecedent objects. Or they may pursue a *non-relational learning* strategy, in which case the associated contingencies are tagged to non-relational properties of antecedent objects. Interestingly, this conclusion is obtained without anything being known about how learning works in practice. The choice of relational and non-relational strategies of operation is a property of learning tasks and is thus *necessarily* faced by any learning procedure, regardless of its implementation or biological origin.

As a matter of fact, it turns out that practical learning methods, insofar as they have been identified and characterized, *do* tend to divide up into relational and non-relational groupings, that is, into methods which seek to generate rules of a relational character and methods which seek to generate rules of a non-relational character. (Clark & Thornton, 1997). Relational learning is, in fact, generally considered to be an independent subfield of machine learning research focusing on discovery-oriented learning procedures. Methods from the area of Inductive Logic Programming (Muggleton, 1992) are good examples of this class. The analytical conclusion relating to the relational/non-relational bifurcation thus does seem to carry over into the empirical domain.

THE NEED FOR RECURSIVE RELATIONAL LEARNING

A key observation for the argument to be developed is that the identification of a relationship within certain data effectively *recodes* those data. For example, imagine that the data are integer values and the relationship identified is *greater-than*. The identification offers us a recoding of the data in which the original set of integer values are transformed into a set of truth values, which are the results of evaluating the greater-than relationship within the given data.

Relational learning is thus a process which *potentially* generates new data. And like Kekulé's snake which can turn around and eat its own tail, the relational learner can turn around and treat the outputs it has generated as if they were a fresh set of inputs. This will not necessarily happen, of course, but we can easily envisage situations in which "recursion" of this form will be advantageous.

For example, imagine that the antecedent objects (in some behavior) exist at one or more levels of description below that of the consequent objects. This would occur, for instance, if the antecedent objects were words and the consequent objects were sentence meanings relating to actions involving real-world objects. On the assumption that an object at one level of description is made up of a set of *related,* lower-level objects, we know that contingencies in this situation necessarily associate consequent objects with some *relational* property of the antecedent objects. If there are several levels of description interposed between antecedent and consequent levels, then we know that the contingencies associate consequent objects with a hierarchy of relational effects, that is, exactly the structure which can only be identified through a process of *recursive* relational learning.

The situation is particularly straightforward in the case of visual perception. Take any visual concept and think of another concept in which it plays a role—the concepts of "surface" and "box," for instance. A box is made up of surfaces arranged in certain relationships. So if learning needs to generate the concept of a box working only from descriptions of surfaces then it *must* identify the relevant relationship.

The implications of this are quite interesting. If learning ever confronts a situation in which antecedent and consequent objects are at different levels of description—and this is, arguably, the *expected* situation for agents using low-level stimuli for purposes of dealing with macroscopic objects—recursive relational learning of some sort is a *necessity.*

To summarize the last few paragraphs:

- Learners may utilize relational or non-relational strategies.
- If learning agents tend to use low-level stimuli for dealing with high-level objects and events, then the level of description of antecedent objects will typically be several levels lower than that of consequent objects. In this case, learners must necessarily utilize a recursive, relational strategy.

The bottom line here is that *realistic* learners will tend to pursue the recursive relational strategy. That is, they will tend to turn around and treat generated outputs as the inputs for further rounds of learning. But in executing this strategy, learners may be doing much more than mere learning. Note that a learner pursuing any sort of relational strategy has to be able to identify relationships. This type of learner must utilize "knowledge" of some sort concerning possible relationships. Succeeding at recursive relational learning involves applying the right relationships in the right way. Successful learners will be those which attempt to identify those relationships that are "really there," that is, actually instantiated in the learner's sensory data stream. The learning is then tantamount to the incremental discovery of successive levels of description—a kind of constructive representation-building operation.

Furthermore, it is natural to assume that a learner of this type will continue the learning process up to the point at which the antecedent and consequent levels of description have been "brought into alignment." Every time the learner recurses (that is, treats generated outputs as new inputs) it generates concepts at a higher level of description. This process continues to yield dividends until the point at which concepts have been generated which are at the same level of description as the consequent objects. Consider the reactionary politics case. If the original inputs for the learning are descriptions of simple words, the recursion should ideally continue until concepts have been generated which identify not particular types of word, but specific types of viewpoint (e.g., the concept of a knee-jerk statement).

At this point, the relevant contingencies potentially cease to have a relational basis and the learner obtains no advantage from continuing. However, termination of the process at this point is not *inevitable*. From the theoretical point of view there is no reason why the process should not continue. In practice, it may even be difficult to determine when full alignment has been achieved. For example, when learning the "reactionary politics" concept, is it best to stop the recursion once the "knee-jerk statement" concept has been generated, or is it better to press on to obtain the "hot-headed-politician-who-issues-knee-jerk-responses-more-strongly-than-reactionary-responses" concept?

But letting the process run on is likely to have some unexpected effects. The generation of internal data will continue to instantiate successive levels of description, but these levels of description will now become increasingly divorced from reality. Initially, the discontinuity will be relatively modest (cf. the "hot-headed-politician . . ." concept above). There will be some initial, post-termination, level of description containing objects made up of components—themselves real objects—tied together within familiar and realistic relationships. However, as the data-generation process continues, the familiarity and realism of the objects populating new levels of description will gradually diminish. Eventually a point will be reached where the process is effectively "fantasizing," that is, building constructs out of "imaginary" objects tied together in "unwordly" relationships. An example might be "expressionist reactionary politics."

What is happening here is that our learning process is starting to run away with itself. It is beginning to flesh out the possible hierarchical constructs that can be built out of known objects and relationships. Put another way, the process is beginning to explore the space of possible ways of reconstructing reality. This is a form of activity that is, in some sense, "creative." And when we look at the dynamics more carefully we find that the process is a plausible instantiation of Margaret Boden's model of creativity (Boden, 1990) as the development and exploration of conceptual spaces. This is effectively the task performed by recursive, relational learning in the runaway phase. The learning strategy meets Boden's creativity criterion fairly well. I think the implication is that our process model has a split personality. On the one hand it is a learning procedure dealing with certain types of problematic behavior. On the other hand it is a *creative* procedure pursuing the exploration and development of new conceptual spaces. The learning personality is built-in by design, but the creative personality is a simple consequence of the fact that termination in recursive learning may not occur when alignment has been achieved.

AN EXAMPLE OF RUNAWAY RELATIONAL LEARNING

Let me illustrate the creative effects of runaway relational learning with a more detailed example. Consider the poker dataset shown in Table 7.1.

Each row in Table 7.1 is an input/output pair representing a particular hand in the card game poker. Each odd-numbered variable contains the face value for a particular card, represented as a number (where 10 = jack, 11 = queen, 12 = king, and 13 = ace). The adjacent even-numbered variable holds the corresponding suit value (1 = hearts, 2 = spades, 3 = clubs, and 4 = diamonds). Values of the output variable represent the rank of the hand, using the following scheme.

1 two of a kind (a pair)

2 two pairs

3 three of a kind

4 straight

5 flush

6 full house

7 four of a kind

8 straight flush

Let us think about the way in which a relational learner might tackle these data. Initially, it might try different ways of applying relevant relationships to the data. For example, the learner might search for instantiations of the *equality* relationship. As a first step, the equality of all ten input values might be considered. In the data at hand there are, in fact, no cases in which all the input values are identical. Thus the application evaluates to false in all cases. A next step might be to try applying the equality relationship across subsets of variables. This produces slightly more interesting results. Cases 8 and 16 both exhibit equality among the same selection of variables. In fact, every even-numbered variable in both data has the same value.

The learner might also investigate the possibilities of applying the equality relationship in a more flexible way. In particular, it might see whether there are cases in which arbitrary selections of *values* from particular data satisfy the relationship. This approach might lead to the discovery that each of the cases 9, 10, 11, 12, and 13 contains at least three identical values, that is, three values that mutually satisfy the equality relationship. (It might also reveal that in each case the relevant values come from the odd-numbered variables.)

TABLE 7.1
Simplified poker data.

Case	Card 1		Card 2		Card 3		Card 4		Card 5		Value
	Card	*Suit*	*Card*	*Suit*	*Card*	*Suit*	*Card*	*Suit*	*Card*	*Suit*	
1	13	2	2	3	8	2	2	1	2	4	3
2	8	3	6	4	6	2	8	3	8	1	6
3	12	1	5	2	3	3	3	2	3	1	3
4	13	4	13	3	8	2	8	1	8	3	6
5	9	3	10	1	11	2	12	1	13	4	4
6	10	4	10	3	1	3	1	4	10	2	6
7	13	4	11	4	11	3	13	4	13	4	6
8	9	2	4	2	5	2	13	2	10	2	5
9	7	4	12	4	12	2	4	2	12	1	3
10	13	2	8	2	1	3	1	3	1	4	3
11	10	3	10	1	5	2	13	2	10	2	3
12	13	4	3	4	4	1	3	4	3	4	3
13	11	2	8	4	4	4	4	2	4	4	3
14	11	3	11	4	13	1	13	1	13	3	6
15	2	3	2	1	2	1	2	2	1	4	7
16	8	2	2	2	9	2	11	2	13	2	5

These initial experiments with equality reveal that even using a single relationship in a single application protocol, there are many different results that can be produced. A tendency to focus on equality relationships among specific variables tends to lead to the identification of effects corresponding to the existence of *flushes,* since in these cases the values exhibiting equality will always be sited in the same variables. A tendency to consider equality among arbitrary collections of values, on the other hand, leads more directly to the identification of n-*of-a-kind* hands.

In a recursive learning process the effects of any bias (i.e., the search strategy used) are cumulative. A bias which leads to the identification of flushes will—in the next round—lead to the identification of hands which are built out of flushes, for example, *straight flushes,* where the hand is both a flush and a straight. A bias favoring n-*of-a-kind* hands, conversely, will lead to the identification of hands which are built out of n-*of-a-kind* hands, for example, *full houses* (three of a kind and two of a kind). The learner with one bias will discover one set of phenomena in the data, while the learner with a different bias will find a different set. In poker the possibilities are particularly numerous. A learner whose bias gave it a predisposition to consider integer sequences, for example, would be led to discover straights rather than flushes or *n*-of-a-kind.

Relational learners thus always have a hand in the creation of their own input data. To some degree, the "worlds" they inhabit are self-built. The original data start out as the most influential factors. But as the learning proceeds, the accumulated consequences of the learner's own bias become increasingly dominant. The learner is led in a particular direction and discovers a certain subset of relational effects in the data. A given relational learner confronted with the poker data will thus identify a certain *subset* of the full range of poker hands, these being the hands that may be constructed using relationships available to the learner.

But let us imagine that we have an *ideal* learner which succeeds in generating the full range of known poker hands, and ask what will happen if the learning is not terminated at this point. The process of searching for relational effects continues on. But now it applies to internal data generated in previous iterations and the objects over which relationships are sought are identified *patterns* of card combination. The inevitable consequence is the generation of imaginary poker hands: "full houses" comprising two-card and three-card runs, "straights" involving ascending sequences of pairs, "flushes" involving alternating suits, and so on. The mechanical procedure used to discover genuine poker hands now begins to generate imaginary hands.

What is happening, in effect, is that the process is starting to explore the space of possible "poker-like" hands. It is doing this in a relatively unguided way. But there is an element of selectivity, in the sense that new objects are explored contingently depending on their grounding in the original data. This selection process might be viewed as a very rudimentary form of "aesthetic filtering" which prioritizes new interpretations of reality over pure fantasy.

The poker example is a very simple one, but it should be sufficient to show how the creative potential of runaway learning may be cashed out in a reasonably realistic context. It also helps us to understand what type of creativity is generated by runaway learning.

CONCLUSION

This chapter has presented a logical analysis of learning which suggests that the learning process has the potential to make a transition from a characteristically objective to a characteristically subjective mode. Once past this transition point, the products of the process have an increasingly creative character while the dynamics become increasingly interpretable in terms of the conceptual-exploration activity suggested by Boden as a model of generic, intellectual creativity. According to this view, then, learning and certain types of creativity are to be treated as extreme points on a single dimension. And we should begin to think in terms of a generic, constructive procedure whose operations are initially "close to the ground" but later achieve something akin to "free flight." From the technological point of view, the argument suggests that those wishing to devise artificial, creative agents should pay close attention to work going on in the learning sciences. The scientific implications are also worthy of note. The argument provides us with the beginnings of what looks to be a theoretically well-grounded process model for certain types of creative action. Whether this model can be provided with any empirical support remains to be seen.

DISCUSSION

TD: You begin by distinguishing between relational and non-relational learning. But isn't all learning implicitly relational? Can we really learn integer values, for instance, without learning relationships between integers?

CT: Well, I take your point. But most computational work on concept learning focuses on non-relational learning, which really amounts to different ways of forming concepts by seeing what objects have in common. The learning of relationships is a much harder nut to crack. There's always this difficult question of working out which relationships to look for.

By the way, you shouldn't try to focus on human learning here. Just think in terms of an arbitrary concept-learning process. This process can identify commonalities between objects (non-relational case) or it can seek to identify relationships between objects (relational case). It's a clear-cut distinction as long as you don't try to drag human learning into it.

TD: And relational learning recodes the data?

CT: That's crucial. I argue that relational learning always implicitly recodes the data, thus generates new data, and thus can potentially be applied recursively.

TD: In what sense is it recursive? Your example is that recursive learning in poker might give us flushes on the first iteration, and straight flushes later on. Strictly speaking this isn't recursive, because on the first iteration the relationship is sameness-of-suit, whereas later on it's integer-sequence, which enables the system to find the straight flushes among the flushes.

CT: Right. A better example would be learning the concept of a full house. This involves having the concepts "pair" and "three of a kind." So here the recursion would first generate data written in terms of "pair," and so on, and then in the next round you would get "full house."

TD: Or a pair and then two pairs. You suggest that recursive learning can "run away" and process information more than necessary, so that it builds castles in the air, imaginary constructions—it fantasizes.

CT: Yes.

TD: Suppose the system looks for relationships between cards (say, sameness-of-suit and integer-sequence), and discovers straights and flushes. It can now recurse and find relationships between the patterns it has discovered on the first iteration. This might give it pairs-of-pairs and straight flushes, but your claim that it can come up with imaginary hands such as a "strange full house" (a three-card and two-card straight) highlights an issue. It's a question of the constraints. If the constraint is to look for five-integer-sequences, then the system *can't* come up with two and three cards sequences, and so can't come up with strange full houses later on. This suggests that it is easier to recurse if we have weak constraints. How important is it to have weak constraints in order to get "running away"?

CT: I don't know the answer to that. It's a key issue, of course, but in order to get valuable creative results out of an artificial learning system you would need to work out the answers to all sorts of difficult questions. All I'm trying to show is that the system *could* run away and that if it did it would generate novel conceptual artifacts which in *some* cases seem to have a "creative" character. I'm waiting for someone else to do the hard part!

TD: Let me come at the question from a different angle. In Clark and Thornton (1997) you talk about Elman's (1993) notion of the importance of starting small. Presumably, in the case of human learning, we begin by looking for simple relationships, the real-world analogues of sameness-of-suit and integer-sequence. One reason for doing this is simply that we don't know what the complex relationships are at this stage—we haven't learned them yet. If we begin by looking for simple relationships, if we start small, there's more chance of recursing, and more chance of running away. It's difficult to recurse when we're looking for five-integer-sequences, but a lot easier with just "integer sequence," which might hold between only two integers. Searching for integer-sequences, where the output data might just be a sequence of two numbers, will yield more recoded data than looking for five-integer-sequences, *and* it's easier to find relationships in this data if we're looking for simple relationships.

CT: My chapter isn't any help here. It just shows how the process of exploring conceptual spaces might be founded in some sort of runaway learning process.

TD: In the introduction to this volume I argue that we *construct* representations in the imagination, rather than copy them from experience in the fashion of Classical Empiricism. We do this by redeploying capabilities that we first acquired in problem solving and learning about the world. Here I think we converge, because you show how learning processes, that we would use in making sense of the world, can "run away" and become creative.

CT: Absolutely. I would say that we were articulating variations on a common theme.

TD: In Chapter 6, Derek Partridge and Jon Rowe distinguish between input and output creativity. Input creativity analyzes incoming data (looks for patterns, etc). Output creativity is, for example, writing a requiem. Does this correspond to your distinction between learning and creativity?

CT: I don't think that you can distinguish between input and output creativity. Input creativity is going to produce new concepts that will feed directly into your creative output (look at the way that the concept of a requiem feeds straight into the production of a requiem). I would imagine that this distinction hides a misunderstanding about learning possibilities.

TD: It's interesting that you accept that we construct representations in the imagination by deploying capabilities that we acquired during the learning process, but reject the broad-brushstroke distinction between input and output creativity. I discuss this in my Introduction to your chapter at the beginning of this volume.

Finally, do you have any thoughts about why recursive learning runs away for us, but apparently not for the rest of the animal kingdom? You suggest that creativity might be a natural consequence of recursive learning, yet other species learn recursively and aren't creative. Why are we different?

CT: Maybe you could turn that question around and use it to provide an answer. Maybe you could say that what makes us different is the fact that we engage in runaway learning. I don't have any answers to the bigger questions about why we have evolved the way we have. All I'm saying is that creativity may not be some special thing grafted on the top of cognition. Maybe we can view it, in some cases, as being a simple variation on the learning process.

REFERENCES

Boden, M. (1990). *The creative mind: Myths and mechanisms.* London: Weidenfeld and Nicolson.

Clark, A., & Thornton, C. (1997). Trading spaces: Computation, representation and the limits of uninformed learning. *Behavioral and Brain Sciences, 20,* 57–90.

Elman, J. (1993). Learning and development in neural networks: The importance of starting simple. *Cognition 48,* 71–99.

Halford, G. (1997). Recoding can lead to inaccessible structures, but avoids capacity limitations. *Behavioral and Brain Sciences, 20,* 75.

Koestler, A. (1964). *The Act of Creation.* London: Hutchinson.

Langley, P., Zytkow, J., Simon, H., & Bradshaw, G. (1986). The search for regularity: Four aspects of scientific discovery. In R. Michalski, J. Carbonell, & T. Mitchell (Eds.), *Machine learning: An artificial intelligence approach* (Vol. II, pp. 425–469). Los Altos, CA: Morgan Kaufmann.

Muggleton, S. (Ed.). (1992). *Inductive logic programming.* London: Academic Press.

Schaffer, S. (1994). Making up discovery. In M. A. Boden (Ed.), *Dimensions of Creativity.* Cambridge, MA: MIT/Bradford.

8

Letter Spirit: Perception and Creation of Diverse Alphabetic Styles

Gary McGraw and Douglas Hofstadter

FLUID CONCEPTS AND CREATIVITY

The Letter Spirit project is an attempt to model central aspects of human high-level perception and creativity on a computer. It is based on the belief that creativity is an automatic outcome of the existence of sufficiently flexible and context-sensitive concepts—what we call *fluid concepts* (Hofstadter & FARG, 1995). Accordingly, our goal is to implement a model of fluid concepts in a challenging domain. Not surprisingly, this is a very complex undertaking and requires several types of dynamic memory structures, as well as a sophisticated control structure involving an intimate mixture of bottom-up and top-down processing. The full realization of such a model will, we believe, shed light on human creativity.

The specific focus of Letter Spirit is the creative act of artistic letter design. The aim is to model how the lowercase letters of the Roman alphabet can be rendered in many different but internally coherent styles. Two important and orthogonal aspects of letterforms are basic to the project: the *categorical sameness* possessed by instances of the same letter in different styles (e.g., the letter "a" in Times and Optima) and the *stylistic sameness* possessed by instances of different letters in the same style (e.g., the letters "a" and "k" in Times). Figure 8.1 shows the relationship of these two ideas. The program will start with one or more seed letters representing a style and create the rest in such a way that all share the same style, or *spirit*.

FIGURE 8.1
Items in any column have *letter* in common. Items in any row have *spirit* in common.

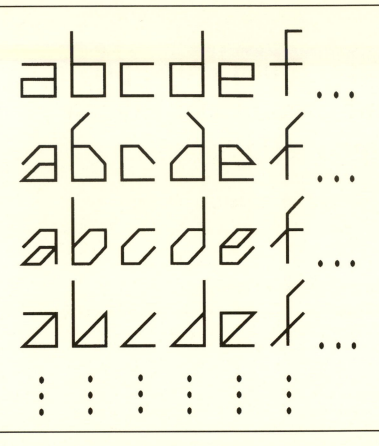

To put the goals of Letter Spirit in perspective, it is enlightening to analyze what is lacking in many AI programs touted as "models of creativity." The problem is that they *don't know anything about what they are doing.* This phrase actually has two meanings, both of which apply to the programs under discussion. The first meaning is "the program has no knowledge about the *domain* in which it is working." The other is "the program has no internal representation of the *actions* it is taking, and no awareness of the *products* it is creating." These gaps are serious defects in anything that purports to be a model of creativity.

We insist that for a design program to be called "creative," it must meet the following requirements:

- The program must arguably *make its own decisions,* not simply carry out a set of design decisions all of which have already been made by a human.

- The program's knowledge must be rich—that is, each concept must on its own be a nontrivial representation of some category, and among diverse concepts there must be explicit connections.

- The program's concepts and their interrelations must not be static, but rather must be flexible and context-dependent.

- The program must be able to judge its own tentative output and be able to accept it, reject it totally, or come up with plausible ideas for improving it.

- The program must gradually converge on a satisfactory solution through a continual process in which suggestions and judgments are interleaved.

We would argue that the deep (and controversial) question raised implicitly by the first point—"What would it mean for a program to make its own decisions?"—is answered by the last four points taken together.

The Letter Spirit architecture is a rudimentary model of these aspects of creativity. As described in this chapter, several of its features—nondeterminism, parallelism, and statistical emergence—are key elements in allowing it to achieve these goals.

THE MOTIVATION OF LETTER SPIRIT

The Grid

To avoid the need for modeling low-level vision and to focus attention on the deeper aspects of letter design, we eliminated all continuous variables, leaving only a small number of discrete decisions affecting each letterform. Letterforms are restricted to short line segments on a fixed grid of points arranged in a 3 × 7 array. Legal line segments, called *quanta,* connect a point to any of its nearest neighbors. There are 56 possible quanta, as shown in Figure 8.2.

Because quanta are either on or off, decisions on the grid are coarse. Surprisingly, the variety among letters of a given category is still huge—hundreds of versions of each letter and full gridfonts have been designed by humans.[1] Almost paradoxically, the domain's limitations engender this diversity.

It is impossible to make tiny changes on the grid, so any two instantiations of a given letter are significantly different. Indeed, because of the coarseness of the grid, designers must tamper with the conceptual essence of letters. Decisions to add or subtract even one quantum often fundamentally affect category membership. Figure 8.3 shows the large distance in letter-space one can travel with minimal changes on the grid. A "small" change—the erasure of just one quantum—changes the first shape from a strong "e" to a strong "z." A one-quantum addition transforms the "z"

FIGURE 8.2
The Letter Spirit grid, with one of the many possible sets of quanta instantiated and "a" turned on.

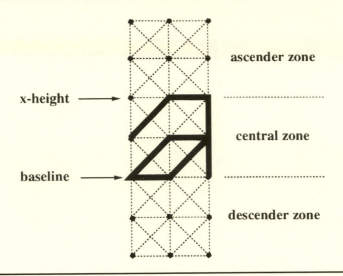

into an "a." So category membership in the Letter Spirit domain is a tricky matter. In fact, modeling the process of deciding which of the 26 categories a given shape on the grid belongs to (if any) is one of the hardest aspects of the project. This problem has been successfully addressed and is reported by McGraw (1995).

As there are no surface features to manipulate at a fine-grained level, one ends up playing at the boundaries of the 26 categories. Consequently, many gridfonts are wild, sometimes having angular, blocky, spiky, sparse, or otherwise bizarre letters. Rather than striving for typefaces with high readability or letterforms beautiful at the surface level, we are attempting to understand the conceptual nature of letterforms and thereby gain insight into what imbues concepts *in general* with their fluidity. Pushing the categories to their edges often results in an intellectual beauty not localized in any single letterform of a gridfont, but spread out over the gridfont as a whole—the beauty of *spirit* rather than of *letter.*

While at first glance, the Letter Spirit domain might be shrugged off as a "toy domain," this would grossly underestimate its subtlety. In spite of, or rather *because* of, the reduction to the grid, the Letter Spirit challenge is, in terms of cognitive-science issues, extremely rich. The cognitive issues are magnified, not reduced, by the act of simplifying the domain. All that has been thrown out is the need for expertise. One need not be a professional typeface designer or lifelong student of letterforms to appreciate the consis-

FIGURE 8.3

Rapid metamorphosis of an "e" into an "a" via "z," with merely a one-quantum change in each step.

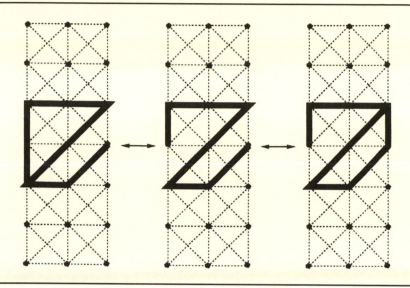

tency of a well-designed gridfont. Even a novice can design a passable grid-font, though doing a sophisticated one is very difficult.

Letters as Concepts

In order to better distinguish the *concept* of a letter from various geometric shapes that may instantiate it, we introduce some terminology. We distinguish three conceptual levels, running from abstract to nearly concrete as they move toward the actual geometric letterform. The term *letter-concept* refers to the most abstract idea for drawing a letter without reference to style. This level is comprised of a set of *letter-conceptualizations*. A typical letter-conceptualization would be the notion that a "b" consists of two "roles"—a *post* on the left side attached in two places to an open *bowl* on the right side, sitting on the baseline. A rival conceptualization for the same letter also consists of two roles—a *post* on the left side attached in one place to a closed *loop* on the right side, sitting on the baseline. These conceptualizations, possibly augmented by others, constitute the *letter-concept* of "b." Once a specific letter-conceptualization has been chosen, notions of style give rise to a more specific and detailed letter-conceptualization that partially specifies how each role should be realized (of course this conceptualization still could be realized in infinitely many ways). This is called a *letter-plan.* A letter-plan is present in a designer's mind before any marks are put on paper. The actual shape drawn on paper is a *letterform*. Letter Spirit is concerned with all these levels: play with letter-conceptualizations, creation of letter-plans, and the design of letterforms based on letter-plans.

A vivid example of the shape/concept distinction involves lowercase "x." For most adults educated in the United States, the only conceptualization for "x" consists of a forward slash and a backward slash of the same size that cross somewhere near the middle. English children, by contrast, are taught to draw a lowercase cursive "x" as a pair of small crescents facing away from each other but "kissing" in the middle. If we look at a printed "x" in this way, we are suddenly struck by this new conceptualization. The shape on our retina is the same, but what is constructed in our mind's eye is very different.

Roles. The conceptual pieces into which a letter is broken in the mind's eye are its *roles*. For example, the two crossing slashes in an imagined "x" are roles. So also are their four tips, and the crossing-point in the middle. Each role has a different degree of *importance* to the letter—the degree to which its presence or absence matters. Of course, different shapes instantiate a given role more strongly or more weakly than others. In other words, roles are also concepts with somewhat nebulous boundaries, just as *wholes* (complete letters) are. The difference is, membership in a role is easier to characterize than in a whole, so that reducing wholes to collections of interacting roles is a step forward in simplification.

The internal structure of a category is represented as a collection of interacting roles. Category membership at the whole-letter level is partially determined by category membership at the lower level of roles. In addition, *stylistic* appropriateness of a shape is judged in terms of how roles are filled—in other words, how norms are violated. Any such violation is a stylistic hallmark that must be propagated (via analogy) to other letters.

The hypothesis that letter-conceptualizations are made up of constituent roles has been empirically validated by several psychological experiments (McGraw, Rehling, & Goldstone, 1994; McGraw, 1995). Comparison of the role hypothesis with other theories of letter perception as well as an implemented model of letter perception based on the role hypothesis has been completed by McGraw (1995).

CREATING A GRIDFONT

For a person, designing a gridfont takes between ten minutes and three hours (after which the font remains potentially subject to scrutiny and minor revision). The process involves myriad small operations, ranging from the mechanical to the inventive. A typical action (e.g., creating a "k" or even changing a single quantum in an already designed letter) sets off repercussions that echo throughout the continuing design process, all over the gridfont, and at all levels of abstraction. This activity is largely guided by a priori notions of the interrelatedness of letter categories (e.g., "d" and "b" are often considered to be near reflections of each other). Many such actions occur, and eventually a stable gridfont emerges.

Dissatisfaction and contradiction either within a given letterform or between letters are the prime movers of the design process. If two or more letters seem to conflict stylistically, the resulting gridfont will be unsatisfying to a human. Letter Spirit must thus be capable of *recognizing* and *resolving* such conflicts, in order to create a coherent style. Sometimes the conflicts are subtle, and require refined artistic judgment calls. Modeling the ability to find conflicts, diagnose them, and convert diagnoses of problems into reasonable suggestions for solutions is a key aspect of the project.

Any design decision will affect not only the letter currently under consideration but also conceptually close letters. For example, a design decision regarding the post of a "b" is likely to have a major effect on the post of the "d," and may also influence the *stems* of the "p" and the "q." Of course, the extent and type of this influence are dependent on the particular style and are in no way mechanical. Most aspects of letterforms are likely to propagate their influence to varying extents through the entire gridfont. The propagating wave will probably cause many retroactive adjustments (major and minor) to some "already finished" letters, and give rise to ideas for letters not yet designed. One design decision will typically spark others, which in turn will spark others, and so on.

Eventually, when enough "decision waves" have washed over the gridfont, letterforms begin to have a high degree of internal consistency, and a style begins to emerge. Once the tension of inconsistency eases up, no more large-scale changes are required. Minor adjustments may continue, but the large-scale creative act will be mostly finished. This temporally-extended, serial process of integration and gradual tightening of internal consistency is an indispensable aspect of creativity, and is a well-known property of such creative acts as musical composition, the writing of poetry and fiction, the activities of painting and sculpture, the evolution of scientific theories, the design of AI programs—even the writing of chapters about creativity and cognitive science!

FOUR GLOBAL MEMORY STRUCTURES

The Letter Spirit program will contain four dynamic memories, each concerned with different levels of concreteness and abstraction of shapes (and concepts pertaining to shapes). These memories are:

- The *Scratchpad,* which is a virtual piece of paper on which all the letters of a font are drawn and modified; as such it is more a type of external memory than an aspect of mental activity.
- The *Visual Focus,* which is the site where perception of a given letterform occurs; in it, perceptual structures are built up and converge to stable categorical and stylistic interpretations.

- The *Thematic Focus*, which is the program's dynamically changing set of ideas about the stylistic essence of the gridfont under way; in it are recorded stylistic observations of all sorts concerning letters already designed, and if and when some of these observations are perceived as falling into patterns, those patterns can be taken as determinant of the style, meaning they can be elevated to the status of explicit *themes*—ideas that play an active role in guiding further design decisions, in the sense of serving as "pressures" on the construction of further letters.

- The *Conceptual Memory*, which is the program's locus of permanent knowledge and understanding of its domain, and which, for each concept, has three facets: (a) a set of *category-membership criteria*, which specify the recognition requirements for instances of the concept in terms of more primitive concepts; (b) a set of *explicit norms*, which encode aspects of the concept's "core"; and (c) an *associative halo*, consisting of links having time-varying lengths connecting the concept with related concepts, thus giving a sense of where the concept is located in "conceptual space" by saying what it most resembles.

A useful perspective is afforded by the following rough equivalencies with familiar types of memory. The Scratchpad can be thought of as an *external memory device*. The Visual Focus can be thought of as a *subcognitive workspace*—that is, a very short-term cache-like working memory in which parallel perceptual processes, mostly occurring below the system's threshold of awareness, collectively give rise to rapid visual classification of a shape, whose final category assignment is made cognitively accessible. (See Hofstadter and FARG 1995.) The Thematic Focus can be thought of as a *cognitive workspace*—that is, a much slower, and thus more conscious, level of working memory in which abstractions derived from more concrete and primary perceptions are stored, compared, and modified. Finally, the Conceptual Memory is a *permanent semantic memory* containing the system's concepts. We now describe each memory in more detail.

The Scratchpad is the place where letterforms are created and critically examined. At the start of a run it is empty; by run's end it contains 26 completed letterforms. The Scratchpad contains an arbitrary number of grids, each being a 56-bit data structure telling which quanta are on and which are off.

The Visual Focus is where recognition of a single letterform takes place. It can be thought of as a busy construction site where quanta belonging to a letterform are fused together in a bottom-up manner into small structures of various sizes and shapes called *parts*. The parts are then interpreted as roles, and possibly modified in the act of "mating" with roles. Any combination of instantiated roles suggests membership in one or more letter-categories.

At the beginning of a run, processing in the Visual Focus is purely bottom-up; gradually, however, as structures are built up, top-down influences enter the picture, with top-down processing guiding the "docking" of syntactic parts into semantic slots. This is fully explained in McGraw (1995).

Structure in the Visual Focus is built up in parallel by many computational micro-agents called *codelets*. A useful image is that of a large structure (like a bridge) being built by a colony of hundreds of ants. The ants work semi-independently, but cooperatively. Codelets correspond to the ants in this metaphor, and perceptual structures to the bridge. So perceptual structures develop nondeterministically but not haphazardly. From hundreds of tiny probabilistic decisions a coherent view emerges.

The Thematic Focus is the site where stylistic attributes come to be recognized, especially if they crop up in one letter after another. The more a stylistic attribute is seen as a systematic pattern, the more chance it has of making an upward shift in status—from being a casual observation, essentially a passive entity, to an active entity: an official guiding principle, or *theme*.

Such "elevation to themehood" is a little-appreciated but pervasive aspect of creative acts. In working on a gridfont, a human designer starts by being inspired by, say, a single seed letter. Aspects of this letter, borrowed analogically, suggest further letters. But each of these new letters, when looked at by a style-conscious eye, will be seen to have stylistic attributes of its own that were not implicit in the seed letter. These unexpected attributes are a result of the interaction of the constraints defining a perceived style with the unrelated constraints defining the given letter category. In other words, these stylistic attributes are unpredictable emergent by-products of the creation of new letters. Once such an attribute is elevated to themehood, it becomes an active force in shaping further letters. This means the process is recursive—new letterforms give rise to new emergent attributes, which in turn give rise to new letterforms, and so on. The upshot is that new stylistic attributes are continually emerging. All of this adds up to an unpredictable meandering in "style space," reflecting the subtlety of the creative act.

Types of stylistic pattern that can characterize a gridfont as a whole include the following:

- A *role trait* characterizes how a specific role tends to be instantiated, independently of the letters it belongs to. A role trait is a "portable norm-violation"—one attached to a specific role (e.g., crossbar or post) and thus capable of affecting several letters.

- A *motif* is a geometric shape used over and over again in many letters. If it is very simple (e.g., a two-quantum backslash crossing the central zone), it may be required to appear in complete form in every letter. If it is a more complicated shape (e.g., a hexagon that looks like a tilted benzene ring), then parts of it may be allowed to be absent from various letters, so long as a reasonably substantial portion of it remains. Some styles allow a motif to appear in reflected, rotated, and/or translated form, others allow translation but no reflection or rotation, and so on.

- An *abstract rule* is a systematic constraint such as: allowing no diagonal quanta, allowing only diagonal quanta, requiring each letter to consist of precisely two disjoint parts, and so on.
- *Levels of enforcement.* The three preceding types of stylistic attribute pertain directly to shapes on the grid. A much more abstract determiner of style—in fact, a kind of "meta-level" aspect of style—is the degree to which any such constraint is considered "unslippable" (i.e., absolute or inviolable), as opposed to being "slippable" (i.e., allowed to be disrespected under sufficiently great pressure). The level of enforcement of a stylistic constraint—strict, lax, or somewhere in between—sets an abstract, almost intangible tone for the entire gridfont.

All these stylistic attributes are explicitly represented in the Thematic Focus and are thus globally accessible, both in the sense of being *observable* and in the sense of being *alterable* by agents in the program. Thus all aspects of style are under the control of the program.

The Conceptual Memory provides every concept in the domain with an internal definitional structure and a conceptual neighborhood. A concept's internal definitional structure consists of its specification in terms of simpler concepts. A concept's conceptual neighborhood consists of its links to peer concepts in conceptual space. The internal definitional structure itself breaks down into two facets: *category-membership criteria* and *explicit norms*. Finally, a concept's conceptual neighborhood is known as its *associative halo,* and one of its main purposes is to serve as the source of conceptual "slippability." What this means is that, in times of severe pressure, the concept may "slip" to some concept in its halo, with closer concepts of course being more likely to slip. This means that the nearby concept is tried out, and possibly accepted, as a substitute for the concept itself. We now say a bit more about each of these three aspects of a concept.

Category-membership criteria specify perceptual attributes that contribute toward membership in the category, with different weights attached to the various attributes, reflecting their levels of importance. This weighted set of criteria reduces the concept to a collection of more primitive notions (e.g., a letter is reduced to a set of interacting roles, or a role to a set of desired properties of a modified part).

By contrast, a set of explicit norms exists (at least for roles and wholes, which are sufficiently semantic concepts), which make the core of the concept explicitly accessible to agents seeking ways to make a weak instance of the concept stronger, or a strong instance somewhat weaker without casting its category membership into limbo. Norms represent the program's explicit knowledge about the internal structure of categories.

A concept's associative halo consists of links of varying lengths connecting it with related concepts. The links encode such information as: standard resemblances between letters, analogical relationships connecting different types of roles, conceptual proximity of various descriptors used in specifying norm violations, and so on. Knowledge of letter-to-letter resemblances serves a dual function: it helps in designing new letters (e.g., a good heuristic for a first stab at "u" is to rotate "n"), and also serves as a warning that one letter tends to be confused with another (e.g., "b" and "h" can easily be confused). The set of links from a given concept effectively gives that concept a halo of conceptually close, potential-substitute concepts—concepts to which it might slip under sufficiently great contextual pressures.

FOUR INTERACTING EMERGENT AGENTS

Four conceptually separable types of large-scale activities emerge from the many small actions of codelets:

1. The high-level conceptual activity of *devising a new letter-plan* (i.e., either an idea for an as-yet undesigned letter or a possibility for improving an already designed letter).

2. The intermediary activity of *translating a new letter-plan into a concrete shape* on the Scratchpad.

3. The relatively concrete perceptual activity of *examining a newly-drawn shape and categorizing it* (i.e., deciding which letter of the alphabet it is, and how unambiguously so).

4. The more abstract perceptual activity of *recognizing the stylistic attributes of a newly drawn letter, and judging them* (i.e., finding "exportable" ways of describing how a given letterform violates norms, and deciding how well the letter's attributes fit with those of other letters in the developing gridfont).

It is convenient to speak as if these emergent activities were carried out by four explicit and cleanly separable modules, together comprising the totality of the program. (These agents could be likened to the agents referred to by Minsky [1985].) We call these hypothetical agents the *Imaginer*, the *Drafter*, the *Examiner*, and the *Adjudicator*, and will briefly describe them. However, it must be kept in mind that these modules are in some sense convenient descriptive fictions, in that each is simply an emergent by-product of the actions of many codelets, and their activities are so intertwined that they cannot be disentangled in a clean way.

The Imaginer does not deal with, or even know anything about, the constraints defined by the grid; rather, it functions exclusively at the abstract level of roles. Its job is to make suggestions regarding roles, which it then hands over to the Drafter (which will attempt to implement them as parts composed of quanta). The Imaginer can make suggestions of two distinct types—*norm-violation* suggestions and *role-regrouping* suggestions. Though both types can lead to highly novel instantiations of letters, suggestions of the first type tend to be tamer than those of the latter type.

A *norm-violation* suggestion assumes a set of interacting roles (i.e., a particular conceptualization for the letter) has been specified. Then, for one or more roles in that set, it suggests one or more ways of violating associated norms. For instance, suggestions such as "Bend the tip of the ascender to the right," "Use a short crossbar," "Make the bowl narrow," and so on (suitably expressed in an internal formalism) would be typical norm-violation suggestions. Though fairly specific, such suggestions require more fleshing out to be realized on the grid.

A *role-regrouping* suggestion is more radical, in that it involves tampering with the very essence of the letter—in other words, coming up with a new conceptualization for the letter. This means taking apart one or more roles and making new roles that combine aspects of the old roles. An easy-to-grasp example is the conceptual move from imagining "x" as two intersecting slashes to imagining it as two kissing angle brackets. Role regrouping is very subtle because it takes place completely at an *abstract* level. That is, no *shapes* are involved at any time. Rather, the Imaginer deals exclusively with abstractions—abstractions that, to be sure, have the general "feel" of shapes, in that they are associated with spatial locations and have spatial functionalities—but such abstractions are not shapes.

Once a new conceptualization has been produced, it can be handed over directly as a suggestion to the Drafter, or norm-violation suggestions can be made in addition, and then the whole thing handed over as a package to the Drafter.

The Drafter, unlike the Imaginer, does know about the grid; indeed, its main function is to take the Imaginer's grid-independent suggestions and adapt them to the grid.

Here is an example that could easily come up in designing a "t" or an "f." A norm-violation suggestion like "Make the crossbar short," which in real-life circumstances would offer a letter designer a full continuum of possibilities, offers much less freedom to a designer restricted to the grid. For a grid-bound "t" or "f," a conventional (i.e., norm-respecting) crossbar would be a horizontal line segment composed of two quanta. Obeying the suggestion to make it short would thus seem to offer just three alternatives: dropping the left quantum, dropping the right one, or dropping both. Dropping both quanta would seem drastic if not outrageous (although possibly the right solution for some very far-out styles); thus in all likelihood, the Drafter should opt for drawing just a single quantum, probably horizontal. Then the question is whether it should draw it to the left or the right of the ascender. This choice will certainly depend in part on precedents in other letters (e.g., if the decision "Draw a quantum on the left side of the ascender" had already been made in the case of "f," then "t" might want to follow suit), but will also depend on how strong the potential letter's category membership will be.

The Examiner has been fully implemented (McGraw, 1995). Its responsibility is to take the specification of a grid letter in terms of its quanta and to determine which (if any) of the 26 letter-categories it belongs to, and how strongly and unambiguously so. It is useful to cast the Examiner's work in terms of *syntactic* and *semantic* operations.

Syntactic operations are purely bottom-up chunking operations. They serve to put quanta together in a way that would be reasonable no matter what type of shape was being recognized. In other words, they are *context-free chunkings* that would presumably arise as the result of any naturally evolved visual system. Semantic operations, on the other hand, depend on the set of categories into which the shapes are being channeled—a writing-system-specific repertoire that, in a person, is acquired through experience. Semantic operations take the output of syntactic actions (which occur earlier in perceptual processing) and adjust it to conform to expected abstract structures. The upshot is a "marriage" of bottom-up structures coming from sensory stimuli with top-down expectations defined by letter-concepts.

All processing in the Examiner takes place in the Visual Focus. Processing begins at the level of quanta and starts out totally bottom-up. Quanta get syntactically chunked into parts, which are then assigned any number of syntactic labels (e.g., "straight," "central-zone," "zigzag," "left-side," "slanting," etc.). Top-down semantic influence enters the picture as the labeled parts are matched up with conceptual roles. As the interpretation rises towards the level of letters (which we call wholes), even more top-down influence is brought to bear.

The Adjudicator is concerned with a more abstract type of category membership—namely, *stylistic consistency*. It is not enough for a candidate letterform to be perceived by the Examiner as a strong member of its intended letter category; that letter must also be judged by the Adjudicator as embodying the same stylistic qualities as the seed letter or letters and any already generated letters. This requires a set of high-level descriptions of stylistic qualities to be manufactured as the alphabet develops. No single letter contains all the information about style, so stylistic attributes from various letters, as they come into existence, must be assembled in a global list belonging to the gridfont as a whole. This is of course the Thematic Focus. Thus whereas the 26 letter categories exist in the Conceptual Memory *prior* to any run, a single stylistic category gradually comes into existence in the Thematic Focus *during* a run.

The types of stylistic attributes the Adjudicator looks at to judge a candidate letterform include *role traits, motifs, abstract rules,* and *levels of enforcement.* A letterform is inspected for the presence of established themes, and is given a "stylistic-coherency rating" according to how many themes are echoed in it.

In addition to looking for attributes that have already been established as part of a style, the Adjudicator tries to extract new stylistic attributes from any new letter, to extend the set of themes defining the emerging style. An attribute discovered in a single new letter may not be considered strong enough to be elevated to themehood, but if that observation is reinforced by finding it echoed in other new letters, it stands a chance of becoming a new theme and thus driving the design of further letters and the retroactive modification of older letters.

Note that stylistic attributes can emerge in a completely unpredictable fashion. If the Adjudicator happens to notice that neither the seed letter nor the first new letter generated contains any vertical strokes, then it may generalize from these two examples and thereafter strictly forbid vertical strokes. Such a decision will of course have global ramifications. On a different run where the same two letters existed, a totally different course could be taken if that observation were not made, or if the interdiction were taken somewhat loosely.

THE CENTRAL FEEDBACK LOOP OF THE CREATIVE PROCESS

The Letter Spirit challenge can be thought of as the problem of attempting to do in one framework something that has already been done in a significantly different framework. Here, the two frameworks are different letter categories, such as "d" and "b." A designer is handed a somewhat off-center member of the first category and the challenge is to transport its eccentricity—its stylistic essence—into the other category, or in other words, to reproduce its *spirit* in the second framework, despite the fact that the second framework is by no means isomorphic to the first. Such transport of spirit cannot be done in a reliable manner except by trial and error. Guesses must be made and their results evaluated, then refined and evaluated again, and so on, until something satisfactory emerges in the end. We refer to this necessarily iterative process of guesswork and evaluation as "the central feedback loop of creativity."

We now run through one example, and a rather simple one at that, in order to give a sense of how all four agents are involved in this loop. We suppose that Letter Spirit is given as its lone seed letter an "f" with a conventional ascender (i.e., a tall vertical stroke on the left side of the grid that curves over to the right at the top), but with no crossbar at all (see Figure 8.4). What kind of grid-letters might this seed inspire? What kind of overall style?

To begin with, the seed's letter category must be identified (in itself a nontrivial task, given the eccentricity of the letterform). To this end, the Examiner is invoked. The quanta in the seed letter are quickly chunked together, and since there is a fairly weak juncture near the top, where the ascending line bends to the right to form an overhang, two distinct syntactic parts are made. After being suitably labeled, these parts wake up two semantic roles: *post* and *hook,* and since there is nothing else to see, no other roles are strongly activated. This pair of activated roles now activates two wholes—the letter categories "f" and "l." Counting against "f" is the lack of cross-

FIGURE 8.4

The "f" with no crossbar (left) gives rise in the Imaginer to a "t" with no crossbar (middle). This is rejected by the Examiner since it is too much like an "l." This leads the Imaginer to slip "no crossbar" to "short crossbar," and a better "t" is created (right).

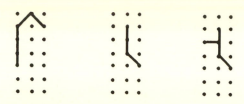

bar, but counting against "l" is the hook at the top. The power of two strongly filled roles overwhelms the pressures for seeing "l," and the shape winds up being seen as an "f" whose primary stylistic attribute is the lack of anything to fill the *crossbar* role. Thus "crossbar suppressed" is the main stylistic note (i.e., norm violation) attached to the letter.

We now move from the perceptual to the generative phase. Given that "f" and "t" are linked as similar letters in the Conceptual Memory, there is a high probability that "t" would be the next letter tackled. An obvious idea for the "t" would be to suppress *its* crossbar. Like any good copycat, the Imaginer would have little trouble coming up with that analogy, since the role crossbar exists in both "f" and "t," all it would need to do is take the norm violation that describes "f" ("crossbar suppressed") and copy it literally into a suggestion for the "t." Upon receiving this norm-violation suggestion, the Drafter would have no problem converting it into a grid-oriented instruction saying, in effect, "Draw no horizontal quanta at the x-height." (Let us assume the ascender for "t" would be conventional.)

The Drafter renders this attempt at "t" on the Scratchpad, leaving it up to the Examiner to look at it and make of it what it can. The quanta are quickly put together into a single perceptual part—a vertical line rising from the baseline to somewhere above the x-height. This wakes up the role *ascender,* and since there is nothing else to see, no other roles are strongly activated. This rather sparse "combination" of activated roles now sharply activates one and only one whole—the category "l." At this point, the Examiner, knowing that "t" was intended, pronounces the attempt at "t" a failure, and provides what is hopefully an accurate diagnosis: the fact that the role of crossbar never got awakened at all.

This information is sent back to the Imaginer, which was, after all, the source of the idea of suppressing the crossbar entirely. So the Imaginer is now caught in the crossfire of Letter and Spirit pressures: on the one hand, it knows that suppressing the crossbar leads to disaster (this is Letter pressure), but on the other hand, it wants to follow the stylistic lead of the "f" (Spirit pressure). Something has to give!

Luckily, there is a way out, provided by *creative slippage*, which involves consulting the Conceptual Memory for potential substitutes provided by conceptual halos. In the halo of "suppress," the Imaginer finds such close neighbor concepts as "austerity," "minimality," "sparsity," as well as the concept "underdo" (or a more formal structure representing that idea). Thus, under the pressure created by the failure of using the concept "suppress," it is quite likely that the Imaginer will make a slippage—namely, it will take the nearby idea "underdo" and try it on for size. In other words, the Imaginer supposes that "underdoing" the crossbar on the "t" is the next-best thing to all-out suppression of it. This slippage is of course the key creative breakthrough. It now just needs some fleshing-out, still to be done by the Imaginer.

In order to translate the rather vague "underdo" into a more specific operation, the Imaginer must have information about the *meaning* of "underdo." This is available through its internal definition, which (in a suitable formalism) is given as "reduce the key dimension of." Now the Imaginer consults the norms attached to "crossbar" to find out if a crossbar has a key dimension, and if so, what it is. It finds that for "crossbar," there is only one norm involving size—horizontal length. This allows the vague "underdo" suggestion to be straightforwardly translated into a norm-violation suggestion that says, in effect, "Make a short crossbar." The Imaginer hands this to the Drafter. From our discussion above, we know that this can lead to a "t" with a one-quantum crossbar—in other words, a perfectly acceptable and style-loaded "t." It is, of course, debatable how faithfully this "t" preserves the austere spirit of the seed letter "f," but certainly it is a reasonable attempt.

Note that this example shows how the program can understand and imitate the spirit of the seed letter, rather than copying it literally. A key role was played here by the conceptual halo of the concept "suppress," which yielded the conceptually close, potential-substitute concept "underdo."

The interaction of these four agents, whereby ideas are suggested, critiqued, revised, possibly abandoned and regenerated, and so on, jibes with our intuitive sense of what human creativity really is. It seems to us fair to say that this kind of emergent, unpredictable processing constitutes a program's *making its own decisions*.

CONCLUSION

The two main predecessors of Letter Spirit are Copycat (Mitchell, 1993) and Tabletop (French, 1995) both of which create microdomain analogies in psychologically plausible ways. Both are based on models of high-level

FIGURE 8.5

Six human-designed gridfonts illustrate various devices for assuring stylistic consistency, such as motifs and abstract rules.

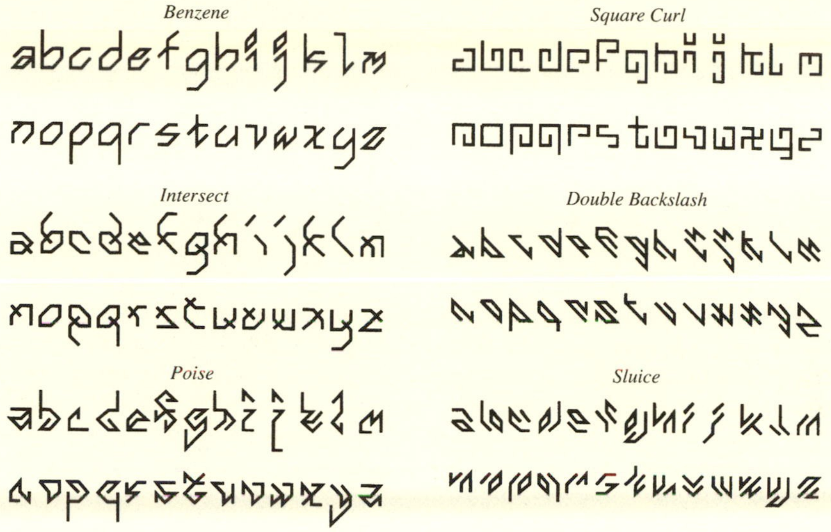

Benzene

Square Curl

Intersect

Double Backslash

Poise

Sluice

perception making use of a novel type of architecture. Top-level behavior emerges from many low-level stochastic computational actions that occur in parallel. Letter Spirit will make use of a similar architecture, but will deal much more with the internal structure of concepts, and will focus on a much larger-scale creative process that unfolds over an extended period of time. Work on the Examiner—reported in McGraw (1995)—shows that the approach of using a similar architecture is sound.

Letter Spirit will test the applicability of our architecture to large-scale creative tasks. Its parallel stochastic processing mechanisms fall under the rubric of *emergent computation* (Forrest, 1991), wherein complex high-level behavior emerges as a statistical consequence of many small computational actions. Like Copycat and Tabletop, Letter Spirit will occupy a level of cognitive modeling somewhere between connectionism and symbolic AI—the level we feel is the most useful for the understanding of high-level perception, the fluidity of concepts, and creativity.

DISCUSSION

TD: You say that a creative program must be able to make its own decisions, and you say that it makes its own decisions if there is sufficient internal dialogue and conceptual play. What worries me is the presence of a Hidden Human Hand in Letter

Spirit. This is ironic because it's something that Doug's always warning us about (e.g. Hofstadter, 1985). The Hidden Human Hand seems to be evident all over Letter Spirit: in the way the architecture and the grid are set up and especially in the fact that the style of the seed-letter that sets the whole process off is provided by a human.

Consider your main example. You say that the "key creative breakthrough" is the conceptual slippage from "suppress crossbar" to "shorten crossbar." But is this true? The key creative factor is the human decision to suppress the crossbar of the "f" in the first place.

DH: Perhaps the most important point in response to your objection that so much human creativity went into the seed letter is simply this: that's wrong! On occasion, a good bit of creativity is involved in coming up with a single seed letter, but by *far* the greatest bit of creativity is in developing out of that seed letter a consistent, appealing style. It's nowhere close to a mechanical task. If one could assign numerical measures of percent of creativity involved to the two tasks—namely, (a) creation of the seed letter, and (b) creation of the remaining letters of the alphabet—I would rank them about this way: 10 percent and 90 percent. It's vague, but it gives you some sense of how much of the creativity lies in the working-out phase. A bit reminiscent, isn't it, of Thomas Alva Edison's famous dictum "Genius is 1 percent inspiration, 99 percent perspiration"? But my main point is that in the case of gridfonts, there's tons of inspiration going on as part and parcel of the "perspiration" of working out the other 25 letters. Inspiration is *not* just in the dreaming up of the seed letter.

To make this clearer, I should point out that the computer could very easily come up with its own seed letters. That's not in any sense a fundamental obstacle. Consider this: I give it an "a." It works out all the other 25 letters, and suppose that along the way it tries out some shape for the "k" and then rejects it. Well, it can remember that shape and say to itself, "How about using that rejected 'k' as the seed letter for a brand new gridfont?" and so off it goes, using that. And, of course, this is recursive—specifically, while creating the remaining 25 letters of this second gridfont, perhaps it considers some shape for the "g" and then winds up rejecting or revising it; then, needless to say, the discarded "g" would make a fine new seed letter to feed in for the next go-round. Every single time one makes a gridfont, one winds up rejecting lots more letters than one accepts, so this is a very simple way to get seed letters as a trivial spin-off of a program that "merely" spins out the consequences of a given seed letter.

There is a final point I would like to make. Your question seems to suggest or imply that you think that, given a particular seed letter, there is just *one* single style that that letter implies. That is a long way from the truth. There are tons of possible styles that a given letter could fit in with. They may all share some kind of "meta-level" style, but that is a very loose thing. You simply have no idea how much freedom is still left once one has the seed letter. This holds also after one has two letters. Also after three letters. The point is, a style only starts to really congeal or gel after a considerable number of letters have been generated and have had a chance to exert lots of mutual influences on each other's shapes. Everything at the outset is fluid and tentative, and only gradually do things start to mutually resonate and support each other and thus to lock in. Probably the only way you or anybody else could come to appreciate the truth of these statements is to try designing one or two or preferably more gridfonts yourself. Then you'd hopefully see how complex, how engaging of the mind, the working-out phase really is.

GM: I think that your confusion may have stemmed from the fact that we provided only one example in the chapter (mostly due to space constraints). The "f" example just happened to involve a seed letter (presumably coming from a human designer). But suppose the "f" had not been a seed letter, but had instead been generated by Letter Spirit earlier on in the run (or in another run altogether, as Doug suggested). Note that the very same sort of "f" → "t" analogy could be made. In any case, I think the confusion was exacerbated by our using a seed letter in the example. The key is to remember that all sorts of slippages, noticings, and elevations to themehood are going to occur throughout the design of a consistent gridfont.

TD: I don't know whether Edison's dictum is true in general. Ideas, solutions, even poems and chunks of novels, seem to "come to us" sometimes, without much perspiration at all. D. H. Lawrence said, "wait for the creative moment, and trust it when it comes."

How does Letter Spirit compare with Copycat (Mitchell, 1993)? How much further does it go?

GM: There are strong architectural similarities between Copycat and Letter Spirit. The same sort of codelet-based architecture is used, and the focus for both projects is on high-level perception and analogical thinking. There are important differences, though. I'll explain some of them with reference to the Examiner that I implemented for my dissertation (McGraw, 1995).

One of Melanie Mitchell and Doug's main claims in Copycat was that analogy making has everything in common with perception (they used the phrase "high-level perception" to get at this notion). Work on the Examiner shows that these claims were on the mark. Because the models we have built work well in a variety of situations, ranging from low-level (letter recognition based on quanta) to high-level (Copycat's structure building and mapping), we feel that claims about the generality and pervasiveness of the mechanisms that we have developed are empirically justified.

Though it shares many architectural features with Copycat and Bob French's Tabletop, the Examiner differs in important ways from them. The task that it carries out involves a somewhat lower level of visual processing than the analogy problems in the other two programs. Letter recognition is by necessity closely tied to low-level vision (though we have avoided some of the problems of low-level vision by starting at the level of quanta). Both Melanie and Bob point out that the mechanisms modeled in their programs should be applicable to categorization and recognition tasks. My work on the Examiner proves that such claims are justified. Collectively, our three theses have shown that the parallel terraced scan models a broad spectrum of cognitive activities, ranging from the mundane and everyday (letter recognition and categorization) to the exalted and "mystical" (feats of insight and creativity, such as when Copycat discovers the wyz answer given the problem: abc → abd; xyz → ?). The power of our architecture will be further tested and explored by future work on the Letter Spirit project.

TD: You coined the term "terraced scan," Doug. Would you like to talk us through it?

DH: When you go into a bookstore, you don't read the first book you come across from cover to cover, and then the next one, and so on. People need to protect themselves from that sort of absurdity! You eliminate books that are of little interest to you, and hone in on the good possibilities. This is the idea of the *terraced scan:* a parallel investigation of many possibilities to different levels of depth, quickly throwing out bad ones and honing in rapidly and accurately on good ones. The scan moves by stages: the first one performs very quick superficial tests, proceeding further only if those tests are passed. Each new stage involves more elaborate and computationally more expensive tests, which, if passed, can lead to a further stage—and so on.

TD: You provide a nice example in Hofstadter & FARG (1995) of a young woman trying to associate herself with a sorority at Indiana University. First she spends half an hour at all 22 sororities, then half an hour at 16 of them, then 45 minutes at eight of them, and so on. And the culling is mutual, sorority-down and student-up.

DH: I had no inkling that such an intricate selection process was involved!

GM: Another important difference between Letter Spirit, on the one hand, and Tabletop and Copycat, on the other, is the level of sophistication in the modeling of concepts. The concepts in the Examiner's Conceptual Memory are more sophisticated than are the concepts in the Slipnets of Copycat and Tabletop. Concepts and subconcepts are modeled in a nested, hierarchical way. The notion of norms and their effects on activation are explored. The concepts that the Examiner includes are highly interrelated and must vigorously compete to explain the same, possibly ambiguous sensory data.

The most important architectural features of the Examiner, however, stand squarely on common ground with Copycat and Tabletop. These features allow for the successful implementation and application of the parallel terraced scan, the modeling of the emergence of structure, and the exploration of high-level perception.

TD: The beautiful gridfonts in Figure 8.5 weren't produced by Letter Spirit, but by one or more human designers, right?

DH: Right. The *design* part of Letter Spirit is simply not yet implemented.

TD: Moreover, close inspection of those gridfonts shows that it is very unlikely that Letter Spirit could produce anything like them. How could it produce the double "v" in *Sluice*, for instance? The one example worked through in the chapter, although beautifully described, is nowhere near as sophisticated as this.

DH: That is a very reasonable criticism. We have no genuine theory as to how a gridfont as complex and daring and multi-themed as *Sluice* is generated (see Figure 8.5). We would aim for something far more modest, such as *Benzene*. However, even building up *Benzene* from its "a" alone would be considerably beyond our expectations for the Letter Spirit program. We discuss this very issue in Chapter 10 of *Fluid Concepts and Creative Analogies* (Hofstadter & FARG, 1995).

TD: How much progress has been made on Letter Spirit to date?

DH: Gary's Ph.D. dissertation program is a good start on the Examiner. His program recognizes lots of letters of greatly varying styles and all 26 lowercase categories (though we wish it performed better in some cases). The program is thoroughly explained in his dissertation. In addition to explaining Letter Spirit's recognizer, Gary's dissertation also maps out the project in much more detail that we went into here.

Work on Letter Spirit is continuing at CRCC (my research center at Indiana University) even though Gary has gone on to do other things. John Rehling has taken on Part 2 of the project, which focuses on design, taking recognition somewhat as solved. He has begun thinking about and working on the Imaginer. Certainly there is lots of work left to do, but the ball is definitely rolling.

[In Chapter 9, we see, in December 1999, what progress John Rehling has made on the design component of Letter Spirit. TD]

NOTE

1. Several human-designed gridfonts are displayed at the end of this paper. For more, see Hofstadter (1987), McGraw (1995), and Hofstadter & FARG (1995).

REFERENCES

Forrest, S. (Ed.). (1991). *Emergent computation*. Cambridge, MA: MIT Press.

French, R. (1995). *The subtlety of sameness: A theory and computer model of analogy-making*. Cambridge, MA: MIT Press/Bradford Books.

Hofstadter, D. R. (1985). *Metamagical themas: Questing for the essence of mind and pattern* (See especially chapters 10, 12, 13, 23, 24, and 26). New York: Basic Books.

Hofstadter, D. R. (1987). Introduction to the Letter Spirit Project and to the idea of "gridfonts" (Technical Report 17). Bloomington, IN: Center for Research on Concepts and Cognition, Indiana University.

Hofstadter, D. R., & FARG (Fluid Analogies Research Group). (1995). *Fluid concepts and creative analogies: Computer models of the fundamental mechanisms of thought*. New York: Basic Books.

McGraw, G. (1995). *Letter Spirit (Part one): Emergent high-level perception of letters using fluid concepts*. Ph.D. dissertation, Department of Computer Science and Cognitive Science Program, Indiana University.

McGraw, G., Rehling, J., & Goldstone, R. (1994). Letter perception: Toward a conceptual approach. In *Proceedings of the Sixteenth Annual Conference of the Cognitive Science Society*, 613–618. Atlanta, GA: Lawrence Erlbaum Associates.

Minsky, M. (1985). *The society of mind*. New York: Simon and Schuster.

Mitchell, M. (1993). *Analogy-making as perception*. Cambridge, MA: MIT Press/Bradford Books.

9

Results in the Letter Spirit Project

John Rehling

Since Chapter 8 was written, work on Letter Spirit has continued, and a working version meeting many of the original goals has been implemented. In this chapter, Letter Spirit refers to the current implementation (as of December 1999), which differs in some respects from the hypothetical program described in Chapter 8.

The Examiner module, which scrutinizes gridletters in order to determine their letter category ("a" through "z"), was implemented by Gary McGraw by 1995, and works very well. During the years 1995–1999, John Rehling built upon this foundation by using the Examiner as one module in a three-module architecture which includes an implementation of both the Adjudicator and the Drafter. A loop coordinating the three modules accepts input gridletters as seeds, and designs complete, stylistically consistent gridfonts based on these seeds.

THE EXAMINER

The Examiner, which was a stand-alone program at the time Chapter 8 was written, has been incorporated as one module within the larger Letter Spirit program. The organization and performance of the Examiner as implemented by Gary McGraw are described in great detail in his dissertation (McGraw, 1995). Some subsequent changes were necessary, especially in that some of the data structures that the other modules reference needed a bit more detail than their use by the Examiner required. These changes were mainly on a level of detail beneath the scope of this chapter; the basic organization was unchanged. Performance is up to and beyond that of subjects who participated in an experiment asking them to identify gridletters—93.5 percent correct for the Examiner versus 84.0 percent correct for people on the given test set.

The Examiner essentially returns three pieces of information. First, and most obviously, there is the program's estimation of the mystery gridletter's letter category ("a" through "z," or an answer that no suitable category was found). Second, the program also returns information indicating how it parsed the gridletter into parts that serve as role fillers for the role set underlying the letter category answer. Third, a score is calculated whose purpose is to indicate how strongly the gridletter serves as a member of the answer letter category; parts that are atypical as fillers of their corresponding roles may explicitly lower this score, as may a lengthy run time needed to derive an answer, as well as unusual ways in which role fillers interact (for example, if they are expected to touch, but do not, or vice versa). All three pieces of information are used by other parts of the full Letter Spirit program.

THE ADJUDICATOR

The second Letter Spirit module, the Adjudicator, performs a number of related tasks, all pertaining to *style* recognition. The Adjudicator runs only on gridletters that the Examiner has already run on, and thus, for computation of norm violations, it relies specifically on the parsing into roles already performed by the Examiner. The Adjudicator compiles a large assortment of stylistic properties. As part of each run, the Adjudicator also creates *bridges,* or matches between the gridletter's stylistic properties and stylistic properties already in the Thematic Focus, which is the representation of the style of the entire gridfont in its current state (see next section). The extent to which the gridletter's style matches the contents of the Thematic Focus forms the basis of a score that expresses how well the gridletter fits the gridfont stylistically.

The collection of bridges between the gridletter's stylistic properties and the Thematic Focus is also made into a list of *promotions,* which can be used to integrate the gridletter's style into the Thematic Focus, should the higher-level control portions of Letter Spirit find the gridletter has been rated highly enough by the Examiner and Adjudicator to recommend it as worthy of inclusion in the gridfont being designed.

THE THEMATIC FOCUS

This brief update focuses on the modules within the Letter Spirit program. The Thematic Focus is not a module: it is a memory structure, as was noted in Chapter 8. Nevertheless, its implementation is interesting enough to merit special attention here.

Essentially, the Thematic Focus is a table that stores stylistic properties—the "atoms" of style—that have been found to be distinguishing characteristics of the gridfont in progress. Its columns are the different types of stylistic properties (norm violations, motifs, and abstract rules—all defined in the previous chapter), while its six rows correspond to different levels of frequency for a stylistic property within the gridfont. Promotion and demotion of stylistic properties throughout a run is probabilistic, so it is not possible to say exactly to what frequency of occurrence in the gridfont each level corresponds. The lowest level is essentially the repository of stylistic properties that have been found in only one gridletter. The next level is the repository of properties found in exactly two gridletters, and so on. The presence of a stylistic property in the sixth and highest level does not necessarily signify that it occurs in *every* gridletter, but that it is nearly universal, at least. A filled Thematic Focus tends to have a pyramidal distribution of stylistic properties, with a few important ones in the highest levels, and many more less important ones in the lower levels. This reflects the way in which people pay special attention to a few items when an overwhelming number of items are put before them, based on which items seem more important to them.

The Thematic Focus is accessed by two modules. The Adjudicator fills it, and uses it as a basis for scoring new gridletters. The Drafter uses it to influence the quantum-by-quantum drafting of new gridletters. In all cases, the action is probabilistic, favoring items in higher levels for influencing action. Because many references of the Thematic Focus are allowed to influence any action at all involving the Thematic Focus, it implements a hazy sort of style, wherein a few stylistic properties may be identifiable in their influence, but many more contribute in smaller and subtler ways.

Currently, the Thematic Focus is filled with stylistic attributes derived solely from the seeds, and once it has been filled, it is no longer updated during a run. This limitation of the program is due to change in the very near future, allowing a gridfont's perceived style to evolve throughout a run, based not just on the seeds but also on gridletters the program itself has created.

THE DRAFTER

In the earlier Letter Spirit proposal, two modules were to carry out the creation of gridletters. The Imaginer would act first, creating an abstract plan for each gridletter, which would not be concerned with the actual grid. In a second phase, the Drafter would render a grid-based version of that plan. In the current implementation, there is only one module, called the Drafter, and it carries out its work directly upon the grid.

The primary mode by which the Drafter works captures the spirit of other FARG architectures, and, like the Examiner and Adjudicator, involves a codelet-based architecture. A letter is drafted, one role at a time. The Drafter selects a point at which to begin drawing the role filler, and also a "target"—a tentative point to aim for as the other end of the role filler (possibly the same point, as in the case of roles that are typically closed, such as "o"). Then quanta are drawn, one by one, as though a pen were drawing the role filler on the grid. As drafting proceeds, there is always a current point to which the pen has drawn on its last step. From that point, the Drafter considers each possible quantum that can be drawn next, by the action of individual codelets which add differing amounts of weight to each. When the queue of codelets (the *Coderack*) is empty, a choice is made probabilistically, biased by the weights. The chosen quantum is then added to the role filler in progress, and the Coderack is then fully loaded anew, to prepare for the next step. Each Drafter codelet adds weights based on one specific kind of pressure influencing the decision. For example, a codelet representing an abstract rule forbidding diagonal quanta might add negative points to each diagonal quantum among the active possibilities, and zero to the non-diagonal quanta. Other types of codelets represent the norms for the role, and all the various kinds of stylistic properties in the Thematic Focus. Thus, when the decision of which quantum to draw is finally made, it reflects all the relevant pressures that should influence the gridletter's design. This method of processing is reminiscent of connectionist models of cognition, which also produce output that is the product of many influences, all combined subtly together.

This is a decidedly low-level approach to incorporating style. Another way the Drafter can create a version of a letter is by borrowing. Entire role fillers can be borrowed from previously created gridletters. For example, the post of a "b" can be used in subsequent attempts to draft "k." However, since the remaining two roles in "k" do not occur in any other letters, the only option for those roles (and other such roles) is to draft them in the quantum-by-quantum fashion described previously.

In addition, an entire gridletter may be created by performing any of a predetermined set of transformations to a previously created gridletter. For example, a mirror reflection of an existing "b" can be used as an attempt at "d." Of course, any letter proposed in this high-level manner must still undergo the standard scrutiny by the Examiner and the Adjudicator, and thus it may well wind up being rejected either as an inadequate member of its intended category or as a poor embodiment of the perceived style of the gridfont. Such borrowing lacks any pretense of modeling human behavior on a low level, but certainly produces the same end result of a process used by human designers in creating gridletters, and it is realistic on the high level if not on the low level. Borrowing, though it lacks any low-level underpinning of interest, is a high-level tool that humans use frequently in design. Borrowing is of great use with certain categories like "b" and "d," while quantum-by-quantum drafting is still essential for other categories, like "v" and "x." The dual modes of drafting, and the ability to try both as appropriate, give the program another commonality with human designers.

THE LETTER SPIRIT LOOP

As we have empirically discovered, none of the just-described modes of drafting has a high rate of creating very good versions of letters on the first try—versions that capture letter and spirit both very well. The overall success of the program lies, rather, in the fact that many versions are drawn for each category, and the best is chosen by the top-level control.

The top-level program is fairly simple. The first phase handles the seed letters given to the program. Each seed is run past the Examiner, which determines the letter category of each seed, and files it away as the final and unrevisable version of that category in the new gridfont. The Adjudicator also runs on each seed, and this builds up, in the Thematic Focus, an assessment of the gridfont's style to be used in subsequent design.

The second phase of the program is a loop, in which a letter category is selected (essentially at random, but favoring any categories for which the program does not have a good version already), and then the Drafter makes an attempt at a gridletter belonging to that category (either by borrowing or by quantum-by-quantum drafting). The attempt is run past the Examiner and the Adjudicator, and if the attempt is judged to be the best version thus far for that category, as determined by the scores that the Examiner and the Adjudicator generate, then the attempt is kept as the current (and tentative) version of that category in the gridfont. The loop runs many more times than there are categories, so multiple attempts are made for each category, and when the program quits (currently, after it reaches the predetermined number of 500 total drafting attempts), the gridfont is considered complete, consisting of the set of all the best attempts made for each category, plus the original seeds.

RESULTS AND FUTURE DIRECTIONS

Some of Letter Spirit's work can be seen in Figure 9.1 on the following page. Each of these gridfonts consists of seeds (created by a human) for "b," "c," "e," "f," and "g," and the 21 gridletters Letter Spirit created to complete the alphabet in the style implied by the five seeds.

Letter Spirit creates gridfonts that have a fair degree of coherence across most letter categories. At times, it overlooks areas where it could make

FIGURE 9.1
Examples of Letter Spirit's work. Each gridfont consists of seeds (created by a human) for "b," "c," "e," "f," and "g," and the 21 gridletters Letter Spirit created to complete the alphabet in the style implied by the five seeds.

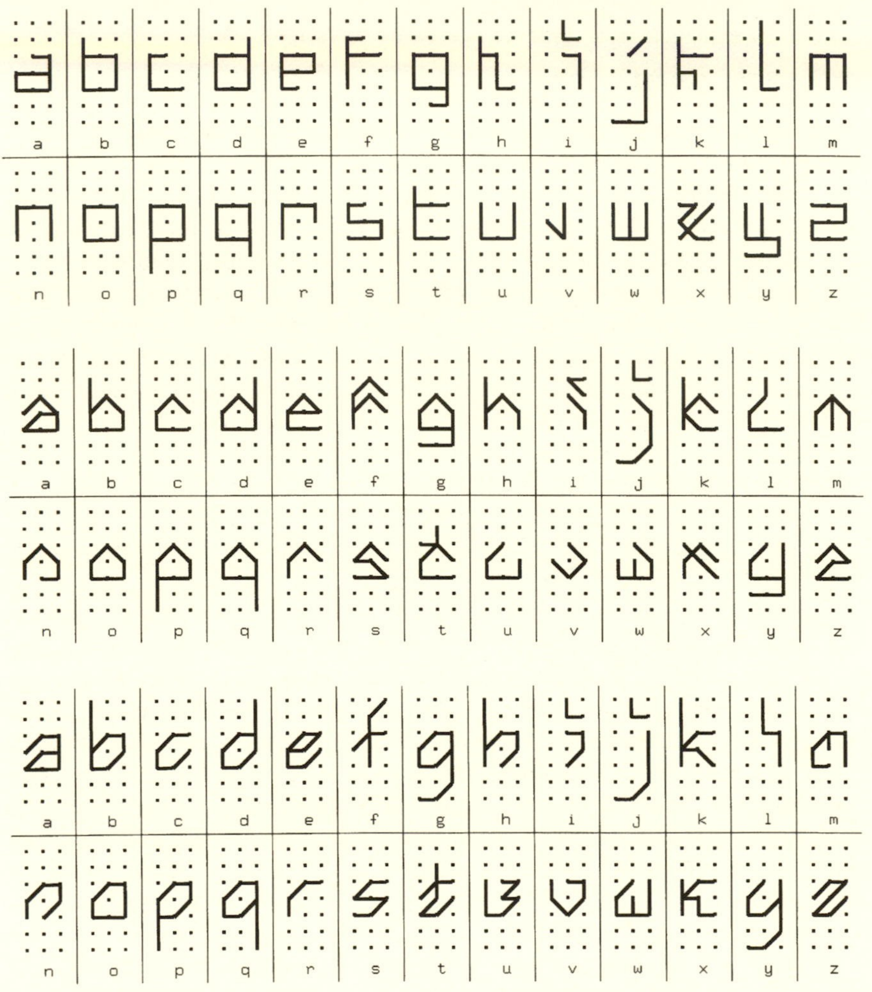

improvements that are, to a human observer, perhaps obvious. Areas where Letter Spirit could benefit most from improvement are:

- The ability to handle slippages between style concepts, as mentioned in Chapter 8, but currently unimplemented.
- The ability to abstract new kinds of stylistic properties, other than the ones programmed into it.

- The ability to take previous attempts it has made at rendering letter categories and to improve upon them by modifying those attempts. Currently, it merely drafts from scratch, ignoring all previous attempts, and simply compares the score of its latest attempt with the scores of older versions.

- The ability to decide when to update the Thematic Focus during a run, based on gridletters that Letter Spirit itself has created. This will allow the program to create entire gridfonts from scratch, without human intervention.

The last item will be included in the current implementation very soon. The other items, and other possible extensions, may be implemented in another wave of Letter Spirit development later on. Clearly there is room to add more sophistication to Letter Spirit, so that the program described in this chapter may be only one step in a long evolution that tries to come ever closer to capturing the complex process of human creativity in the gridfont domain, and in general.

DISCUSSION

TD: I want to ask you about the central, generative-evaluative loop, but first let me see if I've got the picture right. Letter Spirit is given some seed letters. It then goes through two phases. In the first phase, the Examiner identifies the letters and the Adjudicator assesses their style. In the second phase, this information is passed to the Drafter, which generates different letters of the same, or similar, style. Actually there's a loop here, in which the Drafter generates many versions of the same letter, each of which is judged by the Examiner and Adjudicator, and the best one is retained.

In the present version, the style or "spirit" of a generated letter is based on what the system has learned from the seed letters, but you are modifying it so that the style will evolve as new letters are created. Letter Spirit's sense of style will then be based, not only on the seed letters, but on the letters it has created in the current run, so that its sense of style will be more holistic and fluid.

JR: Yes, that's right. In principle, that will let the style it is "aiming" for drift as a run proceeds. This should be especially pronounced when few or no seeds are given.

TD: There seems to be no feedback from the Examiner or Adjudicator to the Drafter in the generative-evaluative loop. The Drafter generates letters of a particular category, and the Examiner and Adjudicator pick out the best one—but they don't give any feedback to the Drafter. That is, despite the codelet-based architecture, which in some ways is similar to connectionism, the Drafter doesn't learn as it drafts new letters, does it? It doesn't get any feedback, such as "give me some more like that," or "that's heading in the right direction." Such feedback would be like back-propagation in connectionism. Would such a modification be difficult to implement?

JR: There are lots of ways that learning could be added. Learning within a run versus permanent between-runs learning are both options. As another way of basing symbolic behavior on subsymbolic underpinnings, Coderack-based architectures do have something in common with back-propagation, but symbolic-level learning is also an option. And there are potentially many ways to try learning on the Coderack level, but we haven't really explored any.

One interesting way to get feedback from the Examiner and Adjudicator directly into drafting, and that doesn't happen to involve "learning" as such, is to have them give reasons why they rated a particular gridletter poorly. Then, have a module that takes the gridletter plus the criticism from the Examiner and Adjudicator, and modifies it into something better, and resubmits it. This is surely something people do sometimes. It can be a lot easier to reach a goal when initial attempts, even if failures, can somehow be used to improve future efforts. That's something the Drafter barely has in it at all. (There is an exception. When a letter category is attempted by the Drafter several times without producing any versions that the Examiner recognizes as a member of that category, fewer codelets involving style are posted in subsequent Drafter runs for that category. Essentially, style is de-emphasized if the program has found, through failure, that it can't find a good way to make the given style fit for that letter category.)

TD: In Chapter 6, Partridge and Rowe distinguish between what they call "input" and "output" creativity. We are *input* creative when we solve problems and make sense of the world—during perception, for instance, or when we listen to music or poetry. We are *output* creative when we run this ability off-line to *produce* music or poetry. Letter Spirit is input creative when it recognizes letters and styles that it hasn't seen before, and it's output creative when it generates new letters of the same style. The Drafter generates letters of the right category and style, on the basis of information acquired by the Examiner and Adjudicator during the input phase, and this output is evaluated by the Examiner and the Adjudicator. Now what is driving what here? Are the Examiner and Adjudicator effectively driving the Drafter? You could see it this way, because they pass a set of constraints to the Drafter, on the basis of which it has to generate appropriate letters on the grid. If this is what is going on, it has implications for the role of judgment and evaluation in cognition. It looks like the kind of thing that traditional rationalism had in mind when it talked about the active role of the intellect in cognition, and how we bring knowledge and judgment to experience.[1]

JR: It may be more accurate to say that the Drafter is not driven or directed by the Examiner and Adjudicator, but that Letter Spirit is. The Drafter and Letter Spirit stand in an unusual relation to one another. All Letter Spirit output, on a gridletter-by-gridletter basis, is Drafter output, but on a gridfont-by-gridfont basis, the two are very different.

I can set the program up to generate a gridfont, based on seeds, that is only Drafter output, and that doesn't have to satisfy the Examiner and Adjudicator. Obviously, the quality of such gridfonts is low. A few good gridletters might be in there, but some will tend to be bad—even horrible.

As a run progresses, and I watch the gridfont that is in progress, I can choose to have it graphically display each attempt the Drafter makes—even those that will be immediately rejected by the Examiner and Adjudicator—or I can have it "hide" them, and represent them internally, but not display them until they pass the Examiner and Adjudicator. In one sense, this is a meaningless variation in the program; it doesn't change the final gridfont at all. But in the latter case, the program *looks* a lot smarter, during a run. And that's because the "input-creative" modules are part of everything being displayed. When it comes down to the final gridfont at the end of the run, that's the only kind of gridletter up on the screen, anyway. Everything has the Examiner's and Adjudicator's "stamp of approval" that they have good Letter and Spirit. So I think you can see Letter Spirit as a black box with "input-creative" ability inside it. If you look inside, you can see how things are modularized, and that there is a stage of drafting which is purely "output-creative," but which doesn't lead to very high quality on its own.

In domains with larger "generative space," I suspect that high quality essentially requires review and revision of some kind. To be a good writer, you have to be a good reader. Systems that have some facility in both directions are going to be the key towards eliminating brittleness in AI.

NOTE

1. But see my comments on this in the Introduction. It might be significant that McGraw and Hofstadter initially planned to have an Imaginer that would play with ideas in an abstract way before drawing anything on the grid, and abandoned this in favor of the Drafter working directly on the grid. This gives us a picture of knowledge tightly integrated with skill, in which we don't plan everything first and execute it later, but constantly monitor and evaluate our creative output.

REFERENCE

McGraw, G. (1995). *Letter Spirit (Part One): Emergent high-level perception of letters using fluid concepts.* Ph.D. dissertation, Department of Computer Science and Cognitive Science Program, Indiana University.

10

Emergence and Creativity: Five Degrees of Freedom

Richard McDonough

> A great deal of the discussion of metaphysics and philosophy of religion
> . . . in our time has been rendered idle by the assumption that if meta-
> physics (meaning, an *a priori* theory of reality) were possible it would
> have to be the sort of thing that Hume and Kant . . . criticized . . . On
> the contrary, what I take to be the great metaphysical issues were not
> clearly seen by Kant or Hume . . . What these authors dealt with [was]
> the metaphysics of being or substance. There is another form . . . the
> metaphysics of becoming or creativity. (Hartshorne, 1991, p. ix)

Although the view that people are machines has become commonplace
(Clark, 1990; Dartnall, 1994; McDonough, 1999a, 1999b), many people
continue to feel the force of Lady Lovelace's intuition that, unlike people,
machines cannot be genuinely creative because "they cannot originate anything" (Turing, 1964). This chapter explores the relevance of emergentism
to the question whether human beings are creative in a sense that distinguishes them from machines. The most basic idea in emergentism is that
what emerges is genuinely *novel* (relative to the base system B). Emergence
is a relative notion (Margolis, 1986) in the sense that a characteristic C is
said to be emergent, or "an emergent," when it is felt that there is an
explanatory gap between C and B. Although it is an important question
what, precisely, is supposed to be emergent, for example, properties, laws,
substances, boundary conditions, and so on (see Klee, 1984), I initially refer
to emergent *characteristics* and later distinguish specific types of emergents
as this becomes necessary.

The best known species of emergentism is *emergent materialism,* the view that life and mind are emergent characteristics of matter. Emergent materialists see their view as a moderate middle position between extreme mechanistic materialism, which I call "mechanism," and substantive vitalism and dualism which posit non-physical forces or entities (Passmore, 1957; Margolis, 1978; Beckermann, 1992; Kim, 1992). While there are certain kinds of wholes, such as machines, whose characteristics are the sum of the characteristics of their parts, emergentists hold that there are other kinds of wholes, most notably organisms, which are distinguished by the fact that "the whole is greater than the sum of their parts" (Nagel, 1979). Whereas persons of a scientific cast of mind generally try to define creativity as the rearrangement of pre-existing elements (Boden, 1994), emergentism offers the possibility of a kind of creativity that involves the birth of something genuinely new, and, therefore, would seem to provide a robust metaphysical answer which supports Lady Lovelace's intuition that organisms are creative in a sense in which mere machines cannot be.

Most emergent materialists hold that emergentism is an empirical doctrine, though some emergentists, such as Broad, hold that it is a priori that certain characteristics are emergent (a view to which I return later). Since emergent materialism represents only one branch of the emergentist tree, I describe some of the alternative branches sufficiently to indicate the direction in which divergent notions of emergence might be developed.

Despite its aspirations to scientific respectability, emergentism has often been viewed as an "unsavory," "kooky," unscientific, obscure, or even mystical doctrine (McLaughlin, 1992; Kim, 1998). Since our dominant world conception is largely reductive insofar as it holds that one can explain the larger systems in terms of their smaller parts (Searle, 1992; also see Butterfield, 1998), there has long existed a strong bias against emergentism. This is illustrated by Hempel's view (1965) (supported by an appeal to fear, that emergentism tends to produce an attitude which stifles scientific research) that emergentism is unscientific since the job of science is to eliminate the appearance of emergence. Emergent materialists respond that one must approach nature, to use Alexander's phrase, with "natural piety," that is, one ought to accept nature as one finds it rather than imposing one's epistemological ideals upon it. Emergent materialism has made a comeback in recent years, and the motivations have nothing to do with romanticism, but because it may be just what is needed to defend "a more ambitious physicalism" (Beckermann, 1992b).

This chapter tries to clarify the notion of emergence with the aim of clarifying its connection with the issue of human creativity. In the first section, I elucidate the key notions in reductionism. In the second section, I develop a taxonomy of emergentism with special reference to emergent materialism. In the third section, I define an ascending series of five "degrees" of emergence-based freedom and creativity. In the fourth section, I argue, first, that the standard arguments against emergentism, by Pepper, Klee, Kim, and McLaughlin, are unsuccessful, and, second, that emergence, and with it creativity, are far more fundamental to human intelligence than is currently believed.

REDUCTIONISM AND ANTI-REDUCTIONISM

Since the notion of reduction is highly ambiguous (van Gulick, 1992; Searle, 1998), it is worthwhile beginning with a brief account of the basic ideas. The common notion of reduction assumes that entities are arranged in a hierarchy of higher and lower, for example, mind, life, and matter, and that one attempts to understand entities of the higher type in terms of the lower type. The classic form of reduction is *conceptual reduction,* in which the "higher" *theory* about A's, (T_1), is reduced to the lower *theory* about B's, (T_2), by defining the concepts of T_1 in terms of the concepts of T_2 and deriving the laws of T_1 from the laws of T_2. Such conceptual reduction requires "bridge principles," technically known as *nomological biconditionals,* connecting the key terms in T_1 with those in T_2. A special case is that in which T_1 refers to macro-phenomena, and T_2 is a micro-theory that purports to explain these macro-phenomena by reference to the micro-theory of physics (Beckermann, 1992a, 1992b). The paradigm example of a successful conceptual reduction is the reduction of the theory of heat to the theory of molecules (where the bridge principles connect the thermal characteristics of macro-objects with those of their molecular micro-constituents).

The classical attempt to conceptually reduce mind to matter, the "identity theory," identifies mental state types with neural state types (Place, 1969; Smart, 1969a, 1969b). But not only was it harder than expected to find the required psychological and neural laws, Putnam (1975) argued that it might be impossible. For a person and a dog may both believe the squirrel is up the tree, but since neurophysiological laws in different species are likely to be quite different, there is little likelihood of an identity between mental state types and neural state types. This required the development of a weaker species of reduction.

The weaker species of reduction, known as "functionalism," construes mental states as abstract causal-functional profiles, which can be realized in any number of different material compositions (this is the *multiple realizability thesis,* or MRT). MRT undermines the possibility of the identity theory since it appears to exclude the possibility of nomological biconditionals connecting mental states and physical states. The terminology of *realizability* goes hand in hand with that of *supervenience.* To say that a mental state M is realized in a physical state P is to say that M *supervenes* on P. On this view, even though one cannot identify the mental with the physical it is still true that the mental depends on it. Borrowing Davidson's (1980) words, it is impossible for two creatures to have all their physical properties in common and differ in their mental properties.

Functionalism became known, however, as *non-reductive physicalism*. But that is a misnomer. For functionalists simply replace the idea of conceptual reduction with the idea of model reduction in which they provide a hypothetical mechanism for the phenomenon in question (Clark, 1980). Functionalism presupposes, therefore, an account of the notion of a machine. Typically, a machine is conceived as an organized physical system that obeys the laws of physics, where the functionally defined states of the machine are individuated, not by reference to the laws of physics, but by relation to human interests. A machine, such as a clock, is entirely consistent with the laws of physics, but, since there is no law of nature that causes the second hands on clocks to rotate clockwise, there are no "machine laws" that might be conceptually reduced to the laws of physics. However, to call functionalism "non-reductive physicalism" is misleading. Though functionalism is motivated by the inability to provide a conceptual reduction, it does require that there is some explanatory connection between the mind and the underlying mechanism. Van Gulick (1992) holds that, in principle, functionalists should be able to get one way nomological conditionals connecting mental and physical states. Although the expression "bridge principles" is traditionally associated with biconditionals, I shall call these one way conditionals "bridge principles" as well (since they do effect a one way bridge between the physical and the mental).

In response to the claim that mental states are emergent relative to bodily states, reductionists typically hold that they only claim to describe the conditions under which A's are manifested (Nagel, 1954). Thus, they say, the appearance that even in a successful reduction something "emerges," derives from the trivial verbal fact that one requires bridge principles to connect the terms of the macro-theory with those of the micro-theory.

However, emergentists can reply that in some cases, bridge principles seem to be explainable, while in others, they appear to be brute and inexplicable (McLaughlin, 1992). Whereas one can see why macro-level water, which is composed of such-and-such types of molecules, will behave like a fluid, one cannot see any analogous way to derive the characteristics of consciousness from those of brain states. Thus, Beckermann (1992b; see also Hooker, 1981) argues that it is not necessary for a functionalist reduction to a mechanism that one can deduce the actual laws of the macro-theory from those of the micro-theory, but only that one can deduce an image of those laws from those of the micro-theory. As Beckermann (ibid.) puts it, one needs to show that "there are properties [in the micro-theory] which play (almost) the same role as the properties which are referred to by the terms of [the macro-theory]." For example, given a knowledge of the bonding properties of the H_2O molecule, one can see why the macro-substance composed of such molecules behaves as a fluid rather than a solid in normal conditions. The non-rigid bonding properties of H_2O molecules provide an image of liquidity.

I call a reduction in which the bridge principles are explainable in this sense, as in the case of H_2O molecules and liquidity, a *micro-reduction,* and a reduction in which the bridge principles are brute, as seems to be the case for some vital phenomena, a *non-micro-reduction.* In these terms, the disagreement between the emergent materialists and the reductivists is that the former hold that for certain macro-phenomena, such as consciousness, one cannot micro-reduce them to their micro-constituents, while the latter hold that one can give such a micro-reduction. This coheres with our provisional formulation that A has emergent characteristics if it is a whole which is "greater than the sum of its parts." For to provide a micro-reduction of the properties of A is to deduce the image of A's properties from those of its micro-parts. Let us now look more closely at the notion of emergence.

VARIETIES OF EMERGENCE

Passmore (1957) states that emergence traces as far back as Lewes, a nineteenth-century English polymath with empiricist and positivist tendencies. In fact, it is as old as philosophy.[1] The most basic idea of emergentism is that C emerges relative to its basis B if C is novel relative to B. Consequently, Davidson's (1999) minimalist view that emergence, which I shall call *novel emergence,* occurs when a concept is instantiated for the first time, is a good beginning. Novel emergence may be divided into *epistemological emergence,* where novelty is defined as unpredictability, and *metaphysical emergence.* Epistemological emergence may be further divided into the kind of emergence which is due to difference in vocabulary between the reducing theory and the reduced theory, which I shall call *vocabulary emergence,* and the kind which is due to our ignorance, which I shall call *ignorance emergence.* Searle's emergence is a version of vocabulary emergence.[2] McGinn (1999) defends a type of ignorance emergence. But we are here interested in metaphysical emergence, for example, in the fact that an entire organism or a significant part of one (e.g., a brain) has characteristics such as intelligence or consciousness that are not a mere sum of the characteristics of their components.

Emergent materialism is that species of metaphysical emergence that has traditionally held that reality divides into layers of material entities in a hierarchy, where conditions in one layer cause the emergence of novel characteristics in a higher layer.[3] Metaphysical emergence divides into emergent evolution, or *evolutionary emergence,* and the emergence of characteristics in an organic whole, which I shall call *organic emergence.* Evolutionary emergence, defended by Bergson (1983) and Popper (1982), and probably earlier by Nietzsche (1968) holds that the laws of nature change over time (Nagel, 1979). Organic emergence is concerned with the dependencies among the physical, chemical, biological, and psychological levels of an organism at a time, for example, with the prima facie fact that an entire organism has characteristics such as consciousness which are not the mere sum of its parts at its lower physical or chemical levels of organization. We are primarily concerned with organic emergence.

Each of evolutionary emergence and organic emergence divides into the kind of emergence based only on the intrinsic parts of the organism, which I shall call *intrinsic parts emergence,* and the kind that results from taking account of its relational parts, which I shall call *relational parts emergence.* To illustrate relational parts emergence, one might claim that an organism, such as a woman, has certain characteristics by virtue of her relations to items in her social environment that make her a wife. In such a case it is not by virtue of her intrinsic structure that she is a wife, and has the powers of a wife, but by virtue of her relational properties. Since emergent materialists have usually understood emergence to concern the intrinsic parts of organisms, I ignore the case of relational properties. However, it is worth pointing out that the contemporary views called "externalism" and "anti-individualism" in the philosophy of mind are species of emergence based on an organism's relations to items in its environment (see Hempel, 1965; Teller, 1992).

Intrinsic parts emergence divides into the species of emergence that presumes the existence of intrinsic vital parts, or *intrinsic vital parts emergence,* and that species which invokes only intrinsic material parts, or *intrinsic material parts emergence.* Intrinsic vital parts emergence is the position known as "substantive vitalism." This is the view that an organism manifests certain novel characteristics, such as consciousness, by virtue of its possession of some non-material component (e.g., a soul). However, since it is theoretically possible, though not common, to claim that an organism manifests novel characteristics due to its possession of some intrinsic material part, such as a certain kind of crystal, it is necessary to make conceptual room for a materialist species of intrinsic parts emergence, but this is more the subject of science fiction than of serious philosophy or science. Both intrinsic vital parts emergence and intrinsic material parts emergence are species of component theories, the view that an organism possesses vital properties due to its possession of some intrinsic component. The problem with component theories is that they do not explain much. They may, however, have some limited explanatory content (see Beckner, 1968). Evolutionary emergence may similarly be divided into vitalist and materialist versions but these do not concern us here.

Finally, we are here interested in that species of emergence in which the principle of emergence is causal, hence, *causal emergence,* in the sense of causality which, as von Wright (1971) points out, derives from the Galilean tradition. However, it is worth noting that some emergentists, such as Hegel and Marx, hold that the principle of change in nature is quasi-logical rather than causal (see von Wright, 1971). Although this is foreign to most recent materialist thinking, Marx holds that the regularities in nature which we

FIGURE 10.1
Types of emergence.

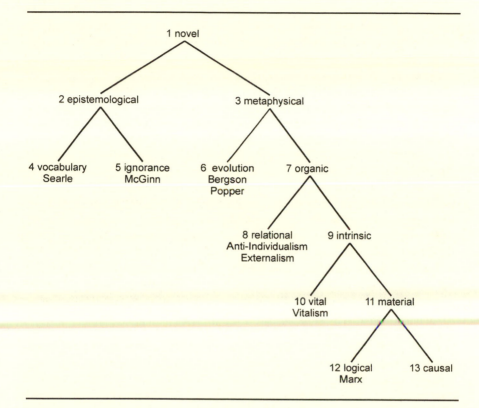

regard as causal are, in fact, something like the logical unfolding of an essence in time (see Meikle, 1985). Since our interest here is emergent materialism in its modern forms, I ignore these relatively exotic species of "logical" emergence.

A representation of this taxonomy is provided in Figure 10.1. The species of emergence with which we shall be most concerned, at node 13, involves the emergence of an organism's macro-characteristics relative to its micro-composition. Consequently, causal emergence divides into the species of emergence in which the connection between the macro- and micro-levels is lawlike, which I shall call *lawlike emergence,* and the species in which it is not, which I shall call *non-lawlike emergence.* Although we are more interested in lawlike emergence, Davidson's "anomalous monism" (1980; see Beckermann, 1992a), which holds that there are no "psychophysical laws," satisfies the conditions of non-lawlike emergence.

Although emergence is generally claimed when there appears to be an ineliminable explanatory gap between the emergent C and the base system B, one should not infer that emergent phenomena are inexplicable. Although that may be true of Davidson's anomalous monism, lawlike emergence holds that since there is a lawlike connection between C and B, the former can be explained by reference to these laws. There is an explanatory gap in such cases only in the specific sense that any mechanisms at B are not sufficient to explain C. This is important because some of the hostility to emergentism may derive from the misconception that since it asserts the existence of an explanatory gap between C and B, it is anti-scientific and committed to skepticism or mysticism.

Lawlike emergence divides into *deterministic emergence,* where the law of emergence is deterministic, and *indeterministic emergence,* where it is not. Popper and Eccles (1977; see Achim, 1992) defends indeterministic emergence.

Deterministic emergence divides into *brute emergence,* where the law connecting the micro-structure and the macro-characteristic is brute, and *non-brute emergence,* where it is not. The case in which the bridge principle connecting A and B is non-brute is the case, discussed in the preceding section, in which A is *micro-reducible* to B, that is, where an image of A is deducible from B. The case in which the law connecting A and B is brute is the case in which A is *non-micro-reducible* to B. Thus, Nagel's (1954) ad hominem complaint that discontent with reductionism derives from a "willful romanticism" which misunderstands the nature of science, is wrong. The emergentist's discontent with reductionism derives from the quite rational point that unexplained bridge principles leave an unacceptable explanatory gap between A and B.

However, the issue of micro-reduction has not been the only debate about emergence in this century. For brute and non-brute emergence can each be divided into *epiphenomenal emergence,* where what emerges is epiphenomenal, and *non-epiphenomenal emergence,* where it is not. The latter is the case in which the emergent characteristic has causal powers that are not the sum of the causal powers of its material parts. The important case here is the case of *downward causation,* or *downwardly causal emergence,* in which, as Sellars and Meehl (1956, p. 251) put it, the emergent phenomena "break the laws" at the lower level. In other words, if the laws which govern the behavior of sodium are understood to consist in the laws which hold at the inorganic level, then the downwardly causal emergentist holds that sodium may behave differently when it occurs within the context of a living organism. Downwardly causal emergentism corresponds to the position traditionally know as "emergent vitalism." Unfortunately, many contemporary philosophers and scientists, such as Paul Churchland (see McDonough, 1998b), dismiss "vitalism" in general, failing to distinguish emergent vitalism from its far more problematic cousin, substantive vitalism. Although downwardly causal emergence is most important for our purposes, it is worth noting that Moore's view that moral properties supervene on physical properties, is a non-trivial version of epiphenomenal emergence.[4]

However, downward causation is still not the only key issue. It may be divided into the species of emergence that must be characterized holistically, or *holistic emergence,* and *non-holistic emergence,* the case in which it is not characterized holistically. Since one common feature of the organismic tradition is that organisms are unitary wholes, we are here most interested in the former. Holistic emergence may be divided into the species in which the whole is a new substance, or *substance emergence,* and the kind of whole that is not. In British Emergentism, this latter is the opinion that what emerges are configurational forces (McLaughlin, 1992). I shall call this kind of emergence *configurational forces emergence.*

Whereas configurational forces emergence merely holds that at certain levels in the organization of matter new forces emerge, R. W. Sellars (1922), whose view may be analogous to Aristotle's position (see McDonough, 2001a), holds that what emerges is a new substance, the emergence of a unitary agent; hence, *agential emergence.* The two important species of agential emergence are the view that the emergent is an instance of a repeatable organic type, for example a tiger, or *subpersonal emergence,* and the species in which what emerges is a person, or *personal emergence.* While configurational forces emergence holds that a configuration of particles acts as a unity in the sense that it exerts forces which are not the sum of the forces of its parts, agential emergence holds that the emergent acts as a unity in the stronger sense that it is a single unitary agent.

The notion of personal-level emergence warrants special comment. A person is not merely an individual in the sense of an individual instance of a repeatable organic type, but an individual in the sense that is expressed by the word "I." Numerous philosophical accounts of this difficult notion have been attempted. What I have in mind for present purposes is the idea that a person is a unique individual in the sense that their agency is inseparable from their historical and cultural context, where, since these are always unique, it cannot be captured in universal rules.

Personal emergence requires that the notion of matter be freed from the requirement that its causal powers are specifiable in universal rules independent of the cultural context. Although I do not believe that the later Wittgenstein is an emergent materialist *simpliciter,* he is an emergentist of a sort insofar as he holds that meaning and mental content are emergent relative to their neurophysiological system (see Wittgenstein, 1970; McDonough, 1989). In addition, his view that since language and thought are embedded in social contexts, they cannot be captured in universal rules, is analogous to personal emergence. Thus, although Wittgenstein's position may not be completely or adequately characterized as a species of emergent materialism, and my own view is similar to Wittgenstein's view (see McDonough, 2001b), his position in Zettel, §608, would seem to endorse a version of emergent materialism. I will, therefore, count Wittgenstein as a qualified (with a question mark) emergent materialist.[5] Since a person is an instance of the organic type *human being,* the claim is not that persons do not engage in any type-specifiable behavior. It is that since a person is not merely an organism, but an "I," then it also exhibits unique person-level behavior.[6] On my (1998a) view, Heidegger's view is analogous in some ways to personal emergence.

We began this branch at node 13 with emergence metaphysical→ organic→intrinsic-parts→material-parts→causal. We now have the further taxonomy shown in Figure 10.2. This gives us five species of emergence that are of special interest to the account of creativity:

- The emergence of epiphenomenal characteristics:
  metaphysical→organic→intrinsic→material→causal→lawlike→
  deterministic→brute→epiphenomenal.
- The emergence of characteristics where the principle of emergence is indeterministic:
  metaphysical→organic→intrinsic→material→causal→lawlike→
  indeterministic.
- The emergence in British Emergentism, which holds that what emerges are configurational forces:
  metaphysical→organic→intrinsic→material→causal→lawlike→
  deterministic→brute→downwardly causal→holistic→configurational forces.
- The emergence in which what emerges is a new natural subpersonal agent:
  metaphysical→organic→intrinsic→material→causal→lawlike→deterministic→
  brute→downwardly causal→holistic→agential→sub-personal.
- The emergence, perhaps found in Heidegger and Wittgenstein, in which what emerges are individuals such as persons:
  metaphysical→organic→intrinsic→material→causal→lawlike→
  deterministic→brute→downwardly causal→holistic→agential→personal.

Each of these supports a different degree of metaphysical freedom and creativity. Although some thinkers have urged that the notion of emergence is vague or empty (Birch & Cobb, 1984), the content of any notion of emergence is given by these stacked suffixes, the length of which indicates that these notions are far from empty. At the same time it can be seen that Kim (1992) exaggerates when he claims that downward causation is the very *raison d'être* of emergence. For there are many non-trivial species of emergence which do not involve downward causation. But it is certainly true that it is the raison d'être of a certain branch of the emergentist tree, specifically, that branch below node 24. Although there are problems explicating some of the required notions on this branch, such as the notion of a person, these problems derive from these notions themselves, not from emergence. Thus, the primary question should be whether one needs such notions in order to characterize human life in all its richness. If one does, then all parties will have to face up to them, but emergentism would seem to have a dis-

FIGURE 10.2
Types of emergence (continued).

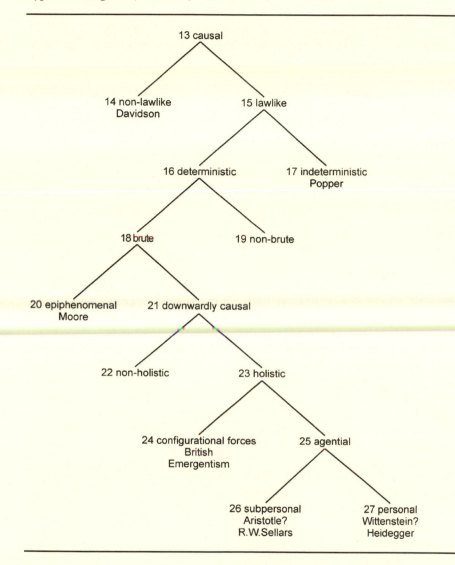

tinct advantage on this score since it is motivated precisely by the attempt to conceptualize the higher features of life and mind (such as human creativity). As Silberstein and McGeever (1999) point out, "Naturalism almost demands the view that minds are emergent features of neurochemical processes and their environments."

FIVE DEGREES OF FREEDOM AND CREATIVITY

Epiphenomenal Creativity

First, even the emergence at the personal level of mere epiphenomenal characteristics would be significant. For this would mean that the world of human experience is not a mere sum of a human being's material characteristics. In this case, persons are *epiphenomenally creative* in the sense that they produce experience which, though epiphenomenal, is emergent relative to their mechanical composition. As Hartshorne (1991, p. 232) puts a version of this idea, "each of us is an artist who produces life or experience itself." So when a poet, novelist, or psychologist describes "the world of human experience," they are describing an emergent world of human creation. Thus, the job of the humanities, including psychology, which, on this view, are autonomous relative to the physical sciences, is to describe this emergent phenomenology.

Indeterministic Creativity

The second case, indeterministic emergence, based on indeterminism, does not necessarily involve downward causation. For indeterministic emergence only holds that matter is characterized by the emergence of states and regularities that are novel relative to its mechanical composition. Thus, indeterministic emergence holds that organisms are *indeterministically creative* insofar as they manifest regularities in their behavior that cannot be explained as the mere sum of the causal powers of their material parts. It does not, however, necessarily hold that these "break the laws" at the lower levels. For example, in quantum mechanics, novel regularities emerge in the behavior of quantum systems, but these are not because the laws at the lower material level are broken, but because the whole point of indeterminism is that the laws at the lower level are not determinate. The emergence here is because the system has become more determinate than its lower level laws themselves require. Furthermore, the indeterministic emergence is different from epiphenomenal emergence because the emergent states, as in quantum mechanics, do possess genuine emergent causal powers. However, since indeterminism is familiar from quantum mechanics, and has been much discussed elsewhere (Pap, 1962), I do not discuss it further here.

Each of the remaining notions of emergent creativity (configurational forces emergence, subpersonal emergence, and personal emergence) are significant in an even greater sense. Since these attribute downward causal powers to the organism, each defines a sense in which the organism can "defy" mechanical nature (McDonough, 1994). As Sellars and Meehle put it, it "breaks the laws" at the lower levels.

Configurational Creativity

The first species of downward causation is the view of the British Emergentists that at certain levels in the organization of matter there emerge configurational forces. One might apply this to human beings in a variety of ways, so I consider only the most likely scenerio here. A proponent of configurational-forces emergence might hold that a complex configuration at the level of the human central nervous system exhibits causal powers that are not the mere sum of those of its neural components. Rather, the neural system as a whole exerts forces that cause its material constituents to behave differently than they would behave according to mere mechanical laws. This defines a sense in which a person (via their central nervous system) *creatively* controls their mechanical body, rather than being controlled by it. I call this *configurational creativity*.

Subpersonal Agential Creativity

Although the British Emergentists can hold that an organism is an agent in the sense that it is the appropriate logical subject for the ascription of causal powers, they do not hold that this *logical subject* has any ontological reality of its own, for they must hold that an organism is merely a configuration of particles. For R. W. Sellars, by contrast, an organism is one unified substance that exerts downward causation on its material composition. Whereas British Emergentism supports the configurational creativity of the whole field of particles relative to its parts, agential emergentism supports the creativity of a single unified agent relative to its material configuration. Although the notion of configurational creativity seems well suited to inorganic systems, such as clouds of particles, *subpersonal agential creativity* seems better suited to the sort of *creativity* observed in the higher animals.

Personal-Level Creativity

Finally, to the degree that the agent's causality cannot be captured by culture-independent rules, the agent is an emergent individual in the sense of a person. Thus, a person is *personally creative* in the sense that its individual causality cannot, in principle, be fixed by universal rules independent of the person's cultural context. In my 1998a opinion, Heidegger and Wittgenstein hold that persons are creative in something like this sense. Note that I here classify personal creativity as a species of agential creativity. That is, I treat the person as a special case of an organismic agent. One might, given more exotic philosophical views about the nature of persons, or even theological views, wish to separate persons from natural agents (material organisms), as, for example, Heidegger may do, but my classification is sufficient for present purposes.

In summary, we have five degrees of metaphysical freedom and creativity by means of our five degrees of emergence. In these definitions, for simplicity, I leave out the clause that each species is relative to the organism's mechanical basis:

- An organism is *epiphenomenally creative* if its experience or behavior is epiphenomenally emergent; that is, though these characteristics are without causal potencies of their own, they cannot be explained as a sum of the organism's micro-parts.
- An organism is *indeterministically creative* if its behavior is not explainable as the sum of the causal powers of its micro-parts but is only the result of indeterministic laws.
- An organism is *configurationally creative* if it consists of a configuration of particles that exert emergent downward causal forces on its mechanical composition.
- An organism is *subpersonally creative* if it exerts subpersonally emergent causal forces on its mechanical composition, that is, if it has the kind of organismic causal unity that cannot be analyzed without loss into its material parts.
- An organism is *personally creative* if it exerts downwardly causal agential forces that are not specifiable in universal laws independent of its cultural context.

One begins with a relatively mundane notion of a matter present in mechanistic materialism, and defines each of these five notions of creativity by relaxing a feature of that starting notion of matter.

Epiphenomenal emergence is materialistic in the sense that it holds, with mechanistic materialism, that all the causal potencies of matter are fixed by the basic constituents of matter, but it frees materialism from the requirement that the nature of matter is exhausted by these causal-mechanical potencies, and holds that these "novel" features of matter are expressed in its epiphenomenal properties.

Indeterministic emergence is materialistic insofar as it retains the idea of exclusive upwards determination by matter, but it frees materialism from the requirement of deterministic upwards determination.

Configurational emergence is materialistic insofar as it retains the notion of upwards determination by matter, but it frees the notion of matter from the idea that upwards determination precludes downward determination, that is, it allows the materialist to hold that lower conditions may determine when higher downward causation occurs.

Subpersonal emergence is materialist in the sense that it retains the view that all the causal powers are material powers, but, in addition to accepting the relaxation on the notion of matter in configurational forces emergence, it frees materialism from the view that the higher types of matter are decomposable without loss into arrangements of the basic material parts.

Personal emergence is materialist in the basic sense accepted by agential emergence, but it also frees matter from the idea that the causal powers of matter are specifiable in universal rules independent of the cultural context of the organism. That is, it holds that the causal powers of matter are completely realizable only in higher culture (see Putnam 1990; Adams 1975).

Although the last three of these notions permit one to say that the organism defies mechanical nature, none of these five notions of creativity allows one to say that the organism may defy material nature. Since all five of these notions of emergent creativity are modifications of materialism, each species of creativity *expresses* the nature of matter rather than contradicts it.

I have not here argued that any of these species of emergence actually exist. The case is different for each one. First, virtually no one argues that some emergent epiphenomenal characteristics, in a suitable broad sense of "epiphenomenal," do not exist (see the following section). The recent arguments tend to focus on downward causation, and these tend to be either conceptual arguments, based on the harmony of the scientific worldview with common sense, or empirical arguments concerning the present state of scientific evidence. But there are conceptual issues about the latter as well. In the following section I first consider the tradition of conceptual objection to downwardly causal emergence in Pepper (1926), Klee (1984), and Kim (1992, 1993a, 1993b, 1998), and then consider the different and seemingly more tolerant kind of objection to emergentism, based on empirical considerations, in McLaughlin (1992).

CRITICISMS OF EMERGENT MATERIALISM

Pepper (1926) initiates the modern assault on emergence with the claim that any emergent characteristic must be epiphenomenal. That is, the recent objection is not to emergence per se but to any causally significant notion of emergence. Sellars and Meehl (1956) note that Pepper's criticism is symptomatic of much contemporary thinking about emergentism.

Since Klee and Kim both develop updated versions of Pepper's criticism, I do not say much about his argument except to point out that Sellars and Meehl (ibid., p. 243) argue that Pepper considers a narrower range of alternatives than is possible. Thus, his argument that the theory of emergence is "palpably" a theory of epiphenomena is a non sequitur; in fact they represent it as a *petitio principii* (a question-begging argument) in which he simply assumes the denial of downward causation. They do not argue that downwardly causal emergence exists, but that its truth is an empirical issue and is consistent with determinism.

Klee considers four recent theories of emergence, the views, respectively, that the marks of emergence are unpredictability, novelty, invariant order and constancy, and macro-determination. He argues that all four theories fail because all are consistent with the view of the world as micro-determined. I focus on Klee's treatment of his fourth case because he considers it the most troublesome. However, I later identify an assumption which underlies his entire discussion and argue that he too begs the question against all four kinds of emergentism.

In his treatment of the fourth case, Klee considers two versions, one by Campbell and the other by Sperry. Campbell (1974) argues that natural selection involves downwardly causal macro-determination. Klee (1984) admits that though, at first glance, this kind of macro-determination would seem to be legitimate, he argues that once one examines *all* the causes operating between different systems, Campbell's emergence is seen to be consistent with micro-determination. For example, if one represents the organism in its environment as the system in natural selection, then it appears as if this system "causes" its own lower level adaptations. But this ignores the fact that "the environment" is itself resolvable into a set of systems, climatic, chemical, ecological, and so on—and that when these are taken into account, the case is consistent with micro-determination. Causey (1969, 1977) argues for the same conclusion, where Campbell's macro-determination is ultimately resolvable into indirect micro-determinations which detour through higher levels.

Klee admits that Sperry's (1970) view that consciousness is an emergent phenomenon in the brain which exerts downward causal force on neural states presents more problems for the micro-determinist, because there is, in this case, no obvious way to resolve the appearance of macro-determination into micro-determination by some larger more embracing system. For consciousness is an intrinsic property of the person. But Klee (1984) rejects Sperry's case because we "have no model of what a macro-determinative connection would be like." Klee points out that Sperry himself motivates his emergentism by means of analogies, for example, the macro-determinative influence is like the influence that the "whole wheel" has on the individual molecules within it as it rolls along or like the influence which an eddy in water has on molecules in it. But these analogies, Klee points out, are all consistent with a micro-determination.

Klee's criticism is ironic indeed given that emergentism was originally conceived as an alternative to mechanism. Thus, Klee exploits Sperry's own heuristic analogies with wheels and eddies, encouraging him to flesh out his view of macro-determination by providing the kinds of mechanisms that would make emergence consistent with micro-determination. But that requires that emergentists abandon their own most basic intuitions for being emergentists. Klee is, as it were, "natural-piety-challenged," insofar as he requires mechanistic explanations of emergence.

My criticism of Klee's criticism of emergence is not, however, merely that it is ironic. One might have independent reasons for favoring explanation by micro-deterministic mechanisms, and Klee thinks he has such reasons, that is, he thinks the reason micro-determination provides such satisfying explanations is that it "provides us with the effective means or mechanism by which the higher level is determined" (ibid.). But this reveals the deeper problem in his argument. For Klee simply assumes that micro-determination is inconsistent with macro-determination. But emergent materialists typically hold that the micro-deterministic world view is consistent with macro-determination, for example, Sellars and Meehl envisage micro-states determining the lawful conditions under which emergent macro-determination occurs. Klee simply repeats Pepper's *petitio*. His conclusion that "the effective means of macro-determination will involve micro-level mechanisms, and that will serve to preserve micro-determinism as a world view" (ibid.), begs the question against emergent materialism by assuming that micro-determination is inconsistent with downward causation.

Kim continues in this tradition with his argument that downwardly causal emergence is incoherent because it is a disguised form of dualism. Only the second part of Kim's argument is directly relevant here. Kim holds that the "tension arises out of the attempt to combine 'upward determination' with 'downward causation'" (1993b). But what, precisely, is this "tension"? Kim (ibid; also see MacDonald & MacDonald, 1995) argues that downwardly causal emergence violates physical conservation principles, since, if new causal powers emerge at the higher levels of matter, then the physical universe is not closed with regard to force. But this is incorrect. The conservation principles do not say that actual energy is conserved but only that total energy is conserved (McLaughlin, 1992). Emergent materialists need only claim that certain material conditions permit the actualization of powers that, at lower levels of organization, had been potential. There is no reason why the satisfaction of certain conditions in the organization of matter could not bring it about that latent potentialities in matter are actualized, resulting in novel behavior of matter. What conceivable sort of argument could show that this is impossible?

Kim's argument is that at precisely the points at which matter is invested with the exotic capacity for downward causation, it slides into dualism. But the traditional reply of reductivist materialists to the claim that they are denuding the world of all of its dignity is that, on the contrary, the success of their reduction shows that matter has the potential for dignity. If the reductivists are serious about this, then they have no choice but to provide materialist accounts of these dignified characteristics by relaxing their restrictions on matter. Each of our key notions is defined by beginning with a relatively mundane notion of matter in mechanistic materialism, and relaxing one or more of these requirements of that narrow materialism. Although there may be a temptation at each of these stages to hold that matter that is assigned such characteristics is tantamount to dualism, that is no more correct than the view that indeterminism in quantum physics commits it to dualism. But quantum indeterminacy does not read mind back into nature. It merely separates our basic notion of matter from the deterministic paradigm. So too, when Kim attempts to convict emergentism of dualism, he is merely insisting on a narrow (mechanistic) conception of

matter, and, once again, begs the question against the emergent materialism. Kim's argument presupposes a reactionary concept of matter.

It is worthwhile concluding with McLaughlin's critique of emergentism
since it represents a seemingly more tolerant kind of criticism symptomatic
of much contemporary thinking about emergentism, but which stacks the
deck, in a different way, against it. Whereas Pepper, Klee, and Kim all crit-
icize emergentism on conceptual grounds, McLaughlin (1992, p. 90) agrees
with Sellars and Meehl that the existence of emergentism is an empirical
matter. The bad news, however, is that emergentism has been empirically
refuted, for emergentism "flies in face of scientific achievements of this
century" (ibid., p. 75). However, McLaughlin's conclusion is misleading.
McLaughlin himself admits that there are emergent phenomena, first, that
Einstein's field equations involve downward causation, and, second, that
there may be emergent effects in the holistic features of quantum mechanics (ibid., and see van Fraassen, 1995).[7] One must remember that McLaughlin defines British emergentism quite specifically as the view that there are
configurational forces, and admits that he is not considering other species
of emergentism in R. W. Sellars, A. N. Whitehead, and others (1992). When
he claims that emergentism has been shown to be empirically false what he
really means is that British Emergentism has been undermined empirically,
and that the *prima facie* emergence in relativity and quantum mechanics are
not due *specifically* to configurational forces. A hasty generalization from
British Emergentism to Emergentism, aided by a "British" presupposition
about the nature of matter,[8] allows him to read a broader significance into
the setbacks for British Emergentism than is warranted. For R. W. Sellars,
A. N. Whitehead, or the Soviet Emergentists would respond that, of course
British Emergentism failed, because organisms are not merely configurations of particles.[9]

McLaughlin's (ibid.) presuppositions about the nature of matter are
implicit in his remark:

Downward causation from the psychological, biological, or chemical level is . . .
enormously implausible. There is overwhelming reason to reject . . . the existence
of *configurational* [my emphasis] chemical, vital, or psychological forces. (p. 53, n5)

This claim must be read carefully, for it is extremely narrow. Note that
McLaughlin only denies the existence of emergent *configurational forces* in
these disciplines. But if one looks for configurational forces in psychology
(what would it even *mean* to do that?), one will not find them. For this failure is an inevitable consequence of the way in which he looks for it. The
interesting philosophical questions here concern what it can mean to assert
that a new material substance or a person emerges, and how such emergents
would be manifested. But McLaughlin passes by these questions in silence.
Just as Sellars and Meehl complained about Pepper, McLaughlin considers

a smaller range of alternatives than is possible, and thereby begs the question against emergentism, but in a different way from Pepper, Klee, or Kim.

As we have seen, one philosopher after another begs the question against emergentism. Since it would seem to be obvious that emergentism, at minimum, makes sense, this hostility is itself a positive phenomenon which requires explanation. In my opinion, the low status of emergentism is connected with the low status accorded to philosophy, even by philosophers, in the present age. The reason emergentism fails to go away, despite longstanding hostility to it, is that it just seems impossible to eliminate the explanatory gap between the inorganic sciences and vital phenomena, and, therefore, the root intuition behind emergentism is that at least some species of emergence are a priori. Since the core of philosophy is metaphysics, in the sense of an a priori theory of reality, while contemporary philosophers prefer to regard themselves as quasi-scientists (Passmore, 1992), this root intuition behind emergentism is not viewed favorably. It is for such reasons that McLaughlin takes the inorganic sciences, for example, relativity theory and quantum mechanics, as the paradigm of science, and dismisses Broad's view that it is a priori that secondary qualities are emergent: "The Emergentists left the dry land of the a priori to brave the sea of empirical fortune. (The only route is by sea of course)" (1992, p. 90). But if some non-trivial species of emergentism is true, where we are ourselves the preeminent vital beings in whom emergent phenomena are manifested, and if we do have a kind of a priori knowledge of those emergent phenomena constitutive of our own personhood, then philosophy enjoys a distinctive role which is the reverse of its role under the scientistic conception—the task of understanding, not how mind and freedom reduce to the inorganic world, but how science is itself an emergent product of human freedom (see McDonough, 1989).[10] Whereas the natural sciences are primarily concerned with the material-causal conditions of life and mind, the distinctive task of philosophy is a kind of a priori investigation of our own emergent creativity (and the emergent world). Fichte claimed that "mine is the first and only philosophy of freedom" (Breazeale, 1994), though he emphasized that he only took himself to be elucidating Kant's views. Emergentism supports the view that philosophy is, intrinsically, a philosophy of freedom, in the sense that it is its job to determine which, if any, of the aforementioned five notions of emergent freedom and creativity (epiphenomenal creativity, configurational forces creativity, indeterministic creativity, subpersonal creativity and personal creativity), or yet others, are required to characterize human life and knowledge.[11] If this is true, the issue of human creativity is not merely one intellectual problem among many, but is, in a sense, the central problem, not only of philosophy, but of intellectual life in general. For on this view, since science itself is a part of the emergent world, the resistance to emergentism by both philosophy and the sciences is one more chapter in the longstanding story of the resistance to self-knowledge.[12] But, as Plato

(1968) pointed out, someone who is really in love with something "cares for everything related to the object of his love."[13]

ACKNOWLEDGMENT

I wish to thank my former student, Shannon Finegan, for helpful comments on an earlier draft of this chapter.

DISCUSSION

TD: Let me see if I understand your position. You say, "emergentism offers the possibility of a kind of creativity that involves the birth of something genuinely new, and, therefore, would seem to provide a robust metaphysical answer which supports Lady Lovelace's intuition that organisms are creative in a sense in which mere machines cannot be." In personal correspondence you have said:

> The aim is to define a sense in which the behavior of the organism is genuinely creative, i.e., that more comes out of the organism than can be accounted for by what is materially/mechanically internal to the organism. My feeling is that many accounts of creativity are really verbal, i.e., they merely put a new gloss on the same facts acknowledged by everybody. The only way, I think, to get genuine creativity, a kind of creativity that has ontological bite, is via a serious doctrine of emergence.

You limit yourself to *emergent materialism*, which is the view that life and mind are emergent characteristics of matter. A material system has a material base, and you say that it has emergent characteristics if it has characteristics that are more than the sum of the characteristics of the parts of its base. You also say, and I take it that you think that this is another way of saying the same thing, that a characteristic is emergent if there is an *explanatory gap* between the properties of the base and the characteristic. You then outline five types of emergence: (a) the emergence of epiphenomenal properties, (b) emergence based on indeterminism, (c) the emergence of configurational forces, (d) the emergence of new material substances, and (e) the emergence of persons. You use this taxonomy to define "an ascending series of five 'degrees' of emergence-based freedom and creativity."

Have I got you right?

RM: Yes, that seems basically correct, with two minor qualifications. First, as I state in the chapter, the notion of the explanatory gap refers specifically to mechanistic explanation. A characteristic is emergent in an ontologically significant sense if it is emergent with respect to any underlying mechanisms. But that is consistent with the claim that emergent characteristics can be explained in some other more general sense. Second, for related reasons, I may, in private correspondence, have said that behavior is creative if more comes out of the organism than can be accounted for by what is materially/mechanically present inside it. That is loose formulation, which might be appropriate in a very general discussion of emergentism (though it would require a more fine-grained analysis of materialism than I have presented in this chapter). Since in this chapter I focus on several versions of emergent materialism, which is a version of materialism, it would be odd to say that emergent materialism holds that something comes out of the organism which cannot be accounted for by reference to the material organism. Thus, it would be better, given the limits of this chapter, to replace "materially/mechanically" by "mechanically" in that private formulation.

TD: I agree that emergence plays a vital role in human creativity, but I think that in some ways your claim goes too far, while in other ways it doesn't go far enough. It goes too far because the relationship between emergence and creativity isn't as simple as you seem to suggest: emergence by itself is neither necessary nor sufficient for creativity. And it doesn't go far enough because you need to say more about emergent mental content and created products. You need to take your story further, from the emergence of people, which is where your story ends, to what creatively emerges out of people, which is where the important stuff begins. Let's go through those in turn.

The relationship between emergence and creativity can't be as straightforward as you suggest, because emergence is neither necessary nor sufficient for creativity. Let's look at the "not necessary" case first. An example of creativity without emergence is creative problem solving. How do you make four equilateral triangles of the same size out of six matchsticks? The answer is that you build a pyramid consisting of three matchsticks for its base and three for the edges that converge at the apex. Where is the emergence here? Or how about Theseus' way of getting out of the Minotaur's maze by leaving a trail of string behind him as he went in, or Columbus' way of balancing an egg on its end? (He broke the egg!) These are creative solutions, but they don't involve any emergence, as far as I can see. So emergence isn't necessary for creativity.

Now, you might want to say that emergence is only necessary for *some* types of creativity. If that is what you want to say, I agree with you, but now you have to provide a non-circular account of these types of creativity—"non-circular" because you don't want to say that we need emergence "in those cases of creativity where the whole is greater than the sum of the parts." This would be circular, because you've *defined* emergence in terms of the whole being greater than the sum of the parts, so that you would be saying that the whole is greater than the sum of its parts in those of cases of creativity where the whole is greater than the sum of its parts.

Now look at the "not sufficient" case. Your first level of emergence is *epiphenomena*. Standard examples of epiphenomena are the liver secreting bile and locomotives giving off steam. The bile and the steam are epiphenomal inasmuch as they are "spun off" by the material base: they are caused by it, but they don't causally influence it.

I don't think that these epiphenomena are creative, although they are emergent. Your example of epiphenomal creativity is human experience. You say, "persons are *epiphenomenally creative* in the sense that they produce experience which, though epiphenomenal, is emergent relative to their mechanical composition." This is because "the world of human experience is not a mere sum of a human being's material characteristics." Sure, but why does this give us creativity? You quote Hartshorne as saying, "each of us is an artist who produces life or experience itself." But if all of life and experience are "creative" in this sense, then we will need another word for what we normally mean by "creative," because *this* isn't how we use the term! "Creative" doesn't mean "all of life and experience."

My own take on this is that creativity *exploits* emergence. Emergence throws things up (which may be more than the sum of their parts, or may have no parts at all), and we evaluate and select them, and readjust our goals, and repeat the process.

This is very close to what McGraw, Hofstadter, and Rehling call "The Central Feedback Loop of Creativity" in their chapters in this volume. We need to guide and contribute to get creativity. We exploit emergence through judgment and evaluation. Isn't this the crucial difference between creativity and mere emergence?

RM: You raise a wealth of interesting issues here. I will try to deal with the most important of them. But first, let me attempt to get your point about my epiphenomenal emergence out of the way, for this is, I believe, misguided.

You use as examples of epiphenomenalism the secretion of bile by the liver or steam by the steam engine. But bile and steam are far more causally robust entities than the kind envisaged in my epiphenomenalism. My example is G. E. Moore's view (1991) that goodness is supervenient on natural properties, that is, *all* of the causal properties of Moore's good entities derive, not from their emergent goodness, but from their natural physical properties. The idea is that there are kinds of views about meaning and mental properties which view them as more like Moore's goodness than bile or steam. Although I do not think that recent eliminativism (the Churchlands', etc.) are classical epiphenomenalist positions, they may be epiphenomenalist in some *analogous* sense, but to specify this precise sense would require a more detailed discussion of eliminativism than is possible here. Let me now move to your more important claim that emergence is neither necessary nor sufficient for creativity.

Since you do not state specifically which of the various notions of emergence, corresponding to the 27 different nodes on my emergence tree you mean, I assume that you here refer generally to some ontologically significant species of emergence, specifically, that you mean some, but perhaps not all, of the notions of emergence at or below node 7 on my tree, but with special reference to the five notions, at nodes 17, 24, 25, 26 and 27, which I make the basis of my five notions of creativity. I make this assumption in my subsequent remarks.

You say first that emergence is not necessary for creativity because there are cases of creativity, for example, the pyramid-building solution, which do not involve emergence. This seems right. However, it is relatively uninteresting. For the word "creativity" does not designate anything like a natural kind. [A believer in natural kinds holds that nature is divided into naturally occurring kinds and species. (ed.)] As Jacques Barzun puts a related point, "The word 'creative' is so much in honor that it is the clinching term of approval from the schoolroom to the advertiser's studio" (Barzun, 1959, p. 15.). We say that Einstein is creative in his production of relativity theory, that a poet is creative in her choice of a word for a simile, that a wrestler is creative in the moves he makes in a match, that little Susie is creative in her color choice while finger-painting, that an octopus is creative in the way it extracts bait from a trap, and so on. We might even say that a robot on Mars is creative in the way it negotiates obstacles on the Martian landscape—see Barzun (1959) on the political dimensions in the application of this much abused word. There is not, *and cannot be,* any single account of creativity which is suitable for these, and many other, diverse kinds of cases. For this reason, I do not begin with the motley of linguistic applications of the word "creative" and attempt to provide a single kind of account of them. Rather, one must grasp the other end of the organismic stick. There are two interesting questions, first, whether one can define an *ontologically interesting* sense or senses in which an organism is creative, and, second, whether any of these senses can be univocally applied to machines. Thus, I begin at the other end, far removed from the motley of creativity, namely, with a certain kind of traditional claim, in the emergentist tradition, about what is ontologically distinctive about organisms and intelligent creatures, and define a series of senses in which, if an organism exhibits emergent characteristics of such and such types, then it is creative in a way a mere machine cannot be. To revert to your example of the pyramid-building solution, along with the "creative" robot on Mars, it seems to me that both of these cases of "creativity" could be accounted for with no appeal to any ontologically significant species of emergence. Thus, I would *not* expect my key notions of emergence, for example, downward causation, and so on, to be applicable to such cases. Since the word "creativity" does a wealth of different kinds of linguistic and political duty, it is not to be expected that a single kind of account of emergence should be able to deal with all its putative applications, that is, both with Einstein's theorizing and Susie's finger painting. By focusing on the messy applications of "creativity," rather than the, in principle, more easily definable notion of emergence, one can only muddy the waters. This is why, at several places in the chapter, I refer to "emergence-based freedom and creativity," not to creativity simpliciter. We could stipulate a sense in which a robot is creative. But such linguistic legislation, though it might serve certain political agendas deriving from the Enlightenment, sheds no real light on organismic creativity.

Your claim, in addition, that emergence is not sufficient for creativity, is also true. But this is also implicit in my trees. The five species of emergence-based freedom and creativity which I define towards the bottom of the tree, epiphenomenal emergence, indeterministic emergence, configurational-forces emergence, subpersonal-agential emergence, and the emergence of persons, all occur under node 7 (organic emergence). Thus, all five of these species of emergence are defined with reference to the logically prior notion of an organism. There are, however, a plethora of species of emergence on the tree, and many more not on my tree, which do not satisfy this condition. Again, one could define notions of creativity which pertain to these other cases, but since contemporary AI and cognitive science are concerned with understanding creativity in a material organism, I have expended the most effort on the attempt to isolate the specific notions of emergence most directly relevant to those disciplines.

In summary, I agree that emergence is neither necessary nor sufficient for "creativity," but, in brief, this is less a problem with emergence than it is a problem with the word "creativity." Our problem is not (or should not be) creativity in its broadest application, which is a horrific motley of disparate notions, but the creativity characteristic of organisms, and for that we need something like an ontology of organic life.

Let me take this opportunity to make a related point about the interpretation of the trees that may not be obvious. At node 17 we have indeterministic emergence. But since node 17 occurs under node 7 (organic emergence) indeterministic emergence does not concern just any kind of system that exhibits indeterministic emergence. It concerns only that species in which characteristics emerge at the level of a living organism as such. Thus, there may be indeterministic systems which are not organisms, for example, a cloud of electrons, which exhibit indeterministic emergence, and, therefore, exhibit, in a sense which could be defined, "creative" behavior, but which are not covered in my chapter. One could make a similar point, for example, about configurational-forces emergence, namely, that there could be systems that have configurational-forces emergent output, and which are therefore "creative" in a sense, but this has little to do with our problem, in AI and cognitive science, of organismic or human creativity.

Since emergence is neither necessary nor sufficient for creativity, you insist that I give a non-circular account of the kind of creativity, that is, you insist that I cannot simply say that I am dealing with the kind of creativity in which the "whole is greater than the sum of the parts."

I think that this is, in a sense right, and in a sense wrong. Your demand that I provide an account of the kind of creativity to which my account of emergence is directed is appropriate. However, the general direction for my answer to this objection is implicit in my tree. I am dealing with the kind of creativity which is *prima facie* distinctive of organisms, and, to be more specific, the higher organisms. Thus, I agree that I owe an account of the nature of organic life. But this is no mean task, despite the fact that, on my view, this was the central task of philosophy until this was replaced in the Enlightenment by paradigms more akin to the inorganic sciences. As Maritain puts it, "During all of classical antiquity and the Middle ages, the reigning philosophy was inspired not by mechanics, but by life" (Maritain, 1955, p. 103). This changed with the Enlightenment. However, even after the Enlightenment, the whole of German Idealism, and most phenomenology and existentialism, are, in my view, reactions against the mechanicism of the Enlightenment. Thus, in my view, part of this task of delineating the nature of life is already done in Plato, Aristotle, Aquinas, Descartes, Spinoza, Leibniz, Kant, Hegel, Schelling, Marx, Goethe, Dilthey, Bergson, Scheler, Husserl, Heidegger, Sartre, Merleau-Ponty, Wittgenstein, and others. Let me just say here that this account typically involves, in addition to a robust notion of emergence, the view that an organism is self-moving, that it is a certain kind of organic unity, that it has a certain kind of internal telos, that it is embedded in its environment in a certain characteristic way (all construed in a way that is incompatible with mere mechanical constructions). If you really want a definition of the kind of emergence I need, it would be found in connection with these weighty notions. Unfortunately, most of these factors are currently seen from the perspective of the Enlightenment, and have been appropriated by the Enlightenment. Consequently, the fact that the better part of the history of philosophy is fundamentally a history of a certain kind of non-reductionist thinking about the nature of life, which compliments the predominately reductionist thinking in science, has been obscured. It is a corollary of my view that the attempts to reconstruct Plato, Aristotle, Kant, and others, as forerunners of mechanistic cognitive science are simply non-starters, which have far more to do with the popularity of mechanical models than they do with the historical Plato, Aristotle, Kant, etc.. I have attempted to sketch parts of the traditional philosophical accounts of organic life, in several of the major historical figures, in various of my papers, but this remains mostly undone.[14]

Unfortunately, it is not possible to extend the discussion of the nature of organic life here. For present purposes, suffice it to say here that although such an account of organism is required, it would not take the form of a definition. Perhaps a definition could be given, but, even so, it would be parasitic on a much more ambitious account of the nature of life.

Since this may be unsatisfying in the short run, let me revert to a specific strategy that might be more satisfying. In his *Philosophical Investigations* (1963), and other later works, Wittgenstein argues that linguistic meaning, that is, the use of words, is emergent relative to the language user's mechanical composition, and to any formulas, images or pictures, and so on, which they have in their mind or brain. If Wittgenstein is correct, then human linguistic usage is characterized by the sorts of regularities which he describes in his books, and which are, he argues, emergent relative to the language user's body and brain mechanisms. What Wittgenstein purports to provide in these books is not a *definition* of these crucial kinds of linguistic regularities, but, rather, a *description* of the facts of linguistic usage, combined with arguments that they cannot be mechanically explained. What is important, therefore, is not whether we can *define* such organic regularities, but whether they exist, and whether they can be explained by the kinds of (roughly) mechanistic strategies common in AI and cognitive science.

You are, therefore, correct that an account of the kind of emergence at issue in key nodes of my tree is ultimately required, but it is a kind of account that is much larger than a mere definition. In lieu of this account, that is, in lieu of my often threatened reconstruction of the history of philosophy as a distinctive kind of nonreductive thinking concerning the nature of life, one can, like Wittgenstein, build one's case for emergence on descriptions of specific kinds of regularities associated with linguistic meaning and intelligence, coupled with arguments that these cannot be mechanically explained.

I now move to your positive alternative to my emergentism. Given your criticisms of my account of emergence-based creativity, you conclude: "My own take on this is that creativity exploits emergence." You then refer sympathetically to McGraw, Hofstadter, and Rehling's central feedback loop in which "we exploit emergence through judgment and selection." This, you suggest, isolates the kind of emergence that we are after.

First, this account does not define a *kind* of emergence at all—unless one individuates kinds of emergence by reference to the sort of "loop" in which they occur. The point may seem trivial but, in fact, goes to the heart of the matter. Let me illustrate it by pointing out that there may, for all we know, be characteristics which are emergent at the level of an organism by virtue, for example, of the indeterministic effects in quantum mechanics, but which are not emergent characteristics of the organism per se. For example, it may be that the shape of the organism varies slightly due to quantum effects, but this has nothing whatsoever to do with its character as a living being. But when I say that my account of the relevant kind of emergence presupposes an account of the nature of an organism, I do not merely mean that a certain emergent characteristic is manifested in an organism, but that it is a species of emergence associated with an organism as such. Your account cannot provide the kind of emergence we need since it does not provide a *kind* of emergence at all. Rather, your account, like mine, presupposes an account of the nature of organic life. For even if your account were correct, it would still require that this "feedback loop" occur within the context of an organism, as opposed, for example, to being in the context of a new type of tank or a cloud of lifeless particles. Your account presupposes an account of organic life just as does my own. On my account, one could, in principle provide an account of specifically organic emergence in that strong sense, by further clarifying and developing the traditional notion of organism (though, I stress again, I have not done this here).

In addition, I would pose to you this dilemma, to which I return later. Either McGraw, Hofstadter, and Rehling's emergence-exploiting judgment and selection can be mechanically explained or it cannot. If it can be mechanically explained, then emergence still plays a very subsidiary role in intelligence (i.e., the emergent characteristics only provide, at best, some data or condition for a mechanical intelligence). That is relatively small potatoes from the perspective of the classical emergentists who want an emergentist account of intelligence, not merely an account of intelligence that allows a bit of emergence somewhere along the "loop." If, however, the judgment and selection cannot be mechanically explained, then they are themselves either emergent phenomena or are committed to substantive vitalism.

At minimum, McGraw, Hofstadter, and Rehling relegate emergence to a subsidiary role in the "loop." More likely, they simply sidestep the problem and we face the issues of mechanism, vitalism, and emergentism all over again at their higher level of judgement and selection. I return to this point later.

TD: One of the things that surprises me about your chapter is that you limit yourself to emergent *materialism*. You say, "Whereas persons of a scientific cast of mind generally try to define creativity as the rearrangement of pre-existing elements . . . emergentism offers the possibility of a kind of creativity that involves the birth of something genuinely new." But what is to prevent the combinationist from saying that it is exactly the rearrangement of pre-existing elements that gives birth to something that is genuinely *and emergently* new? That is, why isn't combinationism *consistent* with emergent materialism? A combinationist might say that all that we can do is to rearrange the parts and components, and that this can give us emergence. "What else can we do?" a combinationist might say. We put notes together to get music. We put words together to get poetry. Here we are intentionally exploiting emergent phenomena by manipulating the components of the material base.

In this context, can you clarify your position on whether people can be creative in a way that machines cannot be? You say that the characteristics of a machine are just the sum of the characteristics of its parts. But isn't this just a verbal account, that rules out machine intelligence and creativity by definition? If a material base can give rise to emergent properties, and if emergence gives rise to creativity, why can't we have creative machines? Saying that they are now no longer machines *by definition* doesn't seem helpful to me.

RM: It is true that I have focused only on a certain branch of the emergentist tree which is closest to contemporary materialism. I would have liked to broaden my account of emergence to include species of non-materialist emergence. However, since AI and cognitive science are largely materialist, and since it has been difficult to get contemporary theorists to take even a modest emergent materialism seriously, let alone more exotic species of emergence, and because of space limitations in the chapter, I decided to limit this discussion primarily to emergent materialism. But it is also true that my attempt to provide a taxonomy for emergentism is far broader than is usual in contemporary discussions. In fact, I believe that even my broader discussion in this chapter is only the tip of emergentist iceberg. Let me, therefore, take this opportunity to comment more generally on the breadth of the emergentist tradition.

In my view, and following my previous remarks concerning the intimate, but largely neglected, connection between traditional philosophy and a kind of characteristically non-reductionist thinking about life and mind, it is also true that most of the major philosophers, from the ancient Greeks through Kant and Hegel, to Heidegger and Wittgenstein, are ontological emergentists in some serious sense. I believe that even La Mettrie, the patron saint of mechanism, is an ontological emergentist in some significant sense. To take just one important example here, which is very close to my own "quasi-Kantian" heart, see Kant's endorsement of emergentism in his *Anthropology* (Kant, 1996). In fact, Kant's philosophy, like all of German Idealism, is permeated by emergentism through and through, though, in keeping with the distorting nature of Enlightenment historiography (see Gay, 1977), this has been systematically neglected in the English-speaking world in the twentieth century. Indeed, I believe that, in large measure, philosophy has traditionally complimented the natural sciences by emphasizing a kind of non-reductionist emergentist thinking about life as a balance to the predominant scientific tendency to reductionist thinking (until much of enlightened philosophy was seduced by reductionism in the eighteenth century).

Continuing this line of thinking, there are whole species of emergence which do not fit into my present limited taxonomy. For example, whereas most modern philosophers assume that emergence is the emergence of the higher from the lower, I believe that Plato and Plotinus, and with them, much Medieval philosophy, are downward emergentists, that is, they hold that the "material" world emerges, that is, is novel with respect to, the higher world. One cannot "derive" the material world from the higher world because the former contains imperfection, evil, and and so on, which are foreign to the higher world. This sounds strange, that matter emerges from God, or Mind, or Ideas, but, in fact, it captures an aspect of such ancient philosophies which is as fruitful for understanding them as it is neglected. If this is correct, then we are faced with the enormous task of reconstructing the whole history of philosophy giving due credit to emergentist thinking as a compliment to reductionism. That is obviously a matter for other occasions. But this is worth driving home here because I believe that much of the opposition to emergentism is a local (recent) phenomenon, which is more visceral than rational, and derives from a specific, and false, interpretation of what was accomplished in the Enlightenment (or required by it).

Returning to your specific points, you ask why combinationism isn't consistent with emergence. The answer to this important question is that it depends on what one means by combinationism. If by "combinationism," call this C1, one merely means that one builds the big ones out of the little ones, sentences out of words, thoughts out of concepts, and so on, then combinationism is consistent with emergence. But if by "combinationism," call this C2, which, I take it, includes compositional theories of meaning in semantics as a prime example, one means that the *meaning* of the whole is an additive function of the meanings of the parts, then it is not consistent with emergentism. Both C1 and C2 hold that the big ones are built out of the little ones, but C2 makes a stronger claim insofar as it claims, in addition, that the big ones are in a strong sense merely an additive function of the little ones. C2 is reductionist is a sense in which C1 is not.

Given this distinction between two kinds of combinationist theories, look at the sort of rhetoric surrounding compositional theories of meaning, and the psychological theories built on them, over the past half century. Since many of these combinationist theories are designed to serve mechanistic theories, as in Fodor's mechanistic theories of intelligence, these have to be combinationist theories of the C2 (reductionist) type. These would have to be theories of the reductionist type because, if they were not, then providing the combinationist-based mechanistic model would not explain the meaning or intelligence. For in that case the alleged explanation would suffer from the "explanatory gap" inherent in emergentist theories.

Unfortunately, the language in which combinationist theories of meaning, intelligence, and so on, have been formulated for forty years or so has been infected by a disturbing ambiguity between just these two kinds of combinationism. To the degree that compositional theorists of meaning merely hold that meaning is a compositional function of the meaning of the parts (in a sense that is consistent with the emergence of new meaning), then that compositional theory cannot serve a mechanistic explanation of the emergent meaning. But the rhetoric by such theorists has often been to the effect that they cannot even understand what else could possibly need to be explained which is not explained by their theories. This ambiguity has enabled combinationists to avoid the real philosophical issues confronting combinationism.

However, if emergentism is true, then the major burden of explanation falls on the explanatory gap separating the mere meanings of the parts and the meaning which emerges from that arrangement of parts. Compositional theorists of meaning in this century have written as if their theory shows how one can explain the meaning, when they should have asked whether, despite the composition, there is an emergent explanatory gap between the meanings of the parts and the whole meaning.

This is one reason I took some pains in my chapter to point out that, despite disclaimers to the contrary, Fodor is a reductionist, that is, that he is just a model-reductionist rather than a conceptual reductionist. The extensive debate about Fodor's alleged anti-reductionism is a smokescreen that has only served to conceal the interesting philosophical issues involving emergence.

Let me move to your final point in this section, that I rule out creative machines "by definition." Now I certainly cannot do that since, because of the motley character of the concept of creativity, I gave (and can give) no general definition of creativity in the chapter. Rather, grasping the other end of the stick, I first define emergence, and define kinds of creativity by reference to that more precise theoretical notion.

Thus, the definitional problem to which you refer, if there is one, is not with "creative machine," but with something like "emergence machine." But this is not my stipulation. The notions of mechanism and emergence are traditionally opposed, and for good reason, namely, that the very notion of emergence involves an explanatory gap with respect to any underlying mechanism. But, pressing your question further, could we have emergence machines (machines, perhaps the brain, on which meaning or intelligence emerge)? The answer to that question, given that very specific formulation, is that, in a sense, we probably could. However, with the admission of significant emergence one must also admit the explanatory gap which comes with it, and that means that the machine does not explain meaning and/or intelligence. This is why Kim does not directly argue that Fodor is wrong, but, rather, argues that Fodor must distinguish his view from emergentism, and, by that accusation, attempts to drive Fodor back into the conceptual-reductivist fold. For the underlying machine, on an emergence-friendly view, becomes a minor player in the production of meaning and/or intelligence, and that is what Fodor, and cognitive science generally, cannot admit without giving up an enormous amount of their bold claims to be able to explain meaning and/or intelligence.

Finally, if meaning and/or intelligence are emergent on the brain mechanism, then the functioning of this mechanism even becomes downright mysterious. For if the brain, operating on purely mechanical principles, manages in some cultural context to produce the appropriate output, say the word "red," which in a certain context takes the emergent meaning *communist,* as opposed to *color of a firetruck,* the question arises, how does it manage to do this (pre-established harmony)? See my paper (1989) for further remarks on this mystery. Combining emergence with mechanism is not a compromise position that combines the best of both, and escapes the extremism of each side. It is a move that raises new questions, and makes the posited mechanism, along with the whole explanatory point of positing cognitive mechanisms, mysterious in the extreme.

TD: To go back to my own take, I think that we want an emergence that gives us not only something that is greater than the sum of its parts, but richness and complexity without any parts. We find this in painting, sculpture, pottery, and so on. We look at the movement of the brush and see the painting emerge. We see the clay pot emerging in the potter's hands. There are no *parts* or *components* here.

And this is the easy case, I think. More difficult, because more misleading, are situations where there are parts, and where the parts are put together to form a whole, but where the parts are *irrelevant* to the whole. Think of a jigsaw puzzle. This is a collection of parts, and it's put together as a collection of parts, but this fact has nothing to do with the constructed product, with the final, constructed picture. If you stand back or blur your eyes, you don't see the lines or the parts. They are irrelevant to the finished product.

A more difficult example is an identikit, because here it does seem that we put a face together out of its components or microfeatures. Here I think that we construct a face out of its features, but it is our *knowledge about* faces and our *knowledge about* the criminal that makes us put them together to form *this* face. I think that this helps us to see why it's vacuous to say that Hamlet consists of a creative combination of words, or that Verdi's Requiem consists of a creative combination of notes. They do consist of these things, trivially, but only in the way that the jigsaw consists of a set of pieces.

So I suspect that atomism plus emergence takes us up to the person level, but *what people produce,* what comes out of them, can't be wholly accounted for in such terms. I think that to account for human creativity and flexibility we need a non-atomistic, "knowing-about" epistemology that accounts for the way in which we create images and pictures and representations out of our skills and abilities, and out of our knowledge about the world.

RM: I find your remark that "we want an emergence that gives us not only something that is greater than the sum of the parts, but richness and complexity without any parts" somewhat confusing. First, your claim is prima facie inconsistent since your first conjunct, "we want something . . . greater than the sum of its parts," implies the existence of parts while the second, "but richness and complexity without any parts," denies it. This by itself may be a small and easily remedial point, but I suspect that the shifting derives from the difficulty in conceiving something that is really without parts. Perhaps the only item in the history of thought which is really supposed to be without parts is Parmenides' sphere. Parmenides seems to have thought that the only true being is an infinitely extended sphere that cannot be divided, because the whole of it is present everywhere. First, this is a highly fictional kind of notion and, second, it is most difficult to conceive (even Parmenides describes his one entity as if it does have parts, a surface, a center, etc.). Furthermore, your own examples, involving painting and pottery involve plenty of parts. What you describe in these examples is a certain kind of *process,* as opposed to an entity, and the process of painting involves temporal parts, events such as brush strokes, and so on. I believe that your claim that here we have emergence without parts is really the claim that a temporal process does not have spatial parts, which is trivially true. Even so, the temporal parts of these processes are, as a matter of fact, closely connected with certain spatial parts, swabs of color, borders between areas, and so on.

This mistaken emphasis derives, I believe, from a dangerous metaphor in your formulation: "We look at the movement of the brush and see the painting emerge." But the notion of emergence is not an observational concept in this sense. Even if one can see an emergent entity, the ontological notion of emergence is the notion of a certain kind of relation, or lack of the kind of relation sufficient for reductionism, between the parts of a system and the characteristics of that system. The assertion of emergence in a given case is, therefore, a quite abstract claim, and one can no more verify the presence of emergence in any given case by appeal to observation than one can evaluate the claim that a reduction is possible in some case by the claim that we can "see" it. This is worth pointing out because some traditional emergentists, such as C. D. Broad (1925), *may* have thought that we can just see that secondary qualities are emergent relative to material properties of bodies (perhaps there is also a conflation in Broad's view between seeing and seeing-that).

This feeds into your next example, the jigsaw puzzle. This case is puzzling because, you say, there are parts but they are irrelevant to the whole. This is surely too strong. Even if one does not, in some sense, see the individual parts *as individuals,* it does not follow that one does not see them. And even if one does not see them, it does not follow that they are irrelevant, for example, when one hears the roar of the ocean one may not hear the individual waves but that does not mean that the impact of these individual waves is irrelevant to what one does hear. In any case, I think your next example, that of *identikit,* is better, because it incorporates what is good in the jigsaw example, and, in my view, leads better into your penultimate point. In identikit, you say, we construct a face out of its features, but it is our knowledge about faces that makes us put them together to form this face. Here again is the idea from your jigsaw example, that we put together a whole with parts, but that the burden of emergence does not fall on the parts. This, you suggest, falls on our knowledge-about. And this leads into your final point, namely, that you "suspect that atomism plus emergence takes us up to the personal level, but what people produce . . . cannot be wholly accounted for in such terms." Rather, what we need to account for human creativity is a "non-atomistic, 'knowing-about' epistemology that accounts for the way we create images and pictures and representations out of our skills and abilities, and out of our knowledge of the world."

This is a rich remark, gesturing at a whole theory, and I make no pretence to evaluate it in detail. And there are some aspects of it, baldly stated, which I find congenial in some general sense. However, there is one thing that puzzles me. I also have an objection (or, perhaps, a challenge—a challenge which is related directly to my own motivations for preferring a more robust doctrine of emergence than your theory allows).

First, what puzzles me is your remark that atomism plus emergence gets us to the personal level, but not into it. If this is meant to suggest that my own views, or the various species of emergence characterized in my tree, presuppose atomism, then it is incorrect (and in personal correspondence you have suggested that my tree does seem "consistent with atomism"). It may be true that the most general notions of emergence are consistent with atomism, but it is not true that some of the specific versions, lower down the tree, are consistent with it. It may well be that many historical emergence theories hold that the emergent characteristics arise as a result of a combination of parts or of atomic parts. But not all of them do. For example, the two final species of substance-emergence on my tree (the emergence of new material substances and the emergence of persons) do not, unlike British Emergentism, presuppose the atomistic conception of matter. They are probably not even consistent with atomism as ordinarily understood. And even in the case of those species of emergentism which do, such as British Emergentism, and this is the central point, there is a big difference between the view that an entity with emergent properties is composed of atoms, and the view that the emergent is a compositional function of the atoms. (See my earlier discussion of the two kinds of combinationism.) Many emergentists may be atomists in some sense, but the whole point of emergentism is that the characteristics of the whole are not a mere additive function of its parts (atomic or otherwise).

I now move to your central point, that we need a "non-atomistic, 'knowing-about' epistemology" where, I presume, this refers back to your earlier expressions of sympathy with McGraw, Hofstadter and Rehling's vision of a central feedback loop in which "we exploit emergence through judgment and selection." I now repeat the criticism I made earlier of that kind of view updated to include the immediately preceding points.

Either this emergence-exploiting knowledge-about can be mechanically explained or it cannot. If it can be mechanically explained, then emergence plays, at best, a minor subsidiary role in what is still a fundamentally mechanistic theory of intelligence. If it cannot be mechanically explained, then it is itself either an emergent phenomenon or it is committed to substantive vitalism.

As the theory is stated, McGraw, Hofstadter, Rehling, and yourself cannot choose the second alternative, since the aim of this model is to keep the emergence contained at a lower level. But if they, and you, choose the first alternative, then one must ask, if emergence can occur at the subsidiary level, then why can it not occur at the level of the controlling knowledge-about? Furthermore, this is not the mere mooting of a possibility. For, within a generally materialist framework, if emergence is motivated anywhere, it is at the highest levels of life, knowledge and intelligence. For the lower down the organic hierarchy, the more likely one is to be able to effect a reduction.

In my opinion, McGraw, Hofstadter, and Rehling's strategy, as baldly stated, combines the worst features of mechanism and emergentism. Since the notion of a "central feedback system" is couched in mechanistic language, it places a mechanism at the higher level, of judgment and knowledge-about, where it will be hardest to justify, and it places emergence at the lower levels, where it will be easiest to reduce away. In my opinion, by contrast, rather than it being the case that judgment and knowledge-about are embodied in mechanisms that exploit lower level emergence, they are themselves prime candidates for characteristics that emerge, in some ontologically substantive sense most akin, on my taxonomy, to the emergence of persons at their level of engagement in the world. These emergents exploit certain lower level "mechanisms" (much as I, the person, given my knowledge about the mechanical world, exploit that mechanical calculator in my pocket).

Several of your remarks seem to suggest that my account is inadequate because even if we have emergence we need a self (of some kind or other) to exploit the emergence. But in my view, we say that a self is present precisely when a certain characteristic kind of emergence, associated with the higher animals, is present. We don't need a self to exploit the emergence because the presence of a self in a material system is constituted by the emergence of certain kinds of characteristic regularities in organic life. We say that there is a self there, and not a mere robot, when the entity exhibits the kind of emergent behavior characteristic of higher organisms, when, that is, it does not behave like a mere machine. As Paul Ziff puts it, "A robot would behave like a robot" (Ziff, 1969).

It may be worthwhile to emphasize that my own specific views are not developed in the body of the chapter. Although I do accept a version of emergent materialism akin to several species developed in the chapter, I believe that the best way to formulate the notion of emergence insofar as this is directly relevant to understanding mental phenomena, is akin to Wittgenstein's more "linguistic" approach (to which I allude in notes 5 and 11 of this chapter). My point here derives from my conception of the nature of philosophy rather than being a point about emergence per se. Although this "linguistic" view is consistent with a kind of emergent materialism, it represents a new level in the formulation of emergence. From my own point of view, therefore, the views developed in the present chapter are best seen as a preparation, from within the sphere of "natural philosophy," for the more adequate "linguistic" formulation of emergence.

NOTES

1. Bailey (1928) argues that Epicurus is an emergentist. I would argue that Plato, Aristotle, and Plotinus are emergentists in a sense (see Sellars, 1949, p. 548 on Aristotle) and, in fact, that emergentism of one sort or another was the dominant position in philosophy until the Enlightenment. But that historical thesis must be a matter for another occasion.

2. Though Searle was one of the first major contemporary philosophers to use the terminology of emergence, he rejects any "adventurous" notion of emergence which holds that the causal properties of a system are not the sum of the causal powers of its parts. That is, he rejects downward causation (1992). His favorite example of emergence is liquidity (1992, 1997, 1998). But though we can deduce an image of liquidity from atomic theory, we cannot deduce an image of consciousness from it. His notion of emergence is, in fact, the verbal species of epistemological emergence. He says, "irreducibility is a trivial consequence of our definitional practice" (1992). See Margolis (1987) and my note 8 in this chapter. In my opinion, what Searle's view requires, even by virtue of its own internal logic, is an adventurous notion of emergence.

3. As Kim points out, this hierarchical view of reality influences the very way we formulate philosophical problems (1998, pp. 15–16). It is possible to develop a different conception of emergence, and quite different conceptions of freedom and creativity, by challenging this hierarchical picture. In Margolis' view (1986, 1987), organisms are material, but a mental or cultural emergent is not produced by an arrangement of biological or chemical parts. However, since Margolis' view involves major departures from traditional emergent materialism, and may tend towards some kind of property dualism (1987), I do not pursue it further here. It may be true, for all that, and, in my opinion, it represents an important development in emergentism.

4. It is often noted that the physicalist notion of supervenience traces to Moore's view that moral properties are dependent on physical qualities (Beckermann, 1992b). Though Moore (1991) is hostile to the organicist notion of emergence in Hegel, he retains a version of emergence in his view that moral qualities are "more than the sum of their parts."

5. Although it might seem odd to describe Wittgenstein as a materialist, as he generally avoids such labels, it is only meant here that he is a materialist in the minimal sense that he holds that whatever is distinctive about the person does *not* consist in their possession of some non-material component of the sort affirmed by dualism, spiritualism, and so on. In my opinion, the qualified endorsement of emergent materialism in *Zettel* §608, is intended as an analogy, and Wittgenstein would prefer to state his own view in a more "linguistic" form. Whereas emergentism is generally considered as a metaphysical position of the classical type, concerning the nature of reality, or of matter, it is worthwhile considering how one would even formulate emergentism within the framework of "linguistic philosophy." For, availing oneself of the technique of "semantic ascent" (see McDonough, 2000), the emergentist's point would seem to correspond to the fact that when we describe an object in purely inorganic terms, that is, as a certain kind of complex molecule, we ascribe to it only certain kinds of characteristics, while, when we describe it as an organism or a person, we ascribe to it a whole different and richer set of characteristics. We have emergence here because there is no way to infer the second richer set of ascriptions from the first. In such a "linguistic" reconstruction, the emergentist claim is not the classical metaphysical view that novel properties and behavior "emerge" from matter (as bubbles "emerge" from a soft drink). Rather, emergence is reinterpreted as a point about the novelty (emergence) of a given "language game" (e.g., that of persons) relative to another one (e.g., that of inorganic matter). I believe that Wittgenstein would prefer to replace the classical metaphysical questions about the nature of matter with a set of questions concerning the connections between various language games (including an account of the kinds of conditions under which we make the kinds of judgments and ascriptions that we do). It should not be assumed that this latter inquiry would be entirely without "metaphysical" implications though. If what I have said is correct, these will not much resemble classical metaphysics construed as a theory about the nature of objects. I believe that the central point of Wittgenstein's later philosophy might be conceptualized as an account, given his linguistic method, of the naturalness and inevitability of something like emergentism. (And see note 11 for this chapter).

6. The historical precedent for this notion of individuality as historical uniqueness is in Dilthey (1962). It is worth remarking that on a view, such as the one con-

sidered by Dummett (1967), in which a person's character is not determined by any internal character mechanism, it is natural to hold that a person's character emerges in their historical development (see Wittgenstein, 1970; McDonough, 1989, 1993). On these kinds of views, time and history acquire a whole new kind of significance that they do not possess in the inorganic sciences per se.

7. Part of the irony here is that it was quantum mechanics that eliminated the motivation for holding that there are emergent chemical forces and, thereby, killed British Emergentism.

8. In fact, this notion of matter is dominant in the English-speaking world. For example, Searle claims that atomic theory is "so fundamental that [it is] no longer optional for reasonably well-educated citizens; indeed, [it is] in large part constitutive of the modern world view" (1992, p. 86). That atomic theory is fundamental to the modern world view is probably true, but how is it to be understood? Searle (ibid.) endorses the "bottom-up" view of the world which explains macro-systems by reference to micro-systems. But, since this requires the rejection of any "adventurous" notion of emergence, Searle begs the question against downwardly causal emergence. (Also see note 2 for this chapter.)

9. This is why McLaughlin (1992) holds that Whitehead is British and an emergentist but not a "British Emergentist." I cannot avoid making the observation that the meaning of "British Emergentist" is not a compositional function of the meanings of "British" and "emergentist" and, therefore, is emergently novel relative to its semantic parts.

10. For example, Einstein (1934) felt strongly, on "Kantian" grounds, that science is itself a product of human freedom.

11. If the view in note 5 is correct, then Wittgenstein is something like an a priori emergentist, where the "emergence" manifested in our hierarchy of "language games" is a natural and inevitable product of the way language functions (and must function). If this is correct, then Wittgenstein's later philosophy is a kind of "linguistic" version of "a philosophy of freedom," and, thereby, gives us a way of reconciling Einstein's "Kantian" intuition (not to mention Kant's whole a priori intuition) as a point following from the very nature of language as an intrinsically emergent phenomenon (see Eldridge, 1997, on the link between Wittgenstein and nineteenth-century German philosophy).

12. On this view, it is no accident that contemporary philosophers of science hold philosophy in contempt. As Lipton puts it, philosophers, unlike scientists, "make their business out of the insoluble" (1998, pp. 213, 217). However, the poverty of philosophy reflects, not its intrinsic nature, but the limitations of an age that insists on a reductive account of the emergent world. Since, of course, one cannot do that, it appears that philosophers must either act as a cheerleader for the reductive sciences or embrace skepticism or nihilism. This is why, in a "scientific" age, which believes that we know more about the world than we ever did, we have witnessed the rise of a series of ever more radical skepticisms and nihilisms as in Kripke (1982), McGinn (1989).

13. See Bloom (1969) on the translation of Plato.

14. For a list of most of these papers see the bibliography to my "Wittgenstein, German Organicism, Chaos, and the Centre of Life," forthcoming in *The Journal of the History of Philosophy.*

REFERENCES

Achim, S. (1992). Emergence—A systematic view on its historical facets. In A. Beckermann, H. Flohr, & J. Kim (Eds.), *Emergence or reduction?* (pp. 25–48). Berlin: de Gruyter.

Adams, E. M. (1975). *Philosophy and the modern mind.* Chapel Hill: University of North Carolina Press.

Bailey, C. (1928). *The Greek atomists.* New York: Russell and Russell.

Barzun, J. (1959). *The house of intellect.* New York: Harper Torchbooks.

Beckermann, A. (1992a). Introduction—Reductive and non-reductive physicalism. In A. Beckermann, H. Flohr, & J. Kim (Eds.), *Emergence or reduction?* (pp. 1–24). Berlin: de Gruyter.

Beckermann, A. (1992b). Supervenience, emergence, and reduction. In A. Beckermann, H. Flohr, & J. Kim (Eds.), *Emergence or reduction?* (pp. 94–118). Berlin: de Gruyter.

Beckner, M. O. (1968). Vitalism. In *The Encyclopedia of Philosophy* (Vol. 8, pp. 253–256). New York: Collier Macmillan Publishers.

Bergson, H. (1983). *Creative evolution.* (A. Mitchell, Trans.) Lanham, MD: The Free Press.

Birch, C, & Cobb, J. B. (1984). *The liberation of life.* Cambridge, MA: Cambridge University Press.

Bloom, A. (1968). *Notes to Plato's Republic.* (Alan Bloom, Trans.) New York: Basic Books, Inc.

Boden, M. (1994). Creativity and computers. In T. H. Dartnall (Ed.), *Artificial Intelligence and creativity: An interdisciplinary approach* (pp. 3–26). Dordrecht: Kluwer Academic Publishers.

Breazeale, D. (1994). Editor's Introduction. *Introductions to the Wissenschaftslehre* (pp. vii–xxxii). Indianapolis, IN: Hackett Publishing Company.

Broad, C. D. (1925). *The mind and its place in nature.* London: Routledge & Kegan Paul.

Butterfield, J. (1998). Quantum curiosities of psychophysics. In J. Cornwell (Ed.), *Consciousness and human identity* (pp. 122–159). Oxford: Oxford University Press.

Campbell, D.T. (1974). "Downward causation" in hierarchially organized biological systems. In F. Ayala, & T. Dobzhansky (Eds.), *Studies in the philosophy of biology.* Berkeley: University of California Press.

Causey, R. (1969). Polanyi on Structure and Reduction. *Synthese, 20,* 230–237.

Causey, R. (1977). *Unity of Science.* Dordrecht, Netherlands: Reidel.

Clark, Andy. (1990). *Microcognition.* Cambridge: Cambridge University Press.

Clark, Austen. (1980). *Psychological models and neural mechanisms.* Oxford: Oxford University Press.

Dartnall, T. H. (1994). Introduction: On having a mind of your own. In T. H. Dartnall (Ed.), *Artificial Intelligence and creativity: An interdisciplinary approach* (pp. 29–42). Dordrecht, Netherlands: Kluwer Academic Publishers.

Davidson, D. (1980). Mental events. In *Essays on action and events* (pp. 242–252). Oxford: Clarendon Press.

Davidson, D. (1999). The emergence of thought. *Erkentnis, 51,* 7–17.

Dilthey, W. (1962). *Pattern and meaning in history.* New York: Harper and Row.

Dummett, M. (1967). Truth. In P. Strawson (Ed.), *Philosophical logic*. Oxford: Oxford University Press.

Einstein, A. (1934). *The world as I see it*. New York: Covici Publishers.

Eldridge, R. (1997). *Leading a human life*. Chicago: University of Chicago Press.

Gay, P. (1977). *The Enlightenment: The rise of modern paganism*. New York: W.W. Norton & Co.

Hartshorne, C. (1991). *The logic of perfection*. LaSalle, IL: Open Court.

Hempel, C. (1965). *Aspects of scientific explanation*. New York: The Free Press.

Hooker, C. A. (1981). Towards a general theory of reduction, *Dialogue, 20,* 38–60, 201–236, 496–529.

Kant, I. (1996). *Anthropology*. Carbondale, IL: Southern Illinois University Press.

Kim, J. (1992). "Downward causation" in emergentism and non-reductive physicalism. In A. Beckermann, H. Flohr, & J. Kim (Eds.), *Emergence or reduction?* (pp. 119–138). Berlin: de Gruyter.

Kim, J. (1993a). *Supervenience and mind*. Cambridge: Cambridge University Press.

Kim, J. (1993b). The non-reductivists' troubles with mental causation. In J. Heil & A. Mele (Eds.), *Mental causation* (pp. 198-210). Oxford: Clarendon Press.

Kim, J. (1998). *Mind in a physical world: An essay on the mind-body problem and mental causation*. Cambridge, MA: MIT Press.

Klee, P. (1984). Micro-determinism and concepts of emergence. *Philosophy of Science, 51,* 44–63.

Kripke, S. (1982). *Wittgenstein on rules and private language*. Cambridge: Harvard University Press.

Lipton, Peter. (1998). Binding the mind. In J. Cornwell (Ed.), *Consciousness and human identity* (pp. 212–224). Oxford: Oxford University Press.

MacDonald, C., & MacDonald, G. (1995). Introduction: Supervenient causation. In C. MacDonald & G. MacDonald (Eds.), *Philosophy of psychology* (pp. 4–28). Oxford: Blackwell.

Margolis, J. (1978). *Persons and minds: The prospects of non-reductive physicalism*. Dordrecht, Netherlands: Reidel.

Margolis, J. (1986). Emergence. *The Philosophical Forum, XVII,* 271–295.

Margolis, J. (1987). *Science without unity*. Oxford: Basil Blackwell.

Maritain, J. (1955). *Bergsonian philosophy and Thomism*. New York: St. Martins Press.

McDonough, R. (1989). Towards a non-mechanistic theory of meaning. *Mind, XCVIII,* 1–22.

McDonough, R. (1992). The last stand of mechanism. *The Journal of Speculative Philosophy, VI,* 206–225.

McDonough, R. (1993). Linguistic creativity. In R. Harre & R. Harris (Eds.) *Linguistics and philosophy: The controversial interface* (pp. 125–164). Oxford: Pergamon Press.

McDonough, R. (1994). Machine predictability versus human creativity. In T. H. Dartnall (Ed.), *Artificial Intelligence and creativity: An interdisciplinary approach* (pp. 117–138). Dordrecht, Netherlands: Kluwer Academic Publishers.

McDonough, R. (1998a). Heidegger on authenticity, freedom, and individual agency. *International Studies in Philosophy, XXX,* 69–91.

McDonough, R. (1998b). Review of Paul Churchland's *The engine of reason, the seat of the soul*. In *Metascience 7,* 374–379.

McDonough, R. (1999a). Introduction to Special Issue on Wittgenstein and cognitive science. *Idealistic Studies, 29,* 125–138.

McDonough, R. (1999b). Bringing cognitive science back to life. *Idealistic Studies, 29,* 172–214.

McDonough, R. (2000). Review of John Cornwell (Ed.), *Consciousness and human identity.* In *Metascience, 9,* 238–245.

McDonough, R. (2001a). Aristotle's critique of functionalist theories of mind. *Idealistic Studies, 30*(3), 209–232.

McDonough, R. (2001b). Wittgenstein, German organicism, chaos, and the centre of life. In *The Journal of the History of Philosophy.* Manuscript in preparation.

McGinn, C. (1989). Can we solve the mind-body problem? *Mind, XCVIII,* 891.

McGinn, C. (1999). *The mysterious flame.* New York: Basic Books.

McLaughlin B. (1992). The Rise and Fall of British Emergentism, in A. Beckermann, H. Flohr, & J. Kim (Eds.), *Emergence or reduction?* (pp. 139–156). Berlin: de Gruyber.

Meikle, S. (1985). *Essentialism in the thought of Karl Marx.* LaSalle, IL: Open Court.

Moore, G. E. (1991). *Principia ethica.* Cambridge, MA: Cambridge University Press.

Nagel, E. (1954). *Sovereign reason.* Chicago: The Free Press.

Nagel, E. (1979). *The structure of science.* Indianapolis, IN: Hackett.

Nietzsche, F. (1968). *The will to power* (W. Kaufmann and R. J. Hollingdale, Trans.) New York: Random House.

Pap, A. (1962). *An introduction to the philosophy of science.* New York: Free Press of Glencoe.

Passmore, J. (1957). *A hundred years of philosophy.* New York: Basic Books.

Passmore, J. (1992). *Recent philosophers.* LaSalle, IL: Open Court.

Pepper, S. C. (1926). Emergence. *The Journal of Philosophy, 23,* 241–245.

Place, U. T. (1969). Is consciousness a brain process? In J. O'Connor (Ed.), *Modern materialism: Readings on mind-body identity* (pp. 21–31). New York: Harcourt, Brace and World.

Plato. (1968). *Republic.* (Alan Bloom, Trans.) New York: Basic Books, Inc.

Popper, K. (1982). *Unended quest.* LaSalle, IL: Open Court.

Popper, K., & Eccles, J. C. (1977). *The self and its brain.* Berlin: Springer.

Putnam, H. (1975), *Mind, language and reality, 2.* Cambridge, MA: Cambridge University Press.

Putnam, H. (1990). *Realism with a human face.* Cambridge, MA: Cambridge University Press.

Searle, J. (1992). *The rediscovery of the mind.* Cambridge, MA: The MIT Press.

Searle, J. (1997). *The mystery of consciousness.* London: Granta Books.

Searle, J. (1998). How to study consciousness scientifically. In J. Cornwell (Ed.), *Consciousness and human identity* (pp. 21–37). Oxford: Oxford University Press.

Sellars, R. W. (1922). *Evolutionary naturalism.* Chicago: Open Court.

Sellars, W. (1949). Aristotelian philosophies of mind. In R. W. Sellars, V. J. McGill, & M. Farber (Eds.), *Philosophy for the future* (pp. 544–570). New York: Macmillan.

Sellars, W., & Meehl, P. (1956). The concept of emergence. In H. Feigl & M. Scrien (Eds.), *Minnesota studies in the philosophy of science* (Vol. I.) Minneapolis: University of Minnesota Press.

Silberstein, M., & McGeever, J. (1999). The search for ontological emergence. *Philosophical Quarterly 49,* 182–200.

Smart, J. J. C. (1969a). Sensations and brain process. In J. O'Connor (Ed.), *Modern materialism: Readings on mind-body identity* (pp. 32–47). New York: Harcourt, Brace and World.

Smart, J. J. C. (1969b). Man as a physical mechanism. In J. O'Connor (Ed.), *Modern materialism: Readings on mind-body identity* (pp. 48–71). New York: Harcourt, Brace and World.

Sperry, R. W. (1970). An objective approach to subjective experience: Further explanation of a hypothesis. *Psychological Review, 76,* 585–590.

Teller, P. (1992). A contemporary look at emergence. In A. Beckermann, H. Flohr, & J. Kim (Eds.), *Emergence or reduction?* (pp. 139–156). Berlin: de Gruyter.

Turing, A. (1964). Computing machinery and intelligence. In A. R. Anderson (Ed.), *Minds and machines.* Englewood Cliffs, NJ: Prentice Hall.

van Fraassen, B. (1995). *Quantum mechanics: An empiricist's view.* Cambridge, UK: Clarendon Press.

van Gulick, R. (1992). Non-reductive physicalism and the nature of theoretic constraint. In A. Beckermann, H. Flohr, & J. Kim (Eds.), *Emergence or reduction?* (pp. 157–179). Berlin: de Gruyter.

von Wright, G. H. (1971). *Explanation and understanding.* Ithaca, NY: Cornell University Press.

Wittgenstein, L. (1963). *Philosophical investigations.* Oxford: Blackwell.

Wittgenstein, L. (1970) *Zettel.* (G. E. M. Anscombe, Trans.) Berkeley and Los Angeles: University of California Press.

Ziff, P. (1969). The feelings of robots. In A. R. Anderson (Ed.), *Minds and machines.* Englewood Cliffs, NJ: Prentice Hall.

Index

About the Editor
and the Contributors

LAWRENCE W. BARSALOU is Professor of Psychology at Emory University. His research includes the central role of sensory-motor mechanisms in human knowledge, the situated character of concepts, the dynamic online construction of conceptual representations, the development of ad hoc categories to support goal achievement, the structure of knowledge, and category learning.

TERRY DARTNALL is a senior lecturer in the School of Computing and Information Technology at Griffith University, Brisbane, where he teaches Artificial Intelligence and logic. His research interests include the foundations of Artificial Intelligence and cognitive science, and human and machine creativity.

GRAEME S. HALFORD holds a personal chair in Psychology at the University of Queensland. His research interests are in cognition, cognitive development and human factors, with special reference to analysis of cognitive complexity. With his colleagues, he has developed a general complexity metric that is applicable to general cognition, cognitive development, animal cognition and to industrial decision making.

DOUGLAS HOFSTADTER is College of Arts and Sciences Professor of Cognitive Science at Indiana University, where he directs the Center for Research on Concepts and Cognition. His research concerns the cognitive mechanisms underlying analogy-making and the creative process. He has also published in other areas, including poetry translation, sexist language and imagery, the mechanisms underlying human error-making, musical composition, discovery in mathematics, and various types of alphabet-based art.

KEITH J. HOLYOAK is a professor of psychology at the University of California, Los Angeles. His research focuses on human reasoning and decision making, integrating behavioral, neural, and computational approaches.

JOHN E. HUMMEL is a professor in the Department of Psychology at the University of California, Los Angeles. His research interests center on how neural architectures can give rise to explicit symbolic representations and processes, and with the computational and behavioral consequences of the solution(s) to this problem.

RICHARD McDONOUGH is Lecturer in Philosophy and the Humanities at the Overseas Family College in the Republic of Singapore. He has taught philosophy at Bates College, the National University of Singapore, the University of Tulsa, and the University Putra Malaysia. His research interests include the philosophy of mind, the philosophy of language, and the history of philosophy.

GARY McGRAW is Vice President of Corporate Technology at Cigital, Inc., a Software Risk Management company. His research interests include software security, software engineering, mobile code security, automated testing, and machine learning.

DEREK PARTRIDGE is Professor of Computer Science at the University of Exeter in the UK. He has maintained a long-standing interest in AI and software engineering. His current research is based on the formal development of inductive AI technologies to support data mining for software system enhancement.

DONALD M. PETERSON is a lecturer in the Schools of Education and Computer Science at the University of Birmingham. His current research interests are in autism, contextualized cognition and the psychology of e-learning.

JESSE J. PRINZ is an assistant professor in the Philosophy Department and Philosophy-Neuroscience-Psychology Program at Washington University in St. Louis. His research interests include concepts, consciousness and emotion.

JOHN REHLING is a research scientist in the cognitive modeling group at NASA Ames Research Center. His work concerns the creation of accurate models of human behavior in domains such as aircraft flight and air traffic control.

JON ROWE is a lecturer in the School of Computer Science at the University of Birmingham, UK. His research interests are in evolutionary computation and emergent systems.

CHRIS THORNTON is a lecturer in Artificial Intelligence at the School of Cognitive and Computing Sciences, University of Sussex. His research interests include creativity, representation, learning and evolution.

WILLIAM H. WILSON is an associate professor in the School of Computer Science and Engineering at the University of New South Wales, where he teaches Artificial Intelligence and neural networks. His research interests include cognitive modeling, neural networks, and natural language processing.

WITHDRAWN

American Designs